THE STRATEGIC
BOND INVESTOR

THE STRATEGIC BOND INVESTOR

Strategies and Tools to Unlock the Power of the Bond Market

Anthony Crescenzi

McGraw-Hill

New York Chicago San Francisco
Lisbon London Madrid Mexico City
Milan New Delhi San Juan Seoul
Singapore Sydney Toronto

McGraw-Hill

*A Division of The **McGraw·Hill** Companies*

2 3 4 5 6 7 8 9 0   DOC/DOC   0 9 8 7 6 5 4 3 2

ISBN 0-07-138707-2

This book was set in Palatino per the IPROF design by Joanne Morbit of the McGraw-Hill Professional's Hightstown, N.J. composition Unit.

This publication is designed to provide accurate and authoritative information in regard to the subject matter covered. It is sold with the understanding that the publisher is not engaged in rendering legal, accounting or other professional service. If legal advice or other expert assistance is required, the services of a competent professional person should be sought.

> —*From a Declaration of Principles Jointly Adopted by a Committee of the American Bar Association and a Committed of Publishers and Associations.*

McGraw-Hill books are available at special discounts to use as premiums and sales promotions, or for use in corporate training programs. For more information, please write to the Director of Special Sales, Professional Publishing, McGraw-Hill, Two Penn Plaza, New York, NY 10121-2298. Or contact your local bookstore.

This book is printed on recycled, acid-free paper containing a minimum of 50% recycled de-inked paper.

There are many people behind the life of every individual.

*I dedicate this book to my supportive and wonderful wife
and best friend, Cynthia; my three beautiful and enchanting
daughters: Brittany, Victoria, and Isabella; to my mother,
Anita, for her unconditional love, and to my father, Joseph,
for all his encouragement; to my brother, Joe, and my sisters:
Theresa, Gina, and Nicole; to my lovely grandmothers:
Adelaide DiGeorge and Connie Crescenzi; to the memories of
my grandfathers: Philip DiGeorge and Joseph Crescenzi; to
my aunts: Phyllis and Linda; to my wife's parents, Evelyn and
Joseph Montella, and to her sister, Cathy; to my Godparents,
Diane and Jerry Antonellis; to my teachers: Mrs. Merlino,
Mr. Marco Manfre, and Mr. Kircher; to my employers: Jeffrey
Miller and Jeffrey Tabak; to Walter Weil; to all my friends;
and to the great city of New York.*

CONTENTS

CHAPTER ONE

The Importance of the Bond Market

The bond market affects you more than you probably know. In many ways the bond market profoundly affects your personal life and touches the life of nearly everyone else. Its influence stretches well beyond the conventional wisdom in ways that most people are never aware of. In short, the bond market, where interest rates are set, is little understood yet immensely important to the national standard of living. It therefore behooves everyone to gain a better understanding of the bond market even if one is not a bond investor.

Throughout this book I will highlight the many ways in which the bond market affects you. I am convinced that when you have finished reading it, you will be surprised and enlightened and will look at the bond market in a new light. I will show you how you can unlock the power of the bond market. At the same time you will gain valuable insights into how the bond market operates.

You will learn important insights that are absent in other books about the bond market. More often than not those books are filled with information that is of little personal relevance to the reader, and they contain important but uninteresting and overly technical explanations about topics that most people can do without.

Of course, some technical content must be included in any book about bonds and the bond market, but that should not be the central theme of the book. Books about the stock market, for example, rarely delve into the intricacies of stocks and stock investing; they stick to what is relevant to the reader personally while making it interesting. That is what I will do in this book, and I will do my utmost to keep the topics relevant every step of the way.

THE BOND MARKET IS THE DOG THAT WAGS THE TAIL

When most people think about the bond market, it's an after-thought. Bonds are not very sexy to the average investor, and the bond market is either too complex or too uninteresting for most individuals to consider paying it much attention.

This should not be too surprising in this era of financial inno-vations, a secular bull market in the stock market, and a long period of economic prosperity.

But this is where reality and perceptions clash: The bond mar-ket is really the dog that wags the tail. The bond market, and more specifically interest rate levels, significantly influence the behavior of the stock market and the economy, not vice versa. Since the stock market and the economy affect everyone somehow, a great deal of every individual's financial well-being can be traced to the bond market.

Unfortunately, many individuals miss this point and therefore miss the many opportunities that the bond market presents. These opportunities can surface in a wide variety of places, including home mortgages, home equity loans, credit cards, personal loans, car loans, the stock market, interest-bearing assets such as certifi-cates of deposits and money market funds, the economy, interna-tional investments, and even politics.

THE BOND MARKET IS WHERE INTEREST RATES ARE SET

As was mentioned above, the bond market is where interest rates are set. The interest rate levels quoted on loans, credit cards, sav-ings accounts, money market funds, and the like are all linked to the bond market. This is the case because they generally are cor-related with an interest rate level set in the bond market. Most of these interest rate levels are linked to the U.S. Treasury market, the most actively traded debt securities in the bond market. Mort-

F i g u r e   1–1

10-Year Treasury Note versus 30-Year Mortgage Rate

Source: Freddie Mac, Bloomberg

gage rates, for example, are tightly correlated with the yield on the 10-year U.S. Treasury note. Take a look at Figure 1-1.

As you can see from the chart, the 10-year U.S. Treasury note and 30-year fixed-rate mortgages basically move in lockstep with each other, with the 10-year T-note leading a bit. The tight correlation between the two illustrates the notion that interest rates are set in the bond market and shows the importance of following the bond market, especially when obtaining a home mortgage.

The reason so many interest rate instruments are linked to the bond market is the fact that the bond market serves as a reference, or benchmark, for where the investing public believes interest rates should be. In addition, the Federal Reserve sets interest rate levels that are reflected in the bond market. This will be discussed in greater detail in Chapter 6.

Because nearly all interest rate levels are dependent on the bond market in some way and since interest rates affect almost everyone in one way or another, gaining a better understanding of the bond market is a worthwhile endeavor.

Let's take a closer look at how the bond market affects many important facets of our daily lives. As you read on, think about the many ways in which your life has been touched by these powerful forces.

INTEREST RATES AFFECT PERSONAL FINANCES

For most households, interest rates have a large impact on everyday finances. In the United States, where debt is a big part of the way people live, this impact is largely manifested in a household's monthly bills. Americans are simply enamored of debt and use it to fulfill many of their hopes and dreams.

The explosion in consumer debt has resulted from the increased availability of credit and changes in consumer preferences. Demographic influences have been a critical factor too, as baby boomers—those born from 1946 to 1964—have increased their use of debt to tap into every possible means to finance their well-documented love of consumption of goods and services.

Whatever the reason, the fact is that on average most households have a significant amount of debt outstanding in a variety of forms. Table 1-1 highlights the enormous amount of household debt outstanding.

As the table shows, the total amount of mortgage debt outstanding surpasses all other forms of debt. This clearly indicates that the biggest way in which interest rates affect a household's finances is through mortgage rates. The mortgage rate directly affects every homeowner's monthly financial situation. I am sure that many of you can relate to this.

T a b l e   1-1

Liabilities of the Personal Sector
(billions of dollars; source: Federal Reserve)

Type of Debt	Fourth Quarter 2001
Mortgage debt	5,741
Revolving debt	692
Nonrevolving debt	963
Other liabilities	1,883

Let's illustrate one way in which I learned firsthand how important interest rates are.

In 1989, the year before I began my career in the bond market, my wife and I bought our first house, a town house. It was a special time for us, filled with excitement. We were elated to be realizing the American dream of owning one's own home.

While the home itself was a great source of pride and pleasure for us, the financial side of the equation evolved in ways I did not envision at that time. We took out a mortgage at a whopping 11.25 percent, the prevailing rate at that time. I didn't give much thought to the interest rate level because I felt the price of the home would rise, as home prices always had, and offset the interest costs.

Was I wrong! As I came to understand, the Federal Reserve was in the middle of a campaign to slow the economy in an effort to stamp out inflation and a brewing price bubble in the real estate market. The Fed's rate increases therefore hit me with a double-barreled whammy: I was stuck with an 11.25 percent mortgage rate, and my home's price fell when the Fed burst the real estate bubble.

When the real estate bubble burst, the price of my town house fell 25 percent in short order. I tried to refinance for years, but no bank would consider it because my town house had negative equity. Therefore, I was stuck. For years I was saddled with high payments on an investment that had gone awry.

What do I know now that I didn't know then? For starters, I have learned that the interest rate I pay on debt matters—big time. Never again will I borrow money without giving strong consideration to interest rates. That means paying more attention to the bond market. Following the bond market has enabled me to make better financial decisions and plan better.

I have also learned to respect the adage "Don't fight the Fed." The Federal Reserve has enormous influence on the economy and, hence, my financial well-being. I can't emphasize this point enough. We'll learn more about the importance of respecting the power of the Fed in Chapter 6.

So now I have turned the tables. In my new home, my mortgage is just 6.375 percent. Instead of having the highest interest rate of anyone I know, I now have one of the lowest. By staying in tune with the bond market, I have learned to be opportunistic with interest rates when they fall. And by watching the Federal Reserve, I am more on top of the investment climate.

Stay in tune with the bond market as I have and keep the graph in Figure 1-1 fresh in your mind. Let it always remind you that the bond market can have a great impact on your personal finances.

CREDIT CARDS

Aside from home mortgages, interest rate levels have a great impact on the payments that most people make on their credit card balances. Some of you, I am sure, have obtained new credit cards with low introductory interest rate levels on balance transfers. Have you noticed the big difference that the interest rate level makes on the monthly interest charges? It can be staggering.

The attraction of credit cards with low introductory interest rates has been partly responsible for the sharp increase in consumer debt over the past 20 years. Opportunistic financial companies have capitalized on consumers' increased willingness to run up debt by developing various types of creative financing arrangements that entice consumers to take on more debt. And have they! Americans hold hundreds of millions of credit cards and have debit balances of roughly $700 billion. That is well above the level in the mid-1990s, when there was about $500 billion outstanding.

The pervasive use of credit card debt can be used to illustrate the large impact that interest can have in an individual's personal finances.

Consider, for example, a consumer who has $8,000 of credit card debt outstanding carrying an annual financing rate of 18 percent. That consumer will incur roughly $1363 in interest charges through the course of a year, assuming the consumer pays only the minimum payment (of the standard 2.5 percent). If the consumer transfers that balance to a new credit card with an introductory interest rate of 5.9 percent, the consumer will incur just $424 of interest charges over the course of a year. The difference is clearly significant.

Perhaps even more significant is the amount of time it would take for that consumer to eliminate the debt entirely, assuming the consumer pays the minimum monthly payment. If the debit balance is carried at the introductory interest rate, the consumer would eliminate the debt in 16 years. But at 18 percent the consumer would need 30 years. What a difference!

These illustrations clearly show the significant role that interest rates can play in people's personal finances and is another reason to gain a better understanding of the bond market.

THE PROFOUND IMPACT OF INTEREST RATES ON THE STOCK MARKET

The impact of interest rates on your personal finances extends well beyond your debts: Interest rates can affect your equity portfolio too. Indeed, history has proved that interest rates can have a profound impact on the stock market. As a result, the stock market watches the bond market like a hawk. It's no wonder that one of the most famous adages in the stock market is "Don't fight the Fed."

By gaining a better understanding of the bond market, you can empower yourself with an improved ability to recognize the potential risks and opportunities that the gyrations of the bond market present to the stock market every day.

Your goal should be to become less of a casual observer of the goings-on in the bond market and more of a thinker with respect to how the bond market's fluctuations may affect the stocks you own and how the bond market's behavior should be integrated into your investment decisions. This does not mean that you have to become an investor in bonds; it merely means that you should weave your understanding of how the bond market affects the stock market into your investment decision-making process. I will discuss how you can do this throughout the book.

The behavior of the stock market over the years has made one simple fact of investing abundantly clear: The bond market is the dog that wags the tail. When the bond market flutters, the stock market quakes. This has been proved time and time again, as recent events have demonstrated so profoundly.

Think back to 1998, when the world was gripped in a wretched series of financial crises that began in Asia and spread throughout the rest of the world, including the United States. The financial contagion caused markets to swoon lower, and foreign currency and debt markets began to seize up. A liquidity crisis developed as investors shunned foreign markets and avoided financial securities that were not actively traded. U.S. Treasuries, for example, considered the safest financial securities in the world, were partly shunned as older, less active maturities called off-the-runs performed poorly compared with actively traded maturities. For the U.S. Treasury market to have experienced price anomalies was an extraordinary event that highlighted the state of crisis the markets were in at the time.

Enter the Federal Reserve. On September 29, 1998, the Fed responded to the crisis with the first of three rate cuts that year.

In the policy statement that accompanied that first cut, the Fed explained that it decided to lower interest rates "to cushion the effects on prospective economic growth in the United States of increasing weakness in foreign economies and of less accommodative financial conditions domestically." The Fed clearly recognized the deleterious impact that dysfunctional financial markets could ultimately have on the U.S. economy. In addition, the Fed knew that it could use the power of interest rates to help restore investor confidence, which had been shattered throughout the world.

The Fed's interest rate tonic worked its usual magic as the global markets staged a substantial recovery. The Dow Jones Industrial Average, for example, which had fallen from an all-time high of 9367.84 just two months before the Fed's rate cut to a low of 7400.03 on September 1, roared back to a new all-time high two months after the rate cut. That recovery illustrated the powerful impact of interest rates.

While there's no question that the Fed's rate cuts were needed to help restore stability to the financial markets in 1998, the rate cuts arguably sowed the seeds for one of the most explosive and ultimately harrowing periods in economic and financial history.

The problem was that the rate cuts became a classic case of too much of a good thing, a double-edged sword, if you will. Arguably, the rate cuts were meant to address a market problem, not an economic one, and so the Fed should have reversed its rate cuts once the crisis was over. It didn't. What followed in 1999 was a bubble in both the economy and the stock market. The Fed tried to arrest the bubble in June 1999 with the first of six interest rate increases, but it responded slowly and the bubble grew.

You might recall that the Federal Reserve began raising interest rates in June 1999. The stock market, however, was caught in a euphoric mood—a mania, in fact—and turned a blind eye to the Fed. The stock market also turned its back on a critical development in the bond market—an inversion of the yield curve (to be discussed further in Chapter 7), a development normally considered an ominous signal for both the economy and the stock market. However, the equity market continued to plow ahead and chose to ignore historical precedent. For many investors that would turn out to be a disastrous mistake.

When 2000 began, it was the same old story. The Fed was still raising interest rates, yet the equity market was caught in dot-com mania. It was a bubble that was about to burst, and it was the Fed and the bond market that would burst it.

The Fed continued raising interest rates until May 16, 2000, when it decided to increase the size of the rate hikes from a quarter of a percentage point at a time to a half point. The Fed did this to assure that the stock market, which had started to slip, would stay down for the count. It did. As in many earlier eras, the stock market succumbed to the powerful influence of interest rates. And so did the economy.

By the end of 2000 signs of an economic slowdown and talk of recession abounded. The exuberant free-spending consumer gave way to a more cautious, tepid one. Spending during the 2000 holiday season, in fact, was dreadfully weak and the worst since the last recession back in 1990–1991. Businesses responded to the weakness in the economy by cutting production and shedding workers. Indeed, in the country as a whole, layoff announcements in December 2000 totaled 133,713, a record at that time. Layoffs continued in the early part of 2001, averaging 130,000 per month over the first half of the year before escalating by the year's end. Businesses also began to curtail capital spending by lowering spending on new plants and equipment, for example, and by cutting back heavily on technology spending. This contributed to the battering of the technology-laden NASDAQ index.

In 2001, the Federal Reserve faced virtually unprecedented challenges, having to battle not only the busted bubble and the ensuing economic recession that began in March, but also the economic effects of the tragic events of September 11th. As Federal

Reserve Chairman Alan Greenspan put it in February 2002 in testimony before Congress, "If ever a situation existed in which the fabric of business and consumer confidence, both here and abroad, was vulnerable to being torn, the shock of September 11 was surely it."

Led by Chairman Greenspan, the Fed met the unprecedented challenges of 2001 by aggressively lowering interest rates, cutting the Federal Funds rate eleven times to a 40-year low of 1.75 percent at year's end from 6.50 percent at the start of the year. The Fed's interest rate cuts helped to lift key interest-sensitive sectors of the economy, chiefly the housing and automobile sectors, which both grew strongly at the end of 2001. In addition, the Fed's rate cuts spurred a massive wave of mortgage refinancing activity, with nearly $1 trillion of mortgages refinanced, thereby helping to reduce mortgage payments for millions of households. In these and other ways, the Fed's rate cuts helped the economy to recovery in short order. While the indomitable spirit of Americans was no doubt as good a reason as any for the economic rebound, the Federal Reserve's interest rate reduction played an immense role.

These recent episodes in the financial markets should help convince you that when it comes to investing in the stock market, the bond market is a power to be reckoned with. If you can learn to read the bond market's signals, and I will show you ways to do that throughout this book, you can improve your investment performance sharply. You will learn, for example, how to know when to increase or decrease your risk taking and where you should put your money during the different stages of the economic cycle.

THE BOND MARKET'S IMPACT ON THE ECONOMY

The biggest reason the equity market reacts so strongly to developments in the bond market is the fact that equity investors recognize the major role that interest rates play in shaping the health of the economy and the fact that the health of the economy has a direct bearing on corporate profits and, hence, stock prices.

Understanding how the bond market affects the economy is fairly simple. The rule of thumb is that rising interest rates tend to weaken the economy while falling rates tend to strengthen it. High interest rates tend to discourage borrowing while low interest rates encourage it.

Interest rates generally rise or fall, of course, mainly as a result of actions taken by the Federal Reserve. The Fed adjusts the level of interest rates to regulate the health of the economy. It does this by raising or lowering the federal funds rate, which is the interest rate banks charge each other for overnight loans and is considered the anchor for all short-term interest rates. It is therefore one of the most important interest rates. This is discussed in greater detail in Chapters 6 and 9.

While there's no doubt that the Fed is in control of short-term interest rates, the Fed has limited control over long-term interest rates. As a result, the interest rate levels on a wide variety of long-term financial vehicles, such as home mortgages, are anchored against interest rates that are set in the bond market.

This is what makes the bond market so important to the economy. Its daily fluctuations have a direct bearing on the interest rate instruments that directly affect the economy. In many ways, the bond market is as much in control of the economy as the Federal Reserve is.

THE BOND MARKET'S IMPACT ON THE INTEREST-RATE-SENSITIVE SECTORS OF THE ECONOMY

As we will discuss further in Chapter 9, there are three interest-rate-sensitive sectors of the economy that can be greatly affected by developments in the bond market: housing, automobiles, and capital spending. Each sector by itself can have a very big effect on the economy. Collectively, their impact can be enormous. This is why these sectors are the first place you should look to see impact from interest rate fluctuations. When these sectors start to respond to a change in interest rates, look out. At that point many other areas of the economy will be affected through so-called multiplier effects, resulting in a host of economic and investment implications.

Take the automobile sector, for example, a sector that accounts for roughly 7 percent of all industrial production in the United States, but with multiplier effects that can magnify its impact greatly. If, for example, as a result of lower interest rates, automobile sales strengthened, the benefits of that sales increase would ripple through the economy in a variety of ways. Car salespersons, for example, would see their commission income increase. In turn, they probably would use their extra income to buy a variety of goods unrelated to the automobile industry—from clothing, to furniture, to chewing gum—and thus have a positive impact on the economy. Moreover, factory workers would also see their incomes rise as they worked extra overtime and longer workweeks to build new cars to meet the strong demand. This extra income would find its way into the economy too, of course. The impact would extend further to workers in the automobile parts supply industry, and the effect on the economy could be significant. Indeed, in the United States there are more people working in the automobile parts supply industry than there are working in the manufacture of automobiles.

In the housing sector, where multiplier effects are greater than they are in any other sector of the economy, interest rates play a large role in its performance, and the health of the housing sector can have a broad impact on the economy. It is not uncommon for interest rate gyrations to affect homes sales by several hundred thousand units in a very short time. The impact of these gyrations ripples quickly through the economy. For example, as Table 1-2 shows, it is estimated that the construction of an additional 100,000 homes can create 244,800 full-time construction jobs. Obviously, the human impact can be quite large, and construction workers probably recognize better than most people the role interest rates play in the economy. They no doubt recognize that the health of the housing market can have a direct bearing on their standard of living. Moreover, new homeowners tend to spend more of their income than do nonmovers.

The level of interest rates has long affected capital spending, which is business spending on new plants, machinery, equipment,

T a b l e   1-2

The Effect of Changes in Home Construction

Change in Single-Family Housing Starts	Change in Construction and Construction-Related Jobs
25,000	61,200
75,000	183,600
100,000	244,800
150,000	367,200

Source: National Association of Home Builders

and technology products. Interest rates affect capital spending in two ways.

First, businesses are apt to increase capital spending when the cost of doing so is lower. This occurs because capital spending projects are often costly—a new factory, after all, can be quite expensive—and many companies often finance their capital spending projects with borrowed money. The interest rate level can make or break the decision to engage in new capital spending projects.

Second, businesses are more apt to increase capital spending when they believe the interest rate environment will promote economic growth. When businesses feel that interest rates are low enough to spark economic growth, they generally feel compelled to expand their production capacity so that they can meet expected increases in the demand for their goods and services.

WHY THE PERFORMANCE OF THE ECONOMY IS IMPORTANT TO YOU

As you can see by looking at the impact interest rates have on the housing, automobile, and capital spending sectors of the economy, there are a number of ways in which the bond market affects the economy. This is important to everyone in a number of ways.

First, the economy's performance directly affects job creation. Look again at the example of the construction sector in Table 1-2. Job creation has historically been linked directly to the economy's performance. A strong economy, for example, generally will result in the creation of about 200,000 jobs per month. A weak economy, in comparison, could spell job losses, and when the economy contracts, job losses usually total about 200,000 per month.

Second, the economy's performance affects income growth. Wages tend to rise more rapidly when the economy is prospering, as workers share in growing corporate profits by demanding higher wages and working longer hours. In addition, individuals who derive some or all of their income from commissions see their earnings rise too. When the economy weakens, however, income growth slows as the workweek shrinks and individuals work fewer overtime hours and trade wage gains for job security.

Third, the national standard of living is tied directly to the economy's performance not only through job and income growth but also through the innovations companies develop in the products and services that consumers use. Companies innovate more when they are flush with cash than they do when they are strapped for cash. This means that the quality of the products and services that we buy, from cars, to electronics, to medical services, will vary with the economy's performance.

There are many other ways that the economy affects us, as we will see in the Appendix at the end of the book, but these are some of the most prominent. In each case the bond market's role is unmistakable.

THE BOND MARKET IMPACTS THE FORMATION OF CAPITAL

One big way in which the bond market affects the economy is through capital formation. Without capital, the economy would crumble. Basically, capital is to the economy as gasoline is to a car. Money makes the world go round, as they say, and this is particularly true of the economy.

Corporations, municipalities, the U.S. government, and government agencies raise enormous amounts of capital in the bond market every year for a variety of purposes. In 2000, for example, roughly $2.1 trillion in new bonds was issued in the bond market and a whopping $3.2 trillion was issued in 2001—a record pace. Such vast borrowing eventually affects the economy in one way or another.

There is often a long lag between the time when money is raised in the bond market and the time when it is put to work in the economy. For example, a corporation that raises money in the bond market and plans to use it to build a new factory will take time to draw up plans to build and will need still more time to actually build the factory. But it eventually does get built, of course.

Given that money borrowed in the bond market eventually finds its way into the economy, one might say that changes in the level of bond issuance are a good leading indicator for the economy, meaning that those changes tend to foreshadow future economic activity. This is an indicator I recommend you follow closely. Follow the money!

THE BOND MARKET AND POLITICS

The powerful influence of interest rates goes well beyond conventional thinking. As I will argue in Chapter 14, the influence extends to the political arena too. While there's no doubt that many issues can shape the outcome of an election, the impact of interest rates has historically been quite palpable. This is a relatively new phenomenon, but the evidence is compelling.

President Jimmy Carter, for instance, was saddled with high interest rates throughout much of his administration in the late 1970s. Interest rates were high because of rampant inflation rates. Republicans, led by Ronald Reagan, seized on interest rates as a campaign issue, and in 1980 Carter lost his reelection bid partly because of the public's discontent with soaring interest rate levels.

Reagan benefited from the steady decline in interest rates that occurred during his administration. That decline contributed to perceptions that Reagan had restored and revitalized the nation, a perception that continues to this day. In fact, many people agree that the bull market witnessed in the late 1990s actually got its start in 1982 under Reagan's watch.

Similar to Carter, President George Bush, Sr.'s, bid for reelection was stymied by high interest rates. Early in Bush's term the Fed had raised interest rates in an effort to slow the economy and reduce inflation. The Fed's rate hikes eventually slowed the economy significantly and, combined with other factors, led to the recession of 1990–1991. To Bush's dismay, the Fed was slow to respond to the recession and lowered interest rates slowly and in small increments. The poor state of the economy became a campaign issue for the Democrats and helped sweep Bill Clinton into the presidency in 1992.

Bill Clinton, for his part, masterfully used the powerful influence of interest rates as the centerpiece of his economic strategy. He accomplished this by adopting strategies on fiscal policy developed by his astute Treasury secretary, Robert Rubin, that encouraged low market interest rates and, hence, strong economic growth. The result was a historic shift in the government's yearly fiscal balance from deficit to surplus. What followed was an extraordinary drop in interest rates and a virtually unprecedented period of economic prosperity. The economy's strength helped Clinton weather a number of major personal and political challenges.

President George W. Bush may yet benefit from the extraordinary rate cuts implemented by the Federal Reserve in 2001. Time will tell.

It is unconventional to think about the impact of interest rates on politics. However, the evidence clearly suggests that the bond market can play a major role in shaping the political landscape.

SUMMARY

In many ways the bond market touches all of our lives in ways most of us are never aware of. You can see the bond market at work in many of the things that affect us. Whether it's home mortgages, investments, jobs, the economy, or politics, the bond market's reach is unmistakable. Throughout this book I will illustrate the powerful role the bond market plays in our lives and show you ways to use the bond market to your advantage.

If you're a bond investor, this book will help you understand the most essential elements of intelligent bond investing. You'll find strategies and tools that I have no doubt will give you a new perspective on investing that you can use to help improve your investment performance.

But you needn't be a bond investor to benefit from this book. By simply gaining a greater understanding of the many ways the bond market can affect you and utilizing the tools in this book to your advantage, you'll be on your way toward unlocking the power of the bond market. So read on. Delve into the chapters and subjects you believe will help you the most. Find the tools you will need to meet your objectives, whatever they might be. If you keep an open mind and look at the bond market in ways you haven't before, you may be surprised at what you'll find.

Let's get started.

CHAPTER TWO

The Composition and Characteristics of the Bond Market

One of this nation's greatest assets is its entrepreneurial spirit. In our storied history we have had remarkable periods of economic prosperity spurred by the innovations and inventions of our citizens. From one generation to the next, entrepreneurs have opportunistically set their sails to the shifting winds of the American consumer, creating products and services that have boosted the national standard of living significantly. Scores of innovators, including now legendary greats such as Benjamin Franklin, Thomas Edison, the Wright Brothers, J. P. Morgan, and Bill Gates, have helped shape the way we live and usher in new eras.

As important as these and other entrepreneurs have been to the American society over the years, their innovations and inventions would not have had the impact that they had without a plentiful supply of capital. Innovations and inventions by themselves, of course, cannot lift a nation's standard of living; they eventually must be integrated into society on a national scale. For this to happen, mass production is necessary, an endeavor requiring large amounts of capital.

This is where the bond market comes in. In the bond market, vast amounts of capital are raised every day by numerous entities to meet the funding requirements for a variety of needs. Typical borrowers include the federal government, government agencies, local and state governments, and foreign and domestic corporations. The

17

money these entities raise in the bond market is put toward a wide array of spending initiatives. A few examples are consumer products, U.S. Navy ships, local water supplies, and home mortgages. These few examples clearly illustrate the valuable role of the bond market. Without the bond market, the national standard of living would be far different from what it is today. Bonds, which in their simplest form are interest-bearing documents issued or sold by either a government body or a corporation for the purpose of raising capital to meet a financial need, provide these entities with the capital they need to finance numerous endeavors.

BONDS THAT HELPED SAVE THE WORLD

An extraordinary example of the powerful role bonds have historically played in this society is the war bond program established during World War II to help finance the war effort. On May 1, 1941, President Franklin D. Roosevelt bought the first of the so-called war bonds, also known as victory bonds. A massive effort was undertaken to sell substantial amounts of those bonds, and the results were astounding. By the time the program ended and the last proceeds from the sale were deposited into the U.S. Treasury on January 3, 1946, $185.7 billion of war bonds had been sold and over 85 million Americans had invested in them. It is astonishing to consider that 85 million people had invested in war bonds, and the number is even more staggering when one considers that the population was just 130 million at the time. In contrast, today less than 20 percent of the population owns U.S. savings bonds.

War bonds were crucial not only for the role they played in financing the war but in the way they helped unify the nation. The sale of war bonds became a rallying cry, uniting Americans in a common cause and giving those who invested in the bonds a way to express their patriotism. The effort to raise money reached nearly every nook and cranny of the country, and it seemed that nearly everyone was involved. The entertainment industry played an active role, with the nation's best known and most beloved entertainers using their star status to help the common cause.

It's fair to say that bonds have never played a more vital role than they did during World War II. The lives of our soldiers, the welfare of their families, and the state of both the nation and the world were helped immensely by our ability to fight a well-financed campaign. Bonds have never shined more.

TODAY'S BOND MARKET

The immense success of the war bond program helped elevate bonds as a financing vehicle and paved the way for substantial growth in the bond market. Through the years, the bond market has grown rapidly and financial innovations have led to the creation of many different types of bonds. The bond market has become so large that its dollar value now exceeds that of the stock market. Moreover, the bond market has become a bigger source of capital than the banking system.

Despite the bond market's explosive growth and enormous size, it remains elusive, and many people do not have a clue about what "the bond market" really is.

There are many reasons why the bond market seems so elusive. For one thing, there is no centralized marketplace for bond trading. This is the complete opposite of the equity market, where most trading takes place in centralized exchanges such as the New York Stock Exchange.

SPECIALIZATION IN THE BOND MARKET

In the bond market there are no exchanges. Instead, trading takes place over the counter, or between a network of thousands of broker-dealers and the investing public. Broker-dealers are so named because they can act as either brokers, buying and selling securities on behalf of their customers, or a dealer, buying and selling securities for their own accounts.

These broker-dealers generally act as dealers and carry inventories of fixed-income securities that they resell to their clients. The inventories that broker-dealers hold vary widely, as these firms often specialize in trading specific types of fixed-income securities. Some firms, for example, specialize in trading corporate bonds, while others specialize in trading municipal securities.

This specialization has advantages and disadvantages. A key advantage is that individual broker-dealers may have special expertise in the securities they trade. A firm that specializes in municipal securities, for example, is likely to know the ins and outs of the municipal bond market and generally will have more research and other tools available to help the investing public than do firms that don't specialize in trading those securities.

Going to a firm that specializes in trading specific types of fixed-income securities is akin to choosing to shop for automotive supplies in a store that specializes in them instead of going to a supermarket, where there is very little emphasis on automotive supplies.

Perhaps the main disadvantage of specialization in the bond market is the impact it has on the visibility of a bond's price and availability. This lack of visibility is probably the main reason that the bond market seems so elusive to people; people probably would be more comfortable with the bond market if they could track it better. Luckily, the Internet is making this increasingly possible, as we'll see in Chapter 13.

The price of a bond is not always easily obtainable and can vary from dealer to dealer. This is certainly very different from the stock market, where prices are readily available and can be quoted literally to the penny. Not so in the bond market, where there are well over a million different bonds outstanding and some of those bonds "trade by appointment." In other words, they trade so infrequently that they can be difficult to price, value, find, and sell.

PRIMARY DEALERS FACILITATE EFFICIENCY IN THE BOND MARKET

Despite some important disadvantages of the decentralized nature of the bond market, it is a thriving market with vast liquidity. Playing a crucial role in supplying that liquidity are primary dealers. *Primary dealers* are banks and securities broker-dealers that trade in U.S. government securities with the Federal Reserve System. Collectively, primary dealers trade an average of approximately $200 billion in U.S. government securities every business day.

Primary dealers play an important role in the implementation of the Fed's monetary policy. They do this by buying and selling securities from the Fed in the open market. The purchase and sale of securities in the open market adds or removes money from the banking system, and this pushes interest rates to the Fed's desired levels. This process will be discussed in greater detail in Chapter 6.

The Federal Reserve Bank of New York established the primary dealer system in 1960. Many elite banks and broker-dealers have held the respected primary dealer designation since then, starting at 18 in 1960 and peaking at 46 in 1988. The number of primary dealers has fallen over the years, owing mostly to consolidation in the industry, as government securities dealers have either merged or changed the focus of their business. Currently there are 22 primary dealers that include many household names, as shown in Figure 2-1.

F i g u r e   2–1

Primary Dealer List (as of April 2002)
ABN AMRO Incorporated
BNP Paribas Securities Corp.
Banc of America Securities LLC
Banc One Capital, Markets, Inc.
Barclays Capital, Inc.
Bear, Stearns & Co., Inc.
CIBC World Markets Corp.
Credit Suisse First Boston Corporation
Daiwa Securities America, Inc.
Deutsche Bank Securities, Inc.
Dresdner Kleinwort Wasserstein Securities LLC
Goldman, Sachs & Co.
Greenwich Capital Markets, Inc.
HSBC Securities (USA), Inc.
J. P. Morgan Securities, Inc.
Lehman Brothers, Inc.
Merrill Lynch Government Securities Inc.
Mizuho Securities USA, Inc.
Morgan Stanley & Co. Incorporated
Nomura Securities International, Inc.
Salomon Smith Barney, Inc.
UBS Warburg LLC.

Source: Federal Reserve Bank of New York

Becoming a primary dealer is not easy. Recognizing the critical role primary dealers play in the implementation of monetary policy, the Federal Reserve has established very stringent requirements for obtaining the primary dealer designation. For starters, primary dealers must be either a commercial bank subject to supervision by U.S. Federal Reserve Bank supervisors or broker-dealers registered with the Securities and Exchange Commission. There are no restrictions against foreign-owned banks or broker-dealers becoming primary dealers.

There are also very stringent capital requirements for becoming a primary dealer. According to the New York Fed's current criteria, bank-related primary dealers must be in compliance with Tier I and Tier II capital standards under the Basle Capital Accord, with at least $100 million in Tier I capital. Registered broker-dealers must have at least $50 million in Tier II capital and total capital in excess of the regulatory "warning levels" for capital set by the Securities and Exchange Commission and the U.S. Treasury, the two regulatory bodies that oversee nonbank securities trading organizations.

Tier I capital and Tier II capital are simply fancy names for the types of capital needed for firms to obtain the primary dealer designation. Tier I capital includes common stockholders' equity, qualifying noncumulative perpetual preferred stock, and a minority interest in the equity accounts of consolidated subsidiaries. Tier I capital normally is defined as the sum of core capital elements minus goodwill and other intangible assets. The Tier II component of a bank's qualifying total capital may consist of supplementary capital elements such as allowance for loan and lease losses, perpetual preferred stock and a related surplus, hybrid capital instruments and mandatory convertible debt securities, and term-subordinated debt and intermediate-term preferred stock.

These stringent capital requirements are designed to help ensure that primary dealers are able to enter into transactions with the Fed in sufficient size to maintain the efficiency of their trading desk operations.

Primary dealers assist the Fed not only by facilitating the implementation of its directives on monetary policy but also by giving the Fed valuable information. For one thing, the Fed requires primary dealers to make reasonably good markets in their trading relationships with the Fed's trading desk.

In addition, primary dealers must participate meaningfully in auctions of U.S. Treasuries held by the U.S. Treasury Department. Interestingly, primary dealers also must offer market information and analysis to the Fed's trading desk, which the Fed uses in the formulation and implementation of monetary policy. Primary dealers also must report weekly on their trading activities, cash, futures, and financing market positions in Treasury and other securities.

Primary dealers tend to carry larger inventories of fixed-income securities and carry a greater variety of them. They also tend to have a greater ability to participate in offerings of new fixed-income securities.

As you can see, primary dealers have a very big presence in the bond market in terms of both their daily trading volumes and their relationship with the Fed. They therefore play a critical role in the functioning of the bond market, providing the substantial amounts of liquidity needed to keep the bond market running efficiently.

THE BOND MARKET'S SIZE, FROM HEAD TO TOE

It might surprise you to hear that the bond market is far larger than the stock market, but it is. This surprises most people because so much more attention is paid to the stock market than to the bond market. In many venues the stock market grabs the lion's share of media attention and is the subject of most conversations about investing. Similarly, investment-oriented firms such as brokerage firms and mutual fund companies spend far more of their time and money trying to lure individuals who are interested in stocks than they do trying to attract individuals interested in bonds.

This all seems rational, of course, since individuals frequently trade in and out of stocks but rarely make changes to their bond holdings. Most people who buy bonds buy them with the intention of holding on to them for a while.

The relatively low level of attention paid to the bond market has contributed to the public's misconceptions about it and is one reason why the public knows so little about the bond market.

What is the bond market, and who are its participants? This chapter will help answer these questions.

THERE'S NO BIGGER MARKET

The U.S. bond market is the biggest securities market in the world. At $18.5 trillion, the bond market is almost double the size of the U.S. economy and is several trillion dollars larger than the U.S. equity market, which has a market capitalization of about $15 trillion. The bond market's growth has been accelerating in recent years as new issuance of bonds has exploded in the face of growing demand.

There are many reasons for the bond market's rapid growth. First, as the economy grows, demand for credit grows too. This means that during an economic expansion companies need to borrow additional capital to finance their growth. They get this capital by issuing more bonds. Additionally, in an expanding economy new companies are formed, and this increases the universe of companies that tap the bond market for money.

A second reason for the bond market's rapid growth has been the globalization of the financial markets. New technologies and reduced trade barriers have allowed global investors to move money across borders with relative ease, resulting in an increase in both the issuance of foreign bonds and the purchase of U.S. bonds by foreign investors. The audience for bonds has become far vaster than it was not too long ago, and companies have taken advantage of the growing audience by issuing more bonds.

A third contributing factor to the bond market's rapid growth has been a sharp increase in the introduction of new financial products. One example is the market for so-called asset-backed securities, which are basically a repackaging of loans such as home mortgages. The asset-backed securities market has grown sharply in recent years, more than doubling in size to more than $1.3 trillion over the past five years. Financial innovations such as asset-backed securities have been a big factor in the growth of the markets for many other types of fixed-income securities.

There are other reasons why the bond market has grown, of course, but these are the most prominent. These forces appear likely to continue to influence the growth of the bond market for years to come.

SIZING UP THE MARKET

The bond market consists of many different types of fixed-income securities. The most prominent of these securities are, from the largest segments to the smallest, as follows:

- Mortgage-related securities
- Corporate bonds
- U.S. Treasuries
- Money market securities
- U.S. government agency securities
- Municipal bonds
- Asset-backed securities

These securities account for all of the bond market's $18.5 trillion, and the market for each of them is $1.3 trillion or more. They are all therefore large enough to facilitate the needs of investors both large and small.

Knowing the size of each segment of the bond market can give you perspective on their relative importance and put you well on the road to having a well-rounded knowledge of the bond market. To get started, take a look at Figure 2-2.

As you can see in the figure, the largest segment of the bond market is the mortgage securities market. This might surprise you since the mortgage securities market doesn't exactly make the front page of the business news every day, nor is it the focus of financial advertising and literature. Yet it is a thriving market, as we will discuss later.

Aside from the perspective you'll get from knowing the sizes of the various segments of the bond market, there are several other reasons to track its size. First, tracking changes in the bond market's size can help you discern economic and financial trends. For example, an increase in the size of the corporate bond market could be taken as a sign that U.S. corporations are optimistic about the economic outlook. They borrow money, after all, to expand their businesses. In some cases, however, a surge in the growth of corporate debt may raise a red flag by hinting that corporations are accumulating an excessive amount of debt.

A second reason to learn more about the bond market's size is to gain an improved perspective on the impact that developments

Figure 2–2

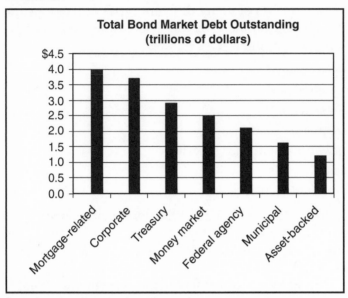

Source: Bond Market Association, Federal Reserve

in each of the market segments may have on the economy and the financial markets. If, for example, dislocation in the municipal bond market were to surface after a municipality's failure to repay its debt obligations, it would be helpful to have a perspective on how large the default was relative to the size of the market. This could help you make a judgment about whether the dislocation was presenting a risk or an opportunity for investments in that market.

A third benefit of tracking the bond market's size is the perspective it provides on both the quote depth and the liquidity of each market segment. The size of the markets has an important bearing on the market's liquidity and quote depth, and this can influence when you buy and sell securities. Basically, the bigger the market is, the more liquid it is likely to be. This should translate into greater quote depth, better visibility on market prices, and prices that are indicative of each security's fair value.

For forecasters and academicians, tracking changes in the sizes of the various segments of the fixed-income market helps provide documentation of the flow of funds between different types of financial assets. This helps them study trends in personal savings, for example.

The Federal Reserve tracks the flow of funds not only between the different segments of the fixed-income market but across other financial assets as well. This helps the Fed quantify the effects that changes in credit conditions may have on real activity. The data on the flow of funds, which is produced by the Federal Reserve in a quarterly survey, helps the Fed develop forecasts on the economy because changes in balance sheets and credit conditions can be important factors that affect the spending decisions of households, businesses, and governments.

Given the value of having a good understanding of the various segments of the bond market, let's take a look at each of the segments and size them up.

Treasury Bonds

For most people the bond market and U.S. Treasuries are synonymous. Public awareness of the Treasury market easily exceeds that of all the other segments of the bond market. You can understand why when you look at its mammoth size and daily trading volume. While the Treasury market is not the biggest segment of the bond market—the mortgage securities market is—Treasuries, which are issued by the U.S. Department of the Treasury, are by far the most active segment, and the Treasury Department is the single largest issuer of debt in the world. In fact, Treasuries are the most actively traded securities in the world.

U.S. Treasury securities are so prominent that their interest rates are used as a benchmark for interest rates in most of the bond markets and throughout the world. This will be discussed in greater detail later in this chapter, and a definitional guide to Treasuries and other types of bonds will be presented in Chapter 4.

As you saw in Figure 2-2, there is almost $3 trillion in Treasuries outstanding, making Treasuries the third largest segment of the bond market in terms of size. Many people might wonder why there is just $3 trillion in Treasuries outstanding when the U.S. government has $5.9 trillion of debt outstanding, or roughly 60 percent of the size of the U.S. economy. There are two main reasons for this. First, approximately $2.5 trillion in nonmarketable securities is held in a trust fund for various programs, particularly the Social Security program. These trust funds are essentially IOUs. Currently, approximately $1.1 trillion is owed to the Social Security trust fund (called the Federal Old-Age and Survivors Insurance Trust Fund) by the U.S. Treasury Department. These IOUs accumulated throughout most of the 1980s and 1990s as the U.S. government essentially dipped into the trust fund's yearly surpluses. The trust fund has been running surpluses for a number of years, as the population of people paying Social Security taxes has exceeded the population of people receiving Social Security benefits. The main reason for this involves favorable demographics: A baby boom took place between 1946 and 1964, resulting in a large pool of taxpayers. The increase in the number of taxpayers has greatly exceeded the increase in the number of Social Security recipients, resulting in large surpluses (as baby boomers retire, this dynamic will work in the opposite direction, carrying with it a bundle of economic, financial, and political ramifications). Through creative accounting and political will, the surpluses have been included in the yearly readings on the U.S. fiscal balance. This has produced smaller reported deficits and larger surpluses than has actually been the case, but the debts owed to the Social Security trust fund and other funds have been kept out of the public eye.

A second reason why the total amount of publicly traded Treasuries differs from the U.S. government's total debt relates to the Federal Reserve. The Fed holds roughly $534 billion in Treasuries for its own account. As will be discussed in Chapter 6, the Fed has been accumulating Treasuries for many years to help it implement monetary policy. Thus, while the Fed's holdings are not included in the $3 trillion tally of publicly traded Treasuries, they are nonetheless part of Uncle Sam's total debt *outstanding*.

It is important to keep in mind that there is a meaningful distinction between the total amount of *publicly traded U.S. Treasuries* outstanding and the total amount of *U.S. debt* outstanding.

The total amount of publicly traded U.S. Treasuries outstanding has been shrinking in recent years as a result of several years of budget surpluses. The surpluses enabled the U.S. Treasury Department to reduce its yearly issuance of Treasuries from a peak of $2.485 trillion in 1996 to $2.001 trillion in 2000. Moreover, in March 2000 the Treasury began a program allowing the use of the surplus to buy back previously issued Treasuries from the public, concentrating on high-yielding long-dated maturities. The Treasury expects to save taxpayers millions of dollars in interest payments by reducing the public debt. In calendar year 2000 the Treasury repurchased approximately $30 billion of Treasuries, and it was expected to buy back a bit more than that by the end of 2001. These buybacks should be good for holders of long-dated maturities, all other factors being equal.

As you can see in Figure 2-3, the total amount of publicly traded U.S. Treasuries outstanding peaked in 1996 at $3.46 trillionand has fallen steadily since 1998, the first year the U.S. government recently began running annual budget surpluses. The market for Treasuries is expected to continue to decline over the next ten years owing to expected yearly budget surpluses and despite the $1.35 trillion tax cut implemented by President George W. Bush in 2001. In fact, one can argue that the tax cut ultimately may boost the yearly budget surpluses by promoting economic growth and thus increasing tax receipts. Tax receipts typically rise when the economy strengthens and incomes rise, resulting in an increase in tax payments by both individuals and businesses.

Many people are wondering whether yearly budget surpluses will result in the eventual elimination of Treasuries. By some estimates, Treasuries will be eliminated by 2012 or so. I doubt that the debt will be eliminated, as the forces that shape the U.S. budget picture have a strong proclivity to work against that possibility. Chiefly, the political temptations to use the budget surpluses for pet projects are likely to erode any chance that the debt will be repaid by 2012. Nevertheless, I believe the federal debt will be reduced steadily in future years.

Volume in Treasury Securities

As was mentioned earlier, U.S. Treasuries are the most actively traded securities in the world. This makes the Treasury market the most liquid financial market in the world. Treasuries trade literally around the clock and around the globe.

Investors are drawn to the Treasury market for its safety element. As obligations of the U.S. government, Treasuries are backed by the full faith and credit of the U.S. government and therefore are considered risk-free. Investors also are drawn to the

Figure 2—3

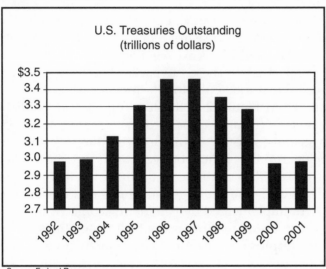

U.S. Treasuries Outstanding
(trillions of dollars)

Source: Federal Reserve

Treasury market because of its deep liquidity and quote depth; large transactions of up to $1 billion or more are commonplace in the Treasury market.

As you can see in Figure 2-4, the daily average trading volume for all Treasuries by primary dealers was $286.1 billion in the first three quarters of 2001—a record. Volume in that quarter was roughly $80 billion above the average daily volume posted in the previous five years. Volume surged in 2001 as investors sought the safety element of Treasuries to shield themselves from global economic and financial uncertainties that resulted from many factors, including the sharp stock market decline in 2000. Volume also surged because of trading activity associated with cuts in interest rates by the Federal Reserve.

The strong trading volume in 2001 provides evidence that three of the biggest determinants of trading volume in Treasuries are the state of the economy, the Federal Reserve, and global economic and financial conditions.

Municipal Securities

The municipal bond market may not be the biggest segment of the bond market in terms of total dollar size, but it is easily the biggest in terms of the total number of bonds outstanding. It's easy to understand why there are so many municipal bonds outstanding when one considers the large number of state and local government entities in the United States: There are over 50,000 government entities that issue municipal bonds. In all, a whopping 1.5 million separate bond issues are outstanding. That stands in stark contrast to the other segments of the bond market, where far fewer securities have been issued. The market for U.S. Treasuries, for example, consists of only about 160 separate securities.

One might think the large number of municipal bonds outstanding would translate into a market bustling with activity, but it doesn't. Daily volume in the municipal bond market is actually quite low. In fact, many municipal bonds "trade by appointment." In other words, they rarely trade.

The municipal bond market is roughly $1.7 trillion in size. It has been growing steadily but slowly over the last five years, increasing from about $1.3 trillion in 1996 to its current level. This puts its average growth rate over the last five years at a little less than 5 percent per year.

Individual investors historically have shown the greatest amount of interest in the municipal bond market, and their continued interest has helped the municipal bond market continue its

Figure 2–4

Average Daily Trading Volume of U.S. Treasury Marketable Securities[1] 1994–2001;Q3

[1] Includes only marketable coupon securities.
Source: Bond Market Association

steady growth. Individuals, in fact, are by far the largest holders of municipal securities, holding about 75 percent of all outstanding issues. The municipal bond market is the only segment of the bond market whose securities are held primarily by individuals rather than institutions. Over 5.1 million households hold municipals in one form or another, either directly or indirectly, through mutual funds and the like.

Individuals are drawn to municipal bonds for their tax advantages; the interest paid on most municipal bonds is exempt from federal taxes. This makes municipal securities most attractive to individuals in high income tax brackets. We will discuss the special tax-exempt status of municipal securities in greater detail in Chapter 4.

The municipal bond market is likely to maintain its current rate of growth for quite some time unless the federal government stops collecting income taxes (in the next millennium perhaps). Individuals therefore are likely to maintain their current level of attraction to municipal bonds for the foreseeable future.

One major factor that almost certainly will contribute to its growth is so-called urban sprawl. Urban sprawl is basically what the name implies; it occurs as a result of the spreading of communities from urban areas to rural areas. This can put great strains on the finances of state and local governments as the sprawl creates a need for new roads, sewers, schools, and so forth. These municipalities turn to the municipal bond market to finance the many projects that result from urban sprawl.

Volume in Municipals

Despite the popularity of municipal bonds among individual investors and the massive number of municipal securities outstanding, the municipal bond market is an illiquid market. The average daily trading volume of municipal securities is just $8 billion per day, less than 3 percent of the daily trading volume in U.S. Treasuries.

Daily trading volume in the municipal bond market is low largely because individuals do not buy and sell municipal securities in the same way they buy and sell stocks. Municipal securities are not trading vehicles and therefore are rarely used for speculative purposes. Individuals generally buy municipals with the intention of holding on to them for a while, often until the bonds mature. As a result, individual investors are apt to be only occasional participants in the municipal bond market.

Trading volume in the municipal bond market can be influenced by a number of factors. For example, individual investors tend to vary in their preference for municipals depending on interest rate levels. Individuals tend to shy away from municipals when interest rates fall and flock to them when interest rates rise. They are apparently very sensitive to the impact that interest rate levels can have on their interest income and, hence, their tax liabilities.

An exception to the notion that individuals shy away from municipals when interest rates decline is the way they behave when the decline is due partly to weakening in the stock market. In cases such as this, rather than shift out of interest-bearing assets, individual investors often shift money out of stocks and into high-quality bonds such as Treasuries, as well as high-quality municipal securities (not all municipal securities are considered high quality). They do this because bonds tend to perform well when the equity market falters.

Another way in which the interest rate environment influences trading volume in municipals is through activity associated with refunded bonds. *Refunded bonds* are previously issued bonds that essentially are refinanced with new bonds at a lower interest rate. In a refunding, an issuer sells new bonds to raise the money needed to eventually "refund" or prepay the older bonds on their first call date (see Chapter 3 for more on call dates and callable bonds). The issuance of new bonds leads to an increase in volume by spurring investors to participate in the market through purchases of the new bonds. In some cases the buyers of the new bonds sell or swap out of their existing holdings of municipal bonds to pay for their purchases of the new bonds. This boosts volume further.

A downside of refunding issuance is that the investors in bonds that are refunded have to find new investments to replace their prepaid bonds. This usually means that they wind up reinvesting the money they receive from the refunded bonds into new bonds that have a lower interest rate than the refunded bonds. This reduces the rate of return on their money.

Refunding issuance often can account for a meaningful percentage of the total issuance of new municipal bonds. In the first
quarter of 2001, for example, refunding issuance was roughly 30
percent of the total issuance of municipal bonds. That was much
higher than a year earlier, when refunding issuance was roughly 15
percent of total issuance. The doubling in refunding issuance was
due to the sharp drop in interest rates that occurred after the Federal
Reserve began a series of interest rate cuts on January 3, 2001.

As you can see, interest rate levels play an important role in
influencing trading volume in the municipal bond market. It is
therefore important to bear in mind that interest rate levels may
affect key investment considerations such as market liquidity,
quote depth, and refunding risk.

Corporate Bonds

At $3.8 trillion, the corporate bond market is the second largest seg-
ment of the bond market. Corporate bonds are widely held, with
most of them in the hands of large institutions such as insurance
companies, pension funds, and foreign entities. Households are
also large holders of corporate bonds, owning more of them than
of any other type of bond.

The corporate bond market is a fairly active market, but exact
figures on its daily volume are not calculated by any of the major
bean counters. It is known, however, that the holders of corporate
bonds are active players, especially compared to participants in the
municipal bond market.

The corporate bond market consists of many names that are
familiar to most people. The likes of General Electric, Procter &
Gamble, General Motors, and Walt Disney Company are just a tiny
sampling of the many familiar names that make up the corporate
bond market. With names like these, it's no wonder that this market is so large. As we have learned, large corporations frequently
issue new debt to finance their expansion, and this contributes to
the growth of the corporate bond market.

Almost daily, corporations issue new bonds to a receptive
audience of investors. In 2000 roughly $600 billion in new corpo-
rate bonds was issued. That was slightly below the pace set in 1999
and roughly equal to the pace in 1998.

New issuance surged to record levels in 2001, with a staggering $258.2 billion of new corporate bonds issued in the first quarter
of that year and a record $879.2 billion issued for the full year,
according to data from the Bond Market Association and Thomson
Financial Securities. The reasons for this surge are a microcosm of
some of the factors that affect the issuance of corporate bonds.

A major influence on the surge in issuance in 2001 was the
Federal Reserve. The Fed began a series of interest rate reductions
on January 3, 2001, and interest rates began to fall. Importantly,
interest rates on corporate bonds fell faster than did those on many
other types of bonds, most notably Treasuries. In turn, prices on
corporate bonds rose faster too, since bond prices and yields move
inversely with each other. This outperformance meant that corporations could take advantage of a two-pronged drop in interest
rates on corporate bonds; they had dropped both outright and on
a spread, or on a relative basis compared to Treasuries. A yield
spread between corporate bonds and Treasuries is common
because of their differences in credit quality, and so the narrowing
of the yield spread between corporate bonds and Treasuries in 2001
was a sign that investors had become more optimistic about the
credit quality of corporate bonds. They no doubt built their optimism on the notion that the Fed's interest rate cuts would
strengthen the economy and thus improve the credit quality of corporate bonds. Indeed, the yield spread between corporate bonds
and Treasuries continued into the early part of 2002 as optimism on
the economy grew further. Seeking to take advantage of that optimism as well as the two-pronged drop in interest rates on corporate bonds, corporations vigorously issued new corporate bonds.
When companies issue new bonds to take advantage of declines in
interest rates, this is referred to as *opportunistic issuance*. This was a
major factor in 2001 and is one of the most important factors that
can affect the issuance of corporate bonds.

Another key factor that affected the surge in issuance in 2001
was the condition of the U.S. equity market. The steep plunge in
prices that had occurred in 2000 led investors to seek the relative
safety of the bond market. That surge in demand facilitated the
sharp increase in new issuance. Thus, weakness in the equity market can affect the demand for corporate bonds. A weak equity
market, however, does not always translate into increased demand

for corporate bonds. In fact, it actually can result in a decrease in the demand. After all, the companies that investors unload in the equity market could be the same as those in the corporate bond market. Thus, there's a fine line between whether weakness in the equity market helps or hurts the demand for corporate bonds. There basically comes a point when investors' concerns about the economy overtake all other investment considerations.

Yet another factor that influenced the 2001 issuance surge was a big shift from the issuance of short-term instruments, such as commercial paper, which are short-term unsecured debt obligations issued in the open market, to that of longer-term bonds. Companies wanted to take advantage of the decline in interest rates to lock in long-term financing at low interest rates. This is akin to a homeowner refinancing an adjustable-rate mortgage, which changes every year, by converting it to a fixed-rate loan of, say, 15 or 30 years. In doing so, the homeowner removes uncertainties about the monthly payments and locks in a low long-term interest rate. Companies refinance their debt in the same way, hoping to remove uncertainties about near-term debt servicing while simultaneously locking in low long-term interest costs. Thus, the interest rate environment and its impact on financing decisions have an important bearing on the level of new issuance.

A fourth factor that affected the level of new issuance in the corporate bond market in 2001 was a surge in the issuance of high-yield bonds, which jumped to $29.3 billion compared with $12.5 billion in 2000. A key factor behind that surge was a change in investors' attitudes. In 2000 risk aversion had sharply increased as a result of the fall in stock prices and a weakening in the U.S. economy. As a result, investors shunned assets deemed to contain high levels of risk. High-yield bonds fit that mold, hence the name "*junk bonds.*" But in 2001 the Fed's interest rate cuts sharply reduced the risk aversion investors had shown in 2000, leading to strong inflows into high-yield bond funds. Companies recognized this renewed appetite for risk, resulting in a sharp increase in new issuance of high-yield bonds. The experiences of 2000 and 2001 clearly illustrate the important role that investor attitudes toward risk play in the growth of the corporate bond market.

As you can see, the size of the corporate bond market is influenced by a variety of factors. At the core, however, the Fed, the interest environment, and the economy are the most critical factors in shaping the corporate bond market. This becomes even more obvious when one takes a closer look at their impact on the various industries within the corporate bond market. We'll do that in Chapter 4.

The corporate bond market is likely to continue its pattern of growing at rates that depend on these critical factors. Its growth trajectory therefore is likely to continue to fluctuate as these factors change. But so long as the economy continues to grow most of the time, as it has for decades, the corporate bond market is likely to continue to grow strongly in the years to come.

Volume in Corporate Bonds

Volume in the corporate bond market is not easy to quantify. The bean counters who tally the daily volume in Treasuries and municipals cannot as easily quantify the volume of bonds that trade in the corporate bond market. There are many reasons for this, but the primary reason relates to the fact that most corporate bond trades are not recorded in ways that can be captured easily. Transactions in Treasuries, for example, can be tracked through *government brokers:* intermediaries that facilitate trading between primary dealers and, to a lesser degree, between broker-dealers. Government brokers post the primary dealers' bids and offers on their computer networks, and all those transactions are visible to the dealer community. The transactions are therefore easily tabulated. No such network exists in the corporate bond market. While some corporate bond transactions are done through brokers, the preponderance of trades takes place over the counter, essentially invisible to the public.

There is, however, one source of data on daily trading volume in corporate bonds, and it comes from an unusual source: the New York Stock Exchange (NYSE). A large number of bonds are listed on the NYSE: about 1600 compared to the nearly 3500 stocks that are listed there. The bonds listed on the NYSE have a combined value of about $2.1 trillion compared to about $12.3 trillion of listed stocks. Daily volume in bonds that trade on the NYSE was just $11.1 million in 2001, with $2.5 billion traded for the full year. These numbers are a far cry from the daily volume in Treasuries, which is estimated at close to $300 billion. These data clearly show the difficulty of tracking daily volume in the corporate bond market and provide further evidence of the lack of transparency that makes the bond market so elusive to the general public.

Although there are no official numbers on the daily trading volume in corporate bonds, institutional investors trade billions of dollars in corporate bonds on a daily basis. There's little doubt, therefore, that the daily trading volume in corporate bonds handily exceeds the trading volume in municipal bonds, but it in no way approaches that of Treasuries.

One indication that volume in corporate bonds is indeed vigorous is the level of new issuance. In all of 2001, for example, daily issuance of U.S. investment-grade corporate bonds averaged roughly $2.32 billion per business day, according to data from IDEAglobal.com. During that time issuance often topped $5 billion in a single day. Since new issuance tends to spur volume in excess of the issuance, as investors shuffle their portfolios to make room for the new securities, it is rational to conclude that the average daily trading volume in corporate bonds is high and that the corporate bond market is an active market.

Agency Securities

At $2.1 trillion, the government agency securities market is not the largest segment of the bond market, but it is easily one of its most active and fastest-growing segments. The agency securities market consists largely of debt issued by eight separate government securities agencies, which commonly are referred to as GSEs (this is discussed in greater detail in Chapter 3). With the exception of one of the eight government-sponsored enterprises, the GSEs are not backed by the full faith and credit of the U.S. government. Importantly, this means that they carry an element of credit risk. Nevertheless, since they are government-sponsored agencies, many investors believe that the GSEs have an implicit guarantee. In other words, investors feel that the U.S. government probably would take extraordinary measures to help the agencies if they encountered financial difficulties.

It's easy to understand why investors would draw such a conclusion even if it is not entirely technically correct. Consider the biggest of the GSEs, the Federal National Mortgage Association, Fannie Mae for short. Since Fannie Mae began in 1938, it has helped millions of Americans buy their own homes. Over the last 30 years alone, Fannie Mae has helped over 30 million families buy their own homes. With numbers like these, it is evident why many investors believe that the government would do its utmost to assure that Fannie Mae and the other GSEs stay in business. Again, I must emphasize that this conclusion is technically incorrect, since there is no true implicit guarantee that would save those agencies from a full-scale financial dilemma. Nevertheless, it is difficult to imagine that the government would sit idly by in the event of a dilemma. Luckily, however, such dilemmas are not on the immediate horizon; GSEs are in very strong financial shape.

Led by the GSEs, the agency securities market has been growing rapidly in recent years. In fact, total federal agency debt outstanding roughly doubled between 1996 and 2000, as Figure 2-5 shows. In 2001 new issuance of long-term federal agency debt (maturities of one year or more) rose sharply to $921.5 billion from $428.1 billion in 2000, according to the Bond Market Association.

The sharp growth in the agency securities market has been fueled partly by the strong growth of the housing market as home ownership has reached record levels. Fueled by an expanding economy and low interest rates, home ownership steadily climbed in the 1990s, and by the late 1990s close to two-thirds of American households owned their own homes. As home ownership expanded, so did the need for financing, since most homeowners take out a mortgage to buy a home. Government agencies such as Fannie Mae play an integral role in providing this financing by issuing debt securities and using the money to purchase pools of mortgage loans and by guaranteeing others.

With home mortgage loans playing such a big role in the growth of the agency securities market, its continued growth therefore depends crucially on the interest rate environment. High interest rate levels, for example, almost certainly would discourage home buying and thus reduce the number of mortgage loans outstanding. In turn, new issuance of agency securities would drop and curtail the growth of the agency securities market.

Similarly, if the U.S. economy weakened dramatically, home buying probably would decline. This would reduce the growth in the number of mortgage loans outstanding. In contrast, a strong economy accompanied by strong growth in personal income and low interest rates probably would fuel strong growth in home buying, thus also fueling growth in the agency securities market.

Figure 2–5

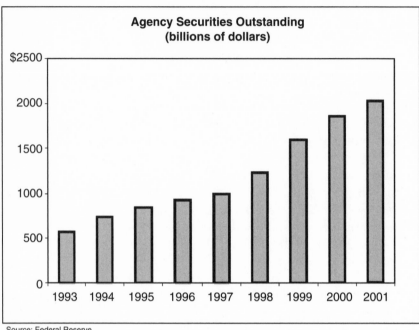

Agency Securities Outstanding
(billions of dollars)

Source: Federal Reserve

Another factor that has influenced the growth of the agency securities market has been favorable demographics. The aging of baby boomers, individuals born between 1946 and 1964, has led to an increase in home buying as baby boomers use the wealth they built during the last few decades to buy larger homes and second homes. Another positive demographic factor for the housing market and hence the agency securities market has been the rise in the number of single-person households and in immigration.

Thus, three critical factors that shape the growth of the agency securities market are the economic climate, the interest rate environment, and demographics. These forces appear likely to influence the growth of the agency securities market positively in the years to come, but cyclical forces almost certainly will interrupt the positive trend occasionally.

As will be discussed in Chapter 3, agency securities could well replace U.S. Treasuries as the benchmark securities of the bond market. Agency securities have very high credit ratings and the agency securities market is highly liquid, making them a good alternative to Treasuries. The agency securities market is growing large enough to overtake the Treasuries market in size if current trends continue, but that's a big if.

Volume in Agency Securities

The strong growth in the size of the agency securities market has been accompanied by strong growth in its daily trading volume. Trading volume in agencies has increased steadily in recent years. In 2001, for example, the daily average trading volume in agency securities was $90.2 billion, a 23.1 percent increase compared to 2000. While that sum falls well short of the daily trading volume in Treasuries, the agency securities market is robust enough to be considered an extremely active, deep, and liquid market.

One clear indication that the agency securities market is an active market is the bid-ask spread on the most active agency securities. Fannie Mae, for example, reports that its benchmark securities have liquidity comparable to that of off-the-run Treasuries (Treasuries that were issued in past auction cycles), with bid-ask spreads of 0.5 to 2.0 basis points. In addition, the bid-ask spread on Fannie Mae's benchmark 10-year note is also comparable to that on Treasuries, with bid-ask spreads usually averaging about $\frac{1}{32}$ of a point.

Another indication that the agency securities market is an active one can be found in the futures market, where futures on agency securities are actively traded. In the futures market, participants actively buy and sell contracts for future delivery. The exchanges that create futures contracts do so only when they feel there will be sufficient interest in them. Therefore, the mere existence of agency futures contracts validates the notion that the agency securities market is an active one. The futures market will be discussed in greater detail in Chapter 11.

A third indication of the growing market for agency securities is the repo market. This is a market where parties exchange collateral for cash with a simultaneous agreement by one of the parties to buy back the collateral at a specified price at some point in the future. Primary dealers often use the repo market to finance the holdings of their positions by exchanging their holdings for cash while simultaneously agreeing to repurchase (hence the term *repo*) at a specified date in the future. An active repo market for agency securities has been developing in recent years, pointing to active conditions in the agency securities market.

In light of the steady growth in the size of the agency securities market, it is likely to continue to become an increasingly active market in the years to come.

Mortgage-Backed Securities

When most people think of debt, they think of mortgage debt. For most people a home mortgage is their biggest debt, and it is usually the biggest debt they will ever incur. When one considers that millions of Americans have a mortgage on their homes, one begins to realize that the total amount of mortgages outstanding is quite large. That is indeed the case; Americans owe approximately $5.3 trillion on their home mortgages, and mortgage debt accounts for over half of all household debt outstanding.

Given the staggering amount of mortgage debt outstanding and the innovative nature of the financial system in the United States, it should not be surprising that the largest segment of the bond market is the market for mortgage-backed securities. At $4.1 trillion, the mortgage-backed securities market is the largest debt market in the world and is roughly one-third larger than the U.S. Treasuries market. The mortgage-backed securities market is also an active market, with average daily trading volume second only to that of U.S. Treasuries.

The mortgage-backed securities market has been growing rapidly in recent years and is now roughly twice as large as it was ten years ago. Its growth has been fueled by many of the same forces that have fueled the rapid growth of the agency securities market. The main driver of growth in both markets has been the sharp growth in the number of mortgage originations, which surged in both 1998 and 2001 as mortgage rates fell in response to interest rate reductions by the Federal Reserve.

New issuance of mortgage-backed securities was particularly strong in 2001 as mortgage rates stayed low for a protracted period. In fact, new issuance reached a record $1.1 trillion in 2001 compared with $483.4 billion in 2000. That sharp increase no doubt was the result of a sharp decrease in mortgage rates, which brought the average 30-year fixed-rate mortgage down to as low as 6.45% in 2001 compared to as high as 8.64% in 2000.

The sharp increase in the number of mortgages outstanding in 1998 and 2001 created a vast pool of mortgages that could be securitized into mortgage-backed securities. *Securitization of mortgages* is the process in which mortgage loans are bundled together and sold to investors as a financial security, with the mortgage loans acting as collateral for the newly created security. This will be explained in greater detail in Chapter 3

Most mortgage-backed securities are issued by three U.S. government agencies: the Federal National Mortgage Association (Fannie Mae), the Federal Home Loan Mortgage Corporation (Freddie Mac), and the Government National Mortgage Association (Ginnie Mae, or GNMA). The biggest issuer of mortgage-backed securities is Fannie Mae, followed by Freddie Mac and then GNMA. As an illustration, note that of the $1.1 trillion of new issuance in the first half of 2001, Fannie Mae issued $528.4 billion, Freddie Mac issued $389.6 billion, and Ginnie Mae issued $170.8 billion.

Clearly, federal agencies play a large role in the issuance of mortgage-backed securities, with Fannie Mae very much at the forefront. By issuing new securities, these agencies fulfill their mission of providing capital to the housing market.

The growth of the mortgage-backed securities market depends largely on the same factors that influence the growth of the agency securities market. As was discussed earlier, these factors include the economic climate, the interest rate climate, and demographics. These factors are likely to continue fueling growth in the mortgage-backed securities market in the years to come, with occasional interruptions caused by cyclical forces.

Another factor that suggests that there is substantial room for continued growth of the mortgage-backed securities market is the fact that only about half of all mortgage debt has been securitized. This means that the long-term growth rate of the mortgage-backed securities market could be maintained even if mortgage originations slowed. All that is needed is continued growth in the percentage of mortgage loans that are securitized.

Volume in Mortgage-Backed Securities

Although the mortgage-backed securities market is the largest debt securities market in the world, it is not the most active. Nevertheless, it is still quite active and is the second most active segment of the bond market after U.S. Treasuries; average daily trading volume in mortgage-backed securities is roughly $100 billion, compared with roughly $300 billion for Treasuries. The relatively low volume in the world's largest debt securities market highlights the enormous volume that takes place in the Treasuries market on a daily basis.

The disparity in daily trading volume between Treasuries and all the other segments of the bond market is so large that Treasuries should not be used as a yardstick to assess the extent to which the other segments of the bond market are active. A comparison would no doubt lead to the incorrect conclusion that most of the bond market is inactive. While this is true of some sectors and of specific bonds, it is not true of the bond market in general and certainly is not true of the mortgage-backed securities market.

To illustrate, note that the $100 billion in average daily trading volume of mortgage-backed securities is nearly double the average daily trading volume of stocks on the NYSE. One would never know that by reading the daily financial newspapers, where there is hardly a mention of the mortgage-backed securities market. Yet the data clearly show that the mortgage-backed securities market is quite active.

As with other segments of the bond market, trading volume in the mortgage-backed securities market is influenced by changes in the level of new issuance that result from fluctuations in interest rates. As was illustrated earlier, when interest rate levels decline, mortgage originations tend to increase, resulting in an increase in the issuance of mortgage-backed securities and spurring trading volume. Conversely, as interest rates rise, mortgage originations tend to decline, bringing volume down.

Despite the big role interest rate levels play in determining daily trading volume in mortgage-backed securities, the long-term trend appears to be up owing to increasing recognition of the many benefits of investing in mortgage-backed securities.

LIQUIDITY: A MEASURE OF THE VIBRANCY, DEPTH, AND EFFICIENCY OF MARKETS

Liquidity is vital for the normal and optimal functioning of markets. *Liquidity* can be defined as the ease or difficulty with which buyers and sellers can transact in small and large quantities at prices that are considered representative of the true market value.

A highly liquid market ensures that observed prices are close to the market consensus on where prices should be and that changes in prices reflect revisions in the market consensus rather than dislocations associated with illiquidity.

Liquidity enhances the efficiency of markets, encouraging broader market participation. In turn, this increases the availability of credit at lowered costs, encouraging the use of credit and spurring economic growth.

In the United States, where the financial markets are both vast and mature, liquidity is generally quite good. This is one of the biggest reasons why the U.S. economy has performed so well for so long. Capitalist societies such as the United States simply cannot thrive without liquid markets.

How to Measure Market Liquidity: Bid-Ask Spreads, Market Depth, and Price Transparency

There are several ways to measure market liquidity, and those methods can be applied to almost any market, including the bond market. One measure of market liquidity is the bid-ask spread on individual securities. The narrower the spread, the more liquid the market; the wider the spread, the less liquid the market. The reason for this is fairly simple: The closer buyers and sellers are in agreement on the price of what they are trying to buy or sell, the more likely it is that they will actually transact with each other. Of course, a wider bid-ask spread indicates that buyers and sellers are in disagreement on the fair market price, and this decreases the likelihood that a transaction will take place.

In the bond market the bid-ask spread varies with the type of fixed-income security and its maturity. In U.S. Treasuries, for example, the bid-ask spread on 10-year notes is typically between $1/64$ and $1/32$ of a point (where 1 point equals 1 percent of par, which is a bond's principal value—usually $1000). Shorter Treasury maturities such as 2-year notes generally trade at a smaller spread of between $1/128$ and $1/64$ of a point owing to their lower level of volatility compared with that of longer maturities and because price changes in short maturities have a greater impact on their yield-to-maturity than do price changes on longer maturities. The impact of price changes on a bond's yield will be discussed in greater detail in Chapter 3.

The bid-ask spread on government agencies is wider than that on U.S. Treasuries but is still relatively narrow. In fact, Fannie Mae, the largest U.S. government agency and the most actively traded government agency market, reports that its actively traded securities have liquidity that is comparable to that of off-the-run Treasury securities (older, less active Treasuries). The yield spread on Fannie Mae's actively traded securities has generally between 50 and 100 basis points over that on Treasuries over the last few years.

Outside of U.S. government and agency securities, the bid-ask spreads on other types of fixed-income securities are generally wider, in some cases much wider. This means that they are much less liquid than Treasuries are.

The bid-ask spread on corporate bonds, for example, can vary greatly, depending on issue-specific factors, with credit risk being one of the biggest determinants of the bid-ask spread.

A *junk bond*, for example, which is a bond that carries a low credit rating and is considered at risk of default (see Chapter 3), generally will have a wide bid-ask spread of as much as a full point or more. Wall Street traders often quip that they could ride a truck through the bid-ask spreads of some junk bonds. AAA-rated bonds, in contrast, which are bonds that carry an exemplary credit rating, tend to have a relatively narrow bid-ask spread and are highly liquid.

The Federal Reserve estimates that in the aggregate the average bid-ask spread on corporate bonds is roughly double the bid-ask spread on U.S. Treasuries. This means that it is usually more difficult to enter into and exit from corporate bonds and to obtain accurate price information on individual securities.

In the municipal bond market liquidity can also vary greatly, depending on issue-specific characteristics and the maturity length of the issues that are trading. In the aggregate the average bid-ask spread on municipals is slightly wider than that on corporates, or roughly double the bid-ask spread on U.S. Treasuries. A major influence on the liquidity of municipal securities is the large amount of municipal securities outstanding. Indeed, there are well over a million municipal bonds outstanding. Many of these bonds are small, issued by small local governments, and therefore are held by a relatively low number of investors. This means that a large number of municipal securities are extremely illiquid and rarely trade. Luckily for municipal bond investors, municipal securities usually are bought with the intention of holding them until maturity, and so those investors do not have to be overly concerned about their ability to resell them if they so choose. If they do choose to sell before maturity, there is a risk that they will not be able to do so at the fair market price. In this case investors should take pains to assure that they are getting a price that is as close to the fair market price as possible.

The bid-ask spread on other types of fixed-income securities differs but is affected by the same principles that dictate the bid-ask spreads on Treasuries, corporate bonds, and municipal bonds. That is, the bid-ask spread is largely influenced by credit risk, maturity length, trading volume, and issuer-specific characteristics.

MARKET DEPTH

Another measure of market liquidity is market depth. *Market depth* refers to the quantity of securities that broker-dealers are willing to buy and sell at various prices. This means that bonds that have larger bids and offers have greater market depth and liquidity than do bonds that have smaller average bids and offers. For example, a bond that averages $5 million in both bids and offers is much more liquid than is a bond that averages just $1 million in bids and offers. When a bond has a large amount of market depth, it is easier for investors to find willing buyers and sellers under a variety of market circumstances. Conversely, bonds with shallow market depth are more difficult to buy and sell, especially when market conditions are adverse. As a gauge of typical market depth, note that the Federal Reserve estimates that 10-year Treasury notes averaged slightly more than $5.5 million in quote depth in 1999 (through October).

Market depth is extremely important to institutional investors, who can buy or sell up to a billion dollars or more of bonds in a single trade. These institutions sometimes need to buy and sell securities on days when the market is volatile and therefore depend on deep quote depths to execute their trades. Luckily, there are usually plenty of institutions on both sides of the market in such situations, and these investors are able to execute most of their trades without a hitch.

It takes great skill on the part of the traders involved in large trade executions to get them done at a price that is indicative of the fair market price. The skill involved in executing large orders is considered valuable on Wall Street and partly explains why bond traders are compensated so well. These skills are sometimes innate and sometimes learned but are no doubt a true commodity to Wall Street firms and their clients in volatile times.

Oddly, deep market depth does not always help the individual investor because the bond market is largely an institutional market (we'll discuss this later in this chapter). In essence, the market is bifurcated, with quote depth differing for institutions and individuals. This means, for example, that on any given day 10-year Treasury notes could have total bids of $5 million yet there could be very few offers of, say, $10,000. This means that the institution may be able to get a better price on the notes than the individual investor can.

The quote depth of the bond market therefore is broken into two parts: separate markets for "odd lots" and "round lots." In the bond market, trades of under $1 million are considered odd lots and trades of $1 million or more are considered round lots. This is in stark contrast to the equity market, where trades of fewer than 100 shares of stock are considered odd lots and trades of 100 shares or more are considered round lots. The inherent message is that institutions dominate the bond market while individuals dominate the stock market. Individual investors therefore should avoid being lulled into thinking that they can obtain good quote depth levels simply because there's a high level of quote depth on an institutional level. In other words, caveat emptor (buyer beware).

PRICE TRANSPARENCY

These days, obtaining a price on a stock is extremely simple and there are numerous ways to do it. Prices can be retrieved easily from the Internet, newspapers, and financial programs on television, for example. In the bond market prices are much more difficult to obtain except on a handful of securities, such as the most actively traded U.S. Treasuries. This lack of transparency poses challenges to fixed-income investors and for anyone trying to track the bond market. It is a challenge that must be constantly overcome.

The reason the bond market lacks transparency is related largely to the fact that there is no centralized location for trading and no centralized location reporting quotes and trade prices. Instead, prices are obtained through phone calls between broker-dealers and by quotes posted on a number of electronic trading systems that are not available to the general public. This lack of price transparency impedes market liquidity and serves as a reminder to investors to be cautious about the quotes and prices they obtain on bonds.

U.S. Treasuries are considered the most transparent securities in the bond market, particularly because they are used as benchmarks for pricing other fixed-income securities (benchmarks will be discussed further later in this chapter). In a recent study, the Securities and Exchange Commission concluded that the Treasury market is indeed the most transparent segment of the fixed-income market and the corporate market is the least, while transparency is improving in the municipal market.

The lack of transparency in the bond market probably has affected the degree to which individual investors have been attracted to the bond market. In other words, individual investors probably would be more attracted to the bond market if it had greater transparency.

The prospects for greater transparency appear to be good, owing largely to new technologies. In particular, the Internet appears likely to increase the transparency of the bond market significantly by essentially creating a centralized location where quotes and prices are aggregated. This is good news for all bond investors and for anyone who wants to track the bond market.

The Financial Crisis of 1998: A Case Study of the Impact of Changes in Market Liquidity

In the fall of 1998 financial problems beset Asia and reverberated throughout the rest of the world. A series of escalating financial crises led to unprecedented turmoil in the global financial markets, spurring investors to seek the safety of U.S. Treasury securities. Surging demand for Treasuries pushed prices to extraordinary heights, and yields plunged (prices move inversely with yields). This so-called flight to quality caused Treasuries to significantly outperform other fixed-income securities as investors shunned riskier assets for the risk-free feature of Treasuries.

While a divergence in the performance of Treasuries and that of other fixed-income securities is not unusual during times when markets are in crisis or when the economy is weak, it would be unusual for two Treasury securities with almost identical characteristics to diverge in performance. Yet in 1998 there was a sharp divergence in the performance of on-the-run Treasuries (the most actively traded Treasuries) and off-the-run Treasuries (the less actively traded Treasuries). This was unusual because both on-the-run and off-the-run Treasuries carry no risk of default, and so there should be little or no variation in their performance, especially if they have other characteristics that are similar, such as the coupon and the maturity date. Assuming all the characteristics of two separate Treasuries are roughly the same, the only factor that could explain the differences in their price performance is liquidity.

The sharp divergence in performance that occurred in 1998 highlights the impact that market liquidity can have on a security. The bid-ask spread on 10-year Treasury notes, for example, increased from its typical $\frac{1}{64}$ to $\frac{1}{32}$ spread to roughly a $\frac{3}{32}$ average spread in the heat of the crisis on October 9, 1998. In addition, market depth was impacted, with the quote depth on the on-the-run 10-year notes falling from $9 to $11 million in the months leading up to the crisis to roughly $6 million in October 1998.

The impact that the financial crisis of 1998 had on U.S. Treasuries probably will endure as a classic case study in which the effects of changes in market liquidity can be isolated and clearly identified. The episode highlights the important role that liquidity plays in the proper functioning of the markets.

SUMMARY

Looking beyond the basics, in this chapter we discussed:

- The bond market plays a vital role in our economy and our nation. It is the spigot that helps supply capital to the nation's dreamers and entrepreneurs. The bond market helps assure that there is plenty of capital available to mass-produce the innovative products and services dreamed by American citizens that raise the national standard of living.
- Bonds probably never played a more vital role than they did when they were used to help finance the war effort in World War II. Over 85 million people bought war bonds and helped lift the nation to victory. For bonds, it was their finest hour.

- The bond market is vast at about $18.5 trillion, and it is composed of a variety of different segments. The best-known segment of the bond market is the U.S. Treasuries market. While it is not the largest segment, it is easily the most active, the most liquid, and the most transparent. Nevertheless, other segments are also quite active as well as liquid, including the agency securities market and the mortgage-backed securities market.

- Primary dealers play an important role in facilitating the hundreds of billions of dollars in trading volume that passes through the bond market every day. Their role is especially vital given the minuscule volume traded on central exchanges every day.

- The bond market is likely to continue growing in the coming years even if cyclical forces slow it down at times. Innovation, securitization, and more widespread use of bonds for funding purposes are a few reasons to expect continued growth of the bond market.

- As important as the bond market is to the American way of life, few people would ever suspect it. Nevertheless, our society is lucky to have a bond market that is mature and vibrant.

CHAPTER THREE

Bond Basics: Building Blocks and Warning Labels

"**F**acts are stubborn things," John Adams once said, referring to our inability to change facts no matter what our wishes or inclinations may be. Since we cannot change facts, we must work with them, around them, and in spite of them. Facts sometimes are misunderstood, however, and often are taken out of context, overblown, or overemphasized, misleading individuals about the subject matter.

That is how it is in the bond market, where investors often are intimidated by the market's apparent array of complexities. Faced with what appear to be numerous hindrances, many investors would rather avoid the bond market altogether than attempt to climb the mountainous learning curve they feel must be surmounted to be successful at bond investing. They feel there is no way around immersing themselves in the numerous facts involved in bond investing, and so they choose to disengage instead.

These investors are missing the forest for the trees, however, focusing too much on the wrong set of facts. Instead of concentrating on the most critical aspects of bond investing, they let themselves get tangled in the bond market's apparent complexities. They forget that the single most important element of successful bond investing is making an accurate assessment of the major fundamental factors that affect the direction of interest rates, the shape of the yield curve, and the level of real interest rates. The factors that affect these key fundamental forces and with which investors should be more concerned include the pace of economic growth, inflation, and the Fed.

It is easy to see how the bond market can intimidate investors. There does seem to be a bit more math involved in buying bonds than there is in buying stocks. Bonds in general also seem to have a plethora of unusual characteristics, and those characteristics seem to differ from one bond to the next. And then there are all those surprise elements that sometimes land at bond investors' proverbial doorsteps when their bonds are called away from them out of the blue. There's also the legal mumbo jumbo that can make it seem that only lawyers can be bond investors. In light of these intimidating factors, some investors see more risk in investing in bonds than in investing in stocks despite the fact that the opposite is generally the case.

Investors should recognize that investing successfully in both stocks and bonds requires a lot of knowledge and that the set of knowledge needed for each type of investment is not materially different from the other. Equity investors who are intimidated by the set of knowledge needed to invest in bonds should look in the mirror and ask themselves whether they have made similar efforts to learn all that is needed to invest successfully in the stock market too. (Unfortunately, many equity investors do not do this and appear to believe that the main prerequisites for investing in stocks are knowing how to open a trading account and knowing how to place an order.) The fact is that regardless of the financial instrument, some degree of legwork is needed for an investor to be successful.

In this book I have placed the most emphasis on the elements of bond investing that are most critical for achieving the highest possible total rate of return. A grasp of critical factors such as the Federal Reserve, inflation, the economy, the yield curve, and real interest rates generally will have a far more substantial impact on your investment returns than will knowledge of what I call "hygienes," or factors that are essential but are not nearly as important as the major factors just mentioned. Some of these hygienes are a bond's indenture, its yield-to-call, and its yield-to-worst. As important as some of these hygienes can be, investors tend to place too much emphasis on them. Nevertheless, it is important for investors to be knowledgeable about them, and they are covered in this book. We will go beyond the basics, however, to give you insights about the bond market that you won't find in other books about the bond market. We will blend the bond basics with insights you can use.

One way to look at these so-called hygienes is to think of them as warning labels similar to those which accompany medical prescriptions. Reading those warning labels is a must, of course, but knowing all the hows and whys of the science behind the warnings serves little purpose for the average consumer. Similarly, individuals need not know everything about the medication they take; they simply need to know how it fits their needs and how to make it work for them. Individuals need only heed the warnings on the label to avoid unexpected complications.

Many bonds have their own warning labels, and those labels should be heeded before one purchases a bond. In this chapter we'll take a look at the most essential elements of a few of them. All the while, keep in mind that your main objective should be to learn about the major influences on the bond market. In other words, don't sweat the small stuff.

Also included in this chapter are definitions of many of the important basics of bond investing. These basics are probably the most frequently cited ones in the literature written about the bond market. Let's start with the simple ones and work our way to some of the more complex topics.

BONDS: WHAT ARE THEY?

In its simplest form, a bond is an interest-bearing document issued or sold by either a government body or a corporation for the purpose of raising capital to meet a financial need. The three largest groups of issuers of bonds are corporations, municipal governments, and the federal government and its agencies. Bonds often are looked at as loans or IOUs because the borrower promises to repay money to investors on a specific *maturity date*, or *term-to-maturity date*, which is the date on which the borrower will repay the face value, or *principal value*, of the bond. The principal value of the bond is merely its dollar value at maturity, usually $1000. Most bonds trade in minimum denominations of a single bond with a principal value of $1000, although many trade in minimum denominations of five bonds with a principal value of $5000 together. The term-to-maturity can span anywhere from 1 day to 30 years and in some cases can be as long as 100 years, although only rarely. When the principal on a bond is repaid, the issuer of the bond has no further obligations from the debt.

An issuer's failure to meet the payment obligations on its debt when the payments are due is a breach of the issuer's contractual obligations and is considered a *default*. In such an instance bondholders can undertake legal actions to enforce the terms of the contract set out in the indenture, which is defined below.

Unlike most loans, bonds are securities because they can be bought and sold in the open market. (The marketplace where bonds are bought and sold is called the bond market, of course.) The bond market is not a marketplace in the literal sense; most bonds do not trade on an exchange but are bought and sold over the counter, with transactions taking place between broker-dealers and between broker-dealers and the investing public.

In the bond market, the term *bonds* is synonymous with most types of fixed-income securities, even though different names are used to distinguish between bonds of varying maturities. For instance, *bills* are fixed-income securities with maturities of 12 months or less, *notes* are fixed-income securities with maturities of 1 to 12 years, and *bonds* are notes with maturities of 12 years or more, although in the Treasury market, securities with a maturity over 10 years usually are considered bonds, not notes. Because Treasuries are considered the benchmark for pricing and quoting most bonds in the bond market, the term *bond market* often is used interchangeably with *Treasuries* since most bonds tend to mirror the behavior of the Treasury market.

As far as what constitutes a short-, intermediate-, or long-term maturity, maturities between 1 and 5 years are considered short-term, maturities between 5 and 12 years are considered intermediates, and maturities greater than 12 years are considered long term. Maturities under 12 months generally are considered money market instruments.

As shown in later in this chapter, there are many different types of bonds representing the three major issuers cited above. Moreover, not all bonds are alike even when they are issued by the same entity. That's why it is particularly important to look closely at the specifics of *every* bond: Their differences make them a bit like fingerprints and DNA at times. One must look closely for differences the same way one should look closely at every warning label on medical prescriptions. It makes no sense to take chances. Let's look at some of the most important characteristics of a bond. Keep in mind that some of these characteristics can differ materially from one bond to the next.

THE INDENTURE: THE CONTRACT BETWEEN THE BOND ISSUER AND THE BONDHOLDER

The *indenture* is an important legal document that sets forth the terms of agreement between the issuer of a bond and the buyers of the issuer's bond. The indenture is legally binding on the issuer until the principal value of the bond is repaid, usually on the maturity date but not always, as you will see later. The indenture contains a significant amount of detailed information that spells out the key characteristics of a particular bond. Some of these features, which will be covered later in this chapter, include the promised interest payment on the debt, the maturity date, the call and refunding provisions, and the period of call protection, put provisions; the number of bonds sold, the collateral put up against the bonds; and sinking fund provisions.

The indenture contains a great deal of legal mumbo jumbo that can confuse the average investor. Luckily, the indenture is made out to a *corporate trustee* who acts as a third party to the indenture contract and acts in a fiduciary capacity on behalf of the bondholders. The corporate trustee monitors whether the bond issuer is complying with the covenants set forth in the indenture and may take action to protect the rights of bondholders, although action on breaches of some covenants in the indenture is not always assured or legally mandated. The indenture provisions are summarized in a document known as a *prospectus*, which is a legally required preliminary statement describing the entity issuing the bond as well as the characteristics of the security. The prospectus is issued to prospective buyers before the sale of the bond. The prospectus spells out some of the legal terms contained in the indenture and is relatively easier reading. It can be obtained from broker-dealers involved in the underwriting of a bond, or, once the bond has been issued, is often available on the Internet. These days the crux of the indenture—the coupon rate, the maturity date, the call provisions, and the like—are available in many places, including the Internet, and from financial information providers such as Bloomberg.

When you buy a bond, you have to think of yourself as a banker and remember that a good banker is always diligent about setting terms that protect the bank's capital. You must do the same thing. Read the indenture or at least find a summary of the terms of the indenture so that you can protect your capital. It's the prudent thing to do.

COUPON RATE: NOT FOR CLIPPING ANYMORE

The *coupon rate* is a term from the days when most bonds were sold in so-called bearer form. A *bearer bond* is a bond that pays interest to the bearer or the presenter of the coupons physically attached to the bond. In the United States the issuance of bonds in bearer form was disallowed in 1982, as it was felt that bearer bonds could be used as payment for illegal activities, could be used for money laundering, and could be easily stolen and converted into cash without the need to prove ownership. Attached to bearer bond certificates issued before 1982 were a series of coupons, one for each coupon payment date stipulated in the bond's indenture. At each coupon payment date the bondholder would clip the appropriate coupon and present it to the trustee for payment, either by mail or in person. This is the reason these issues were known as "coupon" or "bearer" bonds. Today almost all bonds are offered in book-entry registered form, with an increasingly large percentage offered in book-entry form only. In other words, bonds are now held electronically rather than in paper form.

These days the coupon rate refers to the stated interest rate that a bond issuer agrees to pay on a bond to holders of that bond throughout the bond's life. The coupon rate is quoted as a percentage of the bond's principal, or par value. For example, if XYZ Corporation issues a bond with a coupon rate of 6 percent and the bond's principal value is $1000, the issuer has stipulated that it will pay $60 per year to the holder of the bond. Most coupons are paid semiannually, with the semiannual date usually coinciding with the one-year period that follows the original issuance date of the bond.

CALL AND REFUNDING PROVISIONS: A CALL BOND INVESTORS WOULD RATHER NOT TAKE

For some bonds there's a provision in the indenture that allows the issuer to "call," or redeem, the bond before its maturity date. These bonds are known as *callable bonds*. Callable bonds can be redeemed by the issuer either in whole or in part on or after a specific date at a specific price, generally above par (this is known as the *call premium*). Issuers benefit from the call feature on a bond when a borrower can issue new bonds at an interest rate level that is below the interest rate level of the callable bond. This is detrimental to the holder of the callable bond, however, because it exposes the investor to reinvestment risk. As will be described in Chapter 5, reinvestment risk is basically the risk of having to reinvest cash flows at lower and lower interest rate levels. Thus, when a bond is called, the holders of the callable bond will receive cash for their bonds and therefore will have to reinvest that cash at reduced interest rate levels.

Call features are prevalent on corporate and municipal bonds and on older Treasuries (the Treasury last issued callable bonds in the early 1980s). Most entities issues bonds with a call date that assures investors that the bonds will not be called for at least several years. This does not mean, however, that the investor is completely protected. Indeed, this *call protection* is not the same as protection against a bond's possible *refunding*, or early redemption, which can happen well before the call date under conditions specified in the indenture. Read the indenture closely (see Chapter 5 for added risks and strategies related to callable bonds).

YIELD-TO-CALL AND YIELD-TO-WORST: IMPORTANT FOOTNOTES

When some investors buy a bond, they make the mistake of looking exclusively at its yield-to-maturity (to be explained later) when they should be looking at both the *yield-to-call* and the *yield-to-worst* (which are sometimes the same). This is a mistake because both the yield-to-call and the yield-to-worst may be the actual yield the investor receives while holding a bond until it is redeemed. Yield-to-call is computed in the same manner as yield-to-maturity, except that the maturity date is replaced by the call date and the principal value at maturity is replaced by the call price.

Just as with the yield-to-maturity, the yield-to-call assumes that the investor will reinvest the cash flows from the bond at the computed yield-to-call. In addition, it is assumed that the investor will hold the bond until its call date.

Another mistake investors sometimes make with callable bonds is to compare the yield-to-call on one bond with the yield-to-maturity on another bond that has the same maturity date but no call feature. Investors who do this run the risk of mistakenly believing that the callable bond is the more attractive of the two because of its desirable yield-to-call. These investors sometimes ignore the reinvestment risks that accompany the callable bond and could make the callable bond the worst choice in terms of achieving the highest possible yield-to-maturity over a given time period.

The yield-to-worst is simply the lowest possible yield an investor would earn on a bond if it were redeemed for any reason specified in the bond's indenture, including its call and refunding provisions.

The yield-to-call and the yield-to-worst are like footnotes on the yield-to-maturity and are a must-know when one is buying a bond with provisions for early redemption.

PUT PROVISION

A bond that contains a *put provision* gives the bondholder the right to redeem the bond, or "put" it, by selling it back to the issuer at par on dates specified in the indenture. This has both advantages and disadvantages for the bondholder. The main advantage is that the bondholder can redeem the bond at par when interest rates are rising and therefore avoid the price declines that occur with bonds when interest rates rise. A second advantage is the ability to reinvest the proceeds from the redemption at a more attractive interest rate. The major disadvantage is that bonds with put provisions tend to have a lower yield-to-maturity than do other bonds.

CURRENT YIELD

The *current yield* is a very simple but flawed calculation that gives investors an immediate sense of the rate of return they will achieve on their invested capital. This method is useful for investors who plan to spend the interest they receive on their bonds. It is calculated by dividing the annual coupon on a bond by its price:

$$\text{Current yield} = \frac{\text{annual coupon rate}}{\text{price}}$$

The main flaws in this calculation are twofold: It does not consider the interest on interest that could be received on the reinvested interest payments, and it does not consider the difference between the purchase price and the redemption value, completely ignoring the capital gains and losses that could materially affect a bond's total rate of return. Thus, current yield fails to capture two of the most important elements of a bond's total rate of return.

YIELD-TO-MATURITY: NOT NECESSARILY

Yield-to-maturity traditionally has been defined as the total rate of return that will be achieved on a bond from the date of purchase until the time the bond matures. The yield-to-maturity takes into account all of the bond's cash flows, including its coupon income; gains or losses from the difference between an investor's purchase price and the bond's redemption value; interest earned on interest; and the timing of each cash flow. Put simply, the yield-to-maturity represents all possible income as well as the gains or losses that will be realized from the settlement date to the maturity date. On Wall Street, the terms *yield-to-maturity* and *yield* are generally synonymous.

Here's a critical point to remember: A bond's stated yield-to-maturity will be achieved only if the bond's coupon payments are reinvested at a rate equal to its yield-to-maturity and if the bond is held until its maturity date. Investors often misunderstand this point and incur sharp reductions in the returns on their portfolios. It is critical to remember that one of the most important factors affecting the total return on a bond is the return that stems from interest on interest. Indeed, interest on interest can account for as much as or more than half of a bond's total rate of return, depending on interest rate levels and the bond's maturity length.

Here's an illustration. Assume that an investor purchases a bond in XYZ Corporation maturing in 10 years and paying a semi-annual coupon of 4 percent ($40 every six months). Assume that the investor paid $1000 (par) for the bond for a yield-to-maturity of 8 percent. This investor therefore will receive $80 per year in annual coupon payments for a total of $800 over the ten-year period. In addition, assuming the principal value of the bond is $1000, at the maturity date the investor will realize neither a capital gain nor a capital loss. The cash flows received on this bond therefore will have totaled $800 over ten years. Let's make an additional assumption. Let's say that this investor spent the coupon payments rather than reinvesting them. It may still seem, however, that having received a coupon-return of 8 percent per year for ten years, the yield-to-maturity was still 8 percent. However, the yield-to-maturity on this bond is actually 5.79 percent. If the 8 percent coupon had been reinvested semiannually at an interest rate of 8 percent, the total cash flows would have been $22,787. That's significantly more than the $18,400 in total cash flows that would be received if the coupon payments were spent. Importantly, 52 percent of the return related to interest income stemmed from interest on interest.

Let this example serve as a reminder of the importance of interest on interest and the fallacy of the stated yield-to-maturity calculation, which makes the assumption that the interest payments will be reinvested at an interest rate equal to the yield-to-maturity.

The math behind the yield-to-maturity on a bond can get a bit complicated as it involves calculating the present value of all the bond's cash flows. *Present value* is the amount of money that must be invested today to realize a specified value in the future. Applying this to the example above, the yield-to-maturity basically reflects the interest rate level at which the interest payments must be reinvested to result in the cash flow of $22,787. Put another way, the yield-to-maturity is essentially the discount rate at which the present value of future payments (the coupon payments and the redemption value at maturity) equals the price paid for the security.

It is not necessary or efficient to do the math for a bond's yield-to-maturity by hand; there are a variety of modern means of doing the calculations. These days most investors use financial calculators, many of which contain functions that are specifically designed to do a variety of bond calculations. Investors also can utilize calculators available on financial information providers such as Bloomberg and Reuters. Most brokers have access to these tools. In addition, there are a number of Web sites that enable investors to conduct bond calculations on their own.

No matter how you obtain the yield-to-maturity on a bond, the main point to remember is that the yield-to-maturity can be achieved only if the interest payments are reinvested at the yield-to-maturity and if the bond is held to maturity. This point cannot be stressed enough.

ACCRUED INTEREST

In between the actual coupon payments paid on a bond, bondholders earn what is known as *accrued interest*. Accrued interest is an important part of most bond transactions, and investors should assure that the accrued interest they either pay (when buying a bond) or receive (when selling a bond) is correct. Accrued interest is paid to the holder of a bond on the settlement date regardless of who owned the bond throughout the period since the last interest payment. The calculation for accrued interest is simple:

$$\text{Accrued interest} = \frac{\text{annual interest} \cdot \textit{days in holding period}}{360 \text{ days}}$$

BASIS POINTS: BOND LINGO

A *basis point* is equal to one-hundredth of a percentage point and is a term used frequently in the bond market. It is the smallest measure used to quote yields. A basis point is the distance, say, between a bond that yields 5.75 percent and one that yields 5.74 percent. On Wall Street the yield differences between securities are almost always quoted in basis points, particularly relative to Treasuries and/or securities with similar characteristics. In tracking bonds with different maturities, it's best to look at the basis point changes rather than the price changes. This is the case because even if two bonds with different maturity dates experienced the same price change, their basis point changes could be much different. Looking at the basis point changes between bonds is the best way to track their *relative performance*; look at price differences only if you want to gauge a bond's outright performance in terms of price. Moreover, the Federal Reserve's interest rate changes are announced in basis points. This is a very fungible term that is applicable to a variety of fixed-income instruments.

Price Value of a Basis Point (PVBP), or Basis Point Value (BPV)

The *price value of a basis point (PVBP)*, also known as *basis point value* or *the dollar value of an 01* (DV01, where 01 is equal to 1 basis point), is the price change that will occur in a bond if its yield changes by 1 basis point. The price value of a basis point is a useful tool to determine a bond's volatility. Although this is best measured by a bond's duration (discussed later in this chapter), the price value of a basis point can help an investor convert a bond's yield changes into dollars. For example, if the PVBP of a bond is $1 and the bond's price is $985, a yield decrease of 10 basis points will cause the price of the bond to increase to $995. (prices move inversely with yields, of course). Using this method, it is far easier to assess potential risks and opportunities. The price value of a basis point is used extensively in hedging one security with another. In this case the quantity of the hedge is calibrated to equal the basis point value of the security being hedged. This way, equal basis point changes will cause equal dollar changes in the value of the two bonds. One can obtain the price value of a basis point on a financial calculator or by looking at the price change that occurs in a bond for every basis point change.

DURATION: A KEY GAUGE OF A BOND'S PRICE VOLATILITY

Duration is a measure of a bond's price sensitivity to changes in interest rates. It can be used to gauge the volatility of one bond compared with another and for the purpose of hedging securities. A complex mathematical formula is used to compute duration, and so it is generally best not to compute it by hand. Let's take a look at a simple example before discussing it further.

Assume that the duration on a bond is 5.0. In this case, if the yield on the bond were to change by 100 basis points, the price on the bond would change by approximately 5 percent. That sounds simple enough. There is actually a whole lot more to it, but I want to impress upon you the importance of remembering this simple example before the detailed explanation begins to cloud the main message. If you remember nothing more about duration than the notion that duration is an approximation of a bond's percentage price change for a given change in interest rates, you will have learned enough to help you with most bond investments.

There are, however, a number of important details, so let's get into the nitty-gritty and look at some of the more important elements of the concept of duration.

1. Duration is not an exact measure of a bond's price sensitivity to changes in interest rates, but it is generally a very close approximation if the interest rate changes are small. When interest rate changes are large, the concept of *convexity* must be introduced. Convexity is known in mathematical circles as the second derivative of a bond's price change for given changes in yield. Convexity basically measures the percentage change in a bond's price change for a given change in yield that cannot be explained by duration. In other words, if the duration on a bond is 5.0 and its yield changes by 100 basis points but the price of the bond changes by just 4.9 percent instead of the 5 percent change that should be expected based on the bond's duration, the difference can be explained by the bond's convexity. Convexity generally is used to assist in the approximation of large yield changes in a bond.

2. Duration increases with maturity length (assuming all other characteristics are the same).

3. Bonds with high coupon rates have lower duration than do bonds with low coupon rates (assuming all other characteristics are the same).

4. The duration on a zero coupon bond is always equal to its term to maturity. Thus, a zero coupon bond that matures

in ten years will have a duration of 10.0. This principle indicates that zero coupon bonds are very volatile instruments compared with conventional coupon bonds. That is why aggressive investors such as hedge funds often purchase zero coupon bonds when they sense that interest rates are about to decline. Those investors recognize that zero coupon bonds will appreciate faster in price than will conventional bonds (of the same maturity) and thus maximize capital gains opportunities.

5. There are two popular formulas for duration. *Macaulay's duration*, developed in 1983 by Frederick Macaulay, is defined as the weighted average term to maturity of a security's cash flows. It basically takes the present value of all the cash flows and then adjusts them by weight based on when they are received. The result is stated as the weighted average of the life of the bond in years. As such, it is a good measure for ranking different bonds in regard to their price sensitivity and for constructing portfolios which will fully defease, or immunize a future series of cash flows against market risk (see Chapter 5 for a discussion of market risk). *Modified duration* basically is defined as it was defined above; that is, it is a measure of a bond's price sensitivity to changes in the interest rate.

6. Duration fails to capture the risks associated with bonds of varied credit quality. For example, an AAA-rated company with a duration of 5.0 is likely to be subject to less volatility than is a CCC-rated company with the same duration. The poor creditworthiness of the CCC-rated company tends to make that company's bonds subject to greater yield (and price) volatility owing to both macro and micro risks. Thus, duration should not be taken on its own to mean that one company will be more or less volatile than another.

7. Duration increases when a bond's yield decreases and decreases when its yield increases. The exception to this is callable and puttable bonds. On callable bonds, duration decreases when yields fall because the call feature reduces the price appreciation and thus the duration. Similarly, on puttable bonds, as yields increase, duration increases as

yields increase because the put feature increases the value of the bond (because an investor can sell the bond back to the issuer and reinvest the proceeds at higher market interest rates).

8. A portfolio's price sensitivity to changes in interest rates cannot be determined easily by using its average duration. This is the case because individual bonds can and do have varying degrees of yield fluctuations on a day-to-day basis. Therefore, there is no specific yield change on which the duration level can be used to estimate the aggregate price change in a portfolio. In other words, since the yield changes on each of the portfolio's securities generally will vary, so will the price changes. This will be especially apparent when the yield curve shifts and results in sharply varying performances of short- and long-term maturities.

9. The average duration of the universe of investment portfolios can be used to track market sentiment. This topic is covered in Chapter 10.

As you can see, there are many important elements of the concept of duration. Although there are shortcomings, duration can be an extremely useful tool for gauging market risks in individual bonds as well as market sentiment. For most investors, duration is best used in its simplest form as a gauge of a bond's price sensitivity to changes in interest rates. Don't let the complicated details cloud this message.

SUMMARY

Looking beyond the basics, in this chapter we discussed:

- As with many other investments, it behooves investors to obtain a certain degree of knowledge before they consider investing in bonds. Investors often are intimidated, however, about the knowledge set they feel is needed to be successful at investing in the bond market, leading them to shy away from that market.

- However, the degree of knowledge actually necessary for investors to be successful in the bond market is not materially different from that needed for other markets.

- While endeavoring to learn as much as possible about bonds, bond investors should be mindful of the factors that are most likely to affect their investment performance. Factors such as the Federal Reserve, the economy, and inflation, can have a far more significant impact on a bond investment than do other factors. That is why I have placed a great deal of emphasis on these factors throughout this book.

  Once you've reviewed the "warning labels" that come with each bond, don't sweat the small stuff and keep your focus on the big picture.

CHAPTER FOUR

Types of Bonds

It is much easier to generalize about the types of bonds that exist in the bond market than it is to describe their many differences because unlike stocks, the characteristics of bonds can differ sharply from one bond to the next. Moreover, the performance of each type of bond can differ sharply from one bond to the next regardless of the general direction of interest rates. It is therefore important for investors to understand the types of bonds and their differing degrees of performance before considering the purchase of a bond.

This chapter will provide an overview of the largest segments of the bond market, concentrating on their most important elements. The types of bonds that will be covered are:

- U.S. Treasuries
- Corporate bonds
- Government agency securities
- Mortgage-backed securities
- Municipal bonds

These segments account for the bulk of the bond market's $19 trillion in total size. Although the list is short, there are considerable differences between these types of bond and there are differences within each segment. Most of these differences relate to creditworthiness, taxation, cash flows, maturity date, call and refunding provisions, and collateralization (these topics are covered in Chapter 3). One can't judge a bond by its cover, so look closely at the various features of every bond before considering a purchase.

U.S. TREASURIES

The U.S. Treasury market is the most active and liquid market in the world, with daily volume by primary dealers averaging $297.9 billion in 2001. Treasury securities are issued by the U.S. Treasury Department to meet the funding requirements of the United States. Treasury securities are backed by the full faith and credit of the U.S. government and therefore are perceived to be free of the risk of default. The deep liquidity of the Treasury market and its risk-free characteristics are the primary reasons Treasuries are used as the benchmark for the quoting and pricing of other fixed-income securities.

The Treasury Departments issues three different categories of Treasury securities: discount, coupon, and inflation-linked.

Discount Securities

Discount securities are securities that are sold at a discount to their maturity (face) value. These securities are known as *Treasury bills*. For many years, all Treasury bills matured in 52 weeks or less. Today, however, owing to the discontinuance of 52-week maturities, all new Treasury bills mature in 26 weeks or less. Treasury bills are issued in three maturities: 26 weeks (commonly known as the 6-month bill), 13 weeks (the 3-month bill), and 4 weeks. Occasionally, the Treasury issues bills that mature in different ("oddball") numbers of days or weeks. These bills are sold to meet short-term funding needs, particularly before April, when the Treasury rakes in tens of billions of dollars in tax payments from individuals. These bills are called *cash management bills* and have the same characteristics as regularly issued Treasury bills.

Auctions for Treasury bills take place every Monday (except when Monday is a holiday, in which case they take place on Tuesday), and the securities must be paid for by Thursday of that week. The securities actually begin trading *when issued*, on the Tuesday before the Treasury announces its weekly bill auction sizes. Bids for all

Treasury securities may be submitted in minimum denominations of $1000 (face value) to any Federal Reserve bank, to the Treasury's Bureau of the Public Debt in Washington D.C., or over the Internet using *Treasury Direct* (publicdebt.treas.gov/sec/sectrdir.htm), a highly popular program run by the Treasury Department. This program is discussed in Chapter 13. Of course, an investor can always submit bids through a conduit such as a broker-dealer.

Once issued, Treasury bills are quoted at their discounted value in basis points rather than at the price that corresponds to the discounted rate.

Coupon Securities

The preponderance of Treasury issuance is in *coupon securities*, which are securities that pay interest periodically (usually every six months) and pay their principal at maturity. Of the roughly $3.0 trillion in Treasuries outstanding, about $2.2 trillion of that issuance is in coupon securities. The Treasury Department recently decided to reduce its issuance of coupon securities in favor of Treasury bills in an effort to take advantage of low short-term interest rates. This strategy is resulting in a sharp increase in the amount of Treasury bills outstanding relative to coupons. This strategy is fraught with danger, however, as the Treasury is bypassing an opportunity to lock in low long-term financing on its mammoth amount of debt outstanding. The Treasury's strategy is akin to a homeowner refinancing a mortgage with a 1-year adjustable rate rather than taking advantage of historically low 30-year rates. This is a strategy that creates enormous uncertainties about future liabilities and one that I hope the Treasury eventually reconsiders. It's our money, after all.

The Treasury's coupon issuance currently consists of 2-, 5-, and 10-year maturities. That's a far cry from the Treasury's issuance ten years ago, when it regularly sold maturities of 2, 3, 5, 7, 10, and 30 years. The Treasury simply does not need to issue as much debt as it did when the United States was running large budget deficits. Nevertheless, budget deficits are expected to return as a result of the recession of 2001 and increased government spending. This return to deficits underscores the risks of the Treasury's current financing strategy.

The Treasury sells its 2-year notes every around the third week of every month for settlement on the final day of the month. The Treasury's 5- and 10-year notes are sold quarterly in February, May, August, and November. They are sold before the middle of the month for settlement on the fifteenth of that month.

Treasury auctions are conducted on a *competitive* and a *noncompetitive* basis. That is, competitive bidders submit bids at yields they would like to receive, and noncompetitive bidders submit bids for a yield that will be determined at the auction. Noncompetitive bidders receive a yield that is equal to the average of all the competitive bids placed at the auction. Competitive bidders, in contrast, can receive only the yield that they bid except in the case of a *Dutch auction*, or *single-price auction*, in which all bidders receive the same yield regardless of the bid submitted (unless they bid at a yield above the *stopout yield*, the highest yield needed to clear all the securities being sold at the auction). Therein lies the risk of submitting a competitive bid: A competitive bidder that places a bid at a yield that is above the stopout yield will not be awarded any securities at the auction. This risk explains why most individuals submit noncompetitive bids. However, noncompetitive bids cannot be larger than $1 million in a bill auction or $5 million in a note or bond auction. That's why most institutional investors submit competitive bids.

The difference between the average yield and the stopout yield is known as the *tail*. This is used as a gauge of the success of an auction. A large tail indicates that the Treasury had to sell securities to low bidders in order to sell all the securities being auctioned; it is therefore an indication of a weak auction. A small tail, by comparison, occurs when there is a plentiful supply of aggressive bidders. Before the Treasury switched to the Dutch auction method for most of its coupon issues in the mid-1990s, the tail was an extremely important gauge of market sentiment. These days, however, it is more of a footnote, but it is still a relevant gauge of the degree of vigor shown by bidders at the auctions.

Newly auctioned Treasuries are known as *on-the-run issues*, and previously auctioned Treasuries are known as *off-the-run* issues. On-the-run issues are far more actively traded than are off-the-run issues and therefore tend to be much more liquid, as shown by their bid-ask spreads and quote depth.

The Treasury's 10-year maturity is now considered the benchmark maturity with which to gauge daily price movements in the bond market, but there is still a considerable amount of longer-dated maturities outstanding beyond 10 years. These securities are therefore worthy of attention both from an investment perspective and as a gauge of market sentiment on a variety of fronts. Moreover, as is discussed in Chapter 9, there are other maturities along the yield curve that are extremely useful gauges of market sentiment.

Inflation-Linked Securities

In January 1997 the Treasury began issuing bonds that provided investors with protection against inflation. These bonds are commonly known as *TIPS*, or *Treasury Inflation Protected Securities*. They are also known as *inflation-indexed* or *inflation-linked bonds*. TIPS provide protection against inflation by indexing interest and principal payments to the inflation rate. Thus, the cash flows on TIPS increases along with the inflation rate. With TIPS, an investor is protected against inflation risk (discussed in Chapter 5), one of the biggest risks facing bond investors.

TIPS are indexed to the Consumer Price Index for All Urban Consumers (CPI-U), a monthly index released by the Bureau of Labor Statistics with its widely followed CPI statistics. As the CPI-U increases, the face value of TIPS increases. For example, if you purchased an inflation-indexed security on its issuance date at a face value of $1000 and the CPI-U increased 3 percent over the subsequent year, the face value of that security would increase to $1030. Assuming the security paid a coupon rate of 3 percent (it stays fixed throughout the life of the bond), your interest income would rise from $30 per year ($1000 × 3 percent), to $30.90 ($1030 × 3 percent). Each year the face value would increase along with the inflation rate, resulting in an increase in coupon payments. At maturity, the security would be redeemed at the inflation-adjusted face value or the face value at issuance, whichever was greater. This assures that even if the CPI-U declines as a result of deflation, the maturity value of inflation-indexed bonds on their maturity date will be no less than the initial face value.

It is important to keep in mind that at any point before the maturity date on an inflation-indexed bond, the inflation-adjusted principal value of the bond could fall below the initial face value. This should not concern investors who plan to hold TIPS until their maturity date because the Treasury Department would implement its "minimum guarantee" if deflation persisted long enough; the Treasury will never repay less than the bond's initial face value ($1000).

Inflation-indexed bonds have a distinct advantage over conventional Treasuries because of their indexation to the inflation rate. The principal value of conventional Treasuries, by contrast, will not change; it will stay at $1000 throughout the life of the bond. Figure 4-1 provides an illustration of the differing cash flows that the two types of bonds would experience over a ten-year horizon. Note that even though the inflation-indexed bond receives a smaller interest payment during the ten years, the purchasing power of the money received at maturity is higher for the inflation-indexed bond.

In deciding whether to purchase an inflation-indexed bond, one of the first things to look at is the *breakeven rate*. The breakeven rate can be defined as the inflation rate that would make the rate of return on an inflation-indexed Treasury equal to the rate of return on a conventional Treasury if the two securities had the same maturity date and both were held to maturity. An inflation rate higher than the breakeven rate would make the purchase of the TIPS superior in terms of its rate of return compared to a conventional Treasury. Similarly, if the inflation rate averaged less than the breakeven rate until the bonds matured, the rate of return on the TIPS would be less than that on the conventional Treasury.

This may seem a bit tricky, but it is actually quite simple. A key principle in the analysis is that the yield-to-maturity on most conventional bonds consists of three main components:

- A real rate of return
- Compensation for inflation
- Compensation for credit risk

On a conventional Treasury the yield consists of just the first two components, since Treasuries are considered free of the risk of default. This makes the analysis even simpler. Working with this premise, since the yield on a conventional Treasury consists of both

F i g u r e   4–1

Example of Payments on Nominal and Indexed Bonds

Consider a 10-year conventional nominal bond and a 10-year inflation-indexed bond. Each bond is purchased at its face, or principal, value of $1000. Although Treasury notes and bonds provide semiannual payments, the bonds in this example are assumed to provide annual coupon payments. Each coupon payment on a conventional bond is the coupon rate stated on the bond times the principal. Each coupon payment on an indexed bond is the coupon rate times the indexed principal. The indexed principal is simply the beginning principal of $1000 scaled up through time at the rate of inflation. We'll assume that the coupon rate on the indexed bond is 3 percent and that actual inflation over the 10-year horizon turns out to be a steady 2 percent, equal to expected inflation, and that the coupon rate on the conventional bond is 5.06 percent so that its expected real rate of return equals the coupon rate on the indexed bond.

A schedule of nominal and real values of payments on the bonds is given below. The real values give the purchasing power of the nominal payments. For example, suppose a given item today cost $1. With 2 percent inflation, at the end of the year the same item will cost $1.02, and $1 will purchase .98 (1/1.02) units of the item. So, $50.60 received at the end of year 1 from the nominal bond will purchase 49.61 units.

As the schedule of payments shows, the nominal value of the conventional bond's principal stays fixed. The real value is eroding through time because of inflation. When received at maturity, the $1000 principal can purchase 820.35 units of the good. In contrast, when the bond was first purchased, that $1000 could buy 1000 units. The payment schedule also shows how the fixed nominal payment of $50.60 per year on the nominal bond has a smaller real value over time because of inflation. Note that for the indexed bond, the real values of the principal and interest payments are preserved for the life of the bond. The nominal principal gets scaled up year by year according to inflation. As the principal gets scaled up, so too does the nominal coupon payment to preserve the real return of 3 percent. The indexed bond pays less interest than the nominal bond each year, but that is offset by its larger payment of principal at maturity.

Schedule of Payments

	Conventional Bond				Indexed Bond			
Year	Nominal Value of Principal	Real Value of Principal	Nominal Interest Payment	Real Value of Interest Payment	Nominal Value of Principal	Real Value of Principal	Nominal Interest Payment	Real Value
1	$1000	980.39	$50.60	49.61	$1020.00	1000	$30.60	30
2	$1000	961.17	$50.60	48.64	$1040.40	1000	$31.21	30
3	$1000	942.32	$50.60	47.68	$1061.21	1000	$31.84	30
4	$1000	923.85	$50.60	46.75	$1082.43	1000	$32.47	30
5	$1000	905.73	$50.60	45.83	$1104.08	1000	$33.12	30
6	$1000	887.97	$50.60	44.93	$1126.16	1000	$33.78	30
7	$1000	870.56	$50.60	44.05	$1148.69	1000	$34.46	30
8	$1000	853.49	$50.60	43.19	$1171.66	1000	$35.15	30
9	$1000	836.75	$50.60	42.34	$1195.09	1000	$35.85	30
10	$1000	820.35	$50.60	41.51	$1218.99	1000	$36.60	30

Total nominal receipts: $1506
Real value of principal at maturity: $820.35

Total nominal receipts: $1554.07
Real value of indexed principal at maturity: $1000

Source: Federal Reserve

a real rate of return and compensation for inflation, we need only determine one or the other to find both. This is where TIPS come in. TIPS can help us find both variables because its yield-to-maturity also consists of a real rate of return plus compensation for inflation. In fact, on an inflation-indexed bond, the stated yield-to-maturity is the real rate of return (the actual yield-to-maturity cannot be known in advance because it depends on the inflation rate). The key here is that unlike conventional Treasuries, you know what the real rate of return is. The rest of the return consists of an unknown inflation rate. You can use this real rate of return to find the inflation expectations embedded in the conventional Treasury. With the real rate of return in hand, simply subtract it from the nominal, or stated, yield-to-maturity on the conventional Treasury. The difference represents the market's inflation expectations over the life of the bond. How do we know this? There is no reason to think that investors in TIPS have views of inflation that are different from those of investors in conventional Treasuries, and since both investments have nearly equal real rates of return, the difference between their nominal, or stated, yields must be the market's inflation expectations.

There are caveats to this analysis, however, as the yield differences may reflect more than the market's inflation expectations. For example, TIPS are notoriously illiquid compared with conventional Treasuries. Thus, during periods when investors express a preference for liquid securities, the yield on TIPS could be kept artificially high in compensation for the illiquidity, lowering the breakeven rate. Second, TIPS are subject to a so-called indexation lag. That is, since the principal value of an inflation-indexed bond is based on an inflation rate set as much as three months before the semiannual coupon payment, there is a risk that the holder of an inflation-indexed bond will not be fully compensated for the actual inflation of the prior three months. For example, if you buy an inflation-indexed bond in July, the interest payment that you receive from July through October will be based on the semiannual adjustment made to the price of the bond in October based on the CPI-U from January through June. Therein lies the risk. From July through October you will be paid interest based on an inflation rate in the past (January through June). If inflation rose sharply in those three months, your October interest payment would not reflect the rise.

A third reason to be wary of a strict interpretation of the amount of inflation expectations derived using TIPS is the differences in the tax implications for the cash flows. Because a TIPS investor is compensated for inflation, when inflation accelerates, so does the cash flow on the bonds. In turn, so does the tax liability. Therefore, the TIPS investor is not fully insulated from the effects of inflation. Finally, investors in TIPS may be naturally more averse to inflation risks than are investors in conventional Treasuries. This means that they may be more willing to accept a lower real rate of return. Therefore, the difference between yields on TIPS and those on conventional Treasuries may overstate the market's true inflation expectations.

CORPORATE BONDS

Just a few steps past the comfortable realm of the Treasury market lies a very different bond market. The corporate bond market, which at first blush seems fairly simple to understand, is full of intricacies. Corporate bonds are more than just the bond market's version of familiar stocks. There's a multitude of differences between corporate bonds and Treasuries and between individual corporate bonds. Indeed, there are many twists and turns that investors must be aware of before they consider investing in corporate bonds.

Corporate bonds are bonds issued by corporate entities to raise capital for a variety of purposes. Those entities turn to the corporate bond market for long-term funding as an alternative to borrowing money from financial institutions and issuing stock. Borrowing large amounts of capital from banks for long periods is generally not possible and can be costly, and selling stock can dilute the equity of existing shareholders. The bond market is therefore a superior source of funding for many major companies.

There are five main types of issuers in the corporate bond market:

- Industrials
- Banks and finance companies
- Transportation companies
- Public utilities
- International companies

Of course, within each type of issuer there are many sub-groups. Within the transportation group, for example, issuers include air, rail, and trucking companies. Importantly, each of the five major groups and each of their subgroups has a different level of sensitivity to the economic and financial climate. As with stocks, the investment performance of individual corporate bonds can depend greatly on the group or subgroup of which they are a part. To be sure, company-specific factors are critically important to the performance of a particular corporate bond, but industrywide factors can play a substantial role too and can also have a very large bearing on the market's perceptions of the individual company even if the company is relatively immune to developments in its industry. It is therefore critical to think from the top down before looking at a company from the bottom up. In other words, one should evaluate the macro influences on the company and its industry before looking at the company itself.

How Corporate Bonds Are Collateralized

Corporate bonds are collateralized in many different ways. This is an important aspect of bond investing because if there is a corporate default, bankruptcy, or liquidation, bondholders have legal priority over stockholders in bankruptcy court. It is also important because it will affect the yield-to-maturity on a bond; generally speaking, bonds that are collateralized yield less than do those which are not. Most corporate bonds are not collateralized with any specific assets but are instead backed by the general credit and capacity of the issuing companies. These bonds are called *debentures*. Although debentures are not secured by specific assets, the overall assets of the issuer protect the bonds and there are often pledges to secure the bonds in other ways.

Here are the main types of collateralized bonds:

- *Mortgage bonds.* These bonds are secured by a legal claim on real estate or other real property such as a factory or office building and are used mostly by utility companies. There are many different types of mortgage bonds, reflecting the priority of claims. A "first mortgage" bond, for instance, has priority over a second, third, or junior mortgage bond.

- *Collateral trust bonds.* Collateral trust bonds are issued by companies that have very few real assets to pledge. Instead, they collateralize them with financial assets such as stock or bond holdings.

- *Equipment trust certificates.* As the name suggests, specific types of equipment back equipment trust certificates. These certificates often are called rolling stocks because historically they have been issued by railroad rolling equipment such as the locomotives and cars and are considered a very safe form of collateral.

- *Guaranteed bonds.* Guaranteed bonds are bonds backed by a company other than the issuer. The guarantee is like the guarantee a cosigner makes on a loan for an individual. In both cases the debt is by no means guaranteed and is dependent on the creditworthiness of the guarantor.

These various forms of collateral can be an important source of security to bond investors, but there is no better security than a strong balance sheet and an abundance of cash flow.

Credit Risk: The Key to Corporate Bond Yields

An even more important determinant of a bond's yield-to-maturity than its collateralization and industry-related considerations is its credit rating. A credit rating essentially ranks a company's ability to repay its debts as well as withstand various types of financial and economic stress compared with other companies. Credit ratings are intended to help provide forward-looking opinions on a company's ability and willingness to pay interest and repay principal as scheduled. Credit ratings therefore can help investors assess the likelihood that their money will be returned to them in accordance with the terms on which they invested.

Credit ratings are assigned by four major rating organizations: Moody's Investor Services, Standard & Poor's, Fitch IBCA, and Duff & Phelps. Of the four, Moody's and Standard and Poor's are considered the leading agencies. Each of the four rating agencies follows a very thorough and rigorous methodology for determining a company's creditworthiness

A bond's credit rating has a significant impact on its yield-to-maturity. As one would expect, the lower a bond's credit rating, the higher its yield. On bonds with sharply different credit ratings, the yield differences can be substantial, often more than several percentage points. A high-grade, or investment-grade bond (bonds rated BBB or higher), for example, which is a bond considered to have a low probability of default, will tend to yield much less than will a bond rated below investment grade.

As an investor you must strike a careful balance between choosing bonds deemed safe but low yielding and bonds deemed risky but high yielding. This difficult balancing act is a reminder of the benefits of diversification, which can increase your rate of return while spreading the risks. For many individuals, however, diversification of a portfolio can be difficult to implement because of limited capital, high transaction costs, and difficulty finding suitable bonds. For those investors a bond fund is an excellent way to invest. Bond funds such as those offered by Pacific Investment Management Company (PIMCO), one of the leading fixed-income portfolio management firms in the country, are an excellent choice for investors who would like to diversify their investments and have their money professionally managed.

For more on credit ratings, see Chapter 12.

Covenants: The Fine Print

When a corporate bond is issued, the issuer agrees to abide by a set of promises set forth in a contract known as an indenture. Aside from protecting investors, the indenture also spells out specific rights that protect the issuer in its contract with investors. The issuer's rights can work against investors at times and therefore should be known before an investor considers the purchase of a bond. A good example of these rights is the issuer's right to call, or redeem its bonds before maturity. Issuers typically invoke this so-called call provision when it is advantageous to them but generally disadvantageous to investors. There are many other provisions in a bond's indenture, and they can vary from one bond to the next. It is therefore critical to read the fine print before you purchase a bond because it can have a significant impact on your investment. You can read more about this topic in Chapter 3.

Investing in Corporate Bonds

Investors should buy corporate bonds using essentially the same approach they use to invest in equities. In the same way that an equity investor must be mindful of where the economy is with respect to the business cycle, a corporate bond investor must use the same considerations. For example, when the Federal Reserve begins to raise interest rates, equity investors tend to shun economically sensitive stocks. Corporate bond investors should do the same thing and choose bonds in more defensive industries and higher-quality bonds during such times. Similarly, when the Federal Reserve begins a campaign to lower interest rates, this is a time to consider purchasing corporate bonds in economically sensitive groups such as consumer cyclicals, basic materials, and capital goods. Moreover, since the yield spread between low-grade corporate bonds and investment-grade bonds tends to narrow when the Fed lowers interest rates, low-grade corporate bonds are often a better investment than both Treasuries and investment-grade bonds during such times. This depends, however, on the severity of the economic weakness that provokes the Fed to lower interest rates. If you worry about buying corporate bonds when the economy is weak because you fear you will not be paid the principal and interest that are due, remember this: In the event of bankruptcy, bondholders are first in line; equity investors are way in the back. The conservative bet is therefore to buy a company's bonds rather than its stock.

GOVERNMENT AGENCY SECURITIES

There are two main types of federal agency securities: government-sponsored enterprises (GSEs) and federally related institutions. Most agency securities are issued by GSEs; federally related institutions only rarely issue debt on their own but instead obtain funding from the Federal Financing Bank, which was created in 1973 to help meet the funding needs of a variety of U.S. agencies, such as the General Services Administration, the Farmers Housing Administration, and the Export-Import Bank.

Government-Sponsored Enterprises

Government-sponsored enterprise securities may one day supplant U.S. Treasuries as the benchmark securities of the fixed-income market owing to the size, liquidity, and high credit quality of the GSE market. *Government-sponsored enterprises* are privately owned companies that were created by Congress to provide funding to important sectors of the economy, including housing, farming, and education. GSEs issue debt to raise capital to lend to prospective borrowers, particularly in the housing market. The GSE market has grown rapidly in recent years owing mostly to a surge in debt issued by agencies that provide funding for the housing sector.

There are eight government-sponsored enterprises:

- Federal Farm Credit Bank System
- Farm Credit Financial Assistance Corporation
- Federal Home Loan Bank
- Federal Home Loan Mortgage Corporation (Freddie Mac)
- Federal National Mortgage Association (Fannie Mae)
- Student Loan Marketing Association (Sallie Mae)
- Financing Corporation
- Resolution Trust Corporation

The two largest are Fannie Mae and Freddie Mac, both of which supply funding to borrowers in the housing market. The Federal Loan Bank is the third GSE geared to facilitating activity in the housing market. Let's take a look at how these three entities perform their vital function.

Fannie and Freddie:
The Housing Market's Best Friends

In 1938 the federal government established the Federal National Mortgage Association (Fannie Mae) to help counter the funding problems prospective homebuyers faced during the great depression. Fannie Mae remained a government agency until 1968, when it was divided into a private company (as we know it today) and the Government National Mortgage Association (Ginnie Mae), an institution that is still a government agency. Keep in mind that there is a difference between a government-sponsored agency and a government agency. A GSE is federally chartered, and securities issued by GSEs are not backed by the full faith and credit of the U.S. government, whereas debt issued by agencies such as Ginnie Mae is.

In its own words, Fannie Mae's current mission is "to provide products and services that increase the availability and the affordability of housing for low-, moderate-, and middle-income Americans." Since 1968 Fannie Mae has helped more than 30 million families purchase their own homes. Fannie Mae accomplishes this mission by lending indirectly rather than directly to prospective home buyers. This means that Fannie Mae operates in the secondary market for home mortgages rather than in the primary market. In other words, instead of lending directly to prospective home buyers, Fannie Mae purchases mortgage loans from mortgage lenders such as savings and loan institutions, mortgage companies, and commercial banks. By purchasing existing mortgages, Fannie Mae enables those institutions to lend to a greater number of borrowers by replenishing the money they use for mortgage lending. To finance its mortgage purchasers, Fannie Mae issues debt securities with a variety of maturities. In fact, Fannie Mae is one of the biggest issuers of debt securities in the world and regularly issues bills, notes, and bonds. In recent years Fannie Mae's 10-year notes have yielded about 60 to 110 basis points over Treasuries. This is an attractive yield spread, but investors should be mindful of the fact that the interest on Fannie Mae's (as well as the other GSEs's) debt is subject to state taxes whereas the interest on Treasuries is not (for most individuals).

Freddie Mac operates much in the same way as Fannie Mae. Since Congress chartered it in 1970, Freddie Mac's stated mission has been "to create a continuous flow of funds to mortgage lenders in support of homeownership and rental housing." As with Fannie Mae, Freddie Mac purchases mortgages from lenders and packages them into securities that are sold to investors. In doing so, it ultimately provides homeowners and renters with lower housing costs and better access to home financing.

Prospects for Growth of Agency Securities

The market for agency securities is likely to grow in the years ahead even if the housing market slows from its torrid pace of the last several years. One of the key reasons relates to the sheer size of the mortgage market. At over $5.6 trillion, mortgage debt is the biggest debt in the household sector. Importantly, only about half of all mortgage loans have been securitized. In other words, companies such as Fannie Mae have repackaged only about half of all mortgages into securities. This leaves plenty of room for continued growth.

One potential obstacle to growth of GSEs is the emergence of the concern voiced by members of Congress over the so-called *implicit guarantee* that the GSEs enjoy. This guarantee basically relates to the notion that if there is a default, the U.S. government will step in and rescue the GSEs, which are probably under the umbrella of "too big to fail." Some members of Congress are concerned that the GSEs are borrowing too heavily and that their borrowing binge may one day put taxpayers at risk of having to bail out the GSEs if the housing market goes bust. Many feel that the implicit guarantee is the main reason these agencies enjoy AAA ratings. Nevertheless, the GSEs have strong balance sheets and appear to deserve a high credit rating. Whatever the case, the rumblings out of Washington are not likely to go very far so long as Democrats control any branch of government since the Democrats oppose legislation that would impose new regulations on the GSEs. It might be healthy, however, for the GSEs to be kept on their toes given the important role they play in the U.S. economy and the potential burden that could be imposed on taxpayers if they were to encounter financial difficulties.

Without government-sponsored enterprises such as Fannie Mae and Freddie Mac, far fewer mortgages would be issued, reducing activity in the housing market, one of the most important sectors of the U.S. economy. For investors GSEs provide a means of achieving higher yields than those from Treasuries without a significant increase in risk. Moreover, GSEs are an attractive alternative to high-grade corporate bonds owing to their higher yields and lower risk. Agency securities are also more liquid than corporate bonds, as was discussed in Chapter 2.

MORTGAGE-BACKED SECURITIES

Mortgage-backed securities (MBSs) are perceived as one of the more complex segments of the bond market. This is understandable in light of the considerable differences that exist between mortgage-backed securities and conventional bonds. Two of the biggest differences relate to the very different structures of their cash flows and maturity dates. With most bonds these two characteristics are pretty straightforward and predictable, but they are far more uncertain with MBSs. For investors this presents both risks and opportunities. For most investors, however, a basic understanding is enough to avoid some of the pitfalls of investing in mortgage-backed securities and to capitalize on the attractive yields and many opportunities the MBS market presents.

In its simplest form, a *mortgage-backed security* is pool of mortgages that have been securitized, or repackaged so that they can be sold to investors. Investors in mortgage-backed securities have many of the same experiences that banks do when they issue mortgage loans. For example, both receive regular payments of principal and interest on the mortgage loans, are subject to prepayment risks, and are subject to effects from defaults on mortgage loans. One of the most basic forms of a mortgage-backed security is a *mortgage pass-through* security, also known as a *participation certificate*. A mortgage pass-through security represents pro rata ownership interest in the principal and interest payments of a pool of mortgage loans. The cash flows are said to "pass through" from homeowners and other property owners to the holders of the pass-through securities. The payments are made regularly, generally on a monthly basis, and include both principal and interest. Most pass-through securities are issued by government agencies, including the Federal National Mortgage Association, the Federal Home Loan Mortgage Corporation, and the Government National Mortgage Association. Pass-through securities that are issued by nongovernment entities are called *private-label mortgage-backed securities*. These securities typically are constructed with a pool of large mortgages taken out by individuals with above-average incomes.

The interest paid on a pass-through security is lower than the interest rate paid on the underlying mortgages for a couple of reasons. First, when either a government agency or a private-label company creates a mortgage-backed security, it normally pays a service fee to the institutions from which it purchased the mortgages that underlie the mortgage-backed security. The mortgage lenders that sell their mortgages generally retain servicing of the loans and earn a fee for collecting payments from homeowners and performing other functions. A second factor that reduces the actual interest payment on a pass-through security relates to the fee paid by investors to government agencies for their guarantee of the mortgage loans. Fannie Mae, for example, collects a *guaranty fee* for its guarantee of the timely payment of principal and interest on the securities. Fannie Mae's guaranty is solely its own and does not have the backing of the full faith and credit of the U.S. government. Ginnie Mae's securities, in contrast, have the government's backing.

Collateralized Mortgage Obligations

A more complex type of mortgage-backed security is known as a *collateralized mortgage obligation* (CMO) or, since 1986, a *Real Estate Mortgage Investment Conduit* (REMIC). A CMO is a mortgage-backed security constructed by repackaging and redirecting the cash flows from other mortgage-backed securities. A typical CMO, often called a *plain vanilla or sequential pay* CMO, consists of a few tranches, or classes of securities, that are prioritized to distribute the payments made on the underlying mortgages according to a predetermined payment schedule. In other words, both the scheduled and unscheduled principal payments made on the mortgages will be distributed to holders of a CMO on a predetermined prioritized basis. This is different from a pass-through security, where the principal payments are distributed in a pro rata, or proportionate, basis. CMOs were created to offer investors a wide variety of securities from which to choose. With CMOs, investors are more likely to find a mortgage-backed security that fits their needs and their risk profiles. For example, in a CMO that has four classes of securities, Class A could have first priority on all mortgage prepayments, Class B could have second priority, Class C could be third, and Class D would be last in line to receive prepayments. In this case Class A would be the most likely to be prepaid early, thus making it a relatively short-term security, while Class D would be prepaid last, making it a relatively long-term security. This CMO is structured in a way that gives prospective investors a better sense of when the securities will mature than it would if it were a pass-through security. Investors are therefore more likely to find an MBS that meets their specific needs if they purchase a CMO rather than a pass-through.

Prepayment Risks

One of the biggest risks of holding mortgage-backed securities is prepayment risk. *Prepayment risk* is the risk that a mortgage security will be prepaid early, exposing the investor to reinvestment risk. Mortgages are prepaid for a variety of reasons, including mortgage refinancing, a home sale, and repossession and liquidation of a home, or simply because a homeowner chooses to prepay the mortgage early incrementally or with blocks of money. When the mortgages that underlie an MBS are prepaid, the investors are also prepaid. Investors are therefore at risk of having to reinvest their money at lower interest rates. Prepayment risks are greatest when interest rates decline enough to prompt homeowners to refinance their existing mortgages. In 1998 and 1999, for example, nearly $750 billion of the nearly $4.5 trillion in mortgages that were outstanding at that time were refinanced. In 2001, a plunge in interest rates prompted a record of about $1 trillion in mortgage refinancing. During these periods, investors in mortgage-backed securities had much of their invested principal returned to them. Those investors then faced the unpleasant prospect of reinvesting their capital at interest rate levels that were the lowest in about 40 years. The prospect of early prepayments can cause a mortgage-backed security to perform very much as a callable bond does when interest rates decline. In both cases the securities are subject to negative convexity, or the risk that a bond will perform poorly when a certain interest rate threshold is reached. In the case of an MBS this threshold kicks in when market interest rates decline below the interest rate on the MBS and accelerates as interest rates continue to decline below the threshold. CMOs can give investors in MBSs a greater degree of certainty with respect to prepayment risks but cannot eliminate this critical risk.

One of the best ways to simplify the very complex realm of investing in mortgage-backed securities is to remember that you are holding a pool of mortgages and are therefore apt to have many of the same experiences that a bank does in different interest rate climates. As with many other types of investments, if you first think of the investment in its simplest form—in this case a home mortgage—you will at least have an understanding of the most critical aspect of the investment.

MUNICIPAL BONDS

Municipal bonds are bonds issued by state and local governments as well as other governmental entities to fund a variety of public spending needs, including the construction of new schools, hospitals, utilities, and highways, and to fund a variety of general obligations. Municipal bonds are very popular with individual investors, who own about two times more municipal bonds ($582 billion in direct holdings) than U.S. Treasuries ($260 billion) and about three times more municipal bonds than U.S. savings bonds ($186 billion). In fact, next to corporate bonds, individuals own more municipal bonds than any other fixed-income security, and when indirect holdings of municipal securities are included (mutual funds, mostly), individuals hold over 70 percent of the $1.6 trillion in municipal bonds outstanding.

The reason municipal securities are so popular with individuals is that the interest paid on them is exempt from federal income taxes. U.S. laws are such that the federal government cannot tax the states and vice versa. This is why these securities are tax-exempt. For individuals who purchase municipal bonds issued in the state in which they live, the interest paid on those bonds is likely to be exempt from state and local taxes too. Two tax bills passed by Congress helped boost the popularity of municipal bonds. First, the Tax Reform Act of 1986 reduced many tax deductions that previously had limited tax liabilities for individuals. Municipal bonds therefore became a bastion for tax sheltering. Second, the tax bill of 1993 raised marginal tax rates in the upper income brackets, creating the need for tax shelters. It can be persuasively argued that the Clinton tax increase of 1993 was a leading factor in the rise in the proportion of taxes that individuals paid as a percentage of the gross domestic product (GDP). In the late 1990s, this key statistic reached its highest level in over 40 years. The Bush tax cut implemented in 2001 should begin to reverse this trend, and at the margins eventually could weaken the demand for municipal securities.

Calculating the Taxable Equivalent Yield

In considering the purchase of a municipal bond, it is critically important to know how to compare its yield with the yields on taxable securities. This will help an investor judge which of the two investment choices has the highest after-tax yield-to-maturity. For example, if you were considering the purchase of either a municipal bond with a yield-to-maturity of 5 percent or a corporate bond yielding 7 percent, you would want to know which of the two securities actually produced the best after-tax return. The calculation is very simple:

$$\text{Taxable equivalent yield} = \frac{tax\text{-}exempt\ yield}{1 - \text{marginal tax rate}}$$

The tax-exempt yield is the yield-to-maturity on the municipal bond (or municipal bond fund); the marginal tax rate is the tax rate that you pay on the last dollar of your income. In this example, assuming the marginal tax rate is 39 percent, the calculation is done as follows:

$$\text{Taxable equivalent yield} = \frac{5\%}{(1 - .39)} = 8.20\%$$

In this example, the municipal bond has a greater after-tax yield-to-maturity than does the corporate bond. Put differently, to achieve an after-tax yield-to-maturity that is higher than that of the municipal bond, you would have to find a taxable security yielding more than 8.2 percent.

Keep in mind that if the municipal security is selling at a deep discount to its par value, the yield-to-maturity used in the calculation could overstate its taxable equivalent yield. This is the case because its yield-to-maturity will be inflated by the capital gain that will be realized when the security matures. Since the capital gain is taxable, you want to use a yield-to-maturity that eliminates the capital gain and focuses on the coupon payment instead. Of course, only the coupon payments are tax-exempt.

Types of Municipal Securities

With over 1 million different municipal bonds outstanding and tens of thousands of entities issuing them, there is obviously a wide variety of municipal bonds to choose from. It is therefore very important to look closely at the bond you are considering buying. Although there is an array of municipal bonds outstanding, there are two main types:

General obligation bonds. Also known as GO (gee-oh) bonds, these bonds are backed by the full faith and credit of the issuer, chiefly the issuer's power to tax the public. This means that only an issuer with the power to tax can issue a GO bond. States, cities, counties, and towns are examples of entities that issue GO bonds. Some GO bonds are backed by revenue other than taxes, such as fees. These bonds are known as *double-barreled municipal bonds.* Some GO bonds are backed by an assessment on the entities that benefit directly from the borrowing; these bonds are called *special assessment bonds.* Keep in mind that there is a legal limit on the taxing power used to back some GO bonds. These bonds are called *limited tax general obligation bonds.* When buying GO bonds, investors should inspect the economy of the municipality and the strength of the tax base in the municipality.

Revenue bonds. As the name implies, revenue bonds are backed by revenues generated by projects financed with the bonds. Examples include toll bridges, toll roads, airports, hospitals, and utilities. Revenue bonds are issued by agencies, commissions, and authorities created by legislation passed by state or local governments. Although revenue bonds are backed by specific revenue sources, they can be riskier than GO bonds because the municipality does not back the bonds explicitly. When buying a revenue bond, investors should determine the debt service coverage ratio, which is a measure of the amount of revenue coming in versus the debt payments going out.

Municipal Bond Insurance

Some municipalities are too weak or too small to attract a large group of investors to buy their bonds. To entice investors, these municipalities enter into agreements to have their bonds insured by insurance companies. Municipal bond insurance guarantees that the insurer will pay the interest and principal on the bonds even if the issuer defaults on its debt obligations. The insurance generally lasts for the life of the bond being insured. About half of all newly issued municipal bonds are insured. Insured bonds yield less than do those which are not insured because of the lower risk of holding insured bonds, but they usually yield more than do municipal bonds that are AAA-rated in their own right. The major municipal bond insurance companies are American Municipal Bond Assurance Company (AMBAC), Municipal Bond Insurance Association (MBIA), Financial Guaranty Insurance Company (FGIC), and Financial Assurance Inc. (FSA). These companies are known as *monoline* companies because their focus is primarily on insuring municipal bonds. In recent years large financial companies such as the major property and casualty companies with *multiline* businesses have insured municipal bonds.

HOLDERS OF FIXED-INCOME SECURITIES

In investing in any financial security, it is extremely helpful to know who the players are so that one can both monitor their activities and be aware of factors that could motivate those players to alter their investments. Knowing the major holders of a security can also isolate the causes of sudden market movements and therefore help identify anomalous moves in the markets on which one can capitalize when dislocations arise. Foreign investors are the biggest holders of *Treasuries*, owning over 40 percent of all Treasuries outstanding, followed by the Federal Reserve (about 15 percent) and households (about 8 percent). In *agency securities*, commercial banks are the biggest holders, followed by foreign investors. Individuals are easily the biggest holders of *municipal securities*, holding about 36 percent directly, while another 33 percent is held indirectly through mutual funds. The biggest holders of *corporate bonds* are life insurance companies, followed by foreign investors, individuals, and pension funds.

SUMMARY

Looking beyond the basics, in this chapter we discussed:

- The five largest and most active segments of the bond market are the markets for U.S. Treasuries, corporate bonds, government agency securities, mortgage-backed securities, and municipal bonds.

- The U.S. Treasury market is the most active market and contains largely conventional securities with predictable cash flows and maturities. Treasuries provide investors with a means of investing in fixed-income securities that are perceived to be free of default risks. The Treasury Department is attempting to reduce the average maturity of the nation's outstanding debts, a strategy that is fraught with risks.
- The Treasury's inflation-indexed securities provide a means of protecting oneself against inflation risks and tracking the market's inflation expectations.
- Investors seeking higher yields than those on Treasuries and looking to bet on major sectors of the economy without having to invest in the stock market can choose corporate bonds. Investors should approach purchases of corporate bonds with the same philosophies that work well in investing in stocks. Chiefly, one must be aware of the importance of picking bonds in industries that have the best prospects for economic growth.
- The agency securities market is a large, liquid market with attractive yields in securities that have extremely high credit quality.
- Mortgage-backed securities are complex securities with characteristics that are relatively unconventional in the bond market. The complexities are a key reason for the attractive yields from these securities. Investors can choose from different types of mortgage-backed securities, including the so-called plain vanilla pass-through securities and the more complex but tailor-made collateralized mortgage obligations. Simplify investing in mortgage-backed securities by thinking in terms of owning pools of mortgage loans.
- Municipal bonds are very popular with individual investors because of their tax benefits. The interest paid on the vast majority of municipal bonds is exempt from federal taxes. Investors should compute the after-tax equivalent yield on municipal securities when comparing yields on municipal securities to those on taxable securities such as corporate bonds.

CHAPTER FIVE

Risks Facing Today's Bond Investors: Beware But Be Not Afraid

True or false? Bonds are risk free. Answer: False.

When some people think about bond investing, they conjure up visions of senior citizens comfortably sitting on their nest eggs and bristling with prosperity after years of eschewing risk taking. However, this is a very dusty image decades removed from reality. Bonds are far from risk-free. True, they are less risky than many other types of investments, yet bond investors must be aware of a number of risks that could significantly affect their fixed-income investments. It's simplistic to equate bond investing with risk-free investing.

The degree of risk facing today's bond investors depends on many factors, including the economic climate, the types of strategies investors employ, and the types of fixed-income securities investors choose. Bond investors can control some of the risks they face, but their degree of control is sometimes minimal. As with most risks, however, awareness of the risks involved in bond investing can help minimize the extent to which these risks may have a deleterious effect on a portfolio's investment performance. The benefits of knowing the risks involved in bond investing are akin to the benefits of knowing the risks involved in crossing a street before the light turns green. The main point is that risks can be managed if one is aware of them.

Bonds are at risk of being affected by a variety of risk factors. There are two main ways in which risk factors can affect a bond.

First, some risk factors pose a threat to a bond's current value. In this case the bond's price will fluctuate with the degree to which certain risk factors threaten its value. Second, some risk factors pose a threat to the cash flows on a bond. In this case certain risk factors can affect the timeliness and value of a bond's cash flows.

There are three major risk factors that affect virtually all bonds and many others that affect specific types of bonds and strategies:

Risks to virtually all bonds:

- Market risk
- Reinvestment risk
- Event risk

Risks to specific types of bonds and strategies:

- Sector risk
- Call or prepayment risk
- Liquidity risk
- Credit or default risk
- Yield curve risk
- Inflation risk
- Currency risk
- Hedge risk
- Odd-lot risk

Let's take a look at each of these risks starting with the three most important ones.

MARKET, OR INTEREST RATE, RISK

Ask bond traders on Wall Street or in the futures trading pits in Chicago whether there is much risk in holding bonds and they will give you an earful. Bond prices can and do move sharply, probably more than most people perceive. Make no mistake: Bond investors are by no means immune to market fluctuations and the risk of capital losses. As with most financial assets, bond prices are subject to *market risk*. As the label implies, market risk refers to the risks associated with market fluctuations. In the bond market this risk is also called *interest-rate risk* and is one of the biggest risks a bond investor faces. Interest rate risk arises from the fact that bond prices move inversely with yields. Put simply, when interest rates rise, bond prices fall, and when interest rates fall, bond prices rise. This is a risk for any investor who may sell a bond before its maturity date because the bond is at risk of fluctuating in price. For investors who hold their bonds to maturity, interest rate risks are basically irrelevant because those bonds will be redeemed at their par value regardless of the interest rate volatility that occurs between the date when securities were purchased and the maturity date.

All bonds are subject to interest rate risk regardless of whether they are insured against losses (as is the case with many municipal bonds) or the creditworthiness of the bond issuer is strong. The prices on these bonds respond as other bonds do to fluctuations in interest rates.

Interest rate risk is largely out of a bond investor's control; investors are powerless against the forces that cause interest rates to fluctuate. This does not mean, however, that bond investors are completely helpless in the face of interest rate risks. Indeed, bond investors can control the degree of interest rate risk to which they are subject by varying the maturity length of the bonds in their portfolios. By selecting shorter maturities over longer maturities, bond investors can reduce their interest rate risk. Interest rate risk is greater on long-term maturities than it is on short-term maturities because a bond's price sensitivity to changes in interest rates increases with maturity length. A bond's price sensitivity to changes in interest rates can be quantified by its *duration*. Duration is basically a mathematical means of determining the approximate percentage change that will result when a bond's price changes by 100 basis points. This topic was discussed in greater detail in Chapter 3. Knowing a bond's duration is one of the best ways to control interest rate risk.

Attempting to control interest rate risk by choosing short maturities over long maturities seems simple, but it can introduce new risks. One risk, as discussed below, is a variant of *reinvestment risk*. Reinvestment risk is the risk that the cash flows on a bond will be reinvested at falling interest rate levels. This risk normally applies to a bond's regular interest payments, but it also can apply to an investor who chooses short-term maturities over long-term maturities when that investor engages in the strategy in effort to control interest rate risk. In this case an investor who chooses short-term maturities over long-term maturities will have to reinvest the capital from the maturing bonds more often, increasing the risk that the capital will be invested at a lower interest rate.

A second risk introduced by attempts to control interest rate risk is the possibility that investors will incur opportunity costs by investing in short-term maturities during times when owning long-term maturities would have produced larger capital gains. In this case investors forgo the chance to achieve higher investment returns in order to reduce their interest rate risk. This trade-off is very common in investing; investors recognize that low-risk assets generally have lower investment returns than do riskier assets.

REINVESTMENT RISK

As was just mentioned, *reinvestment risk* is the risk that a bond's cash flows will be reinvested at falling interest rate levels. This risk is of particular concern to investors who invest in short-term maturities and bonds with high coupon rates.

When interest rates decline, bond investors are less likely to be able to invest the interest income they receive on their bonds at the same interest rate level they receive on their bonds. Consider, for example, a bond investor who owns a bond with a par value of $1000 that pays a 6 percent annual coupon. The investor therefore will receive $60 per year in interest income from that bond. Let's say interest rates decline and the investor can no longer find a bond that pays a 6 percent annual coupon and meets his or her investment criteria. The investor must instead reinvest the interest income at 5 percent, and the investor's interest on interest will decline and thus have an impact on a key element of the investment returns. Of course, if interest rates rise, the investor will benefit by being able to reinvest the interest payments at a higher interest rate.

The degree of reinvestment risk for a particular bond depends largely on three key factors. First, the longer the maturity on a bond is, the more the bond's total dollar return will depend on prevailing interest rates to achieve the yield-to-maturity calculated at the time of purchase. This is a critical point because for long-term maturities, interest on interest can account for a large percentage of the total dollar return. In fact, when interest rates are high, interest on interest can account for more than half of a bond's total dollar return. This is why it is extremely important for bond investors to be as diligent with their investment choices as they are with the reinvestment of interest.

A second factor that determines a bond's degree of reinvestment risk is its coupon rate. As was shown above, fluctuations in interest rates can have a direct bearing on the interest on interest received on a bond. The higher the coupon rate on a bond, the greater the reinvestment risk. Bonds with low coupon rates have low reinvestment risk. As with maturity length, the higher the coupon rate on a bond is, the more the bond's total dollar return will depend on prevailing interest rates to achieve the yield-to-maturity that existed at the time of purchase. In light of these risks, bond investors who are concerned about the *dollar* return on their bond portfolios should consider purchasing bonds with high coupon rates when interest rates are rising. Conversely, when interest rates are low, investors should consider investing in low coupon bonds. Zero coupon bonds, for example, have no reinvestment risk except when a bond is sold or matures. However, buying bonds with higher coupons during periods when interest rates are falling could result in opportunity costs since bonds with high coupon rates tend to increase in price more slowly than do bonds with low coupon rates. This is the case because the duration on bonds with high coupon rates tends to be higher than that on bonds with low coupon rates (assuming other aspects of the bond's characteristics are the same).

A bond's maturity length is the third factor that determines the bond's degree of reinvestment risk. The shorter a bond's maturity is, the more it is subject to reinvestment risk. Investors in bonds that have short-term maturities are therefore at risk of having to reinvest the proceeds received on the bonds when they mature. One of the best ways to limit the reinvestment risks in a bond portfolio that result from maturity length is to stagger the maturities so that bonds mature on different dates. This way there will be an opportunity to reinvest the proceeds from maturing bonds at prevailing rates that are likely to reflect both the ups and the downs of the interest rate climate. This strategy also provides a steady flow of capital for reinvestment without the need to sell securities to generate it. This allows for more opportunistic investing and can reduce transaction costs.

Interest Rate Risk and Reinvestment Risk Can Offset Each Other

It is important to note that interest rate risk and reinvestment risk can offset each other. Indeed, many fixed-income portfolio managers recognize this and construct their portfolios to create a high degree of *immunization* against both of these risks. Portfolios constructed in this way benefit when the capital losses that result from rising interest rates (causing prices to fall) are offset by the benefits of higher reinvestment rates on a portfolio's cash flows.

EVENT RISK

There are a number of ways in which unexpected events can affect a bond. After some events, for instance, the ability of an issuer to pay both interest and principal can be seriously affected. In other cases, unexpected events can cause a bond's price to drop sharply. These risks are known as *event risks*. Event risks affect nearly all financial instruments, but the magnitude of the impact depends on the instrument's risk characteristics. A high-yield bond, for example, is likely to be affected more than a Treasury bond when unexpected events occur.

Five types of event risk pose the greatest risk to bond investors:

- Takeover or restructuring risk
- Sudden shifts in market sentiment
- International financial events
- International political or military events
- Systemic risks

Let's take a brief look at each of these event risks.

Takeover or Restructuring Risk

In the 1980s there were a significant number of corporate takeovers, restructurings, and leveraged buyouts that significantly affected the value of many corporate bonds. Companies initiating the acquisition of other companies saw their debt burdens increase sharply as a result of the huge costs of the acquisitions. This resulted in rating downgrades that sent the value of the new company's existing debt spiraling downward, particularly for companies whose ratings were downgraded to below investment grade from investment grade. The flurry of activity that occurred during that period created widespread fears among corporate bond investors who were worried that their bonds might be affected next. In some cases corporate bonds declined in value when companies in related industries were acquired. The reasoning was that there could be further consolidation in the industry. Compared to the 1980s, takeover or restructuring risks have diminished in recent years, but they remain a formidable threat to bond investors. Bond investors should pay close attention to developments in the industries in which they invest and track trends in takeover and restructuring activity to reduce the risks associated with this type of activity.

Sudden Shifts in Market Sentiment

Market sentiment can shift abruptly, affecting the value of bonds in the process. Of course, it is rare for market sentiment to shift in a day's time, but there have been plenty of cases where it shifted in a matter of days or over short spans of time—quickly enough for shifts in market sentiment to qualify as event risk. A clear example of this was the bursting of the financial bubble at the start of 2000. In a very short span of time investors turned sour on the outlook for long-term corporate assets such as stocks and corporate bonds. There was no particular catalyst to prompt the sudden reversal except perhaps the Federal Reserve, which was in the middle of raising interest rates. However, the Fed had started raising interest rates many months earlier, and so it would be incorrect to say that the Fed prompted the sudden shift in sentiment. Figure 5-1 illustrates the large impact the sudden shift in market sentiment in 2000 had on low-grade corporate bonds. There have been many other occasions when market sentiment shifted abruptly; the 1987 stock market crash is a good example.

When market sentiment shifts, this generally is manifested in widening yield spreads between corporate bonds and Treasury bonds. Low-grade corporate bonds tend to act poorly under such circumstances. Investors are powerless against sudden shifts in market sentiment but can control the risk to some extent. The best way is to track market sentiment as closely as possible for signs of excess. This is discussed more thoroughly in Chapter 10.

F i g u r e   5–1

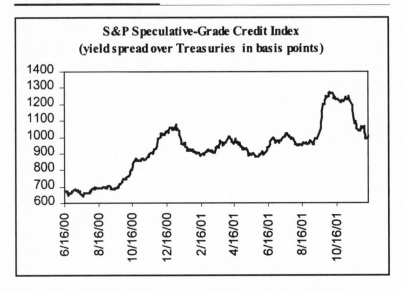

S&P Speculative-Grade Credit Index
(yield spread over Treasuries in basis points)

International Financial Events

Bond prices often are affected by financial events abroad. In recent years the main source of that impact has been the emerging markets, particularly countries in Asia and Latin America. Emerging markets are markets in countries considered undeveloped relative to industrialized nations such as the United States, Japan, and the countries in western Europe. In these relatively undeveloped countries severe weakness in emerging market bonds, which are government bonds in emerging economies rated below investment grade, often spilled over into U.S. markets, sparking weakness in U.S. bond prices. There have been several episodes in recent years in which events in the emerging markets have had a large impact on U.S. bond prices. One of the most dramatic examples was the plunge in emerging market bond prices in 1998 that resulted from the Asian financial crisis and the Russian government's debt default in August 1998. As can be seen in Figure 5-2, lower-tier investment-grade corporate bonds performed poorly during that time, with yield spreads to Treasuries widening dramatically. The impact was so far-reaching that yield spreads have not yet returned to the levels seen just before the crises. For bond investors the impact of past international financial events illustrates the importance of directing at least a modicum of attention toward international markets even though there may appear to be no direct linkage between events abroad and events in the United States. The events in 1998 did not occur overnight; investors were given numerous warnings about the potential for a broadening of the dilemma. Bond investors who recognized those looming risks and acted on them were able to avoid steep losses.

International Political and Military Events

A variety of political and military events can have a direct impact on bond prices. The terrorist attack that saddened and roiled the United States on September 11, 2001, is the most recent example. That event had a large impact on the bond market, spurring sharp weakness in low-grade corporate debt and a surge in U.S. Treasuries. Figure 5-3 shows the large impact of the September 11 tragedy on speculative-grade bonds. As you can see from the chart, the yield spread between speculative-grade bonds and U.S. Treasuries widened dramatically and did not begin to narrow until a string of U.S. military victories in Afghanistan gave the investing public a sense that the crisis was being defused. Yield spreads also widened after Iraq's

F i g u r e   5–2

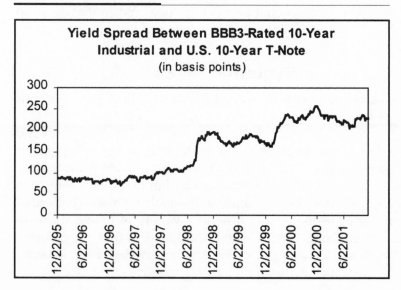

Yield Spread Between BBB3-Rated 10-Year Industrial and U.S. 10-Year T-Note (in basis points)

F i g u r e   5–3

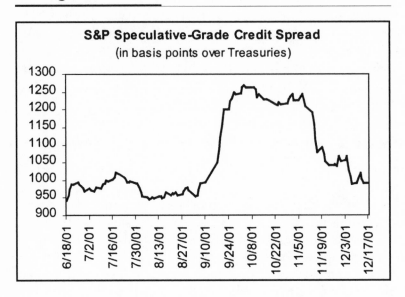

invasion of Kuwait in August 1990 and narrowed when the United States and its allies won the war in early 1991. There is obviously very little that investors can do to prepare themselves for events such as the September 11 tragedy. However, investors should take note of the trading pattern throughout U.S. history in both bonds and stocks when unexpected events have occurred so that they can respond accordingly if the unexpected happens again.

Systemic Risks

On rare occasions events occur that investors believe pose systemic risks to either the U.S. financial system or the world financial system. When this occurs, investors flock to the safety of U.S. Treasuries and move out of riskier assets. A classic example occurred in September 1998, when a hedge fund (hedge funds are investment firms that are structured to avoid certain regulations by limiting their clientele to highly sophisticated, very wealthy individuals who seek high rates of return by investing and trading in a variety of financial instruments) named Long Term Capital Management (LTCM) incurred large investment losses on a variety of highly leveraged investments.

LTCM is thought to have amassed investment positions with a notional value of over $1 trillion on just $4.8 billion of capital by using its $200 billion of borrowing capacity. Investors feared that liquidation of LTCM's highly leveraged investment strategies posed risks to the U.S. financial system because it might create panic selling that would be tantamount to a fire sale. The fear was so great that the Federal Reserve helped arrange what Federal Reserve Chairman Alan Greenspan called "an orderly private-sector adjustment" by gathering major banks and investment firms to raise $3.5 billion of bailout money in exchange for a substantial dilution of the existing shareholders' stake in LTCM. Greenspan described the risks LTCM's potential failure posed to the financial system just a few weeks after the bailout:

> Had the failure of LTCM triggered the seizing up of markets, substantial damage could have been inflicted on many market participants, including some not directly involved with the firm, and could have potentially impaired the economies of many nations, including our own.

Bond investors had similar thoughts and flocked to Treasuries. The desire for safe liquid assets became so great that older, less actively traded Treasuries were shunned in favor of newer, more actively traded Treasuries, causing yield spreads between the two to widen sharply. Figure 5-4 illustrates this widening. Importantly, the widening occurred despite the fact that all Treasuries have the same risk characteristics since they are backed by the full faith and credit of the U.S. government. Investors who recognized this anomalous response in the Treasury market took advantage of the widening spread by buying the older, less actively traded Treasuries and selling the newer, actively traded Treasuries.

Municipal bonds also can be affected by unexpected events in other municipalities. The Orange County, California, bankruptcy in 1994, for example, in which the county lost nearly $2 billion on highly leveraged investments, is a classic example. The sudden bankruptcy spurred weakness in other municipal bonds across the nation, particularly in California, owing to fears that there might be other cases like it.

Concerns over systemic risks arise much more often than those risks actually pose threats to either the U.S. financial system or the world financial system. Investors therefore can benefit by

F i g u r e   5-4

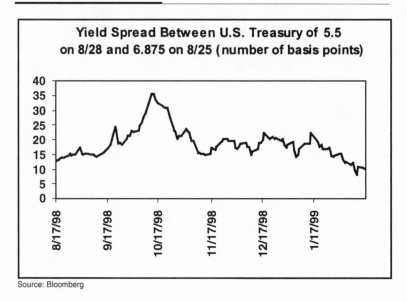

Source: Bloomberg

spotting anomalies that arise in the markets when these unfounded concerns surface.

SECTOR RISK

In the stock market choosing stocks in industries that are prospering can be one of the most important determinants of an equity investor's total return. In fact, many studies suggest that industry selection is the most important aspect of stock selecting. In a study conducted by William J. O'Neil, fully 67 percent of the biggest market movers during the period 1953–1993 were part of group advances. A good example of the powerful influence group moves can have on individual stocks is the behavior of the dot-com stocks between 1999 and 2001. During that time shares in individual dot-com companies were bid sharply higher, often without any basis other than the fact that other dot-com companies were being bid sharply higher. Of course, when the dot-com stocks began to implode, they imploded together, showing clearly that group movement is one of the most important influences on the value of a company's stock. Industry selection is therefore one of the most important elements of investing in stocks as well as corporate bonds. Corporate bond investors therefore should be alert to trends in the industries in which they invest. Failure to be alert will significantly increase the degree of *sector risk* the investor faces.

One of the best things an investor can do to limit sector risk is to be alert to where the economy stands in the business cycle and to potential shifts in monetary policy. These two factors play a very large role in the behavior of the various sectors of the economy. During the later stages of an economic expansion, for example, bonds in economically sensitive industries such as consumer cyclicals (retailers, automotive companies, home building, etc.), basic materials (paper, chemical, and metals companies), financials (commercial banks, brokerages, insurance copmpanies, and savings and loans companies), and transportation (railroads and trucking companies) tend to perform poorly compared to companies in less economically sensitive industries such as utilities, consumer noncyclicals (food, cosmetics, soft drinks, house nondurables), and health care (pharmaceuticals, health care providers, and medical products). During such times it is therefore important to consider shifting money from economically sensitive companies to companies that are less economically sensitive. Similarly, in the early stages of an economic expansion the opposite strategy should be considered.

Staying abreast of the direction of monetary policy is critical to limiting sector risk. Bonds in economically sensitive companies respond directly to changes in monetary policy. When the Federal Reserve is in the process of raising interest rates, that is a good time to reduce an investor's exposure to economically sensitive industries. When the Fed is lowering interest rates, increasing an investor's exposure to economically sensitive industries is likely to be the best strategy.

Another way to limit sector risk is to diversify. This age-old advice can help in the bond market, too, by spreading an investor's exposure among the different sectors of the economy so that when one sector falters, another will be prospering.

CALL OR PREPAYMENT RISK

If it is specified in a bond's indenture, a bond can be "called," or redeemed by the issuer at a predetermined price before its maturity date. Bond issuers use this feature to give themselves an opportunity to refinance their debt if market interest rates decline. For example, suppose an issuer sold a $1000 bond with a yield of 8 percent three years ago but current interest rates are 2 percentage points lower. If this case the issuer would have a strong incentive to refinance its existing debt. Suppose the call feature allowed the issuer to call the bond at 102, or $1020 per bond. The issuer could sell a new bond at $1000 with a yield of 6 percent and use the proceeds to call its existing bonds at $1020 and thus benefit from lower borrowing costs.

What may be good news for bond issuers is not necessarily good news for bond investors. When bonds are called early, an investor must reinvest the principal from the redeemed bond at lower interest rate levels, reducing the investor's rate of return. This risk may make you wonder why an investor would consider purchasing bonds with call risks. One of the advantages of owing callable bonds is that investors are compensated for the added risk by a higher yield. While the opportunity to achieve enhancements to a portfolio's total return by buying callable bonds may appeal to some investors, the disadvantages are strong enough to make some investors loath to buy callable bonds. The most prominent reason relates to the reinvestment risks posed by the call feature. A second big disadvantage of a callable bond is the limited upside potential in the bond's price. Bond prices rise, of course, when interest rates fall, but the interest rate decline raises the odds that the issuer will call a callable bond, limiting the price appreciation in the callable bond. This occurs because bond investors worry that if they purchase a bond at a price that is above the call price, they could be subject to a capital loss (because the purchase price is higher than the call price). The only time an investor would engage in such a purchase would if there was plenty of time remaining before the bond's call date.

The call feature can affect a variety of bonds, including municipal, corporate, agency, and all mortgage-backed securities. Treasury bonds are no longer issued with call features, but a large number of Treasury bonds that were issued in past years have call features. Thus, call risk is a threat to most segments of the bond market.

Investors can limit call risk in a number of ways. First and foremost, investors should determine whether the bonds they are thinking of purchasing have a provision that allows the issuer to call them before the maturity date. An investor can do this by asking his or her broker or by reading the bond's indenture or prospectus. Keep in mind that mortgage securities do not have provisions that specify a call date. Mortgage bonds are not actually "called," they are refunded when the homeowners in the mortgage pools that underlie the mortgage bonds prepay the principal on their mortgage debt. A second way to limit call risk is to be wary of buying bonds with high coupons. Those bonds are generally bonds that were issued at some point in the past when interest rates were higher. In this case there is a greater probability of the bonds being called than there is for bonds with low coupons since it is more likely that an issuer will call bonds that were issued at interest rate levels that are higher than prevailing interest rates. Third, an investor should reduce exposure to mortgage-backed securities when interest rates are falling to limit prepayment risk. Fourth, an investor should avoid buying callable bonds trading at a premium over their par value if the call date is near.

For more on callable bonds, see Chapter 3.

LIQUIDITY RISK

As was shown in Chapter 2, liquidity is an important element of trading fixed-income securities. Low levels of liquidity can create what is known as *liquidity risk*. Liquidity risk is the risk that a bondholder will have difficulty selling bonds at or near their fair value. Liquidity can be defined as the ease or difficulty with which buyers and sellers can transact in small and large quantities at prices that are considered representative of the true market value. Liquidity risk is greatest for bond investors who frequently sell their bond holdings before they mature; investors who generally hold their bonds to maturity do not have to worry much about the liquidity of their bonds.

There are two key measures of market liquidity: the bid-ask spread and market or quote depth. The bid-ask spread is probably the best measure of a bond's liquidity. The narrower a bond's bid-ask spread is, the easier it is to sell the bond. Keep in mind, however, that the bid-ask spread depends a great deal on a bond's market depth. Market depth is the quantity of securities that broker-dealers are willing to buy and sell at various prices. This means that bonds that have larger average bids and offers have greater market depth and liquidity than do bonds that have smaller average bids and offers. Thus, a narrow bid-ask spread on a bond does not necessarily mean that the bond's liquidity will be high on all transactions; the bid-ask spread could well be wider for transactions requiring high levels of market depth.

As was mentioned earlier, a dramatic example of the effects of liquidity on bond prices occurred in 1998 during the LTCM, Russian, and Asian financial crises. As was shown in Figure 5-4, liquidity concerns were so heightened that less actively traded Treasuries performed poorly compared with actively traded Treasuries despite a complete lack of difference in their creditworthiness.

Liquidity risk can be reduced either by investing in bonds that are actively traded or by holding bonds to the maturity date. Transacting with Wall Street's primary dealers, who tend to provide greater quote depth than do nonprimary dealers, also can reduce it. Another way to reduce liquidity risk is to transact early in the trading day, when the bond market is the most active. In addition, one should avoid trading just before the release of important economic reports, when broker-dealers sometimes widen their quotes on bid-ask spreads out of concern that the reports will have a big impact on their fixed-income positions. Broker-dealers often want to avoid the added risk that comes with buying and selling securities from customers who buy and sell securities from those broker-dealers. The broker-dealers do not want their positions to change much when the market might be about to move sharply as a result of the release of economic data.

CREDIT OR DEFAULT RISK

Bond investors loathe few things more than *credit*, or *default*, *risk*. This is the risk that bond issuers will not be able to make timely interest and principal payments on their bonds—in other words, default. Defaults are relatively uncommon. According to a study conducted by Moody's Investor Services, from 1920 to 1997 an average of just 0.17 percent of investment-grade issuers defaulted within one year after the assignment of their investment-grade rating. Speculative-grade credits fared worse, of course, with a default rate of 3.27 percent per year. The study also found that the overall one-year weighted-average default rate for corporate issues during that period was less than 0.01 percent for the highest-rated firms.

Despite the low level of default rates over the years, bond investors shudder when there is even the slightest hint that a bond issuer is at risk of a rating downgrade or at an increased risk of default. Bonds that are downgraded by the rating agencies often fall sharply in price, pushing their yields upward (for a more detailed discussion of credit ratings, see Chapter 12). Given the low likelihood of default on investment-grade bonds, investors may appear to be overreacting

Nearly all bonds are subject to some degree of credit risk with the exception of U.S. Treasuries, which are considered free of default risks. The degree of credit risk inherent in a particular bond depends on a myriad of factors. Because of this, bond investors gauge credit risks primarily by utilizing the credit ratings assigned by the rating agencies. These agencies review the myriad factors that could pose risks to the timely payment of principal and interest on the bonds and assign their ratings accordingly.

Therefore, one of the best ways to reduce credit risk in a portfolio is to utilize credit ratings and stay abreast of any potential changes in the credit ratings on an investor's bonds. A second way to reduce credit risks is to limit one's purchases of speculative-grade bonds in favor of investment-grade bonds, which are bonds rated BBB or higher (see Chapter 12 for ratings definitions). Doing this, of course, could reduce total return since the investor will be foregoing an opportunity to achieve a higher yield in favor of greater stability of the total return. A third way is to either diversify one's bond holdings or invest in mutual funds so that the default of one or more bonds will not substantially impair the investment performance.

YIELD CURVE RISK

Yield curve risk basically involves the risks associated with hedging activity, in which investors use one bond to hedge against the risk of adverse movements in another bond with a different maturity date. Yield curve risks arise when there is a risk that the yield change on the hedged bond will differ from the yield change on the bond used as a hedge. When this occurs, the dollar loss on one bond could exceed the dollar gain on the other one, producing a net loss. Here's an example. Assume a broker-dealer owns a large position in a corporate bond with a maturity of five years. The broker-dealer expects to sell the position to its customers eventually but would like to hedge against interest rate risks until the position is sold. If the broker-dealer chooses to hedge the corporate bond by selling 10-year Treasury notes, the broker-dealer will be subject to yield curve risks. In this case, if the yield change on the corporate bonds rises more than the yield on the Treasury note falls, the broker-dealer will incur a capital loss (assuming the hedge was done in a way that would have resulted in equal dollar gains and losses for equal changes in yield). Yield curve risks can be reduced by setting hedges that are close to the maturity date of the security being hedged.

INFLATION RISK

As has been mentioned a number of times in this book, inflation is the bane of the bond market because it erodes the value of a bond's cash flows. That is why *inflation risks* are one of the biggest risks facing bond investors. Inflation risks that affect the price of a bond pose significant interest rate risks, as was discussed earlier. Inflation risks also pertain to the interest payments on a bond, the value of which can be eroded by inflation. If, for example, a bond paid an annual coupon rate of 6 percent and inflation was also 6 percent, the value of that coupon payment would be completely eroded by inflation. In recent years inflation risks have been low as a result of a long period of relatively low inflation. Investors therefore have had little reason to guard against inflation risks. This cannot be expected to continue indefinitely, however, and so investors should be aware of strategies that can be employed if inflation risks grow. One strategy is to purchase the Treasury's inflation-protected securities commonly known as Treasury Inflation Protected Securities (TIPSs). As was discussed in Chapter 4, TIPSs are securities whose principal value is adjusted upward to compensate investors for inflation (as measured by the U.S. consumer price index). If an investor purchases TIPSs, inflation risks can be sharply reduced.

A second strategy is to purchase floating-rate notes or bonds, commonly known as floaters. The coupon rate on floaters is reset periodically—usually every six months—and uses a short-term interest rate as its benchmark. The benchmark might be Treasury bills, the London Interbank Offering Rate (LIBOR), the prime rate, or another short-term interest rate. Although these instruments are not directly tied to the inflation rate, fluctuations in short-term interest rates tend to be tied to market perceptions about inflation risks and the Fed's possible response to those risks. For this reason, floating-rate securities provide a fairly good hedge against possible inflation risks since their yields are likely to mirror either actual or perceived changes in inflation.

CURRENCY RISK

Many bond investors venture abroad for investment opportunities in foreign bond markets. When they do this, they expose themselves to *currency risk*. Currency risk results from holding bonds denominated in foreign currencies. U.S.-based investors who buy bonds denominated in foreign currencies must convert their dollars into foreign currencies, exposing themselves to the ups and downs of the value of the foreign currencies against the U.S. dollar. This assumes, of course, that an investor in foreign bonds plans to convert the cash flows from the bonds back into U.S. dollars. Individual investors can limit these risks by investing in mutual funds, which often hedge their currency risks by using forward contracts, which are agreements to buy or sell a financial instrument at a specified price on a given date in the future. Institutional investors can limit their currency risks by using forward contracts in the foreign exchange market. The decision to hedge, however, is complicated by questions of just how much of the currency exposure should be hedged; a certain degree of currency risk can be desirable in some cases if there appears to be a good chance that one currency will perform better than another.

HEDGE RISK

Not all hedges are perfect; many simply do not work. (A hedge is a security position bought or sold with the expectation that gains and losses from the hedge will offset gains and losses in another security position.) *Hedge risk* is the risk that the hedge will not offset gains or losses in the hedged position. In the bond market investors use hedges for a variety of purposes. One of the most common strategies is to use Treasuries or Treasury bond futures to hedge against potential losses in other types of bonds. This is known as *cross-hedging*. This strategy works well most of the time since yield changes on most bonds generally tend to mirror yield changes on Treasuries; their prices therefore tend to move in the same direction. This strategy can go awry, however, when the prices of the two securities move in opposite directions, as was the case in late 1998, when the price on corporate bonds fell sharply while Treasury prices soared. This caused a sharp widening in the yield spread between corporate bonds and Treasuries, as was shown in Figure 5-2. Investors who were long corporate bonds and simultaneously short Treasuries incurred large losses. The hedge failed to work primarily because corporate bonds and Treasuries have very different risk characteristics. When risk aversion fell, investors sought the safety of Treasuries and shunned riskier assets such as corporate bonds. In such an environment, investors who needed to hedge against price declines in corporate bonds would have fared better if they had hedged with securities with risk characteristics more like the risk characteristics of corporate bonds. Two examples are agency securities and high-grade corporate bonds. The lesson here is to beware of circumstances where a hedge is not really a hedge.

ODD-LOT RISK

Odd-lot risk is the risk that an investor who buys or sells small quantities of bonds will not be able to obtain a fair market price because of the trading size. In the bond market, which is largely an institutional market, any bond trade under $1 million is considered an odd lot. This is certainly much different from the situation in the stock market, where an odd lot is any stock trade under 100 shares. Odd-lot orders can hurt individual investors because broker-dealers tend to quote wider bid-ask spreads on these small orders and the price is often at a discount (on sales) or a premium (on purchases) compared with prices on orders of $1 million or more. This penalty increases as order size decreases. This puts individual investors at a disadvantage compared with institutional investors. What can an investor do? For one thing, if you are a buyer of Treasuries, you can consider buying Treasuries directly from the Treasury over the Internet (see Chapter 13 for a more detailed discussion). You can buy Treasuries directly from the Treasury Department at the auction prices, and you will pay no commissions or fees. A second measure to take is to buy mutual funds with the lowest possible management fees. This way you will essentially be assured of getting better market prices on the bond holdings and will minimize transaction fees. Be sure to check for fees on buying and selling the funds first. A third measure to take is to call several brokers for a quote on the bonds you wish to buy or sell before placing your order. This way you will have a better chance of getting a better price. It pays to shop around.

SUMMARY

Looking beyond the basics, in this chapter we discussed:

- While bonds are indeed less risky than many other financial assets, they are far from risk-free.
- The biggest risk faced by most bond investors is market risk (also known as interest rate risk), or the risk that the price of a bond will decrease as a result of an increase in the bond's yield. Market risk can be managed by being aware of a bond's duration, a key measure of a bond's price sensitivity to changes in interest rates.
- Reinvestment risk, or the risk that a bond's cash flows will be reinvested at falling interest rate levels, is a concern for bond investors. A significant portion of the total return on a bond—sometimes more than half—comes from interest on interest. It is therefore critical to be very mindful of the reinvestment rate on the cash flows that an investor receives on a bond.
- There are many other risks that bond investors must contend with and that must be assessed before one purchases a bond.
- There is risk in almost everything people do. Whether it's crossing the street, climbing an icy stairway, lifting heavy objects without bending the knees, or buying bonds, risks abound. But these risks need not inhibit investors from taking risks. By being aware of the risks they face, investors can keep them at bay and dance their way between the storms.

CHAPTER SIX

Don't Fight the Fed: The Powerful Role of the Federal Reserve

Don't fight the Fed. There is no better advice I can give you than to heed these words. Time and time again investors have learned that it is dangerous to ignore the powerful influence of the Federal Reserve, yet, many investors put little effort into gaining a better understanding of this powerful institution. They see the Fed as too complex, secretive, and mysterious to be readily understood. Equity investors seem to be even more intimidated than bond investors, often choosing to let the bond market tell them what to expect next rather than doing the thinking for themselves. However, the Fed's impact on the performance of nearly all financial assets is so unmistakable that it behooves every investor to learn more. This is an endeavor that can have great rewards.

This chapter will show you that the notion that Federal Reserve Chairman Alan Greenspan and the Fed are unhittable—throwing the markets curveballs when the market is looking for fastballs—is wrong. I fully believe that Greenspan and the Fed telegraph their pitches so that anyone, including you, can pick them up before they deliver them. When you look closely, both Greenspan and the other Fed members are surprisingly more open and their predictability is far less daunting than you might think. This chapter will show you that the Fed actually strains at times to signal its actions before they happen.

We'll also look at how the Fed works, with an emphasis on the many ways you can use your knowledge of the Fed to formulate an investment strategy. In addition, I will show you the art of Fed watching so that you can anticipate the Fed's actions with greater precision.

Before we examine how the Fed affects the markets, let's take a look at how the Fed works, who its members are, and the crux of its raison d'être.

THE FED'S RAISON D'ETRE: FINANCIAL STABILITY ACROSS THE LAND

Ever since President Woodrow Wilson signed the Federal Reserve Act of 1913 on December 23 of that year, the Federal Reserve has been evolving into one of the most powerful institutions in the United States. The act established the Fed with the goal of providing stability to the U.S. financial system, which at that time had no official backstop in the event of financial crises. The act stated that the Fed would "provide for the establishment of Federal reserve banks, to furnish an elastic currency, to afford means of rediscounting commercial paper, to establish a more effective supervision of banking in the United States, and for other purposes." Other purposes indeed. Ever since that important day in the nation's financial history, the Fed's role has expanded to the point where its influence now stretches around the globe.

Over time new legislation has molded the Fed into the institution we know today. Two particular acts of Congress refined and supplemented the objectives of the Fed as originally stated in the Federal Reserve Act of 1913: the Employment Act of 1946 and the Full Employment and Balanced Growth Act of 1978 (sometimes referred to as the Humphrey-Hawkins Act after its original sponsors). Those two acts restated the Fed's objectives to include economic growth in line with the economy's growth potential, a high level of employment, stable prices (in terms of the purchasing power of the dollar), and moderate long-term interest rates.

From the Fed's vantage point, its duties now fall into four general areas:

- Conducting the nation's monetary policies by influencing the money and credit conditions in the economy in the pursuit of full employment and stable prices

- Supervising and regulating banking institutions to ensure the safety and soundness of the nation's banking and financial system and protect the credit rights of consumers
- Maintaining the stability of the financial system and containing the systemic risk that may arise in financial markets
- Providing certain financial services to the U.S. government, the public, financial institutions, and foreign official institutions, including playing a major role in operating the nation's payment systems

Of the four duties, the first is the most prominent and the one that gets the most attention in the financial markets by far. It also is the main focus of this chapter. Let's take a look at how the Fed conducts its monetary policies and how those policies affect the economy.

FROM THE MINT TO THE GROCERY STORE: HOW THE FED AFFECTS THE ECONOMY

The Fed can directly affect the economy in three main ways:

- Conducting open market operations
- Setting reserve requirements
- Setting interest rates

Open market operations are the Fed's daily buying and selling of Treasury securities in the open market. When the Fed buys and sells securities, it affects the amount of money in the banking system. How? When the Fed buys Treasuries, for example, from a bank or a primary dealer, the Fed has to pay for the securities, and when it does that, the purchase adds money to the banking system. By increasing the amount of money, or reserves, in the banking system, the Fed's securities purchases have the effect of lowering short-term interest rates, particularly the federal-funds rate, the rate banks charge each other for overnight loans and the rate that the Fed essentially controls.

Using this example, which is not far removed from the way the Fed actually implements its monetary policies, understanding how the Fed affects short-term interest rates through its open market operations is pretty easy. It's a matter of applying the laws of supply and demand to the relationship between money and interest rates. Basically, the more money there is, the cheaper money will be. In other words, when the money supply expands, the cost of money (interest rates) falls. The opposite holds true, of course, when the Fed sells securities in the open market and thus decreases the amount of money in the banking system. In this case interest rates will rise. We will get back to these points about the impact of the Fed on short-term interest rates later in this chapter.

The Fed also can affect the economy by altering reserve requirements. *Reserve requirements* are the amount of money banks are required to keep in reserve against their existing capital. This is done to provide a safety net of sorts. Since the early 1990s banks have been required to maintain reserves only against transactions balances (basically interest-bearing and non-interest-bearing checking accounts). Banks keep their reserves either in vault cash or in an account held by a Federal Reserve bank in a bank's Federal Reserve district. By decreasing reserve requirements the Fed can expand the money supply and economic growth. The opposite occurs when the Fed raises reserve requirements. This tool is very rarely used as a means of transmitting the Fed's monetary policies; it is employed mostly as a means of regulating the soundness of the banking system.

The most important way in which the Fed influences the economy is through its ability to set interest rates. These days the Fed accomplishes this task by utilizing its open market operations, as described above, and so in a way the Fed is almost always simultaneously pulling two of its three most important levers.

TAKE A CLOSER LOOK AT THE BUCK

You can remind yourself of the Fed's ability to control the money supply and interest rates by looking closely at a dollar bill or any other denomination of U.S. paper currency. On it you will see that the Federal Reserve is in control of printing money. It says it right there on the bill: "Federal Reserve Note." There's also a stamp that describes which of the Fed's 12 district banks printed the note. Although the Fed does not use its power to print money to control the money supply by handing it out to all who would take it (just about everybody), the Fed nonetheless controls the money supply through its open market operations, using its approximately $650 billion in assets. Put simply, the Fed has enormous resources at its disposal to help regulate interest rates, the economy, and the U.S. financial system.

HOW MONETARY POLICY CHANGES AFFECT THE ECONOMY

When the Federal Reserve alters its stance on interest rates, a whirlwind of change takes place in the financial markets and the economy. With each pull of the interest rate lever, the Fed sets in motion a series of financial and economic responses that make it clear that the Fed has left its mark.

When the Fed changes interest rates, the economy is affected through two primary means of transmission:

- Financial conditions (interest rate levels, stock prices, lending standards, interest rate spreads between high-grade and low-grade debt, the value of the U.S. dollar, and capital formation in the stock and bond markets)
- Consumer and business confidence

Financial conditions can change materially when the Fed adjusts interest rate levels. The primary way this occurs, of course, is through the actual change in interest rates that occurs when the Fed either raises or lowers the federal funds rate. Interest rate changes work their way through the economy in a variety of ways, beginning with their impact on the three most interest-rate-sensitive sectors of the economy:

- Housing
- Automobiles
- Capital spending

These three sectors are the ones I look to first when I want to gauge the effectiveness of the Fed's interest rate changes. These sectors are almost always the first to be affected when the Fed embarks on a course of either raising or lowering interest rates. When these sectors show signs of being affected by changes in interest rates, in due course an additional impact is likely to be seen throughout the economy. Consider the impact of a jump in car sales, for example. When car sales increase, automobile manufacturers raise production schedules, increasing both worker hours and employment. This results in additional income for workers, who spend that income on a variety of goods and services, boosting the incomes of numerous other workers. In this way there is a significant multiplier, or ripple, effect from the increase in car sales, which presumably occurred as a result of the Fed's interest rate actions.

A similar multiplier effect can result from activity in the housing sector, where even slight changes in mortgage rates can have a big impact on the demand for housing. When it does, employment in the construction sector can be affected greatly. An increase of 100,000 units, for example, can result in an increase of about 250,000 full-time construction jobs, according to the National Association of Home Builders. Fluctuations in housing activity are very important not only because of the impact the housing sector can have on construction employment but also because of the impact the housing sector can have on the sales of a variety of goods used to furnish a home. New home buyers often purchase new appliances, for example, and engage in a variety of remodeling projects. This extends the economic benefit well beyond the home purchase. Indeed, the multiplier effects in the housing sector are perhaps greater than in any other sector in the economy. This makes sense when one considers that a home purchase is usually the biggest purchase most people will ever make.

Interest rate levels affect capital spending in two main ways. First, because capital projects are capital-intensive (that is, they are more dependent on capital resources than on labor), the cost of money could have a direct bearing on a business's decision to engage in capital spending projects. Building a new plant or purchasing new equipment, for example, could become more feasible or less feasible depending on the level of interest rates. A second way in which interest rate levels affect capital spending is through their effect on the economic outlook and its impact on business confidence. If businesses feel the economic outlook has worsened as a result of interest rate increases by the Federal Reserve, they are less likely to engage in capital spending. Why, for example, would a business want to expand its capacity to produce goods and services if it felt the demand for its products was about to weaken?

There are cases, of course, in which businesses will continue to raise their capital spending regardless of the Fed's interest rate policies. These businesses feel they can still benefit from the extra productivity they could gain as a result of the capital spending. Nevertheless, on the margins, interest rate levels generally have a large impact on capital spending.

THE FED AFFECTS MORE THAN JUST INTEREST RATES

As was noted earlier, when the Fed pulls the interest rate lever, it can affect more than just interest rates. Indeed, there are a multitude of ways in which the Fed's policies can be amplified. The many ways in which the Fed's interest rate adjustments work their way into the economy are known as *transmission effects*. There are five main ways in which the Fed's interest rate adjustments are transmitted into the economy:

- Stock prices
- Corporate bond yields
- The value of the dollar
- Lending standards
- Capital formation

These so-called transmission effects can have a significant impact on the degree to which interest rate changes have their intended effect. For example, the greater the transmission effects are, the more effective the Fed's rate actions will be and the less the Fed will need to adjust interest rates to achieve its objectives for the economy and inflation. However when the transmission effects are small or somehow wind up offsetting the intended effects of the Fed's rate actions, the magnitude of rate adjustments needed to reach the Fed's objectives probably will be greater. In other words, the collective impact of the transmission effects can have a very large bearing on the magnitude of interest rate adjustments needed to solve a particular economic problem.

The conditions that describe the net effect of all the financial variables that affect the economic climate are known as *financial conditions*. Financial conditions are said to be loose when they are such that they probably will lead to a strengthening of economic activity and are said to be tight when they are most likely to weaken economic activity.

A classic example of two completely different ways in which transmission effects can affect the economy and the difficult task the Fed has in shaping the appropriate monetary policies occurred between 1999 and 2001. In June 1999 the Federal Reserve embarked on a campaign to raise interest rates to quell the rapid pace of economic growth and the rampant pace of speculative fervor that was building up in the equity market. The Fed continued to raise interest rates for many months, and in early 2000 its actions began to be transmitted through a number of channels, causing financial conditions to tighten dramatically. Indeed, the technology bubble of 1999–2000 burst, sending technology stock prices sharply lower and inducing so-called negative wealth effects, resulting in a weakening of consumer spending. In addition, the yield spread between corporate bonds and Treasuries began to widen sharply, particularly on low-grade corporate bonds. In response, credit became scarcer as lenders tightened lending standards and investors refrained from investing in all but the best and most creditworthy companies. This crimped growth in credit and thus reduced the level of business investment. The Fed's rate increases also resulted in a strengthening of the U.S. dollar, which eventually reduced U.S. exports.

Combined, the transmission effect of the Fed's interest rate increases probably went well beyond the intended effects. The result was a far greater weakening of the economy than the Fed probably expected. This episode shows the enormous degree to which the Fed's interest rate changes can be magnified by numerous other financial channels. It also provides evidence of the very difficult task the Fed has in attempting to estimate the full impact of its interest rate adjustments while implementing them and awaiting their impact. One might say that *formulating the appropriate interest rate policy is like trying to walk a dog with a long leash*. The Fed therefore has the unenviable task of providing a remedy to a problem without knowing to what degree the patient will respond to the remedy. As with people, the required remedy and the intended effects can vary greatly. The complications are always difficult to know from the start.

In 2001, when the Fed sought to revive economic growth, it faced a very different set of circumstances that resulted in financial conditions that were completely at odds with the Fed's objectives as well as with historical precedent. In response, the magnitude of interest rate adjustments needed to cure the economy's ills was far greater than what probably would have been necessary if the transmission effects had been more consistent with historical precedent.

That extraordinary episode began on January 3, 2001, when the Fed delivered the first of an unprecedented 11 interest rate cuts that year. The typical response to such aggressiveness normally would entail a number of positive transmission effects, but the opposite occurred. Stock prices, for example, which normally rise when the Fed lowers interest rates, fell throughout the year, with the decline briefly worsening in the aftermath of the September 11 tragedy. The weakness in stock prices contributed to a dampening of consumer confidence and consumer spending. In addition, as shown in Figure 6-1, the yield spread between low-grade corporate bonds and U.S. Treasuries stayed wide most of the year, reaching the widest point exactly ten months after the Fed's first rate cut of the year. The widening in credit spreads made borrowing costs

F i g u r e   6–1

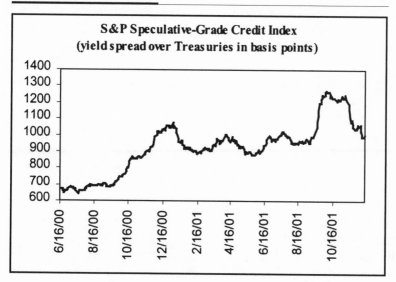

S&P Speculative-Grade Credit Index
(yield spread over Treasuries in basis points)

prohibitive for many fringe borrowers and thus reduced the aggregate level of borrowing and spending. That was the opposite of what normally occurs when the Fed lowers interest rates.

Another uncharacteristic occurrence that followed the Fed's rate cuts was a rise in the value of the dollar. The dollar typically falls when interest rates fall because U.S. fixed-income assets become less attractive to foreign investors. This makes U.S. goods more affordable to foreign investors and therefore tends to increase U.S. exports, stimulating the economy. In 2001 the rise in the value of the dollar hurt U.S. exports and therefore offset some of the positive benefits of the Fed's rate cuts.

Lending standards also remained tight through most of the year before easing at the end of the year. This was also different from the normal response to interest rate cuts. Finally, owing to weak stock prices and weak business lending, capital formation slowed. This slowed the pace of new business creation and business expansion. As a result of these uncharacteristic responses to the Fed's interest rate reductions, financial conditions were actually tighter after the Fed's rate cuts than they were when the cuts began. The lack of positive transmission effects therefore necessitated a more aggressive series of rate cuts that eventually brought the federal-funds rate down to its lowest level in 40 years.

The two sharply different ways in which financial conditions evolved after the Fed's interest rate adjustments in 1999 and 2001 clearly illustrate the importance of assessing the impact of the key transmitters discussed above. It is not sufficient to surmise that interest rate adjustments in and of themselves will succeed in bringing about a desired economic outcome. Moreover, the magnitude of the interest rate adjustments needed to reach a desired economic outcome can vary greatly from one economic cycle to the next, depending on a variety of factors and on the net change in financial conditions that follows the onset of the interest rate adjustments. It is therefore critical to think outside the box and assess the net change in financial conditions as well as the potential impact on the economy rather than fixate on the direct impact of the interest rate adjustments alone. This will assist you in determining the degree of rate adjustments that probably will be necessary to reach a certain economic outcome. The answer to this question will help you judge the extent to which the market's expectations on rates and their impact on the economy will be validated. If after analyzing the net transmission effects you sense that the market's assumptions are unreasonable, you will have a very strong basis for betting against market expectations. If you find that you agree with the market's assumptions, you will have a firm conviction about following market trends.

STRUCTURE OF THE FED

To forecast changes in monetary policy accurately, it is important to understand how the Fed is structured and how it formulates its policies. It is important to note that the Federal Reserve System was designed by Congress in a way that helps assure that the Fed will have a broad perspective on the economy in all parts of the nation. The Federal Reserve System is composed of 12 regional Federal Reserve banks in major cities. Figure 6-2 shows a map of the 12 Federal Reserve districts. The Federal Reserve banks perform a variety of functions that are similar to the services provided by

F i g u r e   6–2

The 12 Federal Reserve Districts

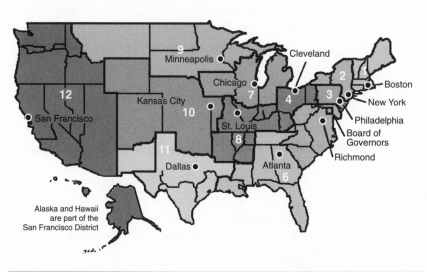

banks and thrift institutions. For example, Federal Reserve banks hold the cash reserves of depository institutions and make loans to those institutions. They also move currency in and out of circulation and process checks. The role of the Federal Reserve banks goes far beyond these relatively mundane tasks, of course, ranging from the actual printing of currency and coin to supervising and examining banks for safety and soundness. To Wall Street the most prominent role of the Federal Reserve banks is the participation of the bank presidents in the formulation of monetary policy. Wall Street watches the bank presidents closely for clues to the direction of monetary policy. Each president is elected to a five-year term by the board of directors of the respective Federal Reserve banks. The terms of all 12 presidents run concurrently, ending on the last day of February in years ending in 6 and 1. The bank presidents are part of the Federal Open Market Committee (FOMC), the committee that sets interest rates.

Wall Street also pays close attention to the seven members of the Board of Governors who are appointed by the President of the United States and confirmed by the Senate for a term of 14 years. A term begins every two years on February 1 of even-numbered years. The chair and the vice chair of the board are named by the President from among the members and are confirmed by the Senate.

The FOMC is composed of five presidents of the Federal Reserve banks and the seven members of the board of governors (including the chair). The presidents of the banks serve one-year terms on a rotating basis beginning on January 1 of each year, with the exception of the president of the Federal Reserve Bank of New York, who serves on a continuous basis.

Figure 6-3 shows the term lengths and appointments of important members of the Federal Reserve System.

FOMC MEETINGS: THE GREAT DEBATE

By law the FOMC must meet at least four times a year in Washington, D.C., but since 1980 it has held eight meetings a year at intervals of five to eight weeks. At each meeting, which is closed to the public and generally begin at 9 in the morning Eastern Standard Time (EST), staff officers of the Federal Reserve System present oral

Figure 6-3

	Appointed by	Term Length	Term Begins	Membership in FOMC
Chair of Federal Reserve Board	President of the United States and confirmed by the Senate	4 years	When confirmed, usually in June of presidential election years	Permanent
Vice chair of Federal Reserve Board	President of the United States and confirmed by the Senate	4 years	When confirmed; month varies	Permanent
Governors (there are six governors, not including the Fed chair, who is also a governor)	President of the United States and confirmed by the Senate	14 years; can serve only one term unless serving unexpired portion of another member's term	Term begins every two years on February 1 of even-numbered years	Permanent
Presidents of the regional Federal Reserve banks	Board of directors of the respective Federal Reserve banks and approved by the Board of Governors	5 years	Terms for all 12 run concurrently, ending in years numbered 1 and 6 (e.g., 2001 and 2006)	Five members serve, but only the New York president is permanent; the rest rotate yearly

reports on the economy, conditions in the financial markets, and international financial developments. Then the manager of the System Open Market Account (SOMA), who is essentially in charge of seeing to it that the Fed's open market operations are carried out in a way that is consistent with the Fed's directive on interest rates, reports on SOMA's transactions since the previous meeting.

After these reports both the committee members and the other Federal Reserve bank presidents discuss their views on the economy as well as the appropriate course to take on monetary policy. Each voting member then votes on a specific policy recommendation to be carried out during the coming intermeeting period. Once a consensus is reached, the committee issues a directive to the Federal Reserve Bank of New York, the bank that handles transactions for the SOMA. The directive provides guidance to the manager of the SOMA for the implementation of the committee's decision on interest rates. Although the Fed's chair has only one vote in this process, his or her power of persuasion goes far beyond that single vote. Federal Reserve Chairman Alan Greenspan, for instance, has been well known to seek a consensus around his own personal views on the appropriate policy stance. There is little doubt that the chair wields immense power at the FOMC even though existing laws do not mandate that power. Rifts can develop, of course, and it takes a chair with astute political skills to negotiate them without undermining the credibility of the committee. Greenspan has shown such skills on many occasions.

The bond market's anticipation of the FOMC meetings and the announcement of the Fed's policy statement are the subject of intense debate and are at the center of many investment strategies. That is easy to understand when one looks at the relationship between the federal funds rate and bond yields. This point is illustrated clearly in Figure 6.4. The focus on the FOMC meetings can reach the point of obsession, with each piece of economic data spurring a new round of intense debate and market volatility. Public comments from Fed officials intensify the debate and are an important aspect of the way in which investors form their opinions on the likely outcome of FOMC meetings. We'll talk more about this later in the chapter.

The Federal Reserve generally announces its decision on interest rates at about 2:15 in the afternoon EST on the day of an FOMC meeting except in the two cases a year when the FOMC meeting spans two days, in which case the announcement is delivered on the second day at about 2:15 in the afternoon EST. The bond market's reaction to the FOMC's decision is often sharp, particularly on the short end of the yield curve, but sometimes is tempered by the market's preparedness for the decision. Nevertheless, the reverberations from the Fed's actions can last for months, especially at the onset of a series of rate moves.

THE FED'S IMPACT ON THE BOND MARKET: RESOUNDING

As is shown in Chapter 9, few factors move the bond market more than the Federal Reserve does. The Fed's power to influence interest rates and the economy has an immense impact on the financial markets in general. There are four main ways in which the Fed's monetary policies tend to affect the behavior of the bond market:

- Nominal interest rates
- Real interest rates
- The yield curve
- The performance of spread products relative to Treasuries

Importantly, the Fed's monetary policies tend to work with an uncanny degree of simultaneity. Although no two financial episodes are alike, especially with respect to the magnitude of reactions to the Fed's policies, the direction of change is generally fairly predictable. For example, when the Federal Reserve raises interest rates, both nominal and real interest tends to rise, the yield curve tends to flatten, and spread products (corporate bonds, agency securities, mortgage-backed securities, and the like) tend to underperform Treasuries. All these responses aid the Fed's efforts to achieve a particular economic objective, providing transmission effects similar to those discussed earlier in this chapter. Let's take a closer look at how the Fed spurs these responses.

Nominal Interest Rates

It is pretty easy to understand how the Fed's rate changes affect *nominal interest rates*. Nominal interest rates, of course, are the actual level of interest rates. When the Fed adjusts short-term interest rates, bond yields adjust accordingly. There are several reasons for this. First, yields on short-term maturities are determined largely by the cost of money, which is determined principally by the federal funds rate, the interest rate the Fed controls. This subject is discussed further in Chapter 10. Figure 6-4 shows the tight relationship between the federal funds rate and short-term maturities. This tight relationship extends beyond short-term maturities, although to a lesser degree. It is important to note that nominal interest rates on short- and long-term bond yields rarely fall below the federal funds rate except in periods that precede imminent rate cuts by the Federal Reserve. Indeed, over the last 12 years the 2-year T-note has dipped below the federal funds rate on only four occasions. On each occasion the Fed lowered interest rates within just a few months. This clearly suggests that the federal-funds rate is an important determinant of nominal interest rates.

Real Interest Rates

As will be shown in Chapter 7, the Federal Reserve has a great deal of influence on the level of *real interest rates*, which are nominal

Figure   6-4

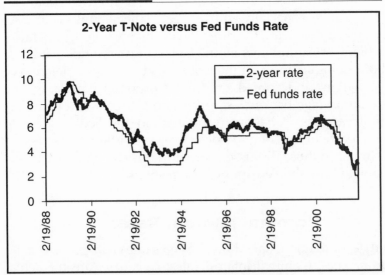

interest rates minus inflation. Real interest rates tend to rise when the Fed raises interest rates and fall when the Fed lowers interest rates. There are a few reasons for this. First, when the Fed decides to move interest rates up or down, bond investors begin to antici- pate additional interest rate adjustments by pushing nominal inter- est rates up or down more quickly than changes occur in the inflation rate. For example, when the Fed is in the process of rais- ing interest rates, it presumably is doing so because of an increase in inflation risks. Bond investors recognize this as well as the Fed's historical tendency to push the federal-funds rate well above the inflation rate during periods when inflation is accelerating or is at risk of doing so. Bond investors respond by pushing up real inter- est rates.

Second, the Fed tends to try to engineer low real interest rates when the economy is weak and high real interest rates when the economy is strong. It does this in an attempt to achieve a certain degree of equilibrium between savings and investment. By varying the real interest rate, the Fed can have an enormous impact on sav- ings and investment. When the savings rate is high (as determined largely by the federal funds rate) and the investment rate is low (as determined by the inflation rate and the level of economic growth), an investor has a greater incentive to save than to invest. Thus, a high real interest rate tends to dampen economic activity because it dampens investment. Similarly, when the savings rate is low and the investment rate is high, an investor has an incentive to invest rather than save, thus spurring economic growth. This is why dur- ing times of economic weakness it is critical for the Fed to move the federal funds rate (the savings rate) down to as close to the inflation rate (the investment rate) as possible. This was the case in 2001, when the Fed pushed the federal-funds rate below the inflation rate. The Fed was attempting to stimulate investment by bringing the savings rate so low that it would serve as a powerful motivation to invest. Figure 6-5 illustrates how the Fed brought real interest rates sharply lower in 2001 in an effort to stimulate the economy.

The Fed's astute recognition of the need to bring the savings rate below the investment rate stands in stark contrast to the situa- tion in Japan, where chronic deflation has kept the investment rate below the savings rate for many years, resulting in extremely weak economic conditions. Investors in Japan have had little reason to

F i g u r e   6–5

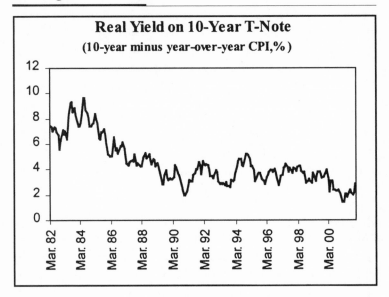

Real Yield on 10-Year T-Note

(10-year minus year-over-year CPI,%)

invest in the economy when deflation is reducing the nominal value of their investments. The deflation in real assets—real estate, for example—has been a powerful disincentive to investment. Investors would rather save their money at interest rate levels that are barely above 0 percent because the return on savings exceeds the return on investments. It therefore behooves Japan's central bank, the Bank of Japan, to make every effort to reduce real interest rates as much as possible and to consider bringing real interest rates into negative territory by raising the inflation rate and keeping short-term interest rates low. Although this is a difficult task, it seems imperative after ten years of recession and meager economic growth.

A third way in which the Fed affects the level of real interest rates is through its credibility as an inflation fighter. When bond investors have confidence in the Fed, real interest rates tend to be low. This is the case because investors tend to demand less of an interest rate premium over and above the inflation rate when they are confident that inflation will stay low. By contrast, when confidence in the Fed's ability to fight inflation is low, bond investors demand a higher real interest rate to compensate them for the risk that inflation will accelerate and erode the value of their bonds.

The Yield Curve

As will be shown in Chapter 7, one of the biggest influences on the yield curve is the Federal Reserve. The Fed affects the yield curve largely through its control of short-term interest rates. When the Federal Reserve raises or lowers the federal-funds rate, yields on short-term maturities tend to follow. Figure 6-4 clearly illustrates this. As a result, the yield curve tends to get steeper when the Fed lowers interest rates, as yields on short-term maturities fall faster than do those on long-term maturities. Yields on long-term maturities respond more slowly to the Fed's interest rate moves because they are affected by a wide variety of other factors, including speculative trading activity, technical factors, and inflation expectations. This brings us to the next point.

A second way in which the Fed has an impact on the yield curve is by affecting inflation expectations. Changes in inflation expectations have a large bearing on the behavior of long-term interest rates, particularly compared with short-term interest rates. The Fed affects inflation expectations in two ways. First, when the Fed adjusts interest rates, the market's outlook on economic growth changes, altering inflation expectations. Second, inflation expectations will be higher or lower depending on the Fed's inflation-fighting credibility. If investors are confident that the Fed will be able to contain inflation, this will tend to keep inflation expectations low, resulting in low long-term interest rates and a relatively flat yield curve. By contrast, if the market lacks confidence in the Fed's ability to fight inflation, the yield curve will be steep, reflecting the market's uncertainty about the inflation outlook.

The yield curve also is affected by the bond market's expectations of future Fed policies. In theory, since long-term interest rates are thought to reflect expectations of future short-term interest rates, the yield curve reflects expectations of future Fed interest rate actions. Thus, when the market expects higher or lower interest rates in the future, long-term interest rates tend to reflect those expectations, having an impact on the shape of the yield curve. There is one important point to remember in this regard. The degree to which the market embeds future Fed interest rate actions in long-term interest rates depends a great deal on the degree to which inflation expectations are well anchored. In other words, if inflation expectations are well anchored, the market will tend to expect a smaller amount of interest rate adjustments. For example, if the Fed begins to raise interest rates at a time when inflation expectations are high or a bit fragile, the rise in long-term interest rates is likely to be larger than it would be if inflation expectations were low. This occurs because the market will assume that a larger magnitude of rate increases will be needed to quash inflation. This type of response occurred in 1994, as will be discussed later in this chapter. The impact of the Fed's rate actions on long-term interest rates is therefore very dependent on inflation expectations. Thus, it can be said that the degree of leverage exerted by short-term rates over long-term rates is regime-dependent. In other words, the impact depends on the market's perception of the degree of interest rate adjustments needed to fight inflation. This can vary from one interest rate cycle to the next but is largely related to the Fed's inflation-fighting credibility over a period of inflation episodes.

The Performance of Spread Products Relative to Treasuries

The Federal Reserve can have a large influence on the performance of *spread products*, or fixed-income securities other than Treasuries, including agency securities, corporate bonds, and mortgage-backed securities. These securities are called spread products because their yields are priced and quoted in terms of their yield *spread* over Treasuries. Since these spread products are deemed to be riskier than Treasuries, their yield spreads tend to fluctuate as perceptions of the risks of holding them change. These perceptions generally change when views about economic growth change. For example, during periods of economic weakness the financial prospects for a wide variety of companies turn sour. Revenues decline, pricing power diminishes, and productivity declines, putting downward pressure on profit margins and in some cases producing outright losses. Bonds in companies with low credit ratings therefore come under pressure as investors worry about the ability of those companies to meet their payment obligations. This causes the yield spreads on these securities to widen. Figure 6-1 clearly illustrates the impact that the economic weakness of 2000 and 2001 had on the credit spreads of low-grade bonds.

Investment-grade bonds are not immune to this effect; only the magnitude of the impact differs.

The Fed affects credit spreads when it adjusts the federal funds rate and thus affects the economy. For example, when the Fed raises interest rates, credit spreads tend to widen because investors fear that the rate increases will weaken the economy. Similarly, when the Fed lowers interest rates, credit spreads tend to narrow in anticipation of a strengthening in economic activity. In early 2001 the Fed's series of interest rate cuts had the usual effect by spurring a narrowing of credit spreads. However, the realization that economic conditions were worse than previously thought and the impact of the September 11 tragedy caused credit spreads to widen again before returning to a more normal pattern by the year's end as confidence in the Fed's ability to revive the economy increased again.

The clear pattern of the Fed's impact on credit spreads is a solid basis on which to formulate investment strategies for buying and selling spread products. In light of the notion that no two financial episodes are alike, spread products should be expected to outperform Treasuries when the Fed is lowering interest rates and should be expected to underperform Treasuries when the Fed raises interest rates. Acting on these principles, it is possible to tailor a fixed-income strategy around the Fed. One must keep in mind, of course, that there can be sharp differences in the performance of the various spread products when interest rates fluctuate. For example, when interest rates fall sharply, mortgage-backed securities tend to underperform other spread products owing to worries that prepayments of the securities will rise as a result of high levels of mortgage refinancing and housing turnover.

DON'T FIGHT THE FED: FOLLOW IT

As I stated earlier, the adage "Don't fight the Fed" is Wall Street lore. History is strewn with periods when the performance of the stock and bond markets was affected significantly by Fed policy. Along the way many investors either profited from or were hammered by the Fed during those periods, depending on the degree to which they showed respect for the Fed's ability to affect their investments.

Despite the unmistakable impact the Fed has had on the markets over the years, investors do not always heed the power of the Fed. Instead, they get caught in bouts of excessive optimism and pessimism, often finding it difficult to see past their emotions. However, investors always seem to come around at some point, eventually recognizing that the Fed's handiwork will have the intended effect in the not too distant future. Investors who show confidence in the Fed's actions early on are likely to have better investment returns than those who choose to bet against the Fed.

A great way to see the very large impact the Fed can have on the markets is to look at the bond market's response to policy speeches made by Federal Reserve Chairman Alan Greenspan. Twice a year the chair delivers testimony to Congress in a report called the Monetary Policy Report to Congress, which was known as the Humphrey-Hawkins testimony until the Humphrey-Hawkins Act of 1978 was altered in July 2000. These testimonies, which are mandated by law, require the Fed to give its view on both monetary policy and the economy to both houses of Congress. In the House the chair delivers testimony to the Committee on Financial Services; in the Senate the chair delivers testimony to the Committee on Banking, Housing and Urban Affairs. The testimonies usually are given in February and July. The reason these testimonies are so revealing is that the detail in which Greenspan describes the Fed's sentiments almost always pushes him into sensitive topics, spurring a sharp response in the bond market. Figure 6-6 illustrates these reactions by highlighting the sharp reactions on the days Greenspan delivered his semiannual reports.

As the chart shows, sharp reactions generally have followed Greenspan's initial testimony (Greenspan delivers his testimony before both the House and the Senate). The chart shows that the most actively traded Treasury bond futures contract has averaged an absolute change of 31/32 on the first day of Greenspan's testimony. That is a big move for one day—the average daily change on T-bond futures is roughly 15/32. Eurodollar contracts, which are basically a reflection of the federal funds rate, also have moved sharply relative to their daily average, although less than more recent daily price swings as a result of the Fed's big rate actions taken in 2001.

The fact that there have been sharp reactions should not be surprising. However, what stands out and what is perhaps more important to remember is the follow-through to these reactions: During the periods shown in the chart, in the week that followed Greenspan's testimony the cumulative reaction has been usually

F i g u r e　6–6

Historical Reactions to Greenspan's Semiannual Reports to Congress
(front-month T-bond future in thirty-two seconds of a point)*

Year	February Testimony	July Testimony
1993	+7	−5
1994	+14	−31
1995	+30	−58
1996	−68	+43
1997	−55	+40
1998	−29	+18
1999	−29	−34
2000	+15	+50
2001	−6	+29

*Average absolute change for all periods = $^{31}/_{32}$.

double that of the initial reaction. And it goes on: One month later the reaction nearly doubles again (also in the same direction as the initial reaction) as the realization of the Fed's policy stance sets in and market participants continue to adjust their positions accordingly. Remember this the next time Greenspan delivers one of these speeches (and read the entire speech, don't just listen to the sound bites). If, for instance, in the aftermath of a Greenspan speech the market trades sharply higher or lower, consider placing a trade in the same direction and wait for there to be follow-through in the market. Give it at least one week. Reassess after one week but keep in mind that the market response to Greenspan's policy speeches can go on for at least a few weeks.

Federal Reserve Chairs since 1934

Eugene R. Black	May 19, 1933–August 15, 1934
Marriner S. Eccles	November 15, 1934–January 31, 1948
Thomas B. McCabe	April 15, 1948–March 31, 1951
William McC. Martin, Jr.	April 2, 1951–January 31, 1970
Arthur Burns	February 1, 1970–January 31, 1978
G. William Miller	March 8, 1978–August 6, 1979
Paul A. Volcker	August 6, 1979–August 11, 1987
Alan Greenspan	August 11, 1987–

Ostensibly, the market reacts so sharply to Greenspan's semiannual report to Congress because it believes that what it hears from him is an unmistakable reflection of Fed policy. And since Fed policy does not change on a dime, the market's reaction generally continues for weeks. Indeed, the Fed generally maintains its monetary policies for many months and sometimes years. The lesson here is to identify the Fed's monetary policy stance and formulate one's investment strategies in ways that are consistent with the Fed's stance. Moreover, one should seize the short- and long-term trading opportunities that arise when the Fed's chair delivers a policy speech by establishing trading positions that anticipate a sustained market response to the speech. Long-term investors can use these principles to time their entries into and exits from their portfolio positions. Investors should use these principles in their consideration of directional bets and bets on the relative performance of the various segments of the bond market. They also can be used to assess the outlook for investment returns in bonds compared with other financial assets.

TRUST THE FED

Greenspan's tenure as chair of the Federal Reserve is filled with episodes in which he has appeared as friend or foe to investors. He often is criticized and singled out when the Fed raises interest rates. Investors wonder why the Fed must raise interest rates at all when good times are rolling.

But in the same way that parents must discipline their children, Greenspan's duty is to act as a disciplinarian—of the U.S. economy. Just as it would be unfair to pass judgment on the disciplinary actions of parents who deploy discipline with the good of their children in mind, it is unfair to criticize Greenspan's disciplinary actions. Importantly, Greenspan has always demonstrated that when the chips are down, he and the Fed are there for us every step of the way. It's his duty to take the proverbial punch bowl away before the party gets out of hand.

A Classic Case of the Fed's Tough Love

A classic example of the Fed's tough love took place in 1994. During that year the economy seemed to be rolling along, but the Fed felt it was growing too strongly and that growth rate could lead to inflation. The Fed implemented a series of interest rate increases, raising rates six times in 1994 and once more in early 1995. Many investors were dismayed by the interest rate increases, and it looked as if the Fed might derail the economy. The Fed's tight grip resulted in a subdued year for the stock market and a wretched one for the bond market. In fact, 1994 was the worst year for the bond market in decades. The yield on the 30-year Treasury bond rose from a low of 5.78 percent on October 15, 1993, to a peak of 8.16 percent on November 7, 1994. The poor performance of the bond market spilled over into the stock market, where the Standard & Poor's (S&P) 500 fell 1.5 percent in 1994.

Although the interest rate increases seemed to be harming the economy, the Fed had good intentions: Inflation looked set to rise and probably undermine the economic expansion. Although inflation never did surface, the Fed's actions made it all possible. In 1994 many more people worried about inflation than is the case today. Late 1990s expressions such as "the new era economy" and the "Goldilocks economy" were themes that very few investors believed in at that time (these themes hold that the economy can grow strongly without inflation because of conditions that are "just right"). In 1994 most investors still believed in the more traditional view that strong economic growth leads to inflation. That is why when economic growth strengthened at the end of 1993 and into early 1994 after several years of sluggish growth, inflation expectations immediately began to rise.

The Fed's challenge in 1994, therefore, was meant to convince investors that it would quash any and all inflation threats. In light of the economic backdrop, the inflation threat that existed was mostly psychological: The unemployment rate was relatively high at 6.6 percent; savings and loans institutions were still recovering from a crisis that had begun several years earlier; worker insecurity was soaring in response to a spate of huge corporate layoffs; businesses were starting to invest heavily in new technology that would dampen inflation pressures by increasing productivity; the budget deficit was falling; and the global economy, led by Japan, was weak. In hindsight, it is striking to think that despite all these factors, inflation fears were strong enough to push the yield on the 30-year bond over 8 percent. It has not come close to that in recent years, averaging about 6.1 percent since 1994.

When the Fed began its inflation fight, it was fighting fears that were not its own. Chairman Alan Greenspan once said that price stability exists only when "the expected rate of change of the general level of prices ceases to be a factor in individual and business decision making." Other Fed officials have expressed similar thoughts. Thus, even though the inflation threat in 1994 did not appear to be as great as investors feared, it nonetheless was affecting the way individuals and investors behaved. The Fed therefore had to convince the public that there was no inflation threat and that inflation was a thing of the past.

Because the Fed did not fully know the extent to which inflation fears might grow, it began the battle against inflation worries by raising interest rates slowly, beginning in February 1994 with three consecutive increases of 25 basis points in the federal funds rate. However, as the extent of inflation fears became evident in the behavior of commodity prices and long-term interest rates (both were rising, indicating inflation fears), the Fed knew it had to do more to reassure investors that inflation would not return. It then opted for larger rate increases in increments of 50 basis points in both May and August 1994. But in November 1994, when it appeared that the new strategy was failing to calm inflation-wary investors, the Fed asserted itself with a large rate hike of 75 basis points. One might think that this would deal the markets a decisive blow and push market interest rates sharply higher, but the opposite occurred. Bond yields peaked that month and began a steady decline that lasted throughout the next year even though the Fed would deliver another rate hike—50 basis points—three months later in February 1995.

The Fed had finally conquered investors' inflation fears and the economic imbalances that created them. The payoff from its efforts quickly followed; in 1995, long-term government bonds returned over 30 percent and the S&P 500 returned 34.1 percent. Inflation rose just 2.6 percent, and inflation fears did not return for the rest of the decade. That year marked the beginning of several years of almost unparalleled prosperity that benefited millions of Americans.

The 1994–1995 episode is one of the best illustrations of how Greenspan and the Fed can give the appearance of being the market's nemesis while acting like its best friend. The episode is a clear illustration of the importance of trusting the Fed, especially if it has a steward at the helm who is as strong and effective as Alan Greenspan. The Fed's mandate, after all, is to conduct its policies in a way that is consistent with the pursuit of full employment and stable prices.

Therefore, when market participants appear to have little faith that the Fed ultimately will be successful in achieving either of its two main objectives (full employment and stable prices), an investor should look to capitalize on the market's wrongheaded conclusions by betting that the Fed will indeed be successful. Countertrend trades are likely to be successful in this instance, although caution must always be taken when an investor is betting against the collective opinions of the market. Nevertheless, if you have evidence that the market is coming around to your view by beginning to show faith in the Fed, you will have a strong basis on which to express your faith in the Fed by betting on the likelihood that it will reach its main objectives.

THE ART OF FED WATCHING

Earlier in this chapter we saw that the bond market reacts very sharply to the semiannual reports to Congress delivered by Chairman Alan Greenspan and that reactions to his testimony tend to be sustained for many weeks after the delivery of those reports in February and July. Predicting the market's behavior during those months is therefore simpler than it is in other months, especially given the large extent to which the Fed chair delves into sensitive topics. During the rest of the year, however, the specificity of the Fed's remarks is not nearly as sharp as it is when the Fed's chair delivers the semiannual reports. It therefore becomes necessary to pick up the Fed's signals through other means, and this requires a bit more inspection. To be able to predict what the Fed will do next one must become an avid Fed watcher.

As was alluded to earlier, Fed watching begins with recognizing that when the Fed's chair delivers a policy speech, the impact is often long-lasting. The clarity that the chair provides on Fed policy leads the markets to behave as though they assumed that those policies will be in place for a while. With this in mind, an investor should tailor his or her trading strategies accordingly, working on the assumption that the chair's policy speeches are a true reflection of the Fed's current stance on monetary policy and that the markets will behave in a way that is consistent with that policy stance.

How can the Fed's policy stance be deciphered on a regular basis? The best way to do that is to follow the Fed regularly and closely. What you need to do is to get in its shadows, so to speak. Being a Fed watcher is quite simple. What it boils down to is tracking the verbiage spewed by the FOMC—that cast of 13, including Greenspan, that votes on whether to raise or lower interest rates at FOMC meetings. There are five additional Federal Reserve officials who attend the Fed's meetings, but they vote only every other year (they are in essence the proverbial flies on the wall at FOMC meetings). While their presence at the meetings means that their views matter, an investor should focus mostly on the voting members. The minutes for each meeting are released to the public about six weeks after the meetings and are a good way to find out what the FOMC discussed.

An investor should think about Fed watching in the following way. Let's say you've been asked to solve a mystery where all the principal players are known, they talk in public all the time, you get a plethora of clues about what they're thinking, they give you verbatim transcripts of what they say in private, and they give you the minutes from all their policy meetings. I bet you can crack that mystery in a jiffy. This is exactly how it is with the Fed, and so there's no reason to be intimidated.

Read the Fed's Speeches

One of the best ways to follow the Fed requires a little bit of homework, but the payoff can be huge and it actually takes very little time. Specifically, I urge you to read the Fed's speeches. Many top investors do this, and when I talk with them and hear them refer to specific lines in those speeches, it always reminds me how valuable it is to read the speeches. The speeches are readily available on the Fed's Web site at www.federalreserve.gov or on the Web site of the Federal Reserve bank an FOMC member represents. Speeches by the presidents of the 12 Federal Reserve banks usually can be found on the Web sites of the individual banks rather than on the Fed's main site.

It is not all that laborious to do this work because most of the Fed's speeches are just a few pages long. Reading the Fed's speeches will give you far greater insight into the Fed than you will get if you simply read headlines from newswires; those headlines largely reflect a reporter's subjective view of the speeches. I have talked to a lot of wire reporters, and I came to the conclusion a long time ago that investors should not rely on reporters to tell them what they should be thinking about what the Fed said; it is really up to you. It is perilous to leave it in the hands of reporters in print, broadcast, and electronic media, who often have very little background on the financial markets and can be novices when it comes to analyzing the Fed in the way that is required of an investor, particularly an institutional investor. Do the work yourself and you will see a dramatic improvement in your mastery over the state of Fed policy.

Watch the Fed's Phraseology

What should you look for when reading the Fed's speeches? Look for key phrases that are repeated in lockstep by several Fed members. When I see a few members collectively repeating a particular phrase either verbatim or nearly so, I always sense that the phrase is a representation of current Fed policy. When Fed members sing the same tune, I envision them meeting with each other either in person or in a telephone conference and drawing conclusions about where they stand on policy and how they should weave their policy sentiments into their public comments.

Of course, each Fed member has his or her personal views about the economy and monetary policy, and they all are free to express them. Wall Street divides the Fed's members into two main camps: hawks and doves. Hawks are members who appear to be wary about the inflation outlook. They therefore tend to express an inclination to raise interest rates when inflation pressures appear to surface or when economic growth is strong. Doves, in comparison, tend to be more positive about the inflation outlook and generally worry less about the implications of strong economic growth than hawks do. Wall Street often measures the degree to which the members are hawkish or dovish by using a hawk/dove scale like the one shown in Figure 6-7.

F i g u r e   6–7

Hawk/Dove Scale

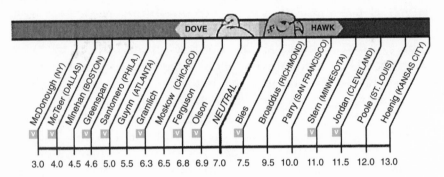

"V" = voting member in 2001.   Source: Bondtalk.com

One might think that hearing a wide range of views from the Fed would make the task of interpreting where the Fed stands on policy more difficult, but these personal opinions help provide insight into Fed policy. Basically, if there's consistency in the use of phraseology by members known to have opposing views on monetary policy (similar to the way in which Democrats and Republicans differ on so many issues), their joint use of a particular phrase is generally a strong indication of agreement about where the Fed stands on a particular issue. The differing views among the Fed's members can help an investor put the individual views in context; this is similar to the way in which knowing whether a politician is a Republican or a Democrat helps put that politician's comments into the proper context.

In 1999, for example, just before the Fed began raising interest rates in June of that year, several Fed members repeatedly used the phrase "the balance of risks have shifted [toward higher inflation]." Some of the members who repeated that phrase were not prone to saying so, given their personal views. Their common use of this phrase therefore suggested that the Fed was in the middle of formulating a new policy designed to counter the risks to which they were referring. Indeed, a hike in interest rates soon followed.

Similar phraseology was used at the opposite end of the spectrum at the end of 2000, indicating that interest rate reductions were in the offing, as indeed they were.

It is always striking to think that by simply following the words of a handful of people at the Fed, an investor can gain insights that can provide an edge over millions of investors. That is why I always include the Fed in my required readings and why you should too.

SUMMARY

Looking beyond the basics, in this chapter we discussed:

- The Fed was created largely to conduct the nation's monetary policies by influencing the money and credit conditions in the pursuit of full employment and stable prices. The Fed's main tool in this regard is the ability to set interest rates.
- The Fed affects the economy primarily by having an impact on the interest-rate-sensitive sectors of the economy, including housing, automobiles, and capital spending. The Fed's impact can be helped or hindered by transmission effects— the many ways in which the Fed's rate changes affect the economy. This includes stock prices and the value of the dollar.
- The Fed is structured in a way that gives it a broad view of the economy. At the Fed's eight meetings per year members debate the need for interest rate adjustments, with the Fed's chair having the most sway.
- The Fed's rate decisions have a significant impact on the bond market, affecting nominal rates, real rates, the yield curve, and spread products.
- The adage "Don't fight the Fed" derives from the cumulative experiences of millions of investors over many decades. History has proved that investors who put their faith in the Fed are likely to achieve much higher investment returns than are those who ignore the Fed. You therefore should incorporate an analysis of monetary policy into your investment decision-making process by

weaving it into your bets on the direction of the markets as well as the relative performances of the different financial securities.

- You can improve your ability to anticipate the Fed's rate actions by becoming an avid Fed watcher. Doing simple things such as reading the Fed's speeches and watching for the repetition of key phrases can go a long way toward putting you ahead of most investors.

CHAPTER SEVEN

The Yield Curve: The Bond Market's Crystal Ball

Investors always seem to be looking for a crystal ball to help them predict the future, but for most of them this is an elusive search. Investors often are confused by the myriad of indicators available to them and the wide variety of messages that the indicators send.

In the bond market there is one indicator that many investors put ahead of all the rest: the yield curve. It is the closest thing the bond market has to a crystal ball. For decades it has reliably foreshadowed major events and turning points in both the financial markets and the economy, and it is one of the most closely watched financial indicators. Few indicators are as reliable as the yield curve. More important, there is significant historical evidence that the yield curve is one of the best forecasting tools available. Let's take a closer look.

For simplicity's sake, assume that for our purposes the term yield curve refers to the yield curve for U.S. Treasuries (we will discuss why the Treasury yield curve is the most widely used later in this chapter).

The yield curve is a chart that plots the yield on bonds against their maturities. The shape of the yield curve is generally upward-sloping, with yields increasing in ascending order as maturities lengthen. In other words, a "normal" yield curve is one in which the yields on long-term maturities are higher than the yields on short-term maturities. The maturities generally included in yield curve graphs range from 3 months to 30 years. For yield curve graphs on the Treasury market, the most commonly included securities are those which are issued regularly by the U.S. Treasury Department. They include 3- and 6-month Treasury bills, 2-year Treasury notes, 5-year Treasury notes, 10-year Treasury notes, and 30-year Treasury bonds.

Market observers focus on the shape of the yield curve as a barometer of the U.S. economy. The focus is generally on the yield spreads between various combinations of short- and long-term maturities. The two most commonly watched spreads are the spread between 3-month T-bills and 10-year T-notes and the spread between 2-year T-notes and 30-year T-bonds. Both spreads have shown a strong historical correlation to the behavior of the economy.

The shape of the yield curve can mean a variety of things to bond investors, but there are two basic ways to look at it. First, if the yield curve is "positively sloped," or steep, this usually is seen as an indication that short-term interest rates are relatively low and are expected to remain low as a result of an accommodating stance on monetary policy by the Federal Reserve. Figure 7-1 shows a normal, or positively sloped, yield curve. In such an environment short-term interest rates are lower than long-term interest rates because the Fed's interest rate reductions put downward pressure on short-term interest rates, the rates the Fed controls. Long-term interest rates, however, do not fall in lockstep with the Fed's rate cuts in the same way that short-term interest rates do. Long-term interest rates are influenced by many other factors, such as inflation expectations and expectations about future short-term interest rates, among many others. This prevents long-term interest rates from falling as much as short-term interest rates do. (We will discuss the many reasons why long-term interest rates tend to be higher than short-term interest rates later in this chapter.) When the Fed lowers short-term interest rates, its monetary policy is considered friendly, and this is usually good news for bonds, stocks, and the economy because it lowers the cost of borrowing. A steep yield curve therefore generally forebodes good times for investors over a horizon of several quarters.

By contrast, a "negatively sloped," or inverted, yield curve usually is seen as an indication that short-term interest rates are relatively high and are expected to remain high, with the Fed engaged

F i g u r e   7–1

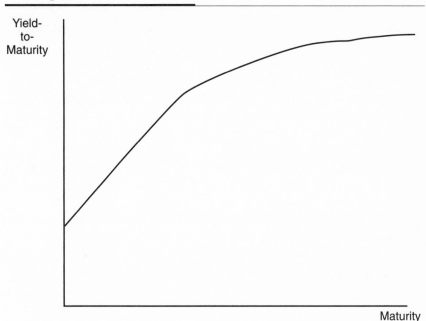

in a strategy of slowing the economy by raising short-term interest rates. Figure 7-2 shows an inverted yield curve. In this type of environment short-term interest rates are higher than long-term interest rates because of interest rate hikes by the Fed. This, of course, generally portends a gloomier set of conditions for bonds, stocks, and the economy because it raises the cost of borrowing. In fact, since 1970 every inverted yield curve has been followed by a period in which Standard and Poor's (S&P) 500 earnings growth was negative and has almost always preceded either an economic slowdown or a recession.

THREE REASONS TO FOLLOW THE YIELD CURVE

There are three solid reasons to follow the yield curve as an economic and financial indicator. First, forecasting with the yield curve is relatively quick and simple and does not require a sophisticated analysis. A quick glance at the yield spread between 2-year

F i g u r e   7–2

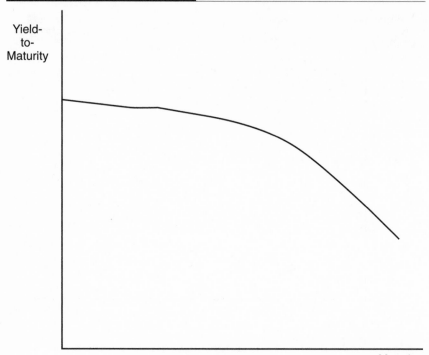

Yield-
to-
Maturity

Maturity

T-notes and 30-year T-bonds is all that is needed to draw a conclusion about the outlook of both the economy and the financial markets. Few indicators with such a stellar forecasting record have the
yield curve's simplicity.

    Second, the simplicity of the yield curve can be used to double-
check conclusions drawn from more sophisticated indicators. If, for
example, the conclusion drawn from the yield curve differs from
the conclusion drawn from other indicators, the yield curve can
serve as a red flag of sorts, perhaps highlighting situations where
the other indicators need rethinking. The yield curve also can be
used to help identify potential flaws in other forecasting indicators
that otherwise might have gone undetected. If the conclusions
drawn from both the yield curve and the other indicators are the
same, this can increase an investor's confidence in the conclusions.

Third, the yield curve serves as a useful gauge of market sentiment. The yield curve's shape, after all, results from the combined judgments of millions of investors. Therefore, its shape tells an investor a great deal about what other investors are thinking. This is important, of course, because market sentiment is an important indicator in and of itself. In addition, market sentiment reflects the preponderance of opinion on the economic outlook, which is also a helpful indicator.

A CRYSTAL BALL INDEED

Throughout the years the yield curve has proved to be one of the best economic indicators among the many that exist. The yield curve is thought to be a better predictor of the economy than the stock market is, for instance, and can give an investor an edge if the investor follows it. Indeed, studies have shown that the yield curve predicts economic events roughly 12 months or more in advance, while the stock market is thought to foretell events only 6 to 9 months in advance. History has proved that the yield curve can be used to make accurate forecasts of future developments in both the economy and the financial markets.

The yield curve is easily on sounder footing than are many other well-known indicators. It is certainly better than basing predictions on the winner of the Super Bowl or measuring hemlines. Incredibly, these so-called indicators are cited year after year as tools for reading the future.

In various studies the yield curve has been proved to be a superior financial indicator. In a study conducted by Haubrich and Dombrosky of the Federal Reserve it was found that from 1965 to 1995 the yield curve performed as well as or better than seven professional forecasting services. In a study by Estrella and Mishkin at the Federal Reserve it was found that the yield curve was superior to the Conference Board's index of leading economic indicators (LEI)(formerly released by the U.S. Commerce Department). That study found that unlike the yield curve, the LEI sent several incorrect signals in the 1982–1990 boom period.

There are a number of reasons why the yield curve is one of the best financial indicators. One of my favorite reasons relates to the Federal Reserve. Since the yield curve largely reflects actions or expected actions by the Fed, it contains a significant amount of information about monetary policy. This explanation of the yield curve's shape is called the *policy anticipation hypothesis*. This hypothesis states that the yield curve captures market expectations of future Fed policy. Since market expectations about the Fed tend to be accurate, the yield curve thus is a terrific tool for forecasting the economy. Accurate assessments of the Fed generally lead to accurate assessments of the economy's performance, since the Fed's actions tend to have a large impact on the economy. In essence, therefore, the yield curve captures a complex intermingling of policy actions, reactions, and real effects.

Another reason the yield curve is such a good financial indicator is that it contains a significant amount of information about the risk premium on long-term assets. The risk premium reflects the risks investors assign to holding various types of assets. For example, the risk premium investors assign to junk bonds is considerably higher than the risk premium they assign to U.S. Treasuries. In the Treasury yield curve investors do not differentiate between the credit risks of holding various maturities, but they do differentiate between the risks of holding Treasuries with different maturity dates. Holding a 10-year T-note, for example, requires greater tolerance for uncertainties about inflation, economic growth, and other factors than is required when one is holding a 3-month T-bill. The yield curve therefore contains a significant amount of information on the risk premium investors are assigning to holding long-term assets. The greater the uncertainties are, the less willing people will be to invest in long-term assets. Conversely, when people are confident about the future, they are far more willing to invest in long-term assets.

There have been many occasions throughout nation's history when the yield curve accurately foreshadowed events in the economy and the financial markets. Let's take a look at a few of them, starting with the events of 2000.

The yield curve's powerful predictive value was clearly illustrated in 2000 when the events of that year were forecast by the inversion of the yield curve that began in January 2000. Investors who heeded the yield curve's warnings at the start of that year are now sitting on a pot of gold. Almost everyone else wound up looking at their stocks like a deer in the headlights.

The inversion that began in January 2000 was the first such inversion since the last recession back in 1990. While many investors and analysts dismissed the inversion as being related to technical factors such as Uncle Sam's buyback of the national debt (which mostly entails the purchase of long-dated maturities), there were clearly other reasons for the inversion.

One reason the inversion occurred was that the bond market was beginning to believe that the Fed would have to raise short-term interest rates aggressively to contain the rapid growth in the economy. That is exactly what happened: The Fed raised rates a full percentage point over the next four months. In turn, bond investors began to believe that economic growth would decelerate. It did. Signs of economic weakness began to pile up by the end of 2000, and there were hints that the economy might enter into a recession in 2001, as it eventually did.

A second message contained in the inversion of the yield curve in 2000 was that stocks might fall. They did. Stock investors initially ignored that message, however, as well as the yield curve's message about what to expect from the Fed. Equity investors finally did get the message, of course, and the stock bubble soon burst. It was no coincidence that the Dow Jones Industrial Average peaked the same month that the yield curve inverted. The S&P 500 and the NASDAQ were not far behind, peaking just a couple of months later in March.

On the three prior occasions when the yield curve inverted—1989, 1982, and 1980—a recession soon followed. These examples clearly illustrate the powerful predictive value of the yield curve. Figure 7-3 shows the yield spread between the 10-year T-note and the 3-month T-bill compared to year-over-year growth in real gross domestic product (GDP). The chart clearly shows that inversions in the yield spread almost always precede recessions. One must keep in mind that investors do not always know that a recession is under way until it is partly over. This means that even a short heads-up on a looming recession can be extremely valuable to investors.

While an inversion in and of itself is a powerful indicator of a recession, the probability of a recession increases with the magnitude of the yield curve's inversion. Estrella and Mishkin of the Federal Reserve, who conducted a study for the period 1960–1995, found values of the yield curve spread that corresponded to

Figure 7-3

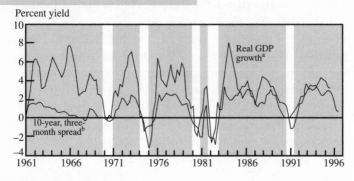

**Real GDP Growth and
Lagged Yield Spread**

Percent yield

a   Four-quarter percentage change.
b   Lagged four quarters.
Note: Shaded areas indicate recessions.
Sources: Board of Governors of the Federal Reserve System and U.S.
Department of Commerce, Bureau of Economic Analysis.

estimated probabilities of recession four quarters into the future.
They found that the yield curve spread between the 10-year
Treasury note and the 3-month T-bill was one of the most successful models of recession four quarters into the future. Table 7-1
shows their findings. As the table illustrates, an inverted spread of
2.4 percentage points implies a 90 percent probability of recession
four quarters into the future. The main message is that the more
inverted the yield curve, the greater the probability of recession in
the future.

The examples shown above clearly suggest that the yield
curve is the bond market's equivalent of a crystal ball. It's a tool
that is so simple to use that almost anyone can use it. I keep it in
my toolbox at all times.

THREE MAIN REASONS THE TREASURY YIELD
CURVE GETS THE MOST ATTENTION

The Treasury yield curve is by far the most closely followed yield
curve. It is the first yield curve that market participants and fore-

TABLE 7-1

Estimated Recession Probabilities for Probit Model Using the Yield Curve Spread (four quarters ahead)

Recession Probability, %	Value of Spread, percentage points
5	1.21
10	0.76
15	0.46
20	0.22
25	0.02
30	−0.17
40	−0.50
50	−0.82
60	−1.13
70	−1.46
80	−1.85
90	−2.40

Note: The yield curve spread is defined as the spread between the interest rates on the 10-year Treasury note and the 3-month Treasury bill.

Source: Federal Reserve.

casters look to for signals on the economy and the financial markets. There are two main reasons for this. First, because Treasuries are not at risk of default, the Treasury yield curve provides a "clean" look at where market participants believe interest rates should be along the various maturities. Unlike other yield curves, such as the yield curve on corporate bonds, the Treasury yield curve is not distorted by differences in creditworthiness. We know, for example, that market participants view the creditworthiness of 2-year Treasury notes as being equivalent to the creditworthiness of 10-year Treasury notes. The same cannot be said for other yield curves, which generally include a mix of different securities and therefore different degrees of creditworthiness.

Second, as was shown in Chapter 2, the U.S. Treasury market is by far the most liquid segment of the bond market. Its vast liquidity assures that the yields seen along the Treasury yield curve accurately reflect the value that market participants place on the securities. In other markets illiquidity and infrequent trading often distort yields and thus lead to inaccuracies in the yield curve.

Third, yields on Treasuries are far more accessible than are yields on other fixed-income securities. It is far simpler, for example, to obtain the yield on a 10-year T-note than it is to obtain the yield on a 10-year corporate bond because price information about Treasuries is far more widely disseminated. Moreover, when one is drawing a yield curve for securities other than Treasuries, choosing the specific security to place on the curve is a subjective decision. For example, deciding which corporate bonds to use in a yield curve for corporate bonds requires choosing between numerous different companies. This subjectivity can alter the reliability of the yield curve.

Largely for these three reasons, it is best to stick with the yield curve on Treasury securities to get the most accurate reflection of market sentiment and the most reliable signals on the outlook for both the economy and the financial markets.

TRADITIONAL EXPLANATIONS FOR THE SHAPE OF THE YIELD CURVE

There are many explanations for the many shapes of the yield curve. Ten factors are most prominent. Before we get into them, let's look at a few of the more traditional theories. There are three that are often cited: the *expectations theory*, the *liquidity preference theory*, and the *market segmentation theory*.

The *expectations theory* is based on the notion that the yield curve's shape is purely a function of investors' expectations of future interest rates. According to this theory, when the yield curve is upward-sloping, it reflects expectations that future short-term interest rates will rise. Similarly, an inverted yield curve reflects expectations that future short-term interest rates will fall. In a flat yield curve environment short-term interest rates are expected to be mostly constant. To some extent the pure expectations theory is similar to the policy anticipation hypothesis described earlier in this chapter because both theories are strongly influenced by expectations about monetary policy.

The *liquidity preference* theory holds that yields on longer-term maturities are higher than yields on short-term maturities because investors want additional compensation for the increased risks associated with holding longer-term maturities. Investors recognize that maturity and price volatility are directly related. They also recognize that there are many other uncertainties in owning longer-term maturities compared with owning short-term maturities. It is therefore rational to think that investors want compensation for the added risks involved in owning long-term maturities. This is a very good explanation for why the yield curve on corporate bonds is almost always upward-sloping. Unlike Treasuries, credit risks on corporate bonds are subject to considerable uncertainties in the distant future. As a result, investors demand compensation for those risks, pushing long-term interest rates above short-term interest rates. This seems to make sense because today's star company may be a laggard or perhaps not even exist 30 years from now. It stands to reason, then, that the yield curve for corporate bonds is almost always upward-sloping.

The *market segmentation* theory is based on the notion that the yield curve's shape is determined by asset-liability constraints, either regulatory or self-imposed, that confine borrowers and creditors to specific maturity sectors. In other words, the shape of the yield curve is determined by the supply and demand for securities in different maturity sectors. Many banks, for example, are permitted by their charters to invest in maturities of no longer than five years. Restrictions such as this largely benefit short-term maturities, resulting in an upward slope to the yield curve.

THE 10 BIGGEST FACTORS THAT AFFECT THE SHAPE OF THE YIELD CURVE

Many factors have an impact on the shape of the yield curve. While the relative importance of each of these factors frequently changes, there are 10 factors that have been and probably will continue to be the most influential for years to come.

By gaining an understanding of the forces that shape the yield curve, you will be better able to spot potential changes in both the economic climate and the financial climate. In addition, you will be able to use your understanding of the yield curve to more deftly select bonds that will perform optimally in different yield curve environments. Bond and stock investors who understand the messages contained in the changing shape of the yield curve are likely to achieve a greater return on their investments than are those who take a more passive approach and ignore it.

Assessing the current and future direction of the yield curve can be simplified by tracking the following 10 factors:

1. Monetary policy and market expectations on future Fed policy. The Fed is perhaps the single most influential factor in shaping the yield curve. This is the case mainly because the Fed essentially controls one part of the yield curve—the short end— and its actions have a big bearing on the other part—the long end.

The Fed affects the short-end of the yield curve when it raises or lowers the federal-funds rate. The fed funds rate, of course, is the rate banks charge each other for overnight loans. The Fed controls this rate by adjusting the amount of money available in the banking system. When the Fed wants to raise the fed-funds rate, it reduces the money supply essentially by selling Treasuries to banks and brokerages (forcing the banks and brokerages to pay for the bonds and hence reducing their cash balances). When the Fed wants to lower interest rates, it increases the money supply by purchasing Treasuries from financial institutions.

By tweaking the money supply, the Fed pushes the fed-funds rate up and down. As the fed funds rate fluctuates, the interest rate on other short-term fixed-income securities moves in lockstep. Short-term maturities closely follow the fed funds rate for a couple of reasons. For one thing, changes in the money supply either increase or decrease the cost of money. This is reflected in short-term interest rates, which are largely a function of the cost of money. A second key reason is that financial institutions usually operate on borrowed money to hold an inventory of notes and bonds. For example, if the fed funds rate is 4 percent, it will cost financial institutions about that amount to borrow the money they need to hold an inventory of notes and bonds (they hold the notes and bonds to resell to their customers). Therefore, these institutions generally will be unwilling to hold securities yielding less than 4 percent they would then incur what is called *negative carry*. Negative carry is incurred when the cost of financing to hold a security exceeds the rate of return on that security. Financial institutions are unwilling to engage in transactions with negative carry unless they feel that the cost of borrowing eventually will fall.

Over the years there have been very few times when borrowing costs exceeded the rates of return on fixed-income securities. Indeed, over the last 12 years the yield on 2-year Treasury notes has dipped below the fed funds rate on only four occasions. On each occasion it did so only months before a Fed rate cut, which lowered the cost of borrowing and hence eliminated the negative carry dilemma that financial institutions try to avoid. Those four occasions provided terrific signals about the future course of Fed policy as well as the outlook on the economy. Importantly, the rarity of periods with negative carry illustrates clearly how closely tied the short end of the yield curve is to Fed policy. The consistency in the yield spread between short maturities and the fed funds rate therefore reinforces the notion that the yield curve is influenced directly by changes in Fed policy.

It is easy to see how the Fed has a major impact on short-term interest rates because the Fed controls the fed-funds rate, a short-term interest rate. In turn, this affects the yield curve. When the market expects the Fed to lower the fed funds rate, short-term maturities tend to outperform long-term maturities because short-term interest rates fall faster than long-term interest rates fall, causing the yield curve to get steeper. When the Fed raises interest rates, shorter maturities rise faster in yield (mostly because financial institutions fear negative carry situations and because investors feel that they can delay their purchases of short-term securities and get a higher interest rate on their investments if they wait). In this case shorter maturities underperform long-term maturities, and so the yield curve flattens.

While the Fed's adjustments of the fed funds rate are the primary way in which the Fed influences the yield curve, the Fed also has a big influence on long-term interest rates. Long-term interest rates tend to be affected less by the negative carry concerns simply because there is much more time for the negative carry situation to reverse itself. Long-term interest rates behave in a way that reflects expectations about where investors believe short-term interest rates will be in the future. One might say that long-term interest rates are a bet on future short-term interest rates. In this way the Fed affects long-term interest rates. In an inverted yield curve environment, for example, where long-term interest rates are lower than short-term interest rates, long-term interest rates reflect a bet that short-term interest rates eventually will decline.

An even more significant way in which the Fed affects long-term interest rates is through inflation expectations. Inflation expectations are generally the main driver of long-term interest rates. The Fed affects inflation expectations by using monetary policy. The Fed can lower inflation expectations by acting quickly and decisively against any emerging buildup of inflation pressures. Staunch anti-inflation measures help keep long-term interest rates relatively low by giving investors confidence that the returns on their bonds will not be diluted by inflation. As a result, investors will demand only a small interest rate premium over and above the inflation rate. However, investors will demand an added premium if they believe that the Fed is soft and slow to act on inflation. In this environment the market will demand a higher interest rate to be compensated for the risk that inflation will rise and chew away at their investment returns.

As you can see, the Fed has a major influence on both ends of the yield curve.

2. Economic growth. The economy affects the yield curve in a number of ways. For starters, it directly affects monetary policy. When the Fed feels that economic growth is too strong (increasing the risk of inflation), it responds by raising short-term interest rates. When economic growth weakens, the Fed lowers short-term interest rates. Both actions affect the yield curve.

Another way in which economic activity affects the yield curve is through the allocation of capital in the economy. For example, when the level of economic activity weakens, banks usually make fewer loans. As a result, banks develop excess capital that they then turn around and invest in fixed-income securities, particularly short-term U.S. Treasury securities. In such an environment shorter maturities tend to outperform longer maturities, causing the yield curve to get steeper. This was illustrated clearly during the recession of 1990–1991, when bank lending stalled and banks were big buyers of short-term Treasuries.

When economic growth strengthens, banks can generate greater returns on their capital by lending it instead of investing in Treasuries. They therefore sell (or just stop buying) some of their holdings of U.S. Treasuries, causing the short end of the yield curve to underperform the rest of the curve and flattening the yield curve.

Also, when the economy is strong, businesses and consumers are less drawn to the safety element of short-term securities. They would rather spend and invest their money in equities and the real economy than buy notes and bonds. This tends to flatten the yield curve as investors shy away from short-term maturities. Of course, when the economic environment sours, businesses and consumers are less driven to spend their free capital and therefore channel more of it into fixed-income securities. In such an environment, the short end outperforms the long end and the curve gets steeper. This occurred in dramatic fashion in 2001.

3. Fiscal policy. Around the globe, numerous countries have illustrated the important role government finances play in the shape of the yield curve. In countries that have big fiscal deficits, for example, interest rates tend to be higher. Conversely, in countries with sound balance sheets, interest rates tend to be lower.

The specific ways in which government finances affect the shape of the yield curve vary, depending on how good or bad a country's fiscal situation is. If a country's fiscal situation is horrendously bad, for example, to the point where the markets are concerned about the possibility that the country will default on its obligations, short-term interest rates tend to be much higher than long-term interest rates. This occurs because investors will demand large compensation for the risk they take in investing in debt that may not be repaid. However, longer-term debt does not yield nearly as much in such a situation because investors will bet that the fiscally challenged government will reform itself eventually and create a better overall interest rate environment in the future. But governments in such situations are the exception and not the rule in the industrialized world. How do fiscal issues affect the yield curve in those countries?

Generally speaking, rising budget deficits tend to make the yield curve steeper while falling budget deficits tend to flatten the curve. Here's why.

If investors believe that a government will have big budget deficits as far as the eye can see, they will demand compensation for the risk that an ever-increasing amount of government securities will be sold in the future to finance the deficits. Investors therefore will tend to push up long-term interest rates more than short-term interest rates (through the laws of supply and demand) because the future is where the risk lies. After all, if an investor bought a 30-year government bond in a country with a shaky fiscal situation, that investor might be able to get a higher interest rate five years from now because the supply of 30-year bonds will have increased (as a result of the soaring budget deficit).

Moreover, in five years the government's finances may be even shakier, putting that 30-year bond at risk. Therefore, the longer the maturity is, the greater the risk is that things could get worse before they get better. Short-term maturities, in contrast, are affected more by short-term considerations, chiefly the government's ability to repay its debt *now*.

4. Inflation expectations. The bond market's perceptions of inflation have a large impact on the shape of the yield curve. That impact is felt in a number of ways. The most important impact is on Fed policy. If the bond market believes that inflation risks are big enough to prompt the Fed to raise interest rates, short-term interest rates will rise faster than will long-term interest rates and thus flatten the yield curve. Of course, this assumes that the market has confidence that the Fed can quash inflation before it becomes a problem.

In addition to the way inflation expectations affect perceptions of Fed policy and, hence, short-term maturities, inflation expectations have a large bearing on the performance of long-term maturities. In fact, inflation expectations are perhaps the most influential factor affecting long-term interest rates. Here's why.

Suppose an investor is considering whether to invest in a 30-year bond yielding 6 percent when inflation is running at 2 percent, for a "real yield" of 4 percent. At the outset, the investor probably is assuming that real yields will hold at around 4 percent or lower throughout his holding period, perhaps for as long as 30 years. The investor has decided that that rate is good enough for him or her. But if the investor began to worry that inflation eventually might rise to 6 percent, he or she would be far less likely to invest in bonds yielding 6 percent and would demand a return of 10 percent instead. In such a situation, the yield curve would get steeper as longer maturities underperformed shorter maturities because of rising inflation *expectations*.

5. The U.S. dollar. The value of the dollar significantly influences the shape of the yield curve largely because of the extent of foreign investment in the United States. Indeed, foreign investors owned a record 44 percent of all U.S. Treasuries outstanding in August 2001 and have been the biggest holders of Treasuries for many years. Since foreign investors are the biggest lenders to Uncle Sam, their level of continued interest in U.S. Treasuries is closely watched. Bond investors recognize that for foreign investors the performance of the U.S. dollar is a critical aspect of the investment decision process. They recognize that foreign investors must sell their own currencies and buy dollars to pay for the Treasuries they purchase, thus incurring currency risks. Fluctuations in the dollar therefore can affect the bond market's perceptions about what foreign investors will do next.

If, for example, the U.S. dollar weakened relative to other currencies, bond investors might become concerned that foreign investors eventually would become less willing to finance Uncle Sam's borrowing needs. They would demand greater compensation when buying long-term Treasuries because they would be concerned that reduced foreign demand for Treasuries in the future would push overall interest rates higher. This would result in a steep yield curve.

Another way the U.S. dollar affects the yield curve is through its impact on inflation expectations. A strong dollar tends to reduce inflation expectations because it reduces the cost of U.S. imports. This tends to contribute to a flattening of the yield curve. A weak dollar, by contrast, tends to raise inflation expectations because it raises the cost of U.S. imports, contributing to a steepening of the yield curve.

6. Flight to quality. In times of political, economic, or financial uncertainty the United States is a magnet for capital. In such times both domestic and global investors express a preference for short-term maturities. They do this because short-term maturities carry the least amount of risk to the invested principal. In times of crisis investors shift their focus from the return *on* capital to the return *of* capital. The best way for investors to assure the return of their capital is to invest in securities with the least amount of risk. When investors have this mind-set, they tend to invest heavily in short-term securities, particularly short-term U.S. Treasuries. As a result, short-term maturities tend to outperform long-term maturities, resulting in a steepening of the yield curve. A few examples of these episodes include the stock market crash of 1987, the savings and loan crisis of the early 1990s, the war with Iraq in 1991, the global financial crisis of 1998, and the terrorist attack on September 11, 2001.

Note that in some of these and other instances investors bought short-term maturities not only to protect their capital but in the expectation that the Federal Reserve would respond to the crisis by lowering short-term interest rates. This further increases the tendency of the yield curve to get steeper in times of crisis.

7. Credit quality. Concerns about credit quality develop when investors worry about the ability of bond issuers to repay their debt obligations. The concerns generally develop when the economy weakens or during times of uncertainty. The effects of credit quality issues on the yield curve are similar to the effects that crises have on it. In fact, concerns about credit quality often go hand in hand with crises episodes. Just as it occurs during times of crisis, when concerns about credit quality arise, the yield curve tends to get steeper.

The market's views of credit quality are not limited to bouts of concern. In fact, there are many situations in which the market's views of the general level of creditworthiness can be quite positive. During such times the yield curve tends to flatten. Indeed, the yield curve often flattens when perceptions of credit quality improve, particularly during times of economic prosperity. The reason is simple: When the economy prospers, investors believe that growing corporate coffers and firming household balance sheets reduce the risks of widespread problems in the financial system. As a result, investors become less interested in owing short-term maturities and are more willing to purchase long-term maturities, flattening the yield curve.

However, when there is concern that corporate defaults and personal bankruptcies will rise, investors become risk-averse and seek safe havens such as short-term Treasuries. In this case the yield curve gets steeper. In 2000 and 2001 concerns about rising corporate defaults and ratings downgrades helped spur a steepening bias in the Treasury yield curve.

8. Competition for capital. All financial assets face competition for capital to one degree or another. The bond market faces no less competition than do other asset classes. In fact, it can be argued that the bond market faces more competition for capital than do other asset classes because bonds historically have a lower rate of return than other asset classes, including equities. As a result, when assets such as equities are deemed attractive, it is usually the bond market that's left out in the cold as investors shun bonds in hopes of receiving a higher rate of return elsewhere.

When the bond market faces high levels of competition for capital from other asset classes, the yield curve typically gets steeper. This occurs because the high rates of return investors are receiving elsewhere tend to prompt investors to demand higher than normal rates of return in the bond market too. They do this by demanding higher real rates of return. This usually is manifested by higher long-term interest rates where real yields tend to be highest. In turn, the yield curve gets steeper.

In contrast, when the competition for capital is low, real yields compress and the yield curve usually flattens.

9. Debt buybacks. A recent phenomenon that has had a significant impact on the shape of the yield curve has been the Treasury department's buyback of older, higher-yielding U.S. Treasury securities. The Treasury has been buying old debt because of the government's improved fiscal situation: Uncle Sam's budget surplus was $237 billion in fiscal year 2000. Although the events of 2001 were likely to reduce or even eliminate future budget surpluses, the Treasury was expected to continue with its buyback program to maintain continuity in it. The Treasury expects budget surpluses to resume once the economy experiences a sustained period of economic growth.

In 2000 the Treasury department repurchased about $30 billion of Treasuries. Importantly, those purchases were concentrated at the long end of the yield curve. As a result, longer-dated securities have become scarcer, and this has lifted their value relative to short-term securities. It is no wonder, then, that in 2000 the Treasury yield curve began to invert for the first time in many years. In fact, the yield curve inverted the very month the U.S. Treasury Department announced the details of its planned buyback program.

The bond market will continue to adjust the yield curve accordingly, depending on the speed at which the Treasury repurchases old Treasuries relative to the market's expectations. Future yield curve bending will depend not only on the rate at which the Treasury Department buys back the government debt but also on the maturities the Treasury Department chooses for its program. Current forecasts assume that the Treasury will increasingly use shorter maturities to avoid an abrupt shrinking of the average maturity of all Treasuries outstanding.

One must keep in mind that Treasury buybacks are largely a technical issue. In the end the yield curve's shape is more likely to be molded by fundamental factors such as the Fed, inflation, and economic growth.

10. Portfolio shifts. When bond portfolio managers want to express their bullishness or bearishness on the bond market, they adjust the average maturity of their portfolios. When portfolio managers are bullish, they extend the average maturity of their bond holdings because extending the average maturity of their bonds increases a portfolio's price sensitivity to changes in interest rates. Portfolios therefore can benefit when yields decline and prices rise. The portfolio extensions often cause the yield curve to flatten as portfolio managers increase their purchases of longer-dated maturities relative to short-term maturities.

When portfolio managers are bearish on the bond market, they decrease the average maturity, get defensive about the bond market, and shorten their average maturity. This increases the demand for shorter maturities and causes the yield curve to get steeper.

There is a caveat to this, however. These examples of portfolio shifts pertain mostly to narrow time periods and short-term shifts in a portfolio manager's maturity selection. Generally, when portfolio managers are bullish in the aggregate, the yield curve gets steeper since yields on short-term maturities typically fall more than do yields on long-term maturities in such an environment.

SUMMARY

Looking beyond the basics, in this chapter we discussed:

- As we have seen, the yield curve has proved to be one of the best financial indicators available. It is a time-tested indicator that shows no signs of losing its predictive value.

- The yield curve is extremely simple to understand and can be used by almost anyone.
- In evaluating the yield curve, stay focused on its shape and evaluate the extent to which the factors listed above may be influencing its shape. This way, you are more likely to pinpoint the message of the market.
- The next time you're looking for a crystal ball, turn to the yield curve.

Real Yields: Where Real Messages Can Be Found

One of the best tools investors can put in their toolboxes is an understanding of *real yields*. Real yields measure the rate of return on bonds minus inflation. In other words, the real yield on a bond is its stated, or quoted, yield-to-maturity minus the current rate of inflation. There is almost always some real yield incorporated into bond yields, largely because investors want compensation for the risks they take in parting with their money. Moreover, in a world where investment choices seem limitless, borrowers recognize that they must provide compensation to entice investors to buy their bonds.

The amount of compensation investors require in the form of real yields for the risks they take and the opportunity costs they bear varies with a wide variety of factors. It is in these variations in real yields that real messages can be found. Put simply, the fluctuations in real yields contain messages about the bond market that are not necessarily evident in nominal rates.

Equity investors look at price-to-earnings ratios (P/Es) and other ratios, using a historical perspective to draw conclusions about the value of stocks and/or the market on any given day; the same thing is done in the bond market. By looking at where real yields have stood in the past, we can answer the question: Is the market overvalued or undervalued? Real rates can give a fixed-income investor a good perspective on whether bond market yields are too high or too low for a given set of fundamentals. They provide a quick and simple method of valuing a bond. Here are a couple of examples.

Suppose the nominal yield on a 10-year U.S. Treasury note moves from 8 percent to 6 percent over a period of three years. On the surface the yield decline might lead some investors to shy away from investing in the 10-year T-note because they think that rates have fallen to unattractive levels. After all, the yield decline here is quite substantial. However, investors who approach it this way are missing the point and probably are not putting their focus where it should be, on real rates. In this example, if the inflation rate over the three-year period fell from 4 percent to 2 percent, real rates would have held steady at 4 percent (8 percent minus 4 percent and 6 percent minus 2 percent). Thus, while it is true that nominal yields became less attractive during the period, the real yields did not.

Consider a situation in which nominal rates rise to 7 percent from 6 percent but inflation also rises, moving to 4 percent from 2 percent. In this case some investors might be misled into thinking that just because interest rates increased a full percentage point to 7 percent, the investment is more attractive than it was when nominal rates were at 6 percent. The reality, however, is that it is a less desirable investment than it was before because real rates fell to 3 percent from 4 percent. There is an obvious caveat to this, however. If investors have a firm conviction that inflation eventually will fall and indeed it does fall, investing when nominal rates are at 7 percent is the more attractive investment.

It pays to look beyond nominal rates when making a judgment about yields. One can't judge a book by its cover, and it's no different in the bond market.

HISTORICAL PERSPECTIVE ON REAL YIELDS

Forming opinions and judgments about the many messages contained in prevailing levels of real yields is relatively simple, but it is necessary to have a perspective on where real yields have been historically. Once you have this perspective, you will be able to quickly form an opinion not only on the valuation of the bond market, but on a wide variety of issues related to the Fed, the economy, inflation, and more.

The best way to gain a perspective on real yields is to focus on U.S. Treasuries. Doing this will help you steer clear of the confusion that can result from having to pinpoint the many possible causes of fluctuations in real yields on other fixed-income securities. This is a must in analyzing real yields because the main objective in this case is to get the big picture and avoid getting bogged down in details. For example, if the real yield on a particular corporate bond increased sharply, the increase could be attributable to many factors, such as company-specific problems or woes in the company's industry. Although that information can be helpful in giving signals about that company and or its industry, it will not reveal much about larger issues such as inflation expectations, the Fed, and inflation. Treasuries have the distinct advantage of being free of micro issues such as creditworthiness. They are also simpler to use than other fixed-income securities partly because prices on Treasuries are more widely available than those on other types of bonds and because of the ease with which you can choose specific Treasuries for your analysis. In contrast, deciding which specific security to choose from among the many other types of bonds is a much more difficult task because of the many differences that exist in their creditworthiness, industry type, and other factors.

Now that we've decided that it's best to use Treasuries when tracking real yields, the next step is to get a perspective on the historical behavior of real yields. By doing this you will be in a much better position to draw conclusions about the messages contained in the level of real yields. It is as simple as knowing the range in which real yields tend to fluctuate and the forces that cause real yields to fluctuate within that range.

The first thing to keep in mind is that real yields are almost always positive except in periods when inflation is much higher than the historical average, such as the 1970s. As was mentioned earlier, this is the case largely because investors want compensation for the risks they take in parting with their money and the opportunity costs of saying no to the many other investment choices available to them. As one might expect, there are exceptions to this, but they are few and far between and generally occur only in times of economic stress.

When tracking real yields, an investor has to decide on a maturity to track. Some observers prefer to look at short maturities, while others prefer long maturities. Which is best? It depends on the type of analysis an investor is conducting. An analysis of the behavior of real yields on both maturities, however, probably will lead an investor to draw similar conclusions. Nevertheless, I believe that real yields on long-dated maturities contain the most messages. Intuitively, this makes sense because long-dated maturities contain information about both the short term and the long term, while short-dated maturities provide information only about the short term.

I like to examine the real yield on both 10-year T-notes and 30-year T-bonds. Let's take a look at where they've been over the last few decades. We can start by looking at Figure 8-1, which shows that the real yield on the 30-year T-bond generally has been slightly higher than the real yield on the 10-year T-note. This can be attributed to its longer maturity; the longer the maturity on a bond is, the more time there is for a wide variety of factors to affect its performance. Uncertainty about the future is therefore the biggest reason for the historical difference in real yields on 10-year and 30-year Treasuries.

Figure 8-1 shows that with the exception of a few outlying periods, real yields tend to be confined to a relatively narrow

F i g u r e   8—1

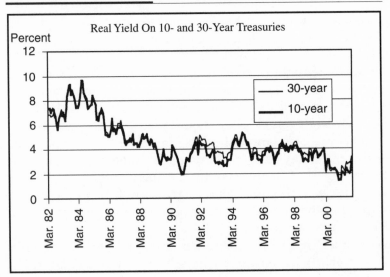

range. Importantly, real yields fluctuate much less than do nominal yields. This suggests that bond investors are fairly consistent in their demands for compensation against future risks.

Figures 8-2 and 8-3 provide an additional perspective on the historical range in real yields. Note that in the 1960s the real yield on the 10-year U.S. Treasury note, as measured by its average yield minus the average year-over-year change in the consumer price index, averaged 2.26 percent. The decade of the 1960s was similar to recent years (the late 1990s) in terms of trends in both economic growth and inflation, and that helped keep interest rates relatively low. In the 1970s real yields fell sharply, averaging just 0.43 percent, as high levels of inflation cut into nominal yields. In the 1980s real yields increased sharply to an average of 4.96 percent owing to rising budget deficits and high levels of competition for

F i g u r e   8–2

Historical Real Yield on 10-Year T-Notes*

Period	Average, %	High, %		Low, %		Standard Deviation, basis points
1960s	2.26	3.50		0.7	(4/69)	69
1970s	.43	3.40		−4.7	(12/74)	288
1980s	4.96	9.64	(6/84)	−4.20	(12/80)	298
1990s	3.63	5.20	(10/94)	1.95	(11/90)	65
Last 30 years	3.07	9.64	(6/84)	−4.90	(12/74)	282
Last 20 years	4.48	9.64	(6/84)	1.39	(2/01)	177
Last 5 years	3.16	4.46	(6/97)	1.39	(2/01)	82
Last 3 years	2.74	3.96	(1/00)	1.39	(2/01)	73

*Recent data through December 2001.

F i g u r e   8–3

Historical Real Yield on 30-Year T-Bonds*

Period	Average, %	High, %		Low, %		Standard Deviation, basis points
1980s	5.71	9.53	(5/84)	−0.42	(12/80)	190
1990s	3.97	5.37	(10/94)	2.15	(12/90)	63
Last 20 years	4.69	9.53	(5/84)	−0.42	(12/80)	166
Last 5 years	3.39	4.70	(5/97)	1.80	(1/01)	80
Last 3 years	2.96	4.00	(7/99)	1.80	(1/01)	69

*Recent data through December 2001.

capital. Also boosting real yields in the 1980s were the extraordinarily high short-term interest rates put in place by the Federal Reserve to combat the double-digit inflation that developed in the late 1970s and early 1980s. In the 1990s, when both inflation and the budget deficit fell, real yields simmered down. A booming stock market created significant competition for capital and probably kept real rates from falling as much as they could have.

Historically, it appears that real yields on the 10-year T-note generally fluctuate in a range of about 2 percent to 4 percent except during extraordinary periods. The long-term range on the 30-year T-bond appears to be a bit higher than that.

These tables and the figures can serve as a useful reference for the general behavior of real rates. By remaining cognizant of both the norms and the extremes, an investor can put almost any level of real yields into perspective.

FACTORS THAT CAUSE REAL YIELDS TO FLUCTUATE

Many factors determine the real yield on a bond. For simplicity, I will focus on government bonds rather than corporate bonds and other types. Here's a list of major factors:

- Inflation expectations
- Opportunity costs
- The economy's growth rate
- The Federal budget
- The Federal Reserve
- Market liquidity

Inflation Expectations

In the long run the most important influence on real yields is the expected inflation rate. When inflation is falling or low, real yields tend to be low because investors are more willing to accept a low real yield in the expectation that inflation will keep falling or stay low and therefore produce an acceptable return after inflation. By contrast, investors demand high real yields when they expect inflation to rise so that they can offset the potential erosion of their capital. Bond investors are always cognizant of the possibility that inflation will erode the value of their money and even take away their returns completely. As a result, when investors are concerned that inflation may accelerate, they demand a higher real rate of return to offset that risk. The degree to which investors demand compensation for inflation risks depends largely on their most recent experience with inflation. In the early 1980s, for example, the double-digit inflation experienced in the 1970s lingered in investors' minds, resulting in very high real yields for several years after inflation peaked. Similarly, as the U.S. economy gathered momentum in 1994, bond investors drove real yields sharply higher partly out of fear that inflation would accelerate. It was a rational fear because inflation had climbed to over 6 percent at the end of the previous expansion in the late 1980s. However, as that fear of inflation proved to be false, real yields began to fall, and by the late 1990s, inflation seemed only a distant memory. Investors demanded very little compensation for inflation risks despite economic growth rates that would have caused bond investors to shudder with inflation concerns years earlier. Investors harbored few worries about inflation because their most recent experience led them to believe that inflation probably would not accelerate. When investors sense that the inflation rate is falling or about to fall, they generally are willing to accept a lower real rate for a while in hopes that the inflation rate will decline.

Opportunity Costs

A second important factor affecting real yields and one that has had a large impact in recent years is the compensation investors demand for the opportunity cost of investing in bonds compared to assets such as stocks. Most bond investors recognize that investment returns on stocks generally have outpaced returns on bonds. This is acceptable to most, of course, because bond investors generally invest in bonds to diversify their portfolios, provide an income stream, and add safety elements to their portfolios. They are therefore somewhat indifferent to lagging returns on bonds compared to those on other asset classes. There is a limit to this indifference, however. When the return on other asset classes far outpaces the return on bonds and when it appears that the returns may be sustained, money almost certainly will be channeled away from the bond market. Bond investors will not pull out en masse, of course, but they will reduce their allocation for bonds to take advantage of better returns elsewhere. This reduced demand for bonds pushes up real yields. Bond investors want compensation for the opportunity costs they incur when the investment returns on other asset classes exceed the returns on bonds. Thus, when the competition for capital is high, bond investors demand higher real yields. This is precisely what happened in the late 1990s, when a roaring stock market prevented real yields from falling as much as many felt they should have as a result of the elimination of the federal budget deficit, rising productivity rates, and disinflation (a slowing in the *rate* of inflation; deflation is defined as an outright decline in prices). When returns on alternative investments sour, as occurred in the stock market in 2000 and 2001 as both the financial bubble and the economic bubble burst, bond investors become less choosy. They turn their focus away from the return *on* capital and toward the return *of* capital. In this case real yields fall as investors basically settle for a low rate of return in exchange for the relative safety of bonds.

The Economy's Growth

The level of economic activity is also a key determinant of real yields. The economy's effect on real yields is similar to the effects of competition for capital on real yields. The pace of economic activity basically affects the allocation of capital in the economy in the same way that competition for capital affects the allocation of capital in the financial markets. When the economy is growing rapidly, for example, all sorts of financial and corporate entities seek capital: banks seek capital for loans, technology companies seek money for research and development, and so forth. The more money these and other entities seek for real economic activity, the less money there is available for investment in the bond market, resulting in higher real yields.

Banks, for example, which typically hold a fairly large amount of bonds, increase their lending activity when the economy is strong. As a result, banks have less money available to allocate for financial investments and therefore reduce their purchases of bonds accordingly, contributing to a rise in real interest rates. In contrast, when the economy is weak, banks reduce their lending activity and increase their purchases of bonds. This is precisely what happened during the savings and loan crisis of the early 1990s when banks sharply curtailed their lending activities and sharply increased their purchases of bonds, contributing to a decline in real interest rates. Similarly, a wide variety of corporate entities shift money in and out of the bond market depending on the economic environment. The level of economic growth basically affects the aggressiveness with which businesses bid for financing. This affects the price of money: interest rate levels.

The Federal Budget

Another important factor that affects real yields is the federal budget. The federal budget does this through its impact on the amount of new Treasury debt that must be sold to finance the government's spending needs. Real yields are apt to be high when the government is running a budget deficit and issuing a lot of debt and are likely to be low when the government is running a budget surplus and issuing less debt. The basic premise here rests on the laws of supply and demand: Since there is a finite amount of capital in the world, the larger the supply of bonds is, the lower bond prices are apt to be, resulting in higher real yields. Conversely, the fewer bonds there are, the higher bond prices are likely to be, resulting in lower real yields. In the 1980s and early 1990s a soaring budget deficit resulted in sharp increases in the issuance of Treasury securities. Real yields no doubt were affected and probably were higher than they would have been otherwise. Investors were demanding compensation for the prospect that the Treasury would issue ever-increasing amounts of debt. The heavy issuance of Treasuries probably kept real rates higher on other types of fixed-income securities too by crowding them out. After all, there are only so many investment dollars to go around.

In the late 1990s the fiscal situation in the United States improved markedly, with the annual fiscal balance turning from deficits to surpluses. The budget improved from a peak deficit of $290.4 billion in fiscal year 1992 to a surplus of $236.9 billion in fiscal year 2000. The surpluses reduced the government's need to issue new Treasury securities. In fact, the surpluses were so large that the government began to repurchase, or buy back, previously issued debt in an effort to reduce the national debt. It is probably not a coincidence that real yields on Treasuries and other fixed-income products began to decline as the government's fiscal situation improved and the supply of both new and existing Treasuries diminished.

The Federal Reserve

Another factor that affects real yields is the Federal Reserve. There are two main ways in which the Fed affects real yields. First, expectations of changes in monetary policy cause interest rates to fluctuate, affecting real yields. If, for example, bond investors expect the Fed to raise interest rates, they will demand higher interest rates as compensation, pushing up real yields. The Fed generally raises interest rates when inflation is accelerating, yet inflation takes time to accelerate and more time to decelerate. Thus, at the onset of Fed rate increases, real yields may rise but the rise can be temporary if inflation eventually accelerates. In a sense, inflation catches up with the Fed's interest rate increase, and real yields eventually decline. Expected changes in monetary policy affect real yields along the entire yield curve but have a disproportionate effect on the short end of the curve. This is the case because the Fed controls short-term interest rates and because long-term interest rates are affected by a wide variety of factors. Nevertheless, the Fed has a large impact on long-term interest rates too, and this is another way in which the Fed affects real yields. When market participants believe that interest rate changes will affect inflation, they adjust interest rates accordingly, affecting the real yields. Changes in inflation expectations that are prompted by actions taken by the Federal Reserve are essentially leaps of faith by investors regarding the future inflation rate. The degree to which investors take that leap of faith depends on the amount of goodwill built up by the central bank. When the Fed has a lot of goodwill, as it has had under Chairman Alan Greenspan, real yields tend to be lower, reflecting investors' optimism about the inflation outlook. This occurs because the Fed's accumulation of goodwill translates into confidence in its ability to prevent inflation. The more confidence investors have in the Fed's ability to keep inflation low, the less real yield they will demand as compensation for inflation risks. In this case investors worry less about the risk that inflation will erode the value of their bonds. The decline in real yields that took place in the late 1990s no doubt had a great deal to do with the tremendous confidence investors had in the Fed's ability to contain inflation. Confidence in Greenspan was particularly high.

Market Liquidity

Another factor that affects real yields is market liquidity. As was discussed in Chapter 2, market liquidity is basically the ease with which an investor can buy or sell securities without paying a premium on purchases or taking a haircut (a reduced price) on the price when selling. A liquid market is one in which there are many buyers and sellers and the bid and ask prices are generally narrow. An illiquid market is the opposite: There are few buyers and sellers, and the bid and ask prices are generally far apart. When market liquidity falls, investors flock to the U.S. Treasury market, where liquidity is almost always high. This capital flight reduces real yields on Treasuries but increases real yields on the securities from which investors flee. In 1998 real yields swung wildly as the Asian financial crisis sparked a virtually unprecedented level of capital flight into Treasuries and out of riskier assets. As a result, real yields on virtually all fixed-income assets other than Treasuries rose while real yields on Treasuries fell sharply. During that period risk aversion increased so sharply that investors also shunned older, less active Treasuries (known as off-the-runs), causing their real yields to rise too. Certainly, the poor performance of the off-the-runs and their subsequent rise in real yields compared to other Treasuries could not be explained by differences in credit quality; all Treasuries have the backing of the full faith and credit of the U.S. government. Therefore, the only explanation for the variation in performance was liquidity. The events of 1998 therefore show the large impact liquidity can have on real yields.

THREE RISKS OF USING REAL INTEREST RATES AS INDICATORS OF FUTURE ECONOMIC PERFORMANCE

Real interest rates historically have been a good gauge of future economic performance. As one would expect, high real interest rates historically have been correlated with weak economic growth while low real interest rates typically have coincided with strong economic growth. While the historical record of real interest rates as an economic forecasting tool has been solid, there are three risks of using real interest rates as indicators of future economic performance.

First, determining whether real yields are "high" or "low" is a bit subjective. While it may be relatively simple to determine whether current levels of real yields are high or low relative to historical levels, one cannot judge with complete accuracy the market's expectations about *future* inflation and, hence, the degree to which current levels of real yields reflect expectations about future levels of inflation. Inflation expectations sometimes are difficult to measure. That said, there are many ways to gauge inflation expectations. For example, the University of Michigan includes data on consumers' inflation expectations in its monthly consumer sentiment survey. Also, the Treasury's inflation-protected securities (described in Chapter 4) can be used to track inflation expectations because their performance is directly affected by inflation expectations. Finally, inflation expectations are largely a function of the most recent experiences. If inflation behaves largely in one way over a multiyear period, there is little reason to believe that inflation expectations will change materially over a short period unless there is an exogenous shock that alters the equation.

A second risk in using real yields as an indicator of future economic performance relates to the difficulty of determining the *equilibrium real yield* that would be consistent with sustainable economic growth. Knowing the equilibrium real interest rate is important because that rate serves as a reference point for the real yield analysis. How, for example, can we say that real yields are "high" or "low" if we do not know what the midpoint of high and low is? That said, the historical range shown in Figure 8-1 provides a good sense of where the equilibrium real rate is.

A third risk in using real yields to forecast the economy is the possibility that the equilibrium real rate will vary over time. It can vary as a result of many different factors, such as changes in the level of risk aversion that investors have, political uncertainties, fiscal policy, inflation, tax rates, competition for capital, and the amount of goodwill investors have toward the Fed. Again, unless one knows what the equilibrium interest rate is, it is difficult to know when interest rates are "high" or "low." However, history provides a good gauge.

WHEN NEGATIVE REAL INTEREST RATES ARE NECESSARY

As the figure and tables in this chapter indicate, negative real interest rates are uncommon. This is the case primarily because just as equity investors expect higher returns on riskier stocks, bond investors want compensation for various risks, particularly for the risk of inflation and expected changes in monetary policy. In a sense, this is the demand side of the equation: The Fed plays a role in determining whether real interest rates should be positive or negative. Although history may have proved that negative real interest rates can lead to inflation and the Fed therefore has tended to avoid such a condition, there is at least one predicament where negative real interest rates are necessary: during a *liquidity trap*.

A liquidity trap is a term used to describe a situation in which reductions in interest rates fail to spur new lending activity either because banks refuse to make new loans or because the demand for new loans is not helped by the low interest rates. A liquidity trap usually occurs when the banking sector is in bad shape or when the economic outlook is poor or uncertain. In such a situation no amount of incentives, including low interest rates, seems to spur lending activity. As a result, when the Federal Reserve cuts short-term interest rates, it is said to be "pushing on a string."

If there is a liquidity trap, as there arguably has been in Japan, where lending activity has been stalled for ten years despite interest rates near 0 percent, the equilibrium real interest rate (the rate that equates savings to investment) is very likely to be negative. How do we know? The fact that lending is falling while real interest rates are in positive territory is evidence that the equilibrium rate is lower than normal. In Japan, zero interest rates have failed to help partly because the inflation rate has actually been *negative*. This means that real rates remain relatively high in Japan despite the fact that nominal interest rates are near zero. Businesses and consumers have no incentive to invest and consume because prices are falling. If you felt that the price of a good that you were contemplating buying would fall every month, wouldn't you delay the purchase if you could? Doesn't it make sense that a business would curtail its borrowing if it knew that the value of the assets in which it invests would fall but the value of its debt would stay the same? When there is deflation, homeowners, for example, must contend with the fact that the value of their homes is falling but their mortgage debt is not. That's certainly not a good environment in which to invest. Deflation is worse than inflation in some ways (as long as inflation is low, of course). To counter a situation such as this, it is imperative for a central bank to endeavor to raise inflation expectations. It can do this by lowering interest rates to low levels and increasing the supply of money. This will result in negative real interest rates, a condition that should spur new lending activity and help restore positive economic growth. With inflation outpacing the rate of return on their investments, consumers will be compelled to spend rather than save and businesses will be compelled to invest rather than save. In this way, the equilibrium between saving and investment is restored.

SUMMARY

Looking beyond the basics, in this chapter we discussed:

- Many factors can affect real yields. All those factors are messages that are embedded in the level of real yields every day. An investor need only look closely.
- First determine the level of real yields by taking the nominal, or stated, yield on a benchmark such as the 10-year U.S. Treasury note and then subtract the current inflation rate (the year-over-year gain in the consumer price index) from that number.
- Then compare the result—the real yield—against the historical average as well as against more recent levels.
- Make a determination of whether you believe that the level of real yields is justified on the basis of the factors described earlier in this chapter. This will tell you whether the bond market is overvalued or undervalued.
- But if you are mostly interested in extracting the message of the bond market, simply determine which of these factors most likely explains the prevailing level of real yields. Once

you feel you have figured out the market's message, this can
be a big help with your investments whether you are
invested in fixed-income securities, equities, or other types.

- A better understanding of real yields will help you see the
big picture better and hear the messages coming from
the bond market loud and clear. The more you know
about the factors that affect real yields, the easier it will
be for you to understand current interest rate levels and
forecast future changes. If, for example, you can explain a
particular level of real yields in terms of one of the factors
described above, you can make a judgment about
whether you believe the condition will persist or diminish. You also can make a judgment about whether you
believe the bond market's assessment of where real yields
should be is built on a reasonable premise. If you decide
that it is not, you have a basis for making a bet against
the market. If it appears to you that real yields are being
unduly affected by one of the factors described earlier
and you sense that there will be a resolution to the factor,
think one thing: opportunity.

The Five Tenets of Successful Interest Rate Forecasting

On Wall Street, bond traders spend most of the day in front of their computer screens, watching bonds bop to and fro. It would be monotonous and dull work if not for the many interesting reasons behind each movement shown on the ticker tape. Bond prices move for reasons that are rooted in the essence of the dynamics of the economy and the way American citizens live, offering traders a new chance every day to view the world from a unique vantage point. Few areas of the financial markets provide this unique macroperspective.

Over the years one of my biggest endeavors has been to learn as much as possible about what makes the bond market move. I have been exposed to a constant flow of information that has given me a solid understanding of the forces that shape the investment decision-making process. I have focused intensely on not only the big secular moves but also on the small incremental moves that are part and parcel of the big moves. I am fascinated by every little wiggle in the market and believe that there is a message and a lesson to be learned in every move.

For decades investors have spoken of the benefits of watching the tape to glean the message of the markets. Those who have fought the tape may have won a few battles now and then, but in the end most of them probably came to realize that it's a losing battle. This is why it is important to understand as much as possible about why markets move. An investor cannot wait for the reasons to come to his or her door in a box with instructions on what to do next. Indeed, the real reasons behind a market's move may not be revealed until after the market has moved. Markets anticipate future events, after all.

THE FIVE CORE ELEMENTS OF SUCCESSFUL INTEREST RATE FORECASTING

In the bond market there are five core reasons behind every move. These are the five elements in developing an accurate interest rate forecast:

- Monetary policy
- Inflation expectations
- The pace of economic growth
- Secular versus cyclical influences
- The market's technical condition

Combined, these factors generally explain the majority of the bond market's moves whether they span ten years or ten minutes. Just how much weight the market will give to each of these factors at any point in time depends on a variety of circumstances and is one of the most important elements in determining the market's next move.

An accurate interest rate forecast requires the ability to dynamically assess how much weight to give to each of the five core elements and to be as open-minded as possible; things can change quickly in the bond market. It is also very important to be extremely persistent in tracking the key elements of the core factors. It takes tremendous discipline, but this is the best way to achieve the best possible forecasting results. It is especially important to incorporate intangibles into the forecasting equation, including an evaluation of the nation's mood and the cultural forces that shape the way people behave. Data and statistics, after all, reflect what people do, not what machines do. Therefore, it's of the utmost importance to stay connected to the real world. Moreover, an investor must always remember that because people are behind the numbers he or she follows, the full gamut of human emotions is present in every observation he or she makes.

Let's take a closer look at each of the five core factors that shape the bond market's movements.

MONETARY POLICY: FED TALK ABOUNDS

Perhaps no measurable factor affects the bond market more than the Federal Reserve's monetary policies do. Indeed, on Wall Street, discussions about the Fed are a daily obsession and not a trading day passes without ruminations about some reference in the financial media to what the Fed may do next. This obsession can seem excessive at times, but Figure 9-1 clearly illustrates the close link between the actions taken by the Federal Reserve and yield changes in the bond market. As the figure shows, the yield on the 2-year Treasury note appears to move in virtual lockstep with the federal-funds rate, the interest rate the Fed controls and uses as its primary means for transmitting changes in monetary policy.

It is significant that the yield on the 2-year T-note is rarely below the federal-funds rate. In fact, if you look closely, you will see that there have been only four occasions in the last 12 years in which the yield on the 2-year T-note dipped below the fed-funds rate. Importantly, on each occasion the Fed lowered interest rates

F i g u r e   9—1

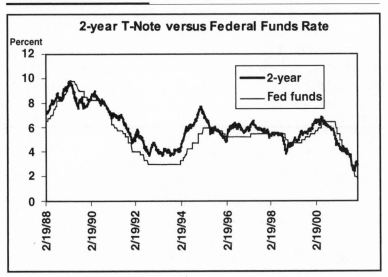

within a few months. This clearly illustrates that the bond market moves in advance of the Fed, anticipating the Fed's every move.

As will be shown in Chapter 10, the close correlation between the 2-year T-note and the fed-funds rate is reason to use the 2-year T-note as one of the top gauges of the bond market's sentiment toward the Federal Reserve. Figure 9-1 provides ample evidence of this strong correlation and is one of the reasons I use the 2-year note as one of my top gauges for forecasting the overall direction of interest rates. The key to using this excellent indicator is to be mindful of the following general principle: If the yield on the 2-year T-note deviates sharply from its normal yield spread to the fed-funds rate, the bond market must expect the possibility of a change in monetary policy and, hence, the fed-funds rate. With this in mind, the next step is to examine whether the market's apparent beliefs have a solid foundation or are a house of cards. The weaker the market's rationale is, the more likely it is that the market will reverse course eventually. If the market appears to have a solid fundamental basis for its rationale, it is more likely that the market's trends will be sustained.

Until late in 2001, the yield on the 2-year T-note fluctuated in a range of 100 basis points below the fed funds rate and 100 basis points above that rate. The average spread was 18 basis points over the fed funds rate. This conveniently simple range made it easy in recent years to judge whether the bond market was "rich" or "cheap." Making this determination first requires a sense of where the Fed is in its interest rate cycle. Note that during periods when the Federal Reserve was raising interest rates, the yield on the 2-year T-note was generally at the upper end of the range, with the yield spread at as much as 100 basis points above the fed funds rate. Conversely, during periods when the Federal Reserve was lowering interest rates, the 2-year generally was at the lower end of the range, with the yield spread at as much as 100 basis points below the fed funds rate.

Whenever the yield on the 2-year T-note is at or moving toward either end of its normal trading range relative to the fed-funds rate, the justification for such moves should be questioned. In other words, operating on the assumption that the 2-year note generally will move to the wide ends of its long-term range only when the Federal Reserve is on the verge of increasing or decreasing the fed-funds rate, you must judge whether actual changes in the fed-funds rate are truly in the offing. That takes some doing, of course, as it requires numerous other judgments about the economy, the Fed, and so forth, but an analysis of the 2-year note's yield relative to the fed funds rate is absolutely necessary to correctly determine the market's expectations about the Fed. Knowing this makes the task of determining the market's richness or cheapness far easier. The Federal Reserve simplifies the task further because it often signals its interest rate changes in advance, validating or invalidating the market's assumptions about its intentions. To detect the Fed's signals you must be an avid Fed watcher, the art of which was discussed in Chapter 6.

The reason for the tight correlation between the 2-year T-note and the federal-funds rate is relatively simple. The correlation exists because yields on short-term maturities are determined largely by the cost of money—which is determined primarily by the federal-funds rate—rather than by the factors that dominate the behavior of long-term maturities, including inflation expectations, hedging activity, speculative flows, and new issuance, to name a few. When the cost of money is higher than the yield on the 2-year T-note, investors who purchase the 2-year note with borrowed money incur what is known as *negative carry* because the interest rate paid on the borrowed money exceeds the yield-to-maturity on the 2-year note. Investors who purchase securities on borrowed money are generally unwilling to engage in investments that incur negative carry unless they believe that borrowing costs eventually will fall and result in *positive carry* on the investment. Investors recognize that there is very little time for an investment in a short-term maturity to evolve from negative carry to positive carry and therefore engage in negative carry trades very rarely, as suggested by the minimal number of occasions over the last 12 years when the 2-year T-note has yielded less than the fed funds rate.

As the 2-Year Note Goes, So Goes the Rest of the Market

Importantly, the correlation between the fed-funds rate and the bond market does not end with the 2-year T-note; there is ample evidence that the forces that shape movement in other maturities and other segments of the bond market are also quite strong. Take a look at Figure 9-2, which shows that the yield on the 5-year T-note closely tracks the yield on the 2-year T-note, which in turn closely tracks the fed funds rate. This clearly suggests that there is a significant correlation between the yield on the 5-year T-note and the fed funds rate. Indeed, the correlation is so strong that I like to think of the 5-year note as the long bond of the short end owing to the sharp price changes often seen in the 5-year note when the market adjusts yield for expected or actual changes in the fed funds rate.

The correlation between the federal funds rate and other maturities along the yield curve extends beyond the 2- and 5-year maturities to as far out as the 30-year bond. Figure 9-3 shows the clear correlation between the 2-year note and the 30-year T-bond. As with the 5-year note, the strong correlation between the 2-year and the 30-year maturities suggests that there is significant correlation between the 30-year bond and the fed funds rate. As was mentioned earlier, however, there are many other factors that affect the behavior of long-term interest rates, and so it is important to avoid putting excessive weight on the Fed as a determinant of long-term interest rates. The other factors need to be assigned weights that depend on their relative importance at a

F i g u r e   9—2

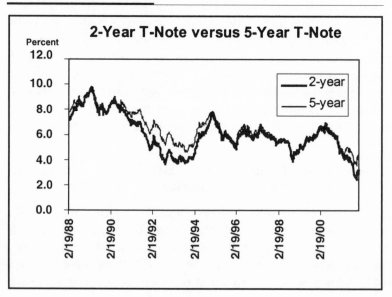

F i g u r e　9–3

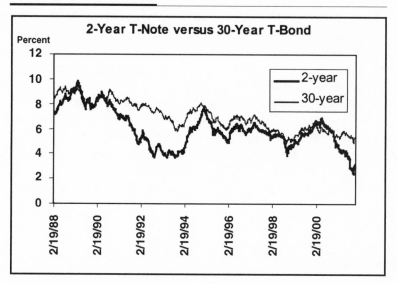

given point in time. Make no mistake, however; the Federal Reserve has an enormous effect on long-term interest rates. Indeed, long-term interest rates are said to be a bet on the future level of short-term interest rates. This is known as the *pure expectations theory*, which postulates that at any given time the yield on all maturities along the yield curve reflects the market's expectations of where short-term interest rates will be in the future.

A great deal of the bond market's time and energy is used to determine the degree to which new news and information may affect the Fed. At times it seems that the market has blinders on and looks at the world only in the context of what it means for the Fed. This helps explain why there is such a high correlation between the fed funds rate and market interest rates.

The most important point about the connection between the Fed and the bond market as it pertains to forecasting interest rates is twofold. First, keep in mind that the bond market moves in advance of the Fed. You therefore must stay abreast of the forces that can shape the bond market's perceptions of future changes in Fed policy. Second, use the 2-year T-note to gauge the market's assumptions about future changes in Fed policy and as a starting point for assessing whether those assumptions are rational in light of the underlying economic fundamentals and financial conditions. The 2-year note can tell you whether the rest of the market is set to rise or fall, since it tends to move in the same direction as the 2-year note and the 2-year note tends to respond primarily to shifts in market sentiment toward the Fed.

As you can see, the Federal Reserve is one of the biggest determinants of the behavior of the bond market. An accurate interest rate forecast is therefore highly dependent on an accurate assessment of the direction of monetary policy. Chapter 6 discussed ways to stay attuned to the Fed and to become a better Fed watcher. That chapter also discussed the many factors that shape the bond market's perception of the Fed.

INFLATION EXPECTATIONS: A WORRY IN CONSTANT FLUX

Next to the Fed, no topic obsesses the bond market more than inflation. Inflation is the bond market's nemesis because it erodes the value of a bond's cash flows. That is why when inflation accelerates, bond prices fall and yields rise: A bond is worth less when inflation is chewing away at its cash flows. Inflation is therefore at the root of *interest rate risk,* the biggest risk facing bond investors. Interest rate risk, or market risk, is defined as the risk of adverse movement in the price of a bond owing to changes in interest rates. (This topic was discussed more thoroughly in Chapter 5.) Inflation creates interest rate risk because it puts a bond investor at risk of incurring capital losses. In light of these risks, it is understandable that the bond market puts so much emphasis on inflation.

In recent times the threat of inflation has been quite low, and inflation has been dormant for a number of years. Indeed, inflation has been on a secular downward trend since the early 1980s and has been close to historical levels for about ten years now. This dormancy has created an opportunity to observe the extent to which inflation expectations play a role in shaping the ups and downs of the bond market. One might think that inflation worries would be all but gone by now, especially since it has been a generation since inflation ran rampant. To the contrary: Inflation worries remain quite measurable. The only difference now is the magnitude of the way in which the market expresses its inflation worries. Today's interest rate fluctuations may be smaller than those in past years, particularly in the 1970s and 1980s, but the fluctuations probably occur just as frequently. Thus, inflation remains a formidable force in determining the direction of interest rates.

One of the more important aspects of the bond market's fear of inflation is that its fears are not always its own. Bond investors often fear inflation not so much because they are worried about inflation themselves but because they are worried that other investors are worried about it. More important, bond investors worry that perceptible changes in inflation risks will prompt the Fed to worry about inflation and thus spur the Fed to raise interest rates in response. Thus, interest rate fluctuations that result from the bond market's concerns about inflation sometimes are related more to fears of the Fed than to fears of inflation.

The source of much of the bond market's inflation fears is the pace of economic growth. Strong economic growth tends to feed inflation fears, while slow economic growth tends to dampen them. When the economy is growing rapidly, bond investors worry that demand will exceed supply and thus result in an acceleration of inflation. Strong economic growth also tends to result in a tightening of the labor market and thus more rapid increases in labor costs. This is important because labor costs account for about 70 percent of the cost of producing goods and services. As labor costs increase, they put pressure on businesses to raise prices. This is why the bond market pays such close attention to economic data. To bond investors each economic report has implications for the pace of economic growth and the inflation outlook. This concept is discussed in greater detail in the section on the economy later in this chapter.

Two Ways to Track the Market's Inflation Expectations

Tracking the bond market's inflation expectations is a crucial part of interest rate forecasting. Gauging the market's inflation expectations is similar to gauging its expectations about the Fed in that in both cases one obtains a reference point with which to compare the market's expectations against reality as well as against the probabilistic outcomes for future events. In other words, quantifying the market's inflation expectations will help you validate or invalidate those expectations on the basis of your own subjective analysis of the underlying fundamentals. From this you can develop an interest rate forecast because you will either agree or disagree with the market's assumptions.

There are two ways to track the bond market's inflation expectations. One method utilizes the Treasury's inflation-indexed bonds, and the other utilize real interest rates. Let's take a look at both.

One of the best ways to track the bond market's assessment of inflation risks is to monitor real interest rates. As was described in Chapter 8, *real interest rates, or real yields,* are nominal interest rates minus inflation. Real yields fluctuate as the bond market's views about inflation fluctuate. Chapter 8 described the many other reasons why real yields fluctuate, but this section will focus on how to use real yields to track the bond market's inflation expectations. Figure 8-1 illustrated how real yields are almost always positive, pointing to the important role inflation plays in setting market interest rate levels. That figure suggested that market interest rates tend to track the inflation rate.

Real yields contain a significant amount of information about the bond market's inflation expectations. The information is not so much quantitative as qualitative, however, because while real yields may provide a numeric value with which to gauge inflation expectations, that numeric value is not an exact measure of those expectations; a qualitative judgment is necessary. This is true partly because real interest rates provide information about a variety of other factors that affect interest rate levels, such as competition for capital, sentiments about the Fed, and external factors. In the end, however, real interest rates tend to reflect inflation expectations more than anything else. Here is an example. Suppose the yield on the 10-year Treasury note is 5.0 percent and inflation (as gauged by the consumer price index) is running at about 2.5 percent. In this case the real yield on the 10-year T-note is 2.5 percent. Let's say that over the last five years the real yield has fluctuated in a range of 2.0 percent to 4.0 percent. With the real yield in this example at 2.5 percent, it is therefore at the lower end of its recent range. This indicates that inflation expectations are low. How do we know this? If investors were worried that the inflation rate might climb to 4.0 percent, that would put the real yield in the

10-year note at just 1.0 percent (if inflation does indeed rise to 4.0 percent), well below the "normal" range. Bond investors are unlikely to accept such a low real interest rate when the inflation rate is trending upward; they are more likely to demand an increase in the compensation for inflation risks. In such a situation investors are more likely to push the real yield up to the wider end of its normal range.

The key point is that real yields tend to be low when inflation expectations are low and high when inflation expectations are high. In addition, investors demand an increasing amount of compensation for inflation risks when the inflation rate is rising but a decreasing amount of compensation when the inflation rate is falling. In a comparison with "normal" levels, a quick glance at real yields can provide an enormous amount of insight into the bond market's inflation expectations.

Using the Treasury's Inflation-Indexed Bonds to Gauge Inflation Expectations

A second way to track the bond market's inflation expectations is to follow the yield spread between the Treasury's inflation-protected securities, commonly known as Treasury Inflation Protected Securities (TIPSs), and conventional Treasuries. As was described in Chapter 4, TIPSs provide compensation for inflation as measured by the Consumer Price Index for all Urban Consumers. The value of these inflation-indexed securities increases at the inflation rate. Holders of these securities therefore are immunized against inflation risks. The yield spread between the quoted yield-to-maturity on TIPSs and that on conventional Treasuries is the *breakeven rate*, which is used as a literal interpretation of the market's inflation expectations. Thus, if the breakeven rate on a 10-year TIPS is 2.0 percent, this indicates that bond investors expect inflation to average 2.0 percent per year over the next ten years. If the breakeven rate on a 5-year TIPS is 1.7 percent, this indicates that bond investors expect inflation to average 1.7 percent over the next five years. The formula looks like this:

Breakeven rate = quoted yield-to-maturity on conventional
Treasury security − quoted yield-to-maturity on TIPS

Let's take a brief look at why the breakeven rate is used as an indication of inflation expectations.

The first thing to note is that all the Treasury's inflation-indexed bonds pay a coupon, usually at a rate of about 3 percent. The dollar value of the cash flows paid on the semiannual coupon rate will vary, however, and will increase as daily adjustments are made to the principal value of the bonds for the indexation of the bond's value to the inflation rate (the increase in the bond's principal value owing to the indexation against inflation is called the inflation accrual). This means that holders of inflation-indexed securities will receive both an incremental return for inflation and a return over and above the inflation accrual; this is the real interest rate, and it is paid via the semiannual coupon payments. As with conventional Treasuries, the real interest rate on TIPSs will vary with the market's view of the economy, the Fed, inflation, and so forth. Both TIPSs and conventional Treasuries contain a real interest rate and compensation for inflation. On TIPSs the inflation compensation can be readily measured by simply tracking the consumer price index (CPI). On conventional Treasuries, however, inflation expectations must be measured differently. This can be calculated by subtracting real yields from nominal, or quoted, yields, with the difference representing investors' inflation expectations. A TIPS provides the information needed to do this simple calculation because its yield-to-maturity is the real yield used in the calculation.

When you look at the yield-to-maturity on a conventional Treasury, always keep in mind that you can gauge the market's inflation expectations by subtracting the yield-to-maturity of the TIPS (the real yield). This difference represents the market's inflation expectations. This method is widely used and has been lauded frequently by officials at the Federal Reserve, including Chairman Alan Greenspan, who often has cited the yield spread between conventional Treasuries and TIPSs to convey his opinions about inflation expectations.

Using the Market's Inflation Expectations to Forecast Interest Rates

Once you have a bead on the market's inflation expectations, you can begin to assess whether you believe that the market's assumptions are rational. This requires a great deal of subjective analysis, of

course, but by knowing as accurately as possible how much inflation the market expects, you will have a basis on which to say you
agree or disagree. It is far easier to say that you agree or disagree
with the market's assumptions when you can assess those assumptions accurately. This makes it easier to judge whether bond prices
are "rich" or "cheap." If, for example, owing to a number of factors,
inflation expectations fall to abnormally low levels, you may conclude that bond prices are too high relative to the inflation outlook.

A classic example of what can happen when the market's inflation expectations reach an extreme occurred in 1998 during the
Asian financial crisis. During that time inflation expectations fell
sharply, as illustrated by the sharp drop in the breakeven rate on
10-year TIPSs. Figure 9-4 clearly shows the sharp drop that occurred
in inflation expectations in 1998. As you can see from the figure, the
breakeven rate fell to as low as 0.7 percent. That meant investors
believed that inflation would average just 0.7 percent over the next
ten years. (while the decline in the breakeven rate also was related
to liquidity concerns, the bulk of the decline was related to a drop
in inflation expectations). With inflation having averaged 3.4 percent over the previous ten years, the market's inflation expectations

F i g u r e   9-4

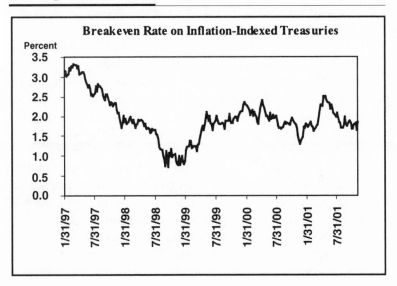

therefore deviated sharply from historical trends. To me and to many other analysts, the market's inflation expectations therefore seemed unreasonable. This provided a solid basis on which to forecast an eventual rise in interest rates. Indeed, a bear market in bonds began soon after the bond market concluded that inflation was a thing of the past. In reality, the market's inflation expectations were a sign of excess market sentiment about the inflation outlook (for more on market sentiment, see Chapter 10).

As you can see, inflation expectations play an important role in the behavior of the bond market. As inflation expectations change, bond prices move accordingly. Like many key indicators that help in formulating an interest rate forecast, inflation expectations are a moving target. However, once you get a bead on them, you are more likely to hit your target with greater precision and derive an accurate interest rate forecast. It is therefore imperative to know the market's expectations when you are developing a forecast along with the appropriate investment strategies.

THE PACE OF ECONOMIC GROWTH: HOW MUCH IS TOO MUCH?

Economic data are the grease that makes the bond market move. With each economic report, the bond market moves another stride along its uneven path. In the bond market the economy is at the root of almost every twist and turn.

As was shown above, the bond market is preoccupied mainly with two dominant influences: the Fed and inflation. These two influences generally explain the majority of the bond market's price movements. At the root of these powerful forces is the pace of economic growth. Bond investors recognize that the pace of economic growth has a direct bearing on both the Fed and inflation. That is why the bond market places so much importance on economic data.

The appendix at the end of the book contains a detailed analysis of the importance of each of the major economic reports and their impact on both the bond market and the individual investor. I feel so strongly about the importance of economic data that I placed extra emphasis on this topic in that appendix.

It is fairly easy to understand how the economy affects the bond market. As was mentioned earlier, when the economy is growing rapidly, bond investors worry that demand for goods and services will exceed available supply and result in an acceleration of inflation. Rapid economic growth worries the bond market particularly because it tends to lead to fast job growth and, hence, faster increases in labor costs, which are one of the most important determinants of inflation. This should not be surprising since labor costs account for about 70 percent of the cost of producing goods and services. In contrast, the cost of parts, raw materials, and the like accounts for only 10 percent of the inflation picture. Commodity prices are important too, of course, but they merely tend to put an exclamation point on the inflation outlook, which depends immensely more upon labor costs. As was mentioned previously, an acceleration of inflation is worrisome to bond investors mainly because inflation erodes the value of a bond's cash flows and creates market risk. However, an even bigger worry for many bond investors is the impact inflation concerns can have on the Federal Reserve, an institution that abhors inflation. Bond investors recognize that if inflation were to rear its ugly head, the Fed would raise interest rates as much as necessary to swat it down. Few things affect the bond market more than interest rate changes by the Federal Reserve.

Thus, when the bond market looks at economic data, it does so not just through its own eyes but also through the eyes of the Fed, constantly assessing inflation risks and their potential impact on monetary policy.

The focus of the bond market on economic data is almost always intense, but the specific economic reports that get the most attention often vary with shifts in the dominant influences on the economy. Occasionally, data that rarely are given more than a passing glance suddenly become a large force in shaping the bond market's direction. At other times big market movers such as the employment report carry little weight in shaping the market's direction. It is therefore important to be open-minded and flexible when one is weighing the potential impact of a set of economic reports. There are many different situations where the market's focus will change, and the changes can occur frequently. It is therefore important to look several steps ahead at the chain of events that will affect the economy in future months. It's not enough to look at the economy's current problems. The way Wall Street works, that is like looking in the past. Instead, an investor must first identify the economy's key problems or key underpinnings and try to envision the chain of events that could alter its direction.

How to Calculate the Economy's Growth Potential

The bond market can tolerate a certain amount of economic growth without sounding the inflation alarm. Specifically, the bond market is generally comfortable when economic growth is at or below the economy's growth potential. The economy's growth potential can be roughly defined as follows:

Economy's annual growth potential = annual labor force growth + annual productivity growth

This simple formula is fairly easy to understand and quite intuitive. Its objective is to measure the economy's added capacity to produce goods and services. That capacity can be measured by adding the annual rate of increase in the number of new workers in the labor force to increases in the productivity of the existing labor force.

Labor force growth can be discerned readily because it is largely related to population growth and generally increases at a pace of a little over 1.1 percent or so annually. The rate of population growth does not change much, of course, and so it is not necessary to worry about finding a value for this part of the equation. As the labor force increases, it obviously adds to the economy's ability to produce goods and services because there are more people to produce goods and services.

Productivity growth results from many factors but is rooted largely in advances in technology. As businesses deploy new technologies such as computers, software, and equipment, output per worker increases. This makes sense when one considers technology even in its most simple form. Typing and editing documents, for instance, is far simpler today than it was 20 years ago, when carbon paper was still widely used. There are many examples like this, of course, but this one should help you more clearly understand that increases in productivity translate into increases in the economy's ability to produce goods and services. In recent years productivity has advanced at a fairly rapid pace compared with previous years. Over the last 5 years, nonfarm worker productivity per hour has grown at an annual rate of about 2.3 percent compared with an average of about 1.5 percent over the previous 10 years and an average of about 2.0 percent over the last 40 years. In light of these trends it is reasonable to assume that productivity generally advances at an annual rate of about 2 percent, with a bias toward a higher figure in current times because of the enormous advances in technology and the likelihood of broadened applications of those technologies in the coming years. Indeed, the current productivity upswing, now going on for about 6 years, is young relative to past cycles, which have averaged over 20 years in length, according to data from the Federal Reserve.

The math for the economy's growth potential therefore goes like this: Add yearly growth of the labor force growth (about 1.1 percentage points) to yearly growth in productivity (about 2.3 percentage points) and we arrive at an estimate of about 3.4 percent for the economy's growth potential. Let's take this a step further to see what happens when the economy grows more slowly than its growth potential. This example will help explain why businesses lay off workers and cut spending when the economy grows slowly. It also will illustrate why bond yields tend to decline in such an environment.

Think about it like this: Say there is an economy with 100 people in the labor force who have the capacity to produce 100 units of goods to meet current demand of 100 units per year. If one new person enters the labor force, the economy's ability to produce will increase by 1 percent to 101 units. And if the same 100 people producing goods somehow become more productive and are collectively able to produce 2 percent more goods, the economy's overall ability to produce goods will increase by 3 percent to 103 units.

Here's the problem: Since the economy is capable of producing more goods than before, if demand grows at a slower pace, say, by only 2 units to reach 102, the economy will have excess capacity of 1 unit (since it has the capacity to produce 103 units). In this case the economy grew, but so did its excess capacity. The longer that trend continues, the more the excess capacity builds.

The excess capacity is manifested in both excess labor and excess capital stock (plants, equipment, technology equipment, etc.). Businesses can deal with the excess capacity in a few ways: They can shed labor, reduce capital spending, or wait for the economy to grow faster. The route they choose generally depends on the severity of the economic slowdown.

The point is that even when the economy grows, if it grows more slowly than the economy's growth potential, that will result in a buildup of excess capacity owing to increases in the labor force and productivity growth. When this happens, businesses feel compelled to reduce the excess capacity with measures that can cause a great deal of economic pain. Of course, bad news for the economy is good news for bond prices because excess capacity tends to dampen inflation pressures. When the economy grows faster than its growth potential, the excess demand for goods and services tends to put upward pressure on inflation, which is bad news for the bond market.

Using the Economy's Growth Potential to Forecast Interest Rates

Many of the bond market's price moves evolve from its sense of the degree to which the economy is growing above or below its growth potential. An accurate interest rate forecast therefore requires an estimate of the economy's growth rate relative to its growth potential as well as an assessment of the market's views on these critical issues. If your views differ from where you sense the market's views are, you can use this as a basis for forecasting a turn in interest rates. As with the Fed and inflation, your interest rate forecast begins by identifying the market's assumptions about both the economy's growth rate and its growth potential and then comparing the market's assumptions with the underlying fundamentals so that you can validate or invalidate those assumptions. From there you can generate a forecast that relies heavily on the extent to which your assumptions appear to differ from those of the market.

SECULAR VERSUS CYCLICAL INFLUENCES: KNOW THE FORCE THAT'S WITH YOU

The reasons bond yields go up and down never cease to amaze me. As Gilda Radner's Roseanne Rosannadanna used to say, "It's always something. If it's not one thing, it's another!" That's how it is in the bond market, or any other market for that matter. There is always something different pushing prices around. It's sometimes as if the proverbial invisible hand were waving its magic wand, telling the market where to go next. In reality, of course, there is a far more substantive explanation of why bond prices sometimes go up and down when there is no tangible explanation. In such cases I believe that either secular or cyclical forces can explain the movement in bond prices.

On Wall Street a *secular trend* is a long-term trend that stems from a set of factors that exert an influence for long periods of time, sometimes as much as decades. These sets of factors sometimes are called *deep fundamentals,* or fundamental forces that are so deeply rooted that they are not likely to be uprooted over short spans of time. An example of a secular trend is the decline in interest rates that began in the early 1980s and has continued to this day. Figure 9-5 shows this trend.

Cyclical trends are short-term trends that stem from short-term influences such as periodic excesses in supply and demand. In the long run cyclical forces tend to be dwarfed by secular ones and

F i g u r e   9–5

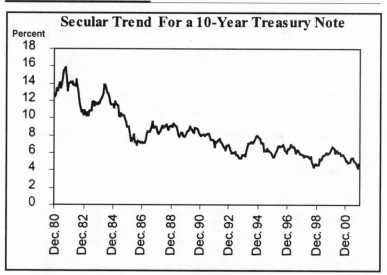

rarely disrupt long-term trends. Examples of cyclical trends include the numerous short-term bear markets in bonds that have occurred throughout the secular bull market in bonds over the last 20 years. When viewed on a long-term chart such as the one in Figure 9-5, cyclical trends appear as relatively minor blips, suggesting that cyclical forces are indeed dwarfed by secular ones. However, when viewed over shorter periods, cyclical trends appear to have a much larger impact. A good example is the bear market in bonds that occurred between the end of 1998 and the start of 2000. Figure 9-6 shows the degree to which cyclical trends can spur movements in bond prices that sometimes last for meaningful periods of time. As the figure shows, the bear market in bonds lasted close to 15 months, an eternity to traders and investors, who sometimes are preoccupied with trading patterns for the next 15 minutes!

Although secular forces are the dominant influence on the behavior of bond prices over the long run, cyclical forces can assert a powerful influence for relatively short periods lasting days, weeks, or even several years. In a sense, secular and cyclical forces alternately exert their influence like a game of Ping-Pong, with one

F i g u r e   9–6

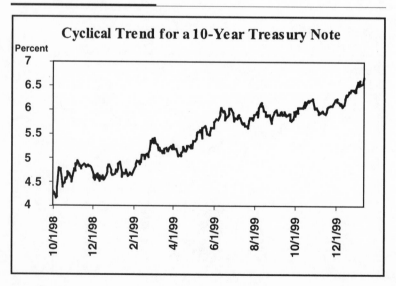

exerting more influence than the other for variable lengths of time. All the while, however, the secular influences are always present, acting as the larger force and taming the cyclical forces with a sort of gravitational pull that keeps market prices from traveling far from the secular trend.

The constant volley between the changing degrees of influence of secular and cyclical forces can be of tremendous value in formulating an interest rate forecast. For example, awareness of secular forces can help establish an idea of where the limitations are on the degree to which cyclical forces can push interest rates higher or lower. Cyclical forces, for their part, are by definition almost always destined to be exhausted at some point, and for a forecaster it is merely a matter of identifying the means by which they will run out of gas. Let's take a look at a couple of examples.

As shown in Figure 9-7, the bond market entered a cyclical bear market at the end of 1993 that lasted about a year. As you can see in the figure, the yield on the 10-year Treasury note went up sharply, rising roughly 2 percentage points. That yield increase equated to a roughly 20 percent drop in price, which was one of the biggest price declines in a generation. There were

F i g u r e   9–7

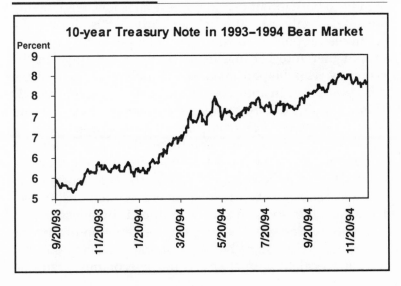

a number of reasons for the decline, most of which were related to factors with a relatively short half-life. In other words, cyclical factors were the main force behind the bear market. Specifically, at the end of 1993, after several years of sluggish economic growth, the U.S. economy began to show signs of gaining vigor. Indeed, in the fourth quarter of 1993 the gross domestic product (GDP) grew at an annualized rate of 6.2 percent, the fastest pace in almost ten years and well above the average growth rate of 2.0 percent seen over the previous five years. The economic performance was led by strength in consumer spending, particularly on new homes and cars, and was supported by strong job growth and declining unemployment. Bond investors worried that the strong demand for goods and services, along with strong job growth, would put upward pressure on inflation. Indeed, a sharp rise in commodity prices seemed to validate that thesis and the cyclical forces behind the inflation pressures appeared to be quite strong. In a way, the bond market's worries appeared to be rational.

The bond market might have been missing the forest from the trees, however, choosing to place more emphasis on cyclical forces than on secular ones. Inflation never did accelerate as much as the bond market had feared, owing to powerful secular forces that limited the actual rise in inflation and thus kept interest rates on a downward track. There were a few secular forces that helped keep both inflation and interest rates low. First, owing to the decline in interest rates in the early 1980s during the Reagan administration, U.S. businesses had a powerful incentive to invest and therefore became increasingly competitive in the global economy. This helped make the United States one of the lowest-cost producers in the world for the first time in over 20 years. This encouraged U.S. companies to keep prices low and grab lost market share back from foreign competitors. Second, lower tax rates fostered economic conditions that were conducive to creating strong economic growth. This helped strengthen the U.S. dollar and reduce the cost of U.S. imports and, hence, inflation pressures. Third, cuts in government regulations implemented during the Reagan years reduced business costs, reducing inflation pressures. Fourth, the combination of low tax rates and reduced regulations helped foster an environment that unleashed the so-called animal spirits in the economy, resulting in product innovations that paved the way for a productivity boom that would help quell inflation pressures.

The bear market in bonds that occurred in 1994 is an excellent illustration of the alternating influences of secular and cyclical forces. In 1994 cyclical forces became immensely important for a while, only to succumb to more powerful secular forces. That episode illustrates the importance of recognizing which of the two forces is likely to be dominant at any given time. This is a difficult task, but it is made easier when the cyclical forces push market prices to levels that begin to go against the secular trend. When this happens, the first step is to question whether there is ample justification for believing that key secular forces have been uprooted. If there is not, and it's generally likely that there will not have been, an investor should consider countertrend investment strategies that take advantage of the apparent dislocation in the market. However, one must beware of the powerful effects of the cyclical influences because they can last a while, as was seen in 1994. In cases such as that an investor must have a basis for believing that the cyclical forces are exhausting themselves before deciding to engage in a risky countertrend trade. When there is ample reason to believe that the cyclical forces will be exhausted, it is time to scale into strategies that will benefit from a return to the secular trend.

Again, the key is to ask yourself which of the two trends is more likely to exert the most influence on the market over a given period. From there you can begin to focus on the forces that are most relevant to the market's trend and on whether they eventually will either peter out or turn the market upside down. When it seems that an invisible hand is pushing bond prices up or down, chalk it up to either secular or cyclical forces. Use the force.

THE MARKET'S TECHNICAL CONDITION: FUNDAMENTALLY IMPORTANT IN FORECASTING INTEREST RATES

In the bond market, as in other markets, there are usually three types of investors. The first relies almost exclusively on market fundamentals such as the Fed, the economy, and inflation, preferring to base investment strategies on qualitative judgments. The second relies mostly on technical factors, preferring to base investment strategies on charts and quantitative analyses. The third combines fundamental and technical analyses, formulating strategies by utilizing the most important elements and signals from the first two approaches.

I must admit to having been a skeptic about technical analysis early on. After all, it seems irrational to think that one could determine the market's next move by using a chart. Yet after a while I came to recognize that technical analysis is about more than charts and includes a wide array of other factors related to market sentiment, capital flows, and so forth. Moreover, it also became clear to me that because many other investors were looking at and acting on technical factors, those factors can become a self-fulfilling prophecy. You would be surprised at how many of some of Wall Street's best-known investors incorporate some form of technical analysis into their formulations of investment strategies.

The fact is that even if you had perfect information about the bond market's underlying fundamentals, you still might not be able to predict where it is headed next. There are simply too many other factors that could exert an influence on the market to rely solely on fundamental factors. I say this, however, firmly believing that the best route to an accurate market forecast requires an accurate assessment of market fundamentals above all else. I am a fundamentalist through and through. However, as I just said, even with perfect information on market fundamentals I could still wind up eating crow. Therefore, it is imperative to incorporate some analysis of the major technical factors that can influence the market's behavior. Doing this will augment your fundamental analyses and thereby help you steer clear of wrongheaded forecasts and investment decisions. It also can strengthen or weaken your convictions about particular investment ideas.

KEY TECHNICAL FACTORS THAT INFLUENCE THE BOND MARKET

Market Sentiment

From tulips to Treasuries, tracking market sentiment has been one of the most reliable ways to forecast future price changes in stocks, bonds, commodities, tulips—you name it. Extreme bullishness and extreme bearishness have foretold key turning points in asset prices for centuries. The same principles apply to the bond market, and there are a number of ways to track bond market sentiment. Chapter 10 thoroughly outlines the most reliable indicators of market sentiment that for many years have reliably pointed to excesses in bullish and bearish sentiment.

When market sentiment reaches an extreme, the bond market often is poised for a reversal. High levels of bullish sentiment, for example, tend to indicate that a large degree of bullish news already has been factored into prices. This makes it difficult for the market to gain further even if additional bullish news materializes. This is an example of how forecasts that are based exclusively on fundamental analysis can go awry because it shows that even with an accurate economic forecast, it is possible to forecast the market's price movements inaccurately. Technical influences such as market sentiment are therefore an essential element of an accurate market forecast.

Mortgage-Backed Hedging Activity

A technical factor that often exerts a great deal of influence on the bond market is the hedging activity tied to the mortgage-backed securities market wherein portfolio managers buy and sell Treasuries to offset prepayment risks. As was described in Chapter 4, mortgage-backed securities are debt instruments backed by a pool of mortgages, generally residential mortgages. These mortgages often are prepaid early as homeowners refinance their homes or move from one home to another. When a mortgage is prepaid, a percentage of the mortgage-backed securities of which that mortgage is a part also are prepaid. This is known as the *constant prepayment rate* (CPR). The prepayment rate increases when interest rates fall as more people refinance their homes or buy new ones. This causes more mortgages to be paid off more frequently. These prepayments have a direct impact on portfolios that include mortgage securities because the prepayments result in an increase in the amount of cash in the portfolios and a decrease in their security holdings. Mortgage portfolios therefore face reinvestment risks associated with having to reinvest the cash from the prepayments at lower and lower interest rates. Moreover, these portfolios are at risk of performing poorly compared with other portfolios as well as against the benchmark indexes that are used to judge their performance. This occurs because portfolios with mortgage-backed securities wind up having relatively more cash and fewer securities than do other fixed-income portfolios. This puts a holder of mortgage-backed securities at risk of missing out on profiting from the increase in bond prices that results from the decline in interest rates.

To guard against the risks associated with falling interest rates, mortgage-backed portfolio managers buy U.S. Treasuries to hedge against the damages caused by rising prepayments. This helps assure that their portfolios will not get stuck with too few securities and too much cash that they must reinvest at lower and lower interest rates. This way, when prepayments rise, holders of mortgage-backed securities in essence have a replacement security waiting in the wings to replace their prepaid mortgage-backed securities.

This buying can have a substantial impact on the bond market because it can accelerate market trends. Thus, during refinancing booms mortgage-related buying of Treasuries increases, putting additional upward pressure on already rising prices. Similarly, when a refinancing boom ends (as a result of a rise in market interest rates that pushes mortgage rates higher), the hedges that were bought by holders of mortgage-backed securities during the refinancing boom begin to be sold because the hedges are no longer needed. This accelerates the downward tract in bond prices. The three most recent examples of this are the refinancing booms of 1993, 1998, and 2001. As can be seen in Figure 9-8, refinancing activity during those periods was extraordinary, as measured by mortgage applications for refinancing. In each case, there were numerous occasions when mortgage-related activity pushed prices sharply higher or sharply lower.

Because of the high degree of influence of big shifts in mortgage refinancing activity, it is important to track refinancing activity for potential market impact. An investor can do this by following the data on mortgage applications released every Wednesday by the Mortgage Bankers Association.

New Supply

In Economics 101 students are taught that increases in supply result in a decrease in price and that decreases in supply result in

F i g u r e   9–8

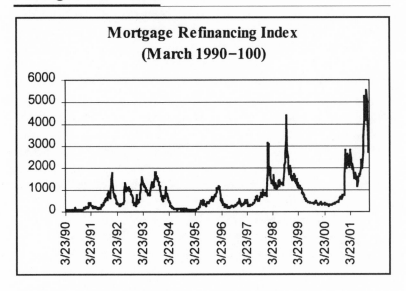

an increase in price. Fitting this theory to the bond market, an increase in the supply of bonds should result in a decrease in bond prices (and a rise in yields), while a decrease in the supply of bonds should result in an increase in bond prices (and a decrease in yields). This makes sense because there is a finite amount of capital in the world. Surprisingly, however, increases and decreases in the supply of bonds do not always have the effect that the laws of supply and demand dictate. Indeed, there are times when the bond market seems to defy those laws. It is therefore important to recognize the various ways in which changes in the supply of bonds affect the bond market.

There are two classic examples of the varying ways in which supply-related factors can influence the bond market. In the 1980s and early 1990s, for example, it was felt that the sharp increase in the U.S. budget deficit and the subsequent rise in the new supply of Treasuries would result in lower prices and thus higher interest rates. However, interest rates fell throughout that period. This was due largely to very positive secular forces that helped tame inflation pressures. The fact that bond prices rose even though supply had increased illustrates how fundamental factors, particularly

with respect to inflation expectations, are significantly more important than technical factors. This said, it is important to note that
throughout the 1980s and early 1990s there were numerous
episodes in which the increase in supply had a large impact on
bond prices, although for short periods. Specifically, there were
occasions when investors needed to be enticed to buy the ever-
increasing supply of Treasuries. On these occasions investors
demanded price markdowns known as *concessions*, in which the
primary dealers basically knocked prices lower to lure investors.
One of the more interesting aspects of those episodes was that
investors rarely sought a concession when market fundamentals
were bullish; however, the more bearish fundamentals were, the
greater the concessions would be.

The fact that investors are indifferent toward a concession
when they are bullish on bond prices is evidence that the laws of
supply and demand do not always apply in the bond market. In
other words, increases or decreases in supply do not always result
in price changes that fit the changes in supply. In the end, inflation
expectations and other key fundamental factors are much more
important. A second example of this is Japan, where there have
been enormous increases in the supply of new Japanese bonds yet
there are extremely low interest rates. Why? Japan has been expe-
riencing deflation for many years. Thus, to investors in Japanese
bonds, the driving force behind their purchase decisions is not supply but inflation expectations.

Therefore, investors must bear in mind that while supply matters, the extent to which it matters depends on the market's attitude toward fundamental factors, particularly inflation.

Foreign Investors Have Hearty Appetites for U.S. Bonds

Foreign investors are the single biggest holders of U.S. Treasuries
and own an increasing share of U.S. corporate and agency securities. Indeed, foreign investors have poured money into U.S. markets since 1996. The reason, of course, relates largely to the strong
performance of the U.S. economy relative to the rest of the world.
Foreign investors have invested in the United States to get superior
rates of return. Figure 9-9 shows the enormous increase in foreign

F i g u r e   9—9

Net Foreign Investment in the United States.

	Equities	Corporate Bonds	Agency Bonds	Foreign Direct Investment
1994	$0.9	$38.0	$21.7	$47.4
1995	$16.6	$58.1	$28.7	$59.6
1996	$11.1	$83.7	$41.7	$89.0
1997	$66.8	$84.0	$49.8	$109.3
1998	$43.8	$122.4	$54.6	$193.4
1999	$94.3	$158.9	$94.1	$275.5
2000	$174.8	$184.1	$152.8	$316.5
12 months ended 8/01	$138.9	$234.0	$169.9	$297.4

Source: Stone & McCarthy, U.S. Treasury, Federal Reserve

investment in U.S. assets that has taken place in recent years. The table helps highlight why it is critical to stay abreast of factors that may affect foreign investment in the United States. Note that while net foreign investment in Treasuries has not changed much in recent years, this partly relates to the fact that the total amount of Treasuries outstanding has decreased in that period. Nevertheless, foreign investors still own over 40 percent of all publicly traded Treasuries.

There are a few key factors to track in judging whether there may be shifts in the level of foreign investment in the United States:

- The U.S. dollar
- U.S. productivity growth
- The inflation rate
- International economic conditions
- The relative performance of the U.S. stock market

By themselves all these factors can have a large impact on the level of foreign investment. One must keep in mind that the most important determinant of foreign investment is the pace of U.S. economic growth compared to the pace abroad. Over the last ten years, for example, economic growth in the United States has consistently and significantly outpaced economic growth in both Europe and Japan. This has provided a powerful incentive for foreign investors to invest in U.S. assets and therefore has helped keep U.S. interest rates low.

TECHNICAL ANALYSIS

As was mentioned earlier, when it comes to fundamental and technical analysis, investors basically can be divided into three camps: the technicians, the fundamentalists, and the hybrids. While one camp may put more or less emphasis on technical analysis than the others, large numbers of investors use technical analysis in one way or another. Collectively, followers of technical analysis therefore can have a large impact on the behavior of bond prices.

The nature of technical analysis increases its impact on markets. Generally this is an exact science, and followers of technical analysis buy and sell securities at prices dictated by the signals sent by the various forms of technical analysis. Since most of these price points are drawn from the same set of analyses, followers of technical analysis often are prompted to buy and sell at the same prices. Because they act virtually in unison, technical analysis often becomes a self-fulfilling prophecy. This is why it is important to be aware of market levels that may trigger technically driven buying and selling.

It is important to keep in mind that technically driven trading is most prevalent in the futures market. As a result, most technical buy and sell signals tend to be based on futures prices rather than on yields. Nevertheless, both prices and yields serve as important support and resistance levels as well as trigger points for purchases and sales.

There are several types of technical analysis I have found to be reliable in terms of conjoining technical analysis with fundamental analysis. I am a fundamentalist at heart, and so I have been very choosy about applying technical analysis to the formulation of investment strategies. Moreover, as a precondition for weaving technical analysis into my fundamental analysis of the market outlook, I first assess whether technical factors may be ascending in importance in the market outlook. This becomes obvious when the market's behavior begins to depart from market fundamentals and/or when market trends accelerate. I have found that the following widely used forms of technical analysis are the important ones in terms of market impact:

- Fibonacci levels
- Benchmark yield levels
- Previous highs and lows
- Relative strength indexes
- Moving averages

The methodology used to compute the prices that correspond to each of these analyses is sometimes a bit complex, so let's take a brief look at each one and focus particularly on the how to apply it to the bond market.

Fibonacci Levels

The origin of Fibonacci analysis is quite interesting. Fibonacci is the name of a mathemetician who lived in Pisa, Italy, around 1170 to 1240; his first name was Leonardo. To investors one of Fibonacci's most important theories relates to the so-called *golden mean*, which is basically a ratio that appears to be present in the growth patterns of many things in nature, including petals on a flower, the spiral formed by a shell, and pinecones. Fibonacci discovered a number series from which the golden mean could be derived. Beginning with the sequence 0, 1, 1, 2, 3, 5, 8, 13, 21, etc., each number is the sum of the two preceding numbers. Dividing each number in the series by the one that precedes it produces a ratio of about 1.618034, which is equal to the golden mean. The inverse of that number is 61.8 percent. What's fascinating is that so much of human nature seems to relate to the golden mean ratio of 1.618034.

From Pisa to Wall Street, Fibonacci's work has found a home. The financial markets use Fibonacci analysis to determine support and resistance levels. In theory, after a specified move in the market—particularly a significant move—market prices will retrace a certain percentage of the original move. This is intuitive and is consistent with the normal patterns of markets. The Fibonacci retracement percentages are 23.6 percent, 38.2 percent, 50.0 percent, and 61.8 percent. Retracements of these percentages are considered normal consolidations of market prices. Retracements beyond these percentages suggest that the previous market move has been invalidated and a full retracement of that move will occur. There is a bit of fuzziness to this, however. In most cases a retracement greater than 50 percent will invalidate a previous market move and thus suggest that a full retracement is under way. In some cases, however, a market can retrace 61.8 percent of a move yet maintain its trend once the consolidation phase has ended. Many analysts believe that a 61.8 percent retracement is normal. I have found, however, that a retracement of more than 50 percent often portends a full retracement.

Here's an example. If the price of a security rises from 90 to 100, a normal Fibonacci retracement could take the security down to 95 (a 50 percent retracement of the 10-point gain). A 61.8 percent Fibonacci retracement could take the security down to 93.82. If the security holds those support levels, the upward trend remains intact. If the levels are breached, the 10-point gain is invalidated and a reversal back to 90 should be expected.

Thus, to use Fibonacci levels, pick a specific market move and do the math. You can pick almost any price move over any period of time, depending on the market move you believe is ripe for or in the middle of consolidation.

Benchmark Yield Levels

As occurs when the Dow Jones Industrial Average reaches round numbers such as 10,000, the bond market tends to place a disproportionate degree of emphasis on round benchmark yield levels. A yield of 6 percent, for example, tends to be looked at as a key support and resistance level. Other key support and resistance levels tend to be in increments of 25 basis points, such as 6.25 percent and 5.75 percent. In light of the widespread recognition of these key levels, a breach of them tends to spark technical buying and selling. Once they are approached, failure to breach benchmark yield levels tends to push the market in the opposite direction. That is why if you are considering liquidating a security at a benchmark yield level, you should consider placing your price a few basis points short of that level. For example, if yields are falling (prices are rising) and you are considering selling your bond at 5.0 percent, consider selling it at 5.03 percent instead so that you will not run the risk of missing the sell point completely because of the market's failure to breach the benchmark level.

Previous Highs and Lows

When traders look for support and resistance levels, a convenient source is the most recent highs and lows in the futures price or the cash yield. For example, in the futures market the previous day's high and low are looked at as resistance and support levels, respectively. Breaks of these levels often spark an acceleration of the market's price movement. Highs and lows for the previous day, week, month, and so on, frequently are used by bond investors as key levels to track and as a basis for buying and selling securities.

Relative Strength Indexes

The math behind the relative strength index (RSI) is quite complex, and so we'll leave it to the mathematicians and computers, but RSIs are nonetheless easy to understand and use. RSIs basically measure the degree to which the bond market is overbought or oversold and are based on a security's past price behavior. RSIs are expressed on a scale of 0 to 100. In the bond market, an RSI of 30 or lower indicates that the market is oversold while a reading of 70 or higher indicates that the market is overbought. I have found that the 9-day RSI gives one of the best signals of the market's condition, and it is one of the most popular parameters. The second most frequently used is the 14-day RSI. There is little room for subjective analysis of the RSI, and so when either the 9-day or the 14-day RSI is in overbought or oversold territory, one should look for the market to reverse course and position oneself accordingly. One must keep in mind that the RSI could stay in overbought or oversold territory long enough to cause a trading position to go awry. Therefore, technical indicators such as the RSI should not carry excessive weight in the investment decision.

Moving Averages

Moving averages serve as support and resistance levels. A moving average is simply the average price (usually the closing price) of a security for a specified number of trading days. For example, a 10-day moving average is the average closing price of the last ten trading sessions. Moving averages are useful because they give investors a sense of the midpoint of the most recent trading range. A break above or below the moving average therefore sends a signal about whether the market may be entering a new trend. The most commonly used moving averages are 20-day, 30-day, 40-day, 100-day, and 200-day averages. The best one to use depends on whether an investor is looking at the market's short-term or long-term trends. The 200-day moving average tends to be very important to investors because it is rarely breached and relates to the long-term trend.

There are many other forms of technical analysis, but I believe the ones mentioned above are some of the most effective. Chapter 11 describes a number of other indicators in the futures market that can be used to gauge the market's technical condition.

SUMMARY AND CONCLUSION

Looking beyond the basics, in this chapter we discussed:

- Understanding the many reasons why bond yields move up and down is an essential part of interest rate forecasting.
- The five elements of an accurate interest rate forecast are monetary policy, inflation expectations, the pace of economic growth, secular versus cyclical influences, and the market's technical condition.
- In assessing each of these major influences, it is important to ask several questions: How much inflation is the bond market priced for, and are its expectations reasonable or do they reflect excesses in market sentiment? How much economic growth is the bond market priced for, and what are the chances that this growth rate will be realized? Are cyclical or secular forces likely to be the dominant influence in the short run, and have cyclical forces pushed bond yields into territory that conflicts with secular trends? What is the market's technical condition, and what are the technical influences that might upend conclusions drawn about the market outlook from an analysis of market fundamentals?
- Combined, the answers to these questions provide a solid basis on which to build an interest rate forecast. From there, a wealth of investment strategies can be formulated along with the convictions needed to implement them.

CHAPTER TEN

From Tulips to Treasuries: Tracking Market Sentiment to Forecast Market Behavior

Tracking market sentiment has been one of the most reliable ways to forecast price changes in stocks, bonds, commodities, tulips—you name it. Extreme bullishness and extreme bearishness have foretold key turning points in asset prices for centuries. The same principles apply to the bond market, and there are a number of ways to track bond market sentiment. In this chapter you will learn about the four indicators that are most closely correlated with key turning points in the bond market. These indicators can be used not only to forecast the future direction of the bond market but also to forecast the future performance of both the stock market and the economy.

On Wall Street one of the best ways to forecast whether the markets are headed up or down is to assess whether investors are bullish or bearish. The theory is that if everyone is bullish, the market is likely to fall. Conversely, if everyone is bearish, the market is likely to rise. Market history is strewn with periods when this time-tested theory has proved true. The demise of the dot-com stocks is the most recent and dramatic example of this and provides a clear illustration of the value of using market sentiment as a contrary indicator.

The reason why extremes in market sentiment typically portend market reversals is fairly simple. If the preponderance of investors is either very bullish or very bearish, this most likely means that market prices fully reflect sentiments about the market's underlying fundamentals. In other words, extreme bullishness or bearishness tends to reflect the digestion of and reaction to a set of bullish or bearish news, respectively, in the past, present, and near future. For example, if over a number of months the equity market falls because of widespread pessimism about the state of the economy, the decline probably means that a large amount of bearish corporate and economic news has already been priced in. Therefore, if more bad news on the economy rolls in, few investors are likely to be surprised and stock prices probably will not move much lower on the news. Here's where smart investors have an opportunity to make money from such a situation: With market pessimism at an extreme and most investors therefore on the lookout for more bad corporate and economic news, even a small degree of good news probably will cause stocks to move sharply higher as investors scramble to get on board. A smart investor buys stocks when pessimism is pervasive and a large amount of bearish news already has been factored into prices. Similarly, when most investors are bullish on stocks or other assets, they become vulnerable to bad news and can readily fall if the news do not fit with investors' notion of a perfect world. Can you say "bubble"? Unfortunately, far too many investors in dot-com stocks know this word all too well.

Blame it on human nature, perhaps. Generations of investors have gone through unavoidable bouts of extreme emotion where rational thinking has been cast aside. In such cases emotions, not fundamentals, drive the market. Fear and greed become the dominant influences on prices, driving the markets to extreme levels.

A classic example of this was the great tulip mania that occurred in Holland in the period 1634–1637. During those years horticultural experiments created new exotic tulips that the common people of Holland craved not only for their beauty but also as a status symbol. Before long buyers who sought tulip bulbs for their beauty gave way to speculators who merely sought financial gain. Local market exchanges developed from the craze, and bulbs were widely traded.

At the height of the tulip mania in 1635 a single bulb was sold for the following items:

4 tons of wheat
8 tons of rye
1 bed

4 oxen

8 pigs

12 sheep

1 suit of clothes

2 casks of wine

4 tons of beer

2 tons of butter

1,000 pounds of cheese

1 silver drinking cup

The present value of these items is roughly $35,000—for a single bulb! What followed, of course, was a reality check in 1637 that brought prices back down to earth, and prices have never looked back.

Modern times have not been without similar bouts of mania-oriented speculation, the most recent of which was the rise and fall of the dot-com stocks in 2000. The fact that the dot-com bubble occurred with such magnitude in an era of tremendous sophistication clearly illustrates that no generation can escape the power of its emotions. It's human nature.

Extreme sentiment results partly because individuals tend to put excessive weight on their most recent experience and unjustifiably extrapolate from recent trends and what those trends say about the future. In other words, when prices move sharply in one direction for a sustained period, individuals tend to believe that the trend will continue even though it may not be supported by underlying fundamentals and may be against statistical odds. Individuals therefore have a tendency to become overly optimistic when prices are rising and overly pessimistic when prices are falling.

Compounding investors' tendency to put too much weight on their most recent experience is their tendency to adopt a herd mentality when the herd starts running. The herd mentality that tends to develop in the financial markets is no different from the herd mentality seen in holiday seasons gone by, when people rushed to the stores to buy Cabbage Patch dolls, Tickle-Me-Elmos, and Pokemons. Individuals have a tendency to adopt the attitudes of other individuals when they observe that large numbers of people have the same attitude.

It is fair to say that human behavior is not going to change anytime soon, and so there is every reason to incorporate an analysis of market sentiment into one's investment strategies. This is one of the essential elements of investing, and it can be applied to virtually every market.

THE BOND MARKET GOES TO EXTREMES TOO

While the type of extreme speculation that has roiled other markets rarely infects the bond market, bouts of speculative excess and extreme emotions frequently play a large role in the bond market's behavior. It is easy to see how when one considers that in a market as large as the bond market there are obviously large numbers of participants who are subject to the same human emotions that create excesses in other markets.

Tracking investor sentiment in the bond market can enhance your investment returns in bonds significantly and help enhance the returns on your other financial investments too. The main benefit is the way it will help you time investments better. If, for example, market sentiment appears to be at a level that historically has indicated that investors may be excessively bullish, you might consider delaying a purchase of bonds until prices retreat a bit. Similarly, if market sentiment appears to indicate excess bearishness, you might want to hasten purchases of bonds or perhaps be opportunistic and buy bonds for a capital gain if achieving capital gains is one of your investment objectives.

Beyond the benefits to bond investors, tracking investor sentiment in the bond market can help an investor forecast changes in stock prices and the economy. The basic premise is this: Because the bond market's behavior tends to be influenced strongly by its expectations about the economy and macroeconomic factors, when bond market sentiment reaches an extreme, that extreme is a reflection of sentiment about the future direction of the economy as well as about bond prices. In other words, when bond market sentiment is at an extreme, sentiment about the economy must be at an extreme too. You therefore can apply your analysis of bond market sentiment to potential turning points in the economy and/or stock prices. Here is an example. Say bond market sentiment is extremely bullish because bond investors are very pessimistic about the economy (bond investors benefit when the economy is weak because inflation tends to be low in such an environment). In such a situation the bond market's pessimism about the economy is likely to be reflected in the stock market too. After all, bond investors also buy stocks and vice versa, and both bond and stock investors are exposed to basically the same information about the economy. Therefore, if bond market sentiment reaches an extreme because of extreme sentiments about the economy, you can assume that sentiments toward the economy in other markets also are likely to be near extremes. Equity investors therefore should track bond market sentiment to help them form judgments about the future direction of stock prices, which are influenced significantly by the economy's performance just as bond prices are.

The tendency of markets to reach extreme valuations will exist as long as humans—not machines—are making the investment decisions. It's human nature for investors to fall victim to fear and greed. Emotions therefore play an important role in the behavior of the markets, and it would be extremely naive to think that this will change anytime soon. Assessing market sentiment is therefore a worthy endeavor. I cannot imagine assessing the markets without including an assessment of market sentiment. After all, a forecast of the direction of market prices is essentially a forecast of the behavior of people. Therefore, it is essential to incorporate the human element into the formulation of investment strategies. You'll spot more risks and opportunities in the process.

IS THE MARKET LONG OR SHORT? THE ANSWER COULD DETERMINE YOUR NEXT TRADE

In the bond market one of the best ways to gauge investor sentiment is to track the aggregate positions of bond investors. In other words, ask yourself if investors are long or short. The answer will give you a sense of whether market sentiment is at an extreme and is poised for a reversal. For example, a market that is very long is not likely to gain much when investors are already fully invested and a large amount of bullish news already has been factored into prices. Similarly, a market that is very short is not likely to fall much further when investors already are holding large short positions and a large amount of bearish news already has been factored into

prices. Historically, and as one might expect, when key indicators
have suggested that the market's aggregate position is either very
long or very short, the market has tended to move in the opposite
direction soon afterward. We will explain how you can tell whether
the market is long or short in this chapter.

FOR EXTREME MARKET SENTIMENT TO REVERSE, CATALYSTS OFTEN ARE NEEDED

The timing of reversals in extreme market sentiment varies, of
course, and knowing when a reversal will occur is one of the more
challenging aspects of using market sentiment to forecast market
behavior. That is why it is extremely important to consider whether
a catalyst may be needed before an extreme market condition is
reversed. In most cases a catalyst of some sort is necessary before
the reversal begins. The form the catalyst will take is often
unknowable and often becomes clear only after the catalyst has
sparked the reversal. This said, when market sentiment is at an
extreme, the market is extremely susceptible to a wide variety of
information that may be at odds with the entrenched views that are
at the root of the extreme sentiment. This is the case because by definition, market sentiment reaches extremes because investors have
taken into account only one possible outcome in regard to future
events. As a result, the market essentially puts itself into a box,
requiring the preponderance of new information to fit its one-sided
view. It therefore becomes increasingly likely that new information
will surface that conflicts with the market's one-sided views and
will upend the market's existing trend. Therefore, while there may
be times when it is important to wait for a catalyst before conclud-
ing that extreme market sentiment will be reversed, it is often not
necessary to wait for one since the very nature of the extreme sentiment increases the likelihood that a catalyst will come along.

Once a catalyst comes along, abrupt reversals often emerge
and price movements can be quite sharp. The depth and duration
of the reversals depend on the extent to which sentiment is at an
extreme and the nature of the catalyst that sparks the reversal.

The behavior of the bond market and other markets in the
aftermath of periods when market sentiment has reached an
extreme has proved time and time again that tracking market sen-

timent is one of the most important elements of formulating invest-ment strategies. In the bond market there are four key indicators that have been excellent indicators of market sentiment and hence reliable indicators of future market behavior. Combined, they send powerful signals about market sentiment:

- The put/call ratio
- The Commodity Futures Trading Commission's Commitments of Traders report
- Aggregate duration surveys
- The spread between 2-year T-notes and the federal funds rate

Let's take a look at each of these indicators. Keep in mind that although each indicator has somewhat different information con-tent, it is best to use the indicators together to get the most reliable signal.

THE PUT/CALL RATIO

The put/call ratio is a popular gauge of market sentiment that is used by stock and bond investors alike. It is simply a measure of the daily trading volume in put options compared with the daily trading volume in call options. Since puts are a bearish bet on the future direction of the market and calls are a bullish bet, extreme volume in either one is a sign of excess sentiment.

A time-tested indicator in the stock market, the put/call ratio has reliably pointed to excesses in bullish and bearish sentiment and, hence, to turning points in stock prices. In early 2000, for example, the put/call ratio accurately pointed to excess optimism about the outlook for equities. The same thing has held true in the bond market, which follows the inverse of the ratio—the call/put ratio—instead. The call/put ratio has been a great guide to spotting tops and bottoms in the bond market.

Bond investors look at the inverse of the put/call ratio because call volume generally exceeds put volume, resulting in a call/put ratio of over 1.0, where 1.0 indicates that one call traded for every put. Investors prefer to quote ratios when they are over 1.0. In the stock market put volume typically exceeds call volume; that is, the put/call ratio is generally greater than 1.0. Equity investors therefore prefer to follow the put/call ratio. Call volume in the bond market tends to be higher than put volume because investors generally are more concerned about sudden increases in prices than about decreases. This is the case because there are many more events that could cause bond prices to suddenly surge than to fall. When bond investors buy call options they are buying protection against unexpected events. This is different from the way it is in the stock market, where most sudden moves tend to be downward and investors buy puts for protection against sudden market declines. After all, who ever heard of a *meltup* in stock prices?

In the bond market, the bond options used most widely to track the call/put ratio is trade at the Chicago Board of Trade (CBOT). Trading volume in the CBOT's contracts is quite high, and participation in T-bond options includes a wide variety of investors. The CBOT's options therefore capture investor sentiment well.

The specific options bond investors use to track market sentiment are the CBOT's options on 30-year Treasury bonds and 10-year T-note futures. Historically, the call/put ratio on T-bonds has been the better indicator of the two mainly because the T-bond contract usually has been more active and most of the speculative flow has resided there. One might wonder why Treasury bond futures are still used when the supply of Treasury bonds is shrinking as a result of the U.S. government's debt reduction program and intention to reduce the issuance of long-term maturities. Although the supply of U.S. Treasury bonds is shrinking relative to the supply of Treasury notes, it is still useful to look at options activity in T-bond futures because there is still a significant amount of speculative activity in that area. After all, there are still hundreds of billions of dollars worth of Treasury bonds maturing in more than ten years. Moreover, the Treasury bond future is more volatile than the 10-year note's future because of differences in maturity. Speculators tend to gravitate toward volatile instruments, and it is the speculative fervor of the market that we are most interested in gauging. Nevertheless, the 10-year T-note also can be used as an indicator of sentiment and is a great gauge of the extent to which mortgage-related activity may be causing excesses in market sentiment (investors with mortgage-backed portfolios tend to buy call options when interest rates are falling to hedge against rising prepayments of their mortgage securities, which are prepaid at an increasing rate when mortgage rates fall and households refinance).

The best way to use the call/put ratio is to compare its 10-day average to its 1-year average. The 10-day average works well because it removes a great deal of daily noise from the analysis. When the 10-day average moves sharply above or below the 1-year average, it generally indicates that market sentiment is moving toward an extreme. For a number of years the 1-year average of the call/put ratio was fairly steady at about 1.15:1. In more recent times, however, it drifted closer to 1.25:1 owing to the bullish climate that developed in the bond market after the decline of the stock market in 2000 and 2001 and the weakening in the economy during that time. Thus, it is best to use a reference point for the 1-year average somewhere between 1.15:1 and 1.25:1 and to vary the reference point depending on the economic and investment climate. Figure 10-1 shows the behavior of the call/put ratio in recent years.

Historically, when the 10-day average has exceeded 1.4:1 (1.4 calls traded for every put), this frequently has foreshadowed an impending decline in the bond market caused by excess optimism. At 0.8:1 or below (0.8 call traded for every put) the bond market generally has been ripe for a rally because of excess pessimism.

F i g u r e   10–1

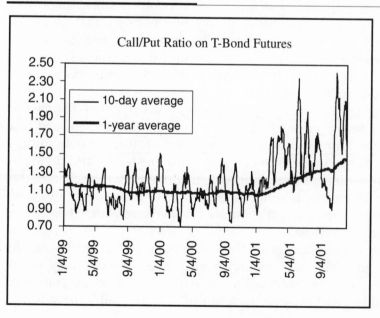

When the call/put ratio is at either of these extremes, it is usually not long before the bond market turns. How long? It is usually a matter of weeks, if not days, before the turn occurs. Therefore, when you see the call/put ratio at either of the two extremes, seek possible catalysts that might send the market in a new direction and formulate your investment strategies accordingly. Typical catalysts include fundamental factors such as economic data and monetary policy. It is important to keep in mind, however, that as with all indicators, it is best to have confirmation from multiple sentiment indicators of the apparent excesses in market sentiment before making final decisions on an investment strategy.

Also keep in mind that when the bond market reverses course, the stock market does not necessarily go in the same direction. This is the case because there are times when the bond market's reversal can be rooted in factors that push the stock market in the opposite direction. For example, if optimism in the bond market is high as a result of pessimism about the economy (interest rates fall and prices rise when the economy is weak), the bond market may be poised to fall, while equities, which are usually weak when the economy is weak, may rise. In this case, a strengthening of the economy would serve as a catalyst for removing the excess bullishness in bonds but would be a boon to stocks because a stronger economy will lift corporate profits. Nevertheless, persistent weakness in bond prices is likely to have negative consequences for the equity market eventually because the resultant rise in interest rates probably will have a deleterious effect on the economy and corporate profits.

Tracking the call/put ratio is easy. You can obtain the data on daily volume from the CBOT's Web site (www.cbot.com) and take the total volume of calls traded on T-bond futures, T-note futures, or both, depending on the one you are interested in, and divide by the total volume of puts. That will give the daily ratio. The 10-day average, of course, is simply the average of the ten previous trading sessions. You should compute this average yourself since it is not readily available.

The core elements of the call/put analysis can be readily applied to other markets and have proved to be a very useful gauge of investor sentiment in the bond market. When combined with other market sentiment indicators, the call/put ratio has pointed to numerous turning points in the bond market for many years, and it probably will be a useful indicator for years to come.

THE COMMODITY FUTURES TRADING COMMISSION'S COMMITMENT OF TRADERS REPORT

A telling indicator of speculative activity in the bond market can be found in government data on the futures market from statistics complied weekly by the Commodity Futures Trading Commission (CTFC) in its Commitments of Traders (COT) report. As will be discussed in greater detail in Chapter 11, the COT report basically sums up and categorizes the holders of futures positions in all existing U.S. futures contracts, including futures for U.S. Treasuries. The COT report is useful for determining the extent to which recent activity in Treasury futures has been driven by speculative activity or commercial activity.

The CFTC separates the holders of bond futures into two main groups: commercials and noncommercials. Commercial traders in bond futures are the true end-users of the contracts: the hedgers and those who are in the business of buying and selling fixed-income securities. Commercial traders are known as "smart money." They can be primary dealers, insurance companies, pension funds, and the like. Noncommercials are considered speculators. This is the group to watch.

Market tops and bottoms frequently have been foreshadowed by extreme positions taken by noncommercial traders. This is the case largely because speculators have relatively less information than do commercial players about market fundamentals and the true level of underlying demand for fixed-income securities. In addition, speculators frequently have a herd mentality and are therefore more likely to alter their positions when commercial players ignite a change in the market's direction. Moreover, speculators have a tendency to accumulate relatively large positions toward the end of a market trend, when they let human nature get the best of them by letting greed dictate their actions. As a group, the noncommercials are most definitely among those people who give too much weight to their most recent experience and extrapolate recent trends that are at odds with long-run averages and statistical odds. Their optimism rises when the market rises and falls when the market falls. As speculators profit from their positions, they have an increasing tendency to remember their successes but not their failures or the risk of failure, unjustifiably increasing their confidence and, hence, their risk taking. Therefore, by following the futures positions held by noncommercials, investors can get a solid lead on possible turning points in the market.

Figure 10-2 shows the net positions in Treasury bond futures contracts (30-year maturity) held by noncommercial traders. As you can see, their positions can swing sharply from extreme long positions to extreme short positions. Take note of the two extremes in 1998 and 2000, two periods that coincided with major reversals in the bond market. In October 1998, just 13 days after noncommercial net long positions reached a record on September 22, bond prices fell over 5 percent in only 4 days, ushering in a long bear market in bonds that would last until early 2000. By then speculative activity had come full circle when on January 25, 2000, noncommercial traders held a record net short position, hinting at excess pessimism and an impending rally in bond prices. Indeed, bond prices bottomed a week later, ushering in a long bull run that would last

F i g u r e   10–2

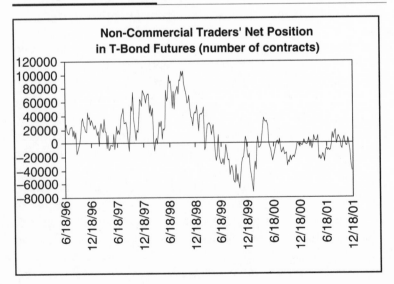

through 2000 and 2001. These are just two examples of many similar episodes over many years. The message to take from the COT data is this: Follow the smart money; don't follow the dumb money. Speculators are seldom right about the market's direction.

AGGREGATE DURATION SURVEYS

The call/put ratio and the CFTC's COT report are great tools for gauging speculative excesses in the bond market because both gauges capture trading activity in the futures market, where speculative trading is high. To get a more complete picture of where bond investors stand as a whole, it is important to look outside the futures market. One of the best things to look at is the activity of portfolio managers, the so-called end users of fixed-income securities, who are the main players in the movement of bond prices. Tracking the extent to which portfolio managers are long or short can yield important clues about whether market sentiment is at an extreme.

It is far easier to track the extent to which portfolio managers are long or short in the bond market than it is in other markets partly because the bond market largely consists of institutional investors rather than individual investors. This makes it easier to get data on portfolio positions. The best way to judge the way in which fixed-income portfolio managers are positioned in the market is to follow surveys on aggregate duration.

The seemingly obtuse term *duration* is less daunting than it seems. As was described in Chapter 3, duration is basically a measure of a bond's price sensitivity to changes in interest rates. It is akin to a stock's beta. The longer the maturity of a bond, the higher its duration and the greater its price sensitivity to changes in interest rates. When portfolio managers want to increase their level of risk, perhaps to benefit from an impending rally in bond prices, they raise their portfolios' duration levels by increasing the average maturity on their bond holdings. In this way they stand to benefit when prices rise, since longer maturities rise faster in price than shorter maturities do when yields fall in equal amounts.

Aggregate duration is basically the average duration of a set of portfolios. Aggregate duration surveys therefore capture the extent to which fixed-income portfolio managers have collectively adjusted their level of risk taking. Since the bond market is largely an institutional business, aggregate duration surveys are a microcosm of the risk profiles of the universe of fixed-income portfolios. Indeed, most duration surveys include portfolios that have a combined total of several hundred billion dollars in assets or more. In fact, a survey conducted weekly by Ried Thunberg, an economic consulting company based in Connecticut, includes portfolios that in total have over $1 trillion in assets. The best and most reliable aggregate duration survey available is conducted weekly by Stone and McCarthy Research Associates (www.smra.com). That survey historically has had the best correlation with turning points in the bond market and therefore appears to capture market sentiment accurately.

When portfolio managers are bullish on bond prices, they increase their portfolios' duration to above the duration of their benchmark—the index their performance is judged against—so that if bond prices rise, their portfolio will outperform the market. Similarly, when portfolio managers are bearish, they decrease their duration to below that of their benchmark, hoping to outperform the benchmark on the way down. Figure 10-3 shows that portfolio

F i g u r e   10–3

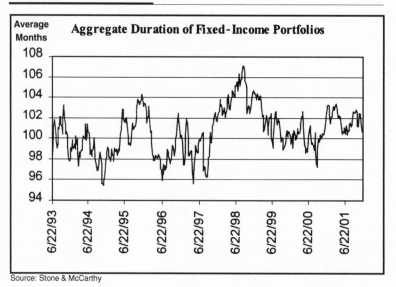

Source: Stone & McCarthy

managers consistently maintain their duration levels between 95 percent and 105 percent of the their target duration (generally the duration of their benchmark, such as the Lehman index).

As the figure shows, aggregate duration generally is maintained between 95 percent and 105 percent except under extraordinary circumstances, such as in 1998, when duration shot up to over 107 percent of target duration during the Asian financial crisis. The steadiness of this duration range probably relates to the conservative nature of fixed-income investors as well as the mandate they give to portfolio managers to stay within a fairly strict range of risk parameters. Moreover, if a portfolio manager takes an extreme position and bets wrong, there is a good chance that the manager will lose investors. Many investors draw comfort from knowing that their investments will not be subject to extreme volatility. A portfolio that sticks to a duration range that is relatively narrow is therefore a big plus. Moreover, it makes the task of judging whether the market is at a bullish or bearish extreme much easier.

Using aggregate duration surveys to spot extreme market sentiment is simple. When aggregate duration falls below 100 percent, this suggests that in the aggregate portfolios are short. The farther aggregate duration falls below 100 percent, the shorter portfolios are. At 95 percent (think of this as portfolios being 95 percent long relative to their benchmark's duration level), bearishness abounds and market sentiment should be considered to be at an extreme. In this case the market is likely to be extremely oversold and ripe for a reversal, and you should consider positioning yourself accordingly in both equities and bonds. When aggregate duration is at 105 percent, bullishness abounds and the market probably is extremely overbought and set to fall.

At 95 percent and 105 percent aggregate duration surveys have reliably pointed to turning points in the bond market, but there are other levels that often foreshadow an impending market reversal. Specifically, 97 percent and 103 percent also can be seen as an extreme at times. This is the case because duration may fluctuate in this range over the short term and the intermediate term simply because conditions that would cause portfolio managers to push their durations to the farthest extremes are less common. Aggregate duration will fluctuate in this more narrow range when few unusual factors are affecting the market. It is therefore important to try to determine whether there may be factors that could push aggregates to their farthest extremes before using the more narrow range as a gauge of whether market sentiment is at an extreme. Keep in mind that even if aggregate duration is at a "neutral" level, you may be able to label the market long or short on the basis of your own subjective analysis of the market's underlying fundamentals.

Aggregate duration can be tracked by following the surveys conducted by several economic and fixed-income services companies, including Ried Thunberg, Stone and McCarthy, IFRmarkets.com, and MCM Moneywatch. In addition, many major brokerage firms, particularly primary dealers, conduct aggregate duration surveys, and you may be able to get the information from them if you have an account or a relationship of some kind with them. As was mentioned earlier, Stone and McCarthy's survey has been the most reliable and the best at capturing extremes in market sentiment and, hence, at forecasting turning points in the bond market. That is why I strongly recommend tracking Stone and McCarthy's duration survey most. Some of the surveys I mentioned are reported by major new services such as Dow Jones, Bloomberg, and Market News and can be tracked that way as well.

THE SPREAD BETWEEN 2-YEAR T-NOTES AND THE FEDERAL FUNDS RATE

Investors often are confused about which U.S. Treasury maturity they should follow as the benchmark for U.S. interest rates. While it is common for most to refer to the 30-year T-bond and increasingly the 10-year T-note, there is an often overlooked maturity that may be a better benchmark than all the rest and may better capture market sentiment and forecast turning points in the market: the 2-year T-note. The case for this benchmark is compelling.

The reason the 2-year T-note captures market sentiment so well is that it may reflect sentiments toward the Federal Reserve better than any other actively traded maturity along the Treasury yield curve. This is the case largely because over time, the 2-year note has had a fairly stable relationship to the federal funds rate, the rate controlled by the Fed. Figure 10-4 harks back to our discussion of the Federal Reserve in Chapter 6.

F i g u r e   10–4

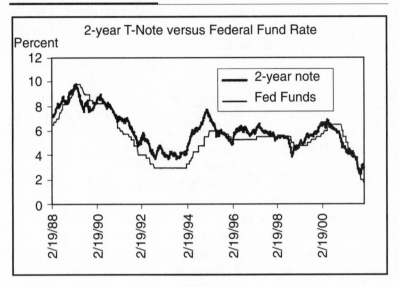

As you can see from the figure, the 2-year T-note has been tightly linked to fluctuations in the fed funds rate. This is the case chiefly because yields on short-term maturities are determined largely by the cost of money and are not affected nearly as much by factors that dominate the behavior of long-term maturities such as inflation expectations, hedging, speculative flows, and new issuance. When the cost of money is higher than the yield on the 2-year T-note, investors who purchase the 2-year note with borrowed money are incurring what is known as *negative carry* because the interest they are paying on the borrowed money exceeds the yield-to-maturity on the 2-year note. Investors who purchase securities by using borrowed money generally are unwilling to engage in investments that incur negative carry unless they believe that borrowing costs eventually will fall and result in positive carry on the investment. Investors recognize that there is very little time for an investment in a short-term maturity to evolve from negative carry to positive carry and therefore engage in negative carry trades very rarely.

As Figure 10-4 shows, over the last 12 years there have been only four occasions when the 2-year note has yielded less than the fed funds rate. On all four occasions, and most recently at the end of 2000, the Fed lowered interest rates soon afterward, usually within a few months. On each occasion investors tolerated negative carry for short periods because they felt the Fed would lower the federal-funds rate, thus reducing borrowing costs and restoring positive carry to their investments. That is why when the yield on the 2-year note is below the fed-funds rate, it indicates that market participants are very bullish on bond prices and expect the Fed to lower interest rates. Similarly, when the yield on the 2-year note is well above the fed-funds rate, it is an indication that market participants are very bearish on bond prices and expect the Fed to raise interest rates. In this case investors worry that positive carry will evolve into negative carry.

During periods when the yield on the 2-year T-note has deviated from its historical relationship to the fed-funds rate, it has given reliable signals about the bond market's true underlying feelings about the direction of the Fed's policy. The degree to which the yield on the 2-year note gravitates away from the fed-funds rate therefore reveals a great deal about market sentiment toward the Fed. This sentiment sometimes reaches extremes owing to either unrealistic hopes for additional interest rate reductions or unrealistic fears of additional interest rate increases.

In many ways the 2-year T-note is therefore a more accurate gauge of the market's sentiment toward the Fed than is any other financial instrument. Longer maturities reflect too many other sentiments toward the market to be used as a proxy for the Fed. This is the case because the longer the maturity on a bond is, the more long-term inflation expectations, speculative flows, and other elements come into play. Longer maturities therefore are best used to gauge speculative excesses in the market rather than the excesses surrounding the market's sentiments toward the Fed. The 2-year T-note is best suited for that role

If there is a maturity other than the 2-year note that is also a good proxy for the market's sentiment toward the Fed, it is the 5-year T-note. The relationship between the 5-year T-note and expectations about the fed funds rate is strong enough that the 5-year note can be called "the long bond of the short end." When sentiment on the Fed shifts, watch out! The 5-year note really moves and will tend to outperform other maturities when prices rise and underperform when prices fall. Nevertheless, the 2-year note historically has had a more stable relationship with the fed-funds rate and is therefore a better gauge of market sentiment toward the Federal Reserve.

The 2-year T-note is a terrific benchmark, and I recommend that it be used in concert with the more commonly employed benchmarks on the long end of the yield curve. The other benchmarks do not capture market sentiment toward the Fed nearly as well, and those sentiments are crucial for determining the direction of maturities across the yield curve as well as the direction of other financial assets.

OTHER USEFUL INDICATORS OF SENTIMENT

There are a couple of other indicators I like to use to gauge market sentiment: real yields and interest rate spreads between low-grade corporate bonds and Treasuries. Both indicators capture sentiment well and frequently can be used to forecast turning points in the bond market. However, they do not signal excesses as often as the indicators I described above do and do not relate directly to the market's net positions.

As was discussed in Chapter 8, the real yield on a bond is its stated, or quoted, yield minus inflation. Bond investors almost always want some degree of real yield to compensate them for a variety of risks, particularly inflation. The fluctuations in real yields therefore reflect changes in market sentiment toward a variety of market fundamentals. When investors are optimistic about inflation, for example, real yields tend to decline. Real yields also tend to decline when the economy is weak and the Fed is lowering interest rates. With this in mind, real yields can be an excellent gauge of market sentiment. When real yields reach extremes, this should be taken as an indication that investors have strong sentiments toward any number of underlying market fundamentals that may be driving the bond market at that time. Whether the sentiments can be deemed extreme depends on whether the market's assumptions appear realistic; determining this is certainly a difficult task. However, if the extremes in real yields are accompanied by extreme positions, as indicated by the indicators above, it is likely that market sentiment is at an extreme and that the risk of a market reversal is higher than normal.

The interest rate spread between low-grade corporate bonds and Treasuries also sends signals about market sentiment that can be used along with the other sentiment indicators to spot excesses. Figure 5-1 in Chapter 5 illustrates the sharp fluctuations that can occur in the yield spread between low-grade corporate bonds and Treasuries. The yield spread is an effective tool because it can capture a wide variety of sentiments toward major influences such as the Federal Reserve, the economy, and external influences such as foreign markets. When the economy weakens, for example, corporate bond investors tend to worry that cash flows will decline and result in an increase in the number of corporate defaults. In turn, corporate bond investors demand compensation through higher interest rates and a wider spread to Treasuries to be enticed to invest in riskier corporate bonds instead of Treasuries, where there is no risk of default. In this way the yield spread between low-grade bonds and Treasuries is a great gauge of market sentiment, particularly with respect to risk aversion. In a sense, the yield spread between low-grade corporate bonds and Treasuries is a reflection of positions held in Treasuries, since it is likely that investors are merely shifting money between low-grade corporate bonds and Treasuries in line with their sentiments toward underlying market fundamentals. Keep in mind that the yield spread between low-grade bonds and Treasuries is probably a better coincident indicator than it is a leading indicator, since the spread's behavior often reflects developments in the economy and other markets and therefore generally follows rather than leads those developments. Nevertheless, I recommend that yield spreads between low-grade corporate bonds and Treasuries be included in your toolbox of indicators of market sentiment.

SUMMARY

Looking beyond the basics, in this chapter we discussed:

- The first four indicators cited in this chapter are just a few of the many indicators available for tracking market sentiment, but they are the best ones. They cast a wide net on investor sentiment by covering both the cash and futures markets, and it is rare indeed when the collective message of the four indicators to send a false signal on the future direction of the bond market.

- As was mentioned earlier, catalysts sometimes are needed before the market's extremes are corrected, but some form of correction is inevitable most of the time. Nevertheless, it is important to be mindful that the depth and duration of market extremes tend to go beyond most investors' expectations. Therefore, it is important to be careful about drawing automatic conclusions about the market outlook when the intelligence you gather from the sentiment indicators points to an impending reversal.

- From tulips to Treasuries, human behavior has played an immense role in the behavior of markets for centuries. Even in these sophisticated times investors continue to show that no amount of sophistication can release them from the grip of their own emotions and clearly remain vulnerable to bouts of fear and greed.

- Many investors probably have experienced the wide range of emotions that come into play in investing and may have affected their investment decisions. You can put your experiences to work for you by recognizing that there are literally millions of other investors who have the same emotions that you have.

- You also can endeavor to turn these emotions into opportunities to spot market extremes. Once you spot them, you will be able to get off the emotional roller coaster before everyone else does and be first in line for the next ride.

CHAPTER ELEVEN

Using the Futures Market to Gather Market Intelligence

In a capitalist society the ability to trade goods and services freely without burdensome taxes and regulations is one of the most important elements. Free trade promotes innovation, risk taking, and an efficient allocation of capital. In the United States free markets have been at the core of a wondrous history of economic growth in which for over two centuries American citizens have sought prosperity wherever it might present itself. The financial markets have come to epitomize these freedoms and have played an immense role in fostering a climate conducive to the spectacular economic prosperity that the nation has enjoyed for so long. The financial markets have been diverse for decades, but when most people think about the history of the financial markets, they typically think of only stocks and bonds. Few ever entertain the thought that more sophisticated financial instruments might have existed before people went to the moon. They should think again.

An established market since the early 1800s and a vibrant one since the mid-1800s, the futures market has played an important role in the growth of the U.S. economy and the financial markets. Indeed, since 1848, when 82 merchants formed the Chicago Board of Trade—a centralized market for exchanging agricultural commodities, futures trading has grown concomitantly with the needs of the marketplace. Since the 1970s futures trading have evolved from trading largely agricultural products to today's market where financial products dominate trading. Indeed, in the early 1970s most of the 13 million futures contracts traded were in agricultural products such as corn, wheat, and soybeans. In 1999, of the 593 million futures contracts traded in the United States, only 11 percent were related to agricultural products. The definition of a futures contract hasn't changed much over the years. Today, as it did many decades ago, a *futures contract* represents an agreement between a buyer and a seller in which the buyer (seller) agrees to take (make) delivery of a specific amount of either a commodity or a financial security at a specific price at a specific time.

The rapid growth of the futures market that has occurred since the 1970s began in the bond market with trading in futures for the Government National Mortgage Association's (GNMA) mortgage-backed certificates. GNMA contracts paved the way for trading in Treasury bond futures, which were launched in August 1977 and became immensely popular and the hallmark product of the Chicago Board of Trade. The success of Treasury futures contracts paved the way for trading in a variety of other financial instruments in a variety of different asset classes, such as equities and foreign currencies.

Interest rate futures remain extremely active and are at the forefront of the futures market. The most active interest rate futures are Treasury contracts and eurodollar contracts. We will discuss both shortly. These contracts are used by a wide variety of investors and by market participants who seek an optimal level of information flow to help them formulate investment strategies.

A wealth of benefits can be obtained from tracking activity in the interest rate futures markets. In addition, interest rate futures can be used as investment vehicles in a wide variety of ways. There are two main ways in which you can use futures to help you with your investments:

- Gathering market intelligence
- Portfolio management

Let's take a closer look at both.

FUTURES PROVIDE SIGNIFICANT MARKET INFORMATION

One of the most important elements of investing is having an accurate assessment of market expectations. If an investor's assumptions regarding market expectations are wrong, an accurate forecast of market fundamentals will not necessarily translate into successful investment strategies. To be a successful investor one has to choose investments that do not yet fully capture, or discount, events in the future. It is therefore imperative to estimate as accurately as possible the various assumptions embedded in market prices. It's the best way to compare an investor's assumptions with the market's so that the investor can decide on an investment strategy.

Interest rate futures can be used to gather market intelligence on three important fronts:

- Market sentiment
- Expectations of future market volatility
- Expectations of future rate actions by the Federal Reserve

Each of these three areas plays an essential role in shaping the direction of bond prices, the shape of the yield curve, the level of real interest rates, and the relative performance of the various segments of the bond market. There are a number of different indicators in the futures market that are an excellent source of market information. These gauges apply to nearly all futures trading, but this discussion pertains to activity in Treasury futures. These indicators are discussed below.

Tracking Market Sentiment

Five main indicators of market sentiment can be found in the futures market:

- Open interest
- Futures trading volume
- Options trading volume
- The Commodity Futures Trading Commission's Commitments of Traders report
- The bond basis

Open Interest

Open interest is a measure of the total number of futures positions that remain open, or outstanding, at a specific point in time. For each open contract there's a long position and a short position held by two different parties, but it is counted as a single contract in the open interest data. Open interest data can be used to gauge the quality of a move in the market. The main way to use this gauge is to compare the daily changes in open interest with the direction of the futures price. In general, when open interest increases on a day when prices rally, this is looked at as an indication that new long positions were behind the rally, not short covering. It is looked at as a sign that market participants are confident that prices will continue to decline.

By contrast, when open interest declines on a day when prices rally, this is seen as a sign that the rally may have been spurred by short covering and is therefore an indication that the rally may not be sustainable. Prices can increase only so much on short covering alone; new buyers eventually will be needed to sustain higher prices.

Similarly, when prices decline and open interest increases, this is looked at as a sign that new short positions spurred the drop in prices and therefore is an indication that market participants expect continued declines in prices. However, when open interest declines as prices fall, this is seen as an indication that existing long positions have been liquidated. Liquidations of long positions cannot continue in perpetuity, of course, and so it is usually only a matter of time before the liquidations are exhausted.

Table 11-1 can be used as a useful reference on the conventional interpretation of changes in open interest.

Futures Trading Volume

A key gauge in most asset classes, trading volume can be used to judge the degree of investor participation in a price trend. A price move that occurs on strong volume helps validate that move and suggests that it probably will continue, but a price move that occurs on light volume suggests that there is very little sponsorship for the price move and that it probably will not be sustained. It is especially critical to track volume when a price trend is well established. In such a case diminishing volume could be a red flag and could portend a reversal or a consolidation of the trend. High levels of volume tend to be associated with increases in commercial activity relative to speculative activity, while low volume levels suggest the opposite. Commercial players are considered "smart money," and I like to say that speculative players are "dumb money." You can

Table 11-1

Interpretation of Changes in Open Interest

Price Direction	Open Interest Change	Interpretation	Reason
Rising prices	Increasing	Bullish	Pattern suggests new longs entered the market
Rising prices	Decreasing	Bearish	Pattern suggests rally due to short covering rather than new long positions
Falling prices	Increasing	Bearish	Pattern suggests new short positions established
Falling prices	Decreasing	Bullish	Pattern suggests selloff due to long liquidations that eventually will be exhausted

track the activity of these two camps more specifically by using the Commodity Futures Trading Commission's (CFTC) Commitments of Traders report, which is discussed below. Tracking volume in the futures market is especially important in the bond market, where there are no other official sources of data on daily volume.

Options Trading Volume

As was shown in Chapter 10, options volume can be used to predict turning points in the market. Specifically, by comparing the daily volume in calls to the daily volume in puts, an investor can spot excesses in bullish and bearish sentiment in the market. This is an excellent indicator that also is employed in the stock market, using stock options, of course. One of the reasons it is such a good indicator is that it captures speculative activity very well, and it is speculative activity that investors want to capture when tracking market sentiment. This is the activity that results from the collective views of short-term traders, who have a tendency to bet wrong on market direction, especially at turning points.

In the bond market the best way to track market sentiment is to use the options on T-bond futures that trade on the Chicago Board of Trade. Although the future issuance of Treasury bonds was put in doubt at the end of 2001 when the Treasury Department announced the elimination of issuance of 30-year bonds, there remains many billions of dollars of bonds outstanding and there is still a great deal of speculative activity in T-bond contracts.

The volume in calls is compared to the volume in puts by using a ten-day average of the *call/put ratio*. This ratio has provided many reliable signals of overbought and oversold conditions in the bond market. Over time the ratio has averaged about 1.25:1. A ratio of about 1.4:1 generally indicates overbought conditions, while a ratio below 0.8:1 generally indicates that conditions are oversold.

The Commodity Futures Trading Commission's Commitments of Traders Report

As was discussed in Chapter 10, the Commodity Futures Trading Commission publishes a very useful report called the *Commitment of Traders (COT) report*. This weekly report basically divides the holders of the existing open interest in a futures contract into two groups: commercial traders and noncommercial traders. Commercial traders in bond futures are the true end users of Treasuries. That is, they are the entities involved in the business of buying and selling fixed-income securities. Examples of commercial traders are primary dealers, insurance companies, and pension funds. The COT report is used as a gauge of speculative activity in various commodities, including Treasuries, and has been a very reliable indicator of extremes in market sentiment.

It is relatively simple to use the COT report as a market indicator. An investor need simply track the net positions of commercial and noncommercial traders. Working on the notion that commercial traders represent smart money and noncommercial traders represent dumb money, one can compare the positions held by the two groups. An investor should pay special attention to the noncommercials; they are the ones who tend to get the market wrong and are trading for short-term profits and therefore will be quick to reverse their positions if market trends reverse.

It is truly helpful to know who is long and who is short in the market, and investors are fortunate to have this information at their disposal. The report is especially useful in the bond market, where trading in interest rate futures is much higher than it is in other financial instruments. The data can be obtained at cftc.gov.

The Bond Basis

Another way to track the quality of a market move is to track the bond basis. The *bond basis* is defined as the difference between the cash price and the converted futures price. The cash price is simply the price of the cash instrument that underlies the future and is eligible for delivery to the buyer of the future. The converted futures price is the price of the futures contract multiplied by the *conversion factor* of the cash instrument. (The conversion factor is the factor used to equate the price of T-bond and T-note futures contracts with the various cash T-bonds and T-notes eligible for delivery.) The conversion factor basically converts the price of all eligible cash bonds to bonds with a 6 percent coupon. The cash instrument's maturity date and call date (if any) are taken into account when the Chicago Board of Trade issues conversion factors.

Basis = (Bond's cash price − futures price) × conversion factor

The basis can be used to track the performance of cash bonds compared to futures. Divergences in performance that cannot be explained by differences in duration can be used as an indicator of commercial and speculative activity. Market trends that appear to be based largely on commercial trading activity are more likely to be sustained than are those that appear to be rooted in speculative activity. Since most speculative activity in the bond market takes place in the futures market, the performance of the cash market relative to the futures market can be used to track the degree to which commercial players are backing a market trend. Thus, if bond prices rise and the basis narrows because the futures market is outperforming the cash market, this indicates that futures, or speculative, activity led the market higher, not commercial activity. This is a low-quality rally and is unlikely to be sustained. Similarly, if bond prices decline but the basis widens, this indicates that futures, or speculative activity, drove prices lower, not commercial activity. One must bear in mind that the basis sometimes can shift because of shifts in the yield curve, as the cash instrument may have a maturity date different from the maturity of the security that underlies the future (this applies to situations where one compares the performance of the benchmark bond to that of the front-month futures contract).

Table 11-2 is a helpful reference on the various interpretations of the behavior of the bond basis.

Table 11-2

Interpretation of the Behavior of the Bond Basis

Price Direction	Basis Change	Interpretation	Reason
Rising prices	Widening	Bullish	Pattern suggests new commercial buyers behind the rally
Rising prices	Narrowing	Bearish	Pattern suggests commercial players are not supporting rally
Falling prices	Widening	Bullish	Pattern suggests speculative activity causing the weakness
Falling prices	Narrowing	Bearish	Pattern suggests selloff due to commercial selling

Expectations of Future Volatility

The market's expectations of future market volatility can be measured by using the implied volatility levels of options on futures
prices. *Implied volatility* is the market's expectations of the future
volatility of a security over a specific period of time. Implied
volatility generally is expressed in percentage terms and is calculated by using options pricing models such as the widely used
Black-Scholes model. A number of benefits result from accurately
assessing the market's expectations of future volatility.

First, this can help you judge whether your expectations about
near-term price behavior are at odds with the market's expectations. This can help you spot opportunities in options trading as
well as temporary dislocations and anomalies in bond prices. For
example, if the performance of low-grade bonds deteriorated
sharply relative to that of high-grade bonds owing to expectations
of sharp increases in market volatility, you might consider purchasing the low-grade bonds if you felt that market volatility probably would diminish and thus stabilize the prices of low-grade
bonds (low-grade bonds tend to weaken in times of uncertainty).

Second, expectations of future volatility have proved to be a
reliable indicator of excesses in bullish and bearish sentiment and
therefore can be used to forecast turning points in the market. For
example, high levels of implied volatility tend to coincide with

market bottoms, as they indicate that there is a high level of fear in the market about additional price declines. High levels of fear are a sign of excess pessimism, of course, and therefore are a contrary indicator. Similarly, low levels of implied volatility tend to coincide with market tops, as they indicate that there is a high level of complacency in the market, with market participants expressing unrealistic expectations about risk.

Third, by knowing the degree to which the market expects to react to certain events, you can form a judgment about its expectations of those events. This can help you plot strategies that capitalize on what you believe are unrealistic expectations of the potential ramifications of a specific event. For example, if implied volatility is low before the release of an economic report that you believe might have a substantial impact on the market, this could indicate to you that the market reaction may be even more significant owing to the market's lack of preparedness.

Fourth, by comparing the implied volatility on call options with the implied volatility on put options you can gauge the market's expectations about the near-term direction of the market. For example if the *skew* on the options for a particular security leans toward higher call premiums when it normally leans toward higher put premiums, this could be taken as a sign of excess optimism. In Treasury bonds, the skew is generally toward slightly higher call premiums.

In the Treasury market, implied volatility on T-bond futures tends to trade at around 9 to 10 percent within a broader range of around 8 to 11 percent. You can track implied volatility by calling your broker, using a professional system such as Bloomberg or Bridge, or purchasing options software. Information also is available on the Web sites of major futures exchanges such as the Chicago Board of Trade (cbot.com) and the Chicago Mercantile Exchange (cme.com).

Expectations of Future Rate Actions by the Federal Reserve Federal Funds Futures

Federal funds futures have evolved into one of the most important and reliable gauges of the bond market's expectations about future rate changes by the Federal Reserve. Understanding how to assess these expectations by using federal funds futures is therefore an essential aspect of investing. Investors who can assess market expectations accurately on a variety of fronts, particularly with respect to the Fed, are more likely to be successful investors than are those who make inaccurate assessments. Tracking federal funds futures is a great way to accurately assess market expectations of the probable outcomes of future Federal Open Market Committee (FOMC) meetings. Indeed, over the last few years federal funds futures have been accurately priced for the outcome of these meetings close to 90 percent of the time.

Using federal funds futures to assess market expectations of the Fed is relatively simple. Here are the steps:

1. Choose a contract month. This step is not as easy as it might seem at first. The contract month that you choose will depend on the date within the month during which the FOMC meeting is scheduled to take place. If the meeting is scheduled for very late in the month and there will be no meeting the next month, it is best to choose the contract in that following month. If you do not choose that month, you will have a lot of math to do. This way, you are getting a clean read on what the market believes the prevailing fed funds rate will be in the month after the meeting. This is the best method for getting a quick, close approximation. One drawback is that the contract of the contract month that follows FOMC meetings could contain expectations about the possibility of an intermeeting rate move. That is why the most accurate way to gauge market expectations about a specific meeting is to choose the contract of the contract month in which the FOMC meeting takes place.

2. Calculate the implied federal funds rate on the futures contract. The implied federal funds rate is found by subtracting the price of the federal funds futures contract from 100. For example, if the FOMC meeting is being held in early November and you choose the November contract to determine the market's expectations of the outcome of that meeting and the price of that contract is 97.07, the implied rate is 2.93 percent.

3. Calculate the weighted average expected of the actual federal funds rate. The next step is to calculate the weighted average of the effective federal funds rate (the daily weighted average) by using both the current federal funds target determined by the Fed when it last changed it and a level that you believe might be implemented at the next FOMC meeting. For example, if the FOMC is scheduled to meet on the tenth of a month that contains 30 days, the weighted average would be as follows:

Weighted average of ff rate =

$$\frac{(n) \text{ effective ff rate} + (n2) \text{ effective ff rate}}{30}$$

where (n) = number of days during the contract month on which the effective federal funds rate is expected to prevail at a given target rate

$(n2)$ = number of days during the contract month on which the effective federal funds rate is expected to prevail at a target rate set at the meeting scheduled for that contract month

4. Assuming that the federal funds rate was at 3.0 percent during the first 10 days of the month and at 2.75 percent during the final 20 days of the month (it is lower because we are assuming that the Fed lowered interest rates at its meeting on the tenth of the month), the weighted average is 2.83 percent. This means that if the Fed cut rates from 3.0 percent to 2.75 percent at the FOMC meeting on the tenth of the month, the federal funds rate would average 2.83 percent. This is the rate that traders in the federal funds futures contract are betting on or against and the rate that is used to pinpoint the probability assigned to the likelihood of that rate cut. Keep this in mind for step 5.

5. Subtract the weighted average of the federal funds rate from the current federal funds target (set by the FOMC when it last changed it; assume in this case that it was 3.0 percent): 3.0 percent − 2.83 percent = 17 basis points.

6. Now that you know the number of basis points it will take for the federal funds contract to fully price in a rate move made at the FOMC meeting (17 basis points in this example), divide the number of basis points in rate cuts priced into the federal funds contract (7 basis points in this example) into the number of basis points that it would take to fully price in the rate cut: 7 divided by 17 = 41 percent. Thus, the contract suggests that the market has assigned a 41 percent probability to the odds of a rate cut at the FOMC meeting.

Here's an important qualifier: First, keep in mind that as you enter the contract month used for your calculation, you must use the actual effective federal funds rate rather than the target federal funds rate, which can differ each day. The target rate is simply that: a target. Where it actually trades is unknowable until it actually trades. Therefore, in your calculation you must substitute the actual rate for the target rate as the month progresses. You can obtain this information from the Fed at federalreserve.gov under the data section on the navigation bar.

The federal funds futures contract is great for assessing the market's expectations over about a six-month time horizon, but it is a poor gauge for longer horizons. The open interest tends to dwindle beyond a six-month time horizon and is usually nil beyond seven to eight months. What should you do? Turn to eurodollar contracts.

Using Eurodollars to Track Expectations of Future Short-Term Rates

Eurodollar futures are one of the most liquid futures contracts in the world and are easily the most liquid contracts based on short-term interest rates. They are used by a wide variety of entities to hedge short-term interest rate exposures. The contract represents rates paid on 3-month eurodollar time deposits, or dollars deposited outside the United States. Eurodollar rates tend to be tightly correlated to the federal funds rate, and this makes the eurodollar contract a great gauge of market expectations about future short-term interest rates.

The method used to determine the market's expectations about the federal funds rate using eurodollar contracts is similar to the steps shown earlier for the federal funds futures contract. There are a couple of twists, however. First, eurodollar futures contracts trade in series of three-month increments (except in the upcoming three months, but the federal funds futures are more reliable in this case). This means that when you are calculating the federal funds rate out into the future, you will not be making a pinpoint assessment. This is not a big problem, however, since you are concerned primarily with making an accurate general assessment during those months anyway.

Second and more important, the spread between the eurodollar time deposit rate and the federal funds rate tends to fluctuate with where the Federal Reserve is expected to be in its interest rate cycle. This means that the implied rate on eurodollar futures contracts is not likely to reflect the market's expectations about the federal funds rate; instead, it is likely to reflect the market's expectations about both the federal funds rate and the spread between the London Interbank Offering Rate (LIBOR), the rate at which major banks in London lend Eurodollar deposits, and the federal funds rate. This spread tends to widen when the Fed is raising interest rates and tends to be very narrow when the Fed is lowering interest rates. Thus, the spread in effect represents a risk premium for the odds that the federal funds rate will rise. Figure 11-1 illustrates the behavior of 3-month LIBOR compared to the federal funds rate. Note how the spread widened when the Fed raised interest rates in 1994 and 1999 and narrowed when the Fed cut rates in 2001.

The behavior of the spread is therefore the most important variable with which an investor must contend when using eurodollar futures to assess the market's expectations of future short-term

F i g u r e   11–1

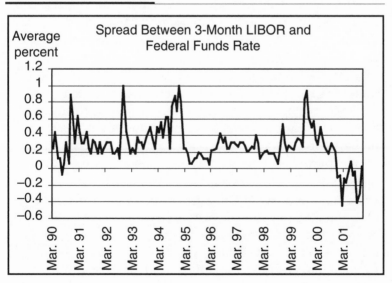

interest rates. Simply assume that the spread will widen when the market has building expectations of interest rate increases and will narrow when the market expects rates to be cut. For example, assume that the federal funds rate is currently 3 percent and that the implied rate on the eurodollar futures contract 12 months hence is at 4 percent. This appears to indicate that the market expects the Fed to raise the federal funds rate next year, but to what level? To find the answer, simply subtract what you think the spread between LIBOR and the federal funds rate will be next year (50 basis points is a reasonable assumption when it is early in a Fed campaign to raise interest rates), and that number will represent the market's expectations of the fed funds rate (3.5 percent in this example).

Uses of Interest Rate Futures

There are many ways in which interest rate futures can be used. While the high degree of leverage involved with futures makes them riskier than most asset classes, there are a number of ways in which futures can be used to allay risks. The most important uses of futures include the following:

- **Speculating.** Speculators actively trade futures to gain a profit by acting on short-term trading opportunities. Speculators play an important role in the futures markets by providing liquidity to those markets, particularly those market participants who use futures for commercial purposes.
- **Hedging.** A wide variety of entities buy and sell futures to offset the risks they incur in their normal business operations. Primary dealers, pension funds, insurance companies, portfolio managers, thrifts, and the like, all use futures to hedge their various risks. Investors who use futures to hedge their risks must take into account basis risks—the risk of unexpected changes in the basis—since the security being hedged and the hedge security are usually different.
- **Duration management.** By increasing or decreasing the duration on a portfolio, investors can attempt to capitalize on expected fluctuations in interest rates. In most portfolios duration can be increased by purchasing Treasury bond futures; conversely, selling futures can decrease duration.

This is a simple and inexpensive way to alter the risk profile of a portfolio.

- **Yield curve bets.** By buying and selling interest rate futures in the various maturities, an investor can make bets on the shape of the yield curve.
- **Asset allocation.** Portfolios that contain a combination of bonds and stocks can use futures to vary their allocations to these asset classes. Insurance companies and pension funds are two examples of users of this strategy. Individuals can use this approach too.
- **Yield enhancement.** Investors can use options on futures to try to add incremental returns to their portfolios.

As you can see, futures can be used in many different ways and can play a valuable role in an investment portfolio.

SUMMARY

Looking beyond the basics, in this chapter we discussed:

- Futures can be extremely useful to those who use them as well as to bond investors who follow trading activity in the futures market to obtain valuable market intelligence. Much of the information in the futures market is unique and is therefore an invaluable source of market intelligence.
- Futures can be used to gain an edge in forecasting turning points in the bond market.
- The futures market contains significant amounts of information on market sentiment, expectations of future market volatility, and expectations of future rate actions by the Federal Reserve, all of which can be extremely helpful tools for bond investors.
- Futures can be used in a number of investment strategies, including duration management, hedging, and asset allocation, among others.

CHAPTER TWELVE

Credit Ratings: An Essential Tool for Bond Investors

Americans love ratings and seem to rate and rank just about everything. This is understandable in light of the plethora of choices consumers and investors face every day.

Ratings help people get a sense of where things stand with respect to each other. They tell people about the quality of the things they buy or plan to buy. They also save busy Americans time by taking a lot of legwork out of the equation. A quick look at a rating or ranking can simplify a purchase decision.

It is no different in the bond market. Bond investors use bond ratings to get a sense of value on the bonds they buy and simplify the investment decision-making process. However, bond ratings are not necessarily for bond investors only; equity investors should use them to increase what they know about the companies in which they invest.

I often think about bond ratings when I see ratings of consumer products. I am reminded how difficult it is to understand why many people invest thousands of dollars in the bonds and stocks of companies they have never heard of without first looking at the ratings on the securities, yet they will not even consider purchasing consumer products such as a washing machine, vacuum, or camera without first reading ratings comparisons produced by companies such as Consumer Reports. This type of behavior clearly suggests that many investors do not have their priorities straight in this regard. It is far more important to be keenly focused when considering financial investments than when making most other types of purchases.

Investors are fortunate to have an extraordinary ratings system at their disposal. That ratings system has been in place for many years and is widely respected. I therefore urge you to put ratings in your financial toolbox. If you are primarily an equities investor, remember that the ratings system used for bonds is suitable for equity investors too and that the information in this chapter is largely transferable to equities.

CREDIT RATINGS CUT AN INVESTOR'S RISK

As was discussed in greater detail in Chapter 5, investors face three main risks when investing in bonds: interest rate risk (the risk that interest rates will rise), purchasing power risk (the risk that inflation will rise and thus erode the value of bonds), and credit risk (the risk that a bond issuer will be unable to meet its debt obligations). While assessing the first two risks requires that individual investors do a significant amount of research on their own, credit risks are arguably the easiest of the risks for investors to assess thanks to credit ratings. Credit ratings make investing in bonds a little easier by augmenting an investor's analysis of bonds in ways that for many people is not possible because they lack the time or expertise to conduct an analysis as extensive as those conducted by the rating agencies. This is especially important for investing in bonds, which often requires a lot of quantitative and qualitative analysis. Credit ratings can help investors assess the likelihood that their money will be returned to them in accordance with the terms on which they invested.

Credit ratings essentially rank a company's ability to repay its debts and withstand various types of financial and economic stress compared to the ability of other companies. Ratings are intended to provide forward-looking opinions about a company's ability and willingness to pay interest and repay principal as scheduled. (For purposes of simplification, this chapter will discuss ratings mainly as they apply to corporations. However, the same general principles apply to government, municipal, and agency debt as well as to other fixed-income securities.)

A primary concern for bond investors is whether they will receive the interest payments that are due on their bond holdings and will be repaid at maturity for the principal they invested in the bonds. Credit ratings help investors assess whether bond issuers can meet those debt obligations. Failure to make an interest payment or repay the principal at maturity (usually $1000 per bond) is considered a *default*. A default is a bond investor's biggest worry and is a risk that exists for almost every bond. The exceptions, of course, are U.S. Treasury securities. Treasuries are considered free of default risks because they are backed by the full faith and credit of the U.S. government.

While there is little doubt that credit ratings can help investors gauge the default risks on a particular bond, it is important to be aware of the limited role credit ratings play in the investment decision-making process. For one thing, credit ratings are not recommendations to buy, sell, or hold a security. In other words, the ratings agencies do not assign credit ratings to signal their investment recommendations in regard to the bonds they rate. That is not why these agencies issue credit ratings. Ratings agencies are interested primarily in providing indications of the ability of an entity to meet its payment obligations.

Another point to remember is that credit ratings do not contain statements on whether a bond is deemed to be "cheap" or "expensive" relative to other bonds in the market. The price of a bond has no direct connection to the ratings that the ratings agencies assign.

Credit ratings also do not comment on the suitability of a bond for a particular investor. The ratings do not tell an investor, for example, whether a particular bond fits with his or her investment profile. Moreover, credit ratings give no indication of the tax implications of owning a particular bond. That is a job best suited for an accountant.

Despite the limited role that credit ratings play in the investment decision-making process, they are an invaluable tool for investors. Let's take a look at where ratings come from, how they are determined, the definitions of the ratings symbols, and the impact they have on the price of a bond.

THE RATING AGENCIES

You probably have heard the names of the four most prominent and nationally recognized private companies that issue credit ratings: Moody's Investor Services, Standard & Poor's, Fitch IBCA, and Duff & Phelps. Of the four, Moody's and Standard and Poor's are considered the leading agencies.

Each of the four agencies follows a very thorough and rigorous methodology for determining a company's creditworthiness. The agencies conduct a thorough credit analysis consisting of a mix of quantitative and qualitative analyses. The agencies' thorough approach and solid track records are responsible for the high degree of confidence and trust investors have in them. The widespread respect the agencies enjoy should give you confidence about putting their credit ratings system in your investment toolbox.

While the credit rating each of the agencies assigns to a particular bond can vary, their assessments are not usually far apart. In fact, it is unusual for the agencies' opinions on a particular bond to be sharply divided. Nevertheless, investors can benefit from utilizing the variety of opinions the various agencies have to offer.

The most prominent and oldest rating agency is Moody's Investor Services. The Moody's of today had its genesis back in 1909, when the founder, John Moody, introduced a simple letter grading system for railroad bonds. Moody's had adopted that system from the mercantile and credit ratings system used by credit-reporting firms in the late 1800s. Soon Moody's began to apply that methodology to other industries, and the ratings system was underway.

Over the years Moody's has extended its reach well beyond its bond ratings. Moody's now provides credit ratings and analyses on over $30 trillion of debt covering 85,000 corporate and government securities, 68,000 public finance obligations, 4200 corporate relationships, and 100 sovereign nations. In the bond market its reach extends to roughly 1500 issuers rated Aaa to Baa (more on these symbols later). Moody's has assigned ratings to 90 percent of public market bonds.

In the 1970s Moody's and the other major rating agencies began charging issuers for their rating services in recognition of the substantial value the issuers were placing on the objective analyses provided by the rating agencies. Issuers increasingly found that objective ratings on the bonds they issued increased the likelihood that investors would participate in their bond offerings, and this tended to lower an issuer's borrowing costs. Charging issuers also become necessary as the financial markets grew in complexity. The increasing size and complexity of the financial markets required many more personnel receiving much higher levels of compensation than could be afforded without the fees.

The growth of Moody's and the other rating agencies thus has been tied directly to the enormous growth in the size and complexity of the financial markets over the last few decades. As the markets have grown, the need for professional services such as those provided by the rating agencies has increased greatly. Luckily for investors, the agencies have grown in size, experience, and sophistication to meet today's challenging investment world.

THE RATINGS SYSTEM

For anyone who can recite the alphabet, the ratings system is simple to learn. One might say that the Moody's ratings system is as easy as ABC. I say this because all the rating agencies use the letters A through D to signify a decreasing level of creditworthiness. The highest credit rating, of course, is AAA, while the lowest is D. This simple approach makes it easy for anyone to understand the system. Investors are fortunate that the ratings agencies have chosen such a simple system, particularly in light of the complex nature of the work involved in generating the ratings.

There are two main categories of investments within the A through D ratings grades: investment grade and below investment grade. Investment-grade bonds are believed to have a low probability of default, whereas below-investment-grade bonds are thought to have a relatively greater probability of default. Most people think of the below-investment-grade category as "junk bonds."

Table 12-1 shows the ratings used by the major rating agencies.

Note that only Moody's uses lowercase letters in its ratings system. In addition, Moody's sometimes attaches a number, or numeric modifier, to its letter ratings. It does this to give its ratings assignment greater specificity with regard to rank and to avoid generalizations within ratings categories. The modifiers are used to refer to a bond's ranking within the group. Here is how Moody's describes the use of numbers within ratings grades: "Moody's applies numerical modifiers 1, 2, and 3 in each generic rating classification from Aa through Caa. The modifier 1 indicates that the obligation ranks in the higher end of its generic rating category; the modifier 2 indicates a midrange ranking; and the modifier 3 indicates a ranking in the

Table 12-1

Credit Ratings

Credit Risk	Moody's	Standard & Poor's	Fitch IBCA	Duff & Phelps
Investment Grade				
Highest quality	Aaa	AAA	AAA	AAA
High quality (very strong)	Aa	AA	AA	AA
Upper medium grade (strong)	A	A	A	A
Medium grade	Baa	BBB	BBB	BBB
Below Investment Grade				
Lower medium grade (somewhat speculative)	Ba	BB	BB	BB
Low grade (speculative)	B	B	B	B
Poor quality (may default)	Caa	CCC	CCC	CCC
Most speculative	Ca	CC	CC	CC
No interest being paid or bankruptcy petition filed	C	C	C	C
In default	C	D	D	D

lower end of that generic rating category." Basically, the numerical modifiers Moody's uses increase the number of ratings grades it can assign. This gives investors even more information to gauge the creditworthiness of the companies Moody's analyzes.

Thus, if you know the alphabet and can count from 1 to 3, you should have no problem understanding the Moody's ratings system.

THE RATINGS CATEGORIES

Investment Grade

Investment-grade ratings reflect expectations of timeliness of payment and a low probability of default. As Table 12-1 shows, investment-grade bonds are bonds rated between AAA and BBB. Many investors prefer to invest solely in these bonds to minimize their investment risks. In fact, many financial institutions, such as banks, are not permitted to invest in bonds rated below investment grade. This is a major reason why bond issuers strive to maintain an investment-grade credit rating. They recognize that demand for their bonds would fall if their credit rating fell below investment grade. This would translate into higher borrowing costs and thus lower corporate profits.

An investment-grade credit rating can have a large bearing on the way investors and other entities treat a particular class of bonds. The Federal Reserve Board, for example, will allow members of the Federal Reserve System to invest only in securities with the four highest rating categories. At the U.S. Department of Labor pension funds can invest in commercial paper only if it is rated in one of the three highest categories. Similar rules are in place for many other pension funds in both the private and public sectors.

The most familiar investment-grade credit rating is, of course, AAA. As one might expect, AAA-rated bonds are considered to have the highest credit quality. Companies that obtain an AAA rating have the highest capacity to meet their financial commitments. AAA-rated bonds are deemed to be protected by a "large and exceptionally stable margin and principal is secure," according to Moody's. While the outlook for AAA-rated companies is, as with all companies, subject to change, such changes are felt to be "unlikely to impair the fundamentally strong position" of these companies. AAA-rated companies have a superior capacity to weather a variety of economic and financial stresses.

Examples of companies that carry the prestigious AAA rating include well-known companies such as General Electric, Exxon, United Parcel Service, Merck, and Johnson & Johnson. All of these companies have very strong balance sheets in industries that are generally not subject to the extremes of the business cycle.

AA-rated bonds "differ from the highest-rated obligations only in small degree," according to Standard & Poor's. Companies with an AA rating are believed to have a very strong capacity to meet their financial obligations. Here is how Moody's characterizes AA bonds: "Bonds which are rated Aa are judged to be of high quality by all standards. Together with the Aaa group, they comprise what are generally known as high-grade bonds. They are rated lower than the best bonds because margins of protection may not be as large as in Aaa securities or fluctuation of protective elements may be of greater amplitude or there may be other elements present which make the long-term risk appear somewhat larger than the Aaa securities."

The AA rating is applied to a diverse group of elite companies in a broad array of industries. Companies that carry an AA rating include AT&T, Procter & Gamble, Kimberly Clark, Motorola, JP Morgan, DuPont, and Eli Lilly. All of these companies have a very strong capacity to meet their debt obligations.

The creditworthiness of companies with lower ratings begins to deteriorate slowly but surely. A-rated bonds, for example, are considered "susceptible" to changing business and economic conditions, and their ability to repay their debts is considered merely "adequate." Thus, investment in A-rated bonds carries a somewhat higher degree of risk than investment in the high-grade categories. However, this does not mean that these companies are highly risky, and bonds rated A generally are considered to be of good quality with favorable investment attributes; these lower-rated bonds yield more than higher-rated bonds do.

Examples of A-rated bonds include companies with somewhat greater sensitivity to cyclical economic conditions than companies rated AAA and AA. In other words, A-rated bonds are more likely to be affected by the ups and downs of the business cycle than high-grade bonds are. Included in A-rated category, for example, are consumer cyclical companies such as retailers, chemical companies, and automotive companies. Financial companies often are placed in this category because their profits and potential losses (from loan losses, bankruptcies, and the like) can vary sharply as economic growth fluctuates.

The lowest investment-grade ratings category is BBB. Bonds in this category are basically on the borderline between investment-grade and speculative-grade debt. As Moody's puts it, they are "neither highly protected nor poorly secured." BBB bonds are felt to have fewer protective elements than higher-rated bonds and are considered vulnerable to potential changes in both an obligor's company business fundamentals and the economic environment.

Companies in this category therefore are likely to have a weakened capacity to repay their debts under changed circumstances.

Below Investment Grade

Obligations rated BB, B, CCC, CC, and C are regarded as having significant speculative characteristics. In this ratings category, bonds rated BB are considered the least speculative and bonds rated C are considered the most speculative. Most of the market for below-investment-grade debt consists of bonds rated BB or B, although in recent years a spate of ratings downgrades has sparked an increase in the number of bonds rated CCC or lower. Moreover, a number of bonds previously rated investment grade have been downgraded to below investment grade. This is known as a *crossover*.

Bonds rated below investment grade are commonly called "high-yield" or "junk" bonds. To individuals who invest in high-yield bonds or make a living from them, high-yield is the preferred nomenclature. To these individuals, high-yield bonds are anything but junk because of the many benefits they believe high-yield bonds can confer to a portfolio.

Not all companies with below-investment-grade ratings are necessarily outright speculative investments. Indeed, many of them have at least some quality and protective characteristics even if those characteristics are outweighed by many uncertainties and vulnerabilities. This is why it is critical to avoid prejudging a bond by looking only at its rating.

Nevertheless, investing in debt rated below investment grade can be risky unless an investor is very familiar with the company. If you are not very familiar with the company you are considering investing in but are still interested in investing in high-yield bonds, you might consider investing in a bond mutual fund offered by a company such as Pacific Investment Management Company (PIMCO). By investing in a high-yield mutual fund you get the benefit of having a professional money manager choose bonds for you. In addition, you get the advantage of diversification without having to invest a lot of money in the process. This helps reduce your transaction fees. However, mutual funds incur transactions charges and generally pass on those charges to the investors in their funds. That is why it is important to compare the fees charged by mutual funds companies.

Diversification is especially important when one is investing in high-yield bonds, particularly when the economy weakens. During such times bonds rated below investment grade tend to underperform investment-grade bonds. For example, nearly 5.8 percent of speculative bonds defaulted in 2000 and nearly 10 percent defaulted in 2001 owing to the weakening of the U.S. economy.

HOW CREDIT RATINGS AFFECT A BOND'S YIELD

The credit rating on a bond has a significant effect on its yield-to-maturity. As one would expect, the lower a bond's credit rating, the higher its yield. This makes sense when one considers that investors deserve to be compensated as they move along the risk spectrum. A bond's credit rating is not the only factor, however, that determines one bond's yield compared to another. One of the most important factors is a bond's industry classification. For example, bonds in economically sensitive sectors such as retail and finance may yield relatively more or less than do bonds in less economically sensitive industries, depending on the economic climate.

Bonds rated below investment grade yield much more than do bonds rated investment grade. Bonds rated BB, for example, yield much more than AAA bonds do. Over the last five years BB-rated 10-year industrial bonds have averaged a yield spread of about 275 basis points over 10-year U.S. Treasuries compared with an average yield spread of about 70 basis points for AAA-rated 10-year industrials.

Junk bonds historically have yielded much more than investment-grade debt has. The reason for this is simple: Junk bonds are more likely to default than other bonds are. Between 1920 and 1927, for example, a study conducted by Moody's found that 3.27 percent of speculative-grade credit issues defaulted within one year of being assigned their speculative-grade credit rating compared with only 0.17 percent of investment-grade issues. The default rate has been even higher when the economy has weakened. During the recession of 1990–1991, for example, the default rate on speculative-grade debt rose sharply to a post-great-depression high of 13 percent in July 1991, according to Moody's.

Similarly, the weak economic conditions that prevailed in 2001 were expected to push the default rate up to a peak of about 10.5 percent in 2002. It should not be surprising, then, that as the economy began to weaken in 2000, yields on junk bonds began to rise sharply compared to the levels seen in prior years. The Standard & Poor's speculative-grade credit index, for example, which averaged a yield spread of roughly 498 basis points, or 4.98 percentage points, over Treasuries in 1999, rose sharply to an average spread of 699 basis points in 2000 and to a whopping 1002 basis points in 2001. That widening reflected investors' concerns over the increased risks of default. Investors demanded compensation for this increased risk, resulting in a sharp rise in yields on junk bonds.

The sharp widening in yield spreads on speculative-grade debt in 2000 and 2001 was far greater than the widening in spreads that occurred in investment-grade debt. AAA-rated debt, for example, widened from an average of 69 basis points over Treasuries in 1999 to an average spread of 107 basis points in 2000 and 92 basis points in 2001, when spreads began to narrow in response to interest rate cuts by the Federal Reserve. This divergence in performance illustrates the varying degree of impact that the economy has on debt rated investment grade and below investment grade. As the rating definitions describe, AAA-rated bonds are "gilt-edged " and are considered strong enough to withstand various types of financial and economic stress without any meaningful impairment of the issuer's ability to pay obligations on such debt. Bonds rated below investment grade, in contrast, are weak at the core, and their ability to withstand numerous types of stress is not assured.

As was mentioned above, while some bonds may have the same maturity and rating designation, this does not necessarily mean that they will have the same yield. Indeed, for a variety of reasons, two companies with identical ratings and maturity dates can have much different yields. Some reasons include the following:

- Industry fundamentals and characteristics such as the extent to which a company's bonds are more or less vulnerable to the ups and downs of the business cycle.
- Total debt. An agency's opinion about a company's management, for example, skepticism about the way a company is managed, will lower that company's credit rating.

- Cash flows. Two companies may have the same balance sheet, but the company generating the most cash will have the higher rating.
- Exposure to various risks, including regulations and international conditions.

THE IMPACT OF RATINGS ANNOUNCEMENTS

The importance of the rating assignments issued by rating agencies can be seen in the behavior of bonds in the aftermath of changes to their credit ratings announced by those agencies. Typically, when a rating agency announces a change in the credit rating on a bond, there tends to be what is known as an announcement effect. An *announcement effect* is the price change that occurs in a bond as a result of an announcement by a rating agency that it is changing the bond's rating assignment. Bonds whose rating assignment is upgraded tend to rise in price (lowering their yield), and bonds that are downgraded tend to fall in price (raising their yield). While the markets generally tend to adjust the price of a bond in advance of announced changes to its credit rating, the actual announcement of the change tends to cause further movement in the bond. The largest degree of movement, however, tends to occur in advance of the announcement. This suggests that the markets are efficient in discounting potential rating changes. This is similar to the stock market, where stock prices move in advance of earnings reports but often respond very little to their actual release, particularly when the reports meet expectations

With the markets often moving in advance of the rating agencies, some people may feel that the agencies are too slow to recognize changes in the conditions that could undermine the credit ratings they issue for particular bonds. A glaring example was the financial crisis that gripped Asia in 1997 and 1998. The agencies maintained investment-grade credit ratings on sovereign debt, or government-issued debt, even as investors began to shun those bonds with a vengeance. Many Asian countries experienced enormous outflows of capital that exposed risks that most bond investors could not have imagined existed in light of those countries' credit ratings. Many investors lost significant amounts of money during the crisis—dubbed the Asian financial crisis—on both the government bonds and the currencies they bought to pay for those bonds.

While criticism of the agencies in this case seems appropriate, it is important to be aware that there were many different aspects of the Asian financial crisis that the agencies could not have expected. The large number of events that took place during the crisis were the result of a snowballing of problems that synergistically resulted in problems that were not likely to have surfaced in most circumstances. Thus, while the agencies probably could have done a better job warning investors about some of the potential risks involved in investing in some of the Asian countries, the agencies cannot be faulted for failing to predict events that were so unlikely.

HOW CREDIT RATINGS AFFECT LIQUIDITY, QUOTE DEPTH, AND BID-ASK SPREADS

As was indicated in Chapter 2, many factors can affect a bond's liquidity, quote depth, and bid-ask spread. These three factors, which are a reflection of the marketability of a bond, are important considerations for bond investors, particularly if they feel they may sell their bonds before their maturity. Along with the factors mentioned in Chapter 2, a factor that affects the way a bond trades in the marketplace is its credit rating. Generally speaking, bonds rated investment grade tend to have greater liquidity and quote depth than do bonds rated below investment grade. They also tend to have more narrow bid-ask spreads. To illustrate this point, consider the marketability of bonds rated AAA compared with that of junk bonds. The AAA-rated bonds are more likely to attract a greater number of investors than are junk bonds simply because many investors are barred from investing in bonds rated below investment grade. As a result, at any given point in time the AAA-rated bonds will have more buyers and sellers present in the marketplace than will be present in the junk bond market. This simple fact will translate into far greater marketability for the AAA-rated bonds. In fact, in a study conducted by the Federal Reserve, it was found that AAA-rated and AA-rated bonds have significantly lower bid-ask spreads relative to junk bonds.

METHODOLOGY USED TO DETERMINE RATING ASSIGNMENTS

The rating agencies conduct a thorough review of the companies they rate, saving investors plenty of legwork. Numerous considerations are weighed, the most important of which is a company's cash flow. Basically, if a company is a cash cow and has a plentiful supply of capital flowing in, that company is very likely to have a high credit rating. Conversely, a company that has difficulty generating cash will tend to have a low credit rating. The rating agencies look closely at the sources of a company's cash flows as well as their variety and availability. Companies with high credit ratings have quickly turning, high-quality accounts receivable, meaning that they are getting paid on time and getting all the money they are due. Rating agencies also consider it important that a company have the ability to sustain its profitability.

Ratings agencies work meticulously when assigning ratings and have a long checklist of considerations they comb through thoroughly. The agencies are largely interested in reflecting their assessment of an issuer's credit risk as well as the degree of legal protection a bondholder has on a specific security based on that security's indenture provisions. An assessment of these two key risks provides valuable information to investors. The assessment of the credit risks involved in investing in a particular bond helps investors gauge the ability of an issuer to pay its debt obligations. The assessment of the legal protections helps investors understand the level of protection provided to them when they invest in a bond. This is important because securities issued by a single issuer could have different ratings because of different legal protections in each security's indenture provisions.

Rating Methodology

Each rating agency strives to give the best indication it can of the risks of investing in a particular bond. The methodology that each agency uses, however, can vary. The variation in the choice of methodology is a reminder that the ratings those agencies issue are merely opinions.

Figure 12-1 illustrates the debt-rating process used by Standard & Poor's (S&P). As you can see, the process it uses is quite thorough, and each step in the process requires an immense amount of work and expertise. What may look like a simple meeting with company management, for example, is anything but that. Standard & Poor's assembles its most experienced staff members

Figure 12-1

Standard & Poor's Debt-Rating Process

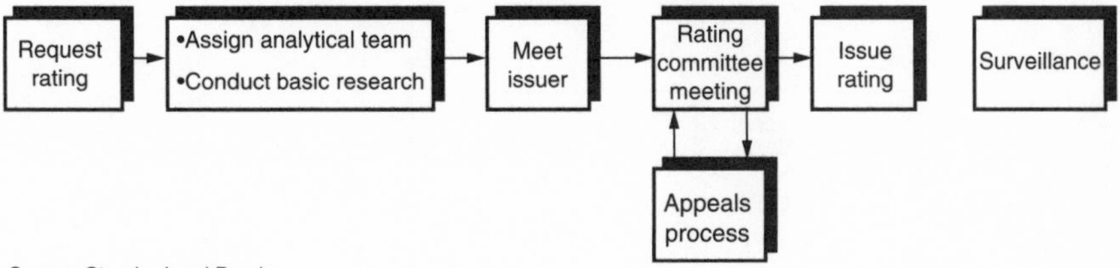

Source: Standard and Poor's

to meet a company's management, and when they meet with management, it's not for cake and coffee. The purpose of the meeting is to "review in detail the company's key operating and financial plans, management policies, and other credit factors that have an impact on the rating." At these meetings the companies are asked to provide significant amounts of information that will help determine the rating assignments. Rating agencies such as S&P scrutinize a company's management for its competence, structure, strategic planning, and composition. It also scrutinizes the company's appetite for risk and often tours a company's facilities, although this is not always a critical factor in the rating process. The many steps carried out in the process quite clearly show that the rating process is quite vigorous, involving many different and intense areas of concentration.

The Agencies Do Their Homework

As was mentioned earlier, the rating agencies endeavor to base their assessments on two key risks: credit risk and indenture protection. Gauging these risks requires a significant amount of financial and legal review. The legal reviews are complex but are less open to interpretation than the financial reviews. The financial reviews therefore must be conducted quite thoroughly. Let's take a look at how the agencies conduct their financial reviews. Table 12-2 details the many factors the agencies consider when conducting their credit analyses.

As the table shows, the two main considerations in a credit analysis are a company's business risk and financial risk. Analysis

Table 12-2

Corporate Credit Analysis Factors

Business Risk

Industry characteristics

Competitive position

　　Marketing

　　Technology

　　Efficiency

　　Regulation

Management

Financial Risk

Financial characteristics

Financial policy

Profitability

Capital structure

Cash-flow protection

Financial flexibility

Source: Standard and Poor's.

of a company's business risk mainly involves an assessment of the industry of which the company is a part. The agencies are primarily interested in assessing the industry's growth potential and sensitivity to the ups and downs of the business cycle. An industry's ability to withstand an economic downturn, for example, is an important factor in the assessment of business risk. The agencies also are interested in assessing the competitive pressures from other companies in the industry as well as the amount of research and development expenses that may be needed for a company to stay competitive. Despite the emphasis on industry considerations, a company's fundamentals always get first consideration and have a far greater bearing on its overall rating. Nevertheless, in recent years rating agencies have increased their responsiveness to and consideration of factors such as the impact of the economic cycle on various industries.

The assessment of a company's financial risk requires greater use of quantitative analysis than is used to assess a company's business risk. In other words, the rating agencies must do enough homework to make a math teacher proud. Scrutiny of a company's cash flows and overall balance sheet, for example, requires a significant amount of mathematical homework. Rating agencies therefore deploy dozens of mathematical formulas and financial ratios to aid them in their rigorous examinations. The ratios are used to gain an understanding of the financial characteristics of a company.

If you are wondering whether an agency places greater emphasis on the assessment of a company's business or financial risks, the answer is: It depends. The rating agencies take pains to meld both quantitative and qualitative analyses to get the most complete picture of a company. Whether a rating agency will depend more heavily on its assessment of one or the other is essentially a case-by-case issue.

The Four Cs

The various elements of the methodology used by the rating agencies to assign credit ratings sometimes are called the four Cs: *capacity, character, collateral,* and *covenants.* The four Cs represent a fairly good summary of the rating process. You might want to remember this system to remind you of the rating methodology described above. Let's briefly look at each of the four Cs.

Capacity refers to an issuer's ability to pay its debt obligations, including both principal and interest. The rating agencies assess this mostly by conducting a review of the issuer's financial situation and the various industry considerations that could affect its financial situation in the future.

Character refers to the issuer's management, management policies, operating plans, and reputation in its industry and with its customers. Personal visits with management are an integral part of the review of a company's character.

Collateral refers to the assets that back an issuer's debt. In a sense, a review of an issuer's collateral can be placed under the umbrella of one of the other Cs: capacity. Capacity, however, refers mostly to an analysis of the cash flows needed for a company to pay its debt obligations. A review of a company's collateral, by contrast, can shed light on the amount of assets that would be available to pay an issuer's debts if the issuer had to liquidate its assets because of a bankruptcy. The review also can indicate the amount of assets available to help fuel a company's expansion.

Covenants refer to the legal protections provided to the bondholder. These legal protections are contained in a bond's indenture. The indenture is essentially a contract between a bond issuer and the investors who buy its bonds. Included in the indenture are promises such as the timing and amount of interest payments, the bond's maturity date, and the call provisions. Indentures were discussed in greater detail in Chapter 3.

The significant amount of homework the agencies do should increase your confidence in the ratings system.

CREDIT RATINGS: A MUST-HAVE FOR EVERY FIXED-INCOME TOOLBOX

As you can see, ratings supply an enormous amount of information to aid in the investment decision-making process. Investors are fortunate to have a few simple ratings grades available to summarize the complex and thorough research conducted by the rating agencies. You need only gain an understanding of the various ratings grades to include them in your research arsenal. Of course, always do a bit of homework on your own too, but regardless of how much work you do on your own, it is comforting to know that the rating agencies have done a good deal of the homework for you.

An interesting exercise to test your understanding of credit ratings would be to make a list of ten diverse companies and try to guess their credit ratings. Once you have finished, see how you fared by checking the actual credit ratings of those companies. Then take a step back and see how the ratings fit with the companies you chose and try to gain a better understanding of why the ratings agencies chose to rate them as they did.

SUMMARY

Looking beyond the basics, in this chapter we discussed:

- Credit ratings are a great tool for gauging a company's ability and willingness to meet its debt obligations.

- The rating system has been in place for decades and has been a reliable way to gauge credit risk, a key risk for bond investors.

- The methodology used by the major rating agencies is extensive and probably is more rigorous than what can be accomplished by most individuals.

- Although credit ratings are a great tool, investors should use them to augment their own investment decision-making tools and consider the many other factors involved in the investment decision.

- Knowledge of credit ratings is very basic yet is essential to investing. The various ratings definitions supplied in this chapter can be used to improve your knowledge of credit ratings.

CHAPTER THIRTEEN

The Internet: The Bond Market Finally Gets a Marketplace of Its Own

Even before the advent of the Internet the bond market was a virtual market; unlike the stock market, the bond market has never had a centralized location—either physical or electronic—for trading and obtaining quotes. Moreover, information about the bond market's trading activity has long been difficult to track. You cannot find daily volume figures in the bond market as you can in the stock market.

Lacking a marketplace of its own, the bond market has grown into a relatively closed market dominated by institutions rather than individuals. One might say that this has been a contributing factor in the growth of the so-called equity culture, which for many years resulted from a climate in which investors spurned bonds in favor of stocks. There are many other reasons for this, of course, but the relatively inaccessible nature of the bond market has had an unmistakable impact on the individual investor. The financial bubble of the late 1990s, for example, might not have grown to the extent that it did if individual investors had held more bonds in their portfolios. Investors would have fared better if they had diversified their assets and purchased more bonds.

Fortunately, the bond market is finally getting a marketplace of its own: the Internet. In many ways the bond market and the Internet are a perfect match. For years individual investors who were looking to buy and sell bonds have had a limited number of choices in regard to where to obtain them. Often this forced investors to buy bonds that did not meet their original specifications, resulting in bond portfolios that were poorly constructed. On other occasions the difficulty of finding a buyer or seller for an inactively traded bond forced investors to pay higher prices on purchases and receive lower prices on sales of their bonds. But now, thanks to the Internet, this is all beginning to change. Greater transparency is finally here, although it is in the early stages. In addition, information about the bond market is now far more readily available than it was before. This is helping investors make more informed decisions and reducing perceptions of the risks associated with bond investing. In short, a new age for bond investing is under way.

BONDS ARE ALREADY THE BIGGEST THING ON THE WEB

You might be surprised to hear that the daily dollar value of bonds traded on the Web exceeds the dollar value of the sales of books, toys, music, and other merchandise combined. In addition, more bonds than stocks trade on the Web in dollar terms. These facts clearly suggest that the Internet is an ideal venue for facilitating numerous aspects of the bond market. There are five main ways in which the Internet is affecting the bond market and fostering conditions that benefit individual investors:

- Electronic trading
- Increased market transparency
- Increased availability of market information and research
- Underwriting and bond issuance
- Added convenience and reduced costs of purchasing Treasuries and U.S. savings bonds

Advances in each of these areas appear likely to continue in the near term and are essentially creating the marketplace that the bond market has never had. Let's take a look at each of these important developments.

ELECTRONIC TRADING

The most important way in which the Internet is affecting the bond market is through the rapid growth of electronic trading. The increased availability of electronic trading systems is giving investors additional ways to buy and sell bonds. The more these systems proliferate, the more efficient bond transactions are likely to get. For example, increased levels of competition are likely to encourage broker-dealers to be more competitive when providing quotes to the investing public. And by creating a virtual marketplace, electronic trading is reducing the need for investors to depend on a small number of broker-dealers to fulfill their trading needs. This is enabling market forces to begin working their magic.

Another way in which electronic trading helps bond investors is by increasing the quote depth on bonds. As was discussed in Chapter 2, quote depth basically refers to the size of the bids and offers on a particular security. The more quote depth a security has, the more likely it is that the bid-ask spread will be narrower. Moreover, quote depth affects the liquidity, or the ease with which a buyer or seller can transact in a security at the fair market price.

The biggest areas of growth in electronic trading have been the municipal, agency, and mortgage-backed securities markets. The electronic market for U.S. Treasuries also remains active, however. For example, on October 31, 2001, TradeWeb LLC, one of the biggest on-line trading firms in the bond market, saw Treasury volume of over $21.5 billion. That is roughly half the average dollar value of daily transactions at the New York Stock Exchange during November 2001.

Types of Electronic Trading Platforms

There are five main types of electronic trading platforms:

- Cross-matching
- Single-dealer
- Auction
- Interdealer
- Multidealer

Of the five types, cross-matching systems are the most prevalent and the fastest-growing. Let's take a brief look at each type. I'll refer to users of these systems as customers.

Cross-Matching Systems
Cross-matching systems enable customers to enter anonymous buy and sell orders with multiple counterparties, increasing the

likelihood of executing their orders at desirable prices. Customer orders are filled when a match is found on the other side of the transaction or when a contraparty decides to buy the bond at the customer's offer or hit the customer's bid. Cross-matching systems bring both dealers and institutional investors together in electronic trading networks that provide either real-time or periodic cross-matching sessions.

Single-Dealer Systems

As the name implies, single-dealer systems enable customers to deal directly with a single dealer, allowing them to execute through an electronic interface, particularly on the Internet. In this type of system the dealers act as principal, which means that they buy and sell securities for their own accounts. The full range of major fixed-income products is being offered through this system. This system enables investors to peruse a dealer's inventory of bonds, helping the customers locate bonds in which they may be interested. The disadvantage here is the lack of competitive bids and offers. For example, would you want to buy stocks from just one firm rather than placing your bids and offers out in the marketplace? Single-dealer systems tend to exist at the large, primary dealer firms such as Goldman Sachs and Merrill Lynch.

Auction Systems

Auction systems are basically on-line systems for auctioning new securities. The auction system functions just as one would expect an auction system to, except that it takes place over the Internet. Users of this system simply post the securities they want to sell and set the guidelines for the auction, including the date of sale and the type of auction (single-price or multiple-price). Bond issuers can use the auction system to reduce the cost of issuing securities. Ford Motor Company was one of the first companies to use the auction system on the Internet.

Interdealer Systems

Interdealer systems enable dealers to trade with one another anonymously through an intermediary known as a broker's broker. Interdealer systems have existed for many years, with Cantor Fitzgerald at the forefront since the 1950s. In the 1970s that company introduced trading in Treasuries on electronic screens. Cantor has since grown into an intermediary with a vast reach and has remained at the forefront of electronic trading despite the devastating impact of the September 11 attacks on the company. In 2000 Cantor processed over $32 trillion in transactions. Interdealer brokers such as Cantor Fitzgerald have been migrating to the Internet in recent years, particularly in the aftermath of the September 11 attacks, enabling hundreds of the world's largest financial institutions to transact in a simpler, more efficient way. The interdealer system is likely to remain robust for years to come, particularly because of the anonymity and liquidity the system provides to its users. Moreover, the Internet facilitates new features such as customized trading screens, user alerts, and the ability to "check out," or review, trading activity for the day.

Multidealer Systems

Multidealer systems have experienced sharp growth in recent years, led by the explosive growth of TradeWeb, a New York–based firm that enables institutional customers to buy and sell various types of fixed-income securities electronically with multiple primary dealers. One of the key advantages of the multidealer system is the ability to obtain prices displayed by multiple dealers. This gives users a better chance at getting a better price on their executions. It is more efficient than the traditional phone method because users can obtain multiple quotes more quickly. The multidealer system differs from the interdealer system in that it facilitates trading between institutional investment management firms and broker-dealers, whereas the interdealer system facilitates trading between broker-dealers.

One of the more salient aspects of these trading platforms is that they cater largely to the institutional investor. What about the individual investor? It is important to note that these platforms can help the individual too, although indirectly. Since trading between institutions has become more efficient, the market should become more efficient in the process and thus benefit individual investors. Moreover, in many cases individual investors may conduct their bond transactions with broker-dealers who may utilize electronic platforms to facilitate the transactions, benefiting the individual investors. Individuals also can benefit from using the single-dealer system if their broker-dealers make the system available to them.

Middleware Trading Platforms

A number of Web sites offer bond trading by utilizing a database of securities from numerous contributing broker-dealers. Those broker-dealers regularly submit their inventories to companies such as Bond Express, a firm that facilitates transactions by providing a searchable database for firms that wish to offer bond trading to the investing public. Some of these companies are purely Internet firms that have entered the realm of electronic trading in hopes of earning a profit. In other cases small broker-dealer firms that lack the resources to build trading systems of their own or have too few securities in their bond inventories turn to companies such as Bond Express to establish a foothold in electronic trading.

There are advantages and disadvantages to using the systems provided by these so-called middlewares. A key advantage is that they enable investors to choose from a far larger database of securities than they would find if they went directly to a small number of broker-dealers. This is especially true in the municipal and corporate bond markets, where finding bonds with specific characteristics can be extremely difficult.

A second advantage of a system that utilizes a database of bonds is the ability it gives investors to search for bonds that fit their criteria. Figure 13-1 shows the type of search screen offered by companies such as Bond Express. As the figure shows, an investor can conduct a bond search that is made to order. An investor can search for bonds with a specific maturity date, coupon rate, credit rating, price, yield, and call protection, among other details. Finding bonds that are tailor-made is a task well suited for the Internet and one which a broker could not easily do.

A third advantage is that these systems enable investors to track and compare prices on bonds. This can be a big help to bond investors who have often traded in the dark, so to speak, with no way of knowing whether the prices they were being quoted were an accurate reflection of the true market prices.

One of the main disadvantages of systems that rely on databases of inventories that are not their own is that often there are multiple entities involved in the transaction. This can raise the actual or implied transaction costs of executing orders on the system. For example, when a bond investor decides to purchase a

Figure 13-1

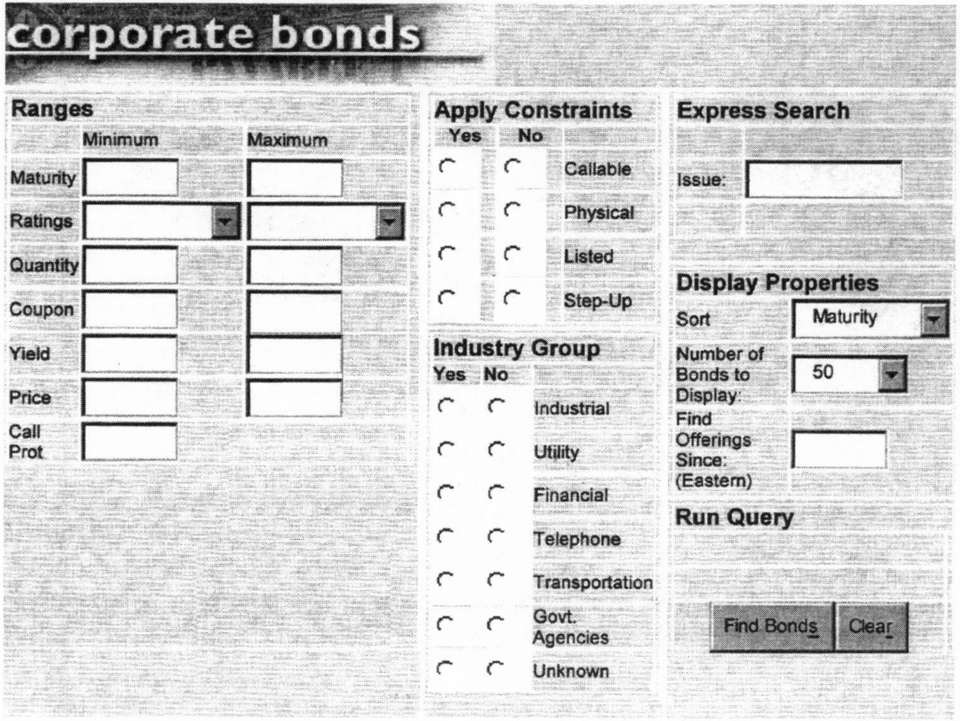

corporate bonds

Ranges

	Minimum	Maximum
Maturity		
Ratings	▸	▸
Quantity		
Coupon		
Yield		
Price		
Call Prot		

Apply Constraints

	Yes	No
Callable	○	○
Physical	○	○
Listed	○	○
Step-Up	○	○

Industry Group

	Yes	No
Industrial	○	○
Utility	○	○
Financial	○	○
Telephone	○	○
Transportation	○	○
Govt. Agencies	○	○
Unknown	○	○

Express Search

Issue:

Display Properties

Sort: Maturity ▸

Number of Bonds to Display: 50 ▸

Find Offerings Since: (Eastern)

Run Query

Find Bonds | Clear

bond on a Web site that uses this type of system, there are likely to be at least two entities with their hands in the kitty. The Web-based company that sells the bond to the investor will mark up the price of the bond to earn a profit from the transaction. The price of the bond will be marked up a second time to reflect the markup it had to pay to obtain the bond from the broker-dealer who listed the bond in the database. On-line brokers do not carry their own inventory. To top it off, those brokers often charge a commission for the transaction, adding to the cost of the transaction.

Despite the disadvantages, the advantages seem to prevail. One key reason for this is the fact that there are often layers of entities involved in transactions that are done off-line too. In addition, the increased transparency can help investors get a better price on the bonds they buy and sell. Moreover, investors are more likely to find bonds in which they are interested by using an on-line search engine designed to find bonds in accordance with an investor's specifications.

In light of the progress made to date and the considerable degree of progress that lies ahead, on-line bond trading seems likely to continue growing in the years ahead and the Internet seems likely to become the venue for the marketplace the bond market has never had.

INCREASED MARKET TRANSPARENCY

As was mentioned above, one of the main problems facing bond investors is the bond market's lack of transparency. For years individual investors essentially have traded in the dark, not knowing whether the prices on their purchases and sales of bonds reflected the fair market prices. In addition, investors have long had difficulty finding bonds that meet their specifications and therefore often have had to resort to buying bonds that were not their first choice. The result has been less participation in the bond market, reducing market liquidity and creating inefficiencies.

The bond market's poor transparency tends to widen the bid-ask spread on individual bonds, particularly in corporate and municipal bonds, where market liquidity is low in comparison to the U.S. Treasury market. Indeed, as was discussed in Chapter 2, the average bid-ask spread on corporate and municipal securities is generally roughly double the spread on Treasuries. The spread is even wider on securities that are traded inactively. Electronic trading is likely to alleviate this problem by making the universe of bonds more accessible.

Increased transparency also will boost the quote depth on individual bonds by increasing the number and size of bids and offers submitted on these bonds. This is important because the greater the quote depth on a bond is, the easier it is for investors to find willing buyers and sellers to take the other side of their trades. Quote depth has long been a greater problem for individual investors than it has been for institutional investors, who generally have much less difficulty finding contraparties to their trades.

The Internet appears likely to increase the transparency of the bond market significantly by essentially creating a centralized location where quotes and prices are aggregated.

INCREASED AVAILABILITY OF MARKET INFORMATION AND RESEARCH

To many investors the bond market has always been a bit of a mystery. One of the main reasons for this has been the relatively small amount of information that flows out of it. Information about trading activity, for example, has been kept largely inside the trading rooms on Wall Street. In addition, much of the crucial information needed to invest with confidence in bonds historically has been difficult to obtain. For example, it often has been difficult to obtain information on the important details contained in a bond's indenture. Investors will never have perfect information, of course, and they will always be challenged to obtain as much information as is necessary to make informed investment decisions. However, these challenges often have been seen as onerous to bond investors, who have had to formulate their investment strategies with far from perfect information.

The Internet is significantly increasing the amount of information available to bond investors. Those investors can now more readily obtain high-quality information on many factors important to the investment decision-making process, including the specifications on a particular bond, daily trading flows, market-moving news, new bond offerings, the Federal Reserve, the yield curve, economic news, and education. This information is available on a variety of Web sites, some of which are mentioned in this chapter.

I have found that investors are very interested in information about the bond market. At Miller Tabak & Co. I built a Web site called Bondtalk.com, now one of the most frequently visited fixed-income Web sites. The most frequently visited section of the site is a section that contains live intraday observations and analysis of the day's events as well the day's trading activity. For example, that section contains analyses of the day's economic reports as well as emerging trends in the bond market. The popularity of this section is an indication that investors are eager for current information about the market and analysis of events that have the potential to materially affect their investments. Few Web sites provide this type of information, since most focus is on the equity market.

Another area that is of interest is education. Investors seem to want to know more about the bond market, particularly important topics such as the yield curve, credit ratings, real interest rates, and market sentiment. These topics are covered in depth in this book. There are many new places where investors can learn about the bond market. Five Web sites that stand out are bondmarkets.com, investinginbonds.com, publicdebt.treas.gov, moodys.com, and standardandpoors.com. Combined, these sites provide a wealth of information about bond investing as well as recent developments in the bond market.

Information about the Fed is also extremely popular. For instance, bondtalk.com's traffic tends to jump significantly on days when the Federal Open Market Committee (FOMC) meets to decide on interest rate policy. This should not be surprising; after all, the Fed is one of the most important influences on the bond market.

Investors also are very interested in interpretations of economic reports that might affect the Fed and the general direction of interest rates. For example, I have the ability to track traffic to my Web site literally by the minute and have always been amazed at the sharp increases in traffic flows that occur in the minutes after the release of an economic report. Investors appear to want a quick interpretation of the data along with the potential investment implications. The intense interest in economic data is clear evidence that investors are clamoring for current information on the market.

Investors also seem to be clamoring for information that helps explain intraday movements in the bond market. Traffic flows to my Web site jumps significantly when there are sharp intraday moves in bond prices. Knowing more about what makes the market move can significantly enhance an investor's ability to forecast future price movements. This topic was covered in Chapter 9.

One area that has always been of interest to investors but has been difficult to track has been information about current market rates. The Internet is making it possible for investors to track market rates in all the major segments of the bond market. This is important because investors have to know where rates are when they are considering making an investment. This is a bit like knowing the price of merchandise in one store when one goes to purchase that merchandise in another store.

The Internet has become a great venue for delivering various forms of fixed-income and economic research. Many large firms, including the primary dealers, provide free research or password access to first-class research previously available largely to institutional investors. This research can assist an investor significantly in the investment decision-making process.

The Internet is opening the door to a world of information that previously was closed to most individual investors, and the opening seems to be widening by the day.

UNDERWRITING AND BOND ISSUANCE

An area which is developing rapidly but in many ways is still in its infancy is the on-line underwriting and issuance of bonds. In a variety of ways the Internet is beginning to transform the way companies issue, or sell, new bonds to investors. In the process investors considering the purchase of a bond sold on-line are getting the benefit of increased transparency, information, and accessibility as well as reduced transaction costs. In short, with on-line bond transactions everyone wins, with the exception of Wall Street's investment bankers.

To issuers of bonds there are a number of distinct advantages to issuing bonds over the Internet that probably will make that practice more prevalent. Already several large companies have made a foray into this new realm. Dow Chemical Company, for example, was the first nonfinancial company to sell its bonds directly to investors over the Internet, selling $300 million in 5-year notes in August 2000, using software developed by WR Hambrecht, a San Francisco–based investment bank. Ford Motor Credit Company has also taken the plunge with several large sales of bonds, including its first foray in January 2000, when they sold $1 billion in 3-year notes. U.S. government agencies could well lead the movement toward more on-line issuance; Freddie Mac, for example, sold $5 billion in 3-year notes on-line in February 2001. Many municipalities have been actively selling their bonds on-line.

To issuers there are several advantages to selling bonds on-line. First, on-line sales reduce an issuer's cost of capital by reducing sales and marketing costs. While the savings can be substantial, pulling off a successful auction still requires a strong effort by professional salespeople. Thus, there is a cap on the savings in this area.

A second advantage is the reduction in the underwriting fees paid by the issuer. In a conventional sale the issuer typically pays a fee to the investment bankers involved in the sale. Sometimes known as a commission, that fee often is expressed as a percentage of the total offering. A typical fee could be about 50 basis points. For example, an entity that sold $100 million in bonds would pay the investment banker $500,000 if the fee was 50 basis points. In cases where the issuer sells bonds on-line but enlists the help of investment bankers, the fee can be cut in half.

Third, an even greater cost saving can result from the increased transparency that comes with selling bonds on-line. In a conventional syndicated offering the investment bankers, or underwriters, often have an incentive to reduce the price of the offering to lure major investors in hopes of strengthening or establishing relationships with them and thus do more business with them. By buying the bonds at a lowered price, these investors can make quick profits by selling them for a profit when the bonds enter the secondary market and begin trading in the open market. New bonds often rise in price after their initial sale because of pent-up demand from buyers who were unable or unwilling to participate in the initial offering. In Internet auctions the so-called book, which is the list of investors who have placed orders to buy the new bonds, can be seen in real time on-line. This helps investors gauge the true level of underlying demand for the bonds, leading them to bid more aggressively than they would if the bonds were sold conventionally. This is the case partly because investors generally will have more confidence that they are not paying too high a price when they submit their bids. Issuers that sell their bonds on-line are therefore able to sell their bonds closer to the true fair market price rather than at a price that largely helps the investment bankers.

A fourth advantage of on-line issuance is that it tends to increase the number of long-term investors relative to short-term investors. The increased transparency of an on-line auction makes it more likely that the investors are going to be long-term investors rather than investors who participate in the auction to reap a short-term profit. The higher a company's bonds trade in the secondary market, the lower that company's cost of capital will be in the long run.

Finally, on-line sales tend to result in increased distribution of a company's bonds. This tends to reduce the volatility of a company's bonds in the secondary market, reducing the company's cost of capital.

ADDED CONVENIENCE AND REDUCED COST OF PURCHASING TREASURIES AND U.S. SAVINGS BONDS

Droves of investors have discovered the benefits of purchasing U.S. Treasuries and savings bonds on-line, directly from the U.S. Treasury Department. Investors can save both time and money by purchasing securities directly from Uncle Sam rather than through a bank or brokerage firm.

Treasury Direct

The Treasury Direct program is intended for investors who plan to hold their Treasuries until the maturity date, but individuals who may need or want to sell their securities for any reason also can use it.

To purchase Treasuries directly from the Treasury Department, an investor can simply go to the Treasury's Web site (publicdebt. treas.gov/sec/sectrdir.htm) to open an account or visit any of the Federal Reserve's 12 district banks either on-line or in person (information about the Fed's 12 district banks is available on the Fed's main

Web site at www.federalreserve.gov). An investor also can call the Treasury Department at 1-800-722-2678. Opening an account is simple and requires very little paperwork.

The main benefit of opening a Treasury Direct account is that no commissions and no fees are involved in the transaction. In addition, you can buy Treasuries in a Treasury Direct account in denominations as small as $1000, and the price you receive on your bonds will be the same as that for institutional investors. The Treasuries you buy will be bought for you at one of the Treasury's regularly scheduled auctions. With a Treasury Direct account you also can perform a variety of maintenance functions with your Treasury holdings, which are held by the Treasury Department in book-entry form. The Treasury will inform you of the impending maturity of your securities about 45 days in advance. This way you will have time to decide what to do with the proceeds and can reinvest the money by informing the Treasury by phone or on-line.

With a Treasury Direct account you can sell your Treasuries in the secondary market under the auspices of the Treasury Department. The Treasury will sell your Treasuries by obtaining quotes from a variety of brokers and then selling the Treasuries to the highest bidder. This is a big help to individual investors, who often have to settle for whatever their brokers quote. Individual investors often are penalized for selling so-called odd lots, or bond orders under $1 million. This is one of the more compelling reasons to do business with the Treasury. The Treasury charges the small fee of $34 for this service, but this is no higher than the commissions charged by most brokerage firms for bond transactions (stock commissions can often be much lower on-line).

U.S. Savings Bonds On-Line

The Internet has taken a tremendous amount of legwork out of buying U.S. savings bonds. This should be welcome news to the millions of investors who buy savings bonds every year. Indeed, nearly 25 million savings bonds are sold every year, and about 55 million people own these bonds. In the past most people had to go through the time-consuming process of going to a bank and waiting in line. Now, however, by simply logging on to the Treasury's Web site at www.savingsbonds.gov you can buy bonds with a credit card. Despite the convenience, there is no fee for the service. By going to a bank you will not get your savings bonds any faster than if you would if you bought the bonds on-line. Banks do not physically give you the savings bonds on the spot. Whether you buy savings bonds on-line or in a bank you still have to wait for them to be delivered in the mail. There's therefore no time saved by going to a bank to buy savings bonds.

Moreover, although savings bonds are a relatively simple instrument, there are complicated aspects to them that require a bit of research. Most bank employees have only a modest understanding of savings bonds and are therefore unable to handle every query about them. On the Internet, however, there's a plethora of information available on the Treasury's Web site, savingsbonds.gov. Investors therefore can make an informed decision before making a purchase. Table 13-1 lists several useful Web sites.

SUMMARY

Looking beyond the basics, in this chapter we discussed the following issues.

In many ways, the Internet is transforming the way the bond market works and giving the bond market a marketplace of its own. The Internet appears to be the perfect venue for creating greater efficiencies in the bond market and giving greater power to the individual investor. Here are a few ways in which you can benefit from the bond market's increased presence on the Internet:

Table 13-1

Useful Web Sites for Bond Investors:

bloomberg.com	federalreserve.gov
publicdebt.treas.gov	investinginbonds.com
bondtalk.com	moodys.com
briefing.com	savingsbonds.gov
cbot.com	standardandpoors.com
cme.com	treas.gov

- **Electronic trading.** By trading on-line individual investors can search for bonds that more closely meet their investment objectives. In addition, using on-line systems that utilize a database of bonds created from the inventories of scores of broker-dealers can increase the odds of finding bonds that may be difficult to obtain from a single dealer. Beware, however, of the potential for several layers of transaction costs. Institutional investors can benefit from the increased liquidity and anonymity and the ability to obtain multiple quotes that come with on-line trading.

- **Transparency.** The Internet is making bond transactions more transparent, and this helps investors know whether their bond transactions are being done at the fair market price. The increased transparency also is causing bid-ask spreads to tighten and increasing the quote depth on bonds.

- **Availability of market information and research.** Far more information about the bond market is now available on the Internet. Useful information on trading activity, new issuance, market-moving news, the Federal Reserve, economic news, the specifications on a particular bond, and education is providing investors with information that can help them formulate their investment strategies. I encourage you to visit some of the Web sites shown in Table 13-1 as well as the links to economic reports shown in the Appendix to learn more about bonds and to stay abreast of the latest developments in the bond market.

- **Underwriting.** Bond issuers can benefit greatly by offering their bonds over the Internet. Reduced sales and marketing costs, reduced underwriting fees, increased transparency, and wider distribution are the main advantages of issuing bonds over the Internet. Individual investors benefit from increased market efficiency and from being able to participate in offerings to which they previously had limited access.

- **Uncle Sam on-line.** Millions of investors have discovered the many benefits of buying Treasuries and savings bonds on-line. You can save time and money by utilizing the Treasury Department's Web sites. It has become especially easy to buy savings bonds, particularly compared to the old way of going to the bank. I strongly recommend giving the new way a try.

CHAPTER FOURTEEN

How Interest Rates Have Shaped the Political Landscape

The powerful role interest rates play in this society goes well beyond conventional thinking. It is simplistic to think that the vast impact of interest rates ends with the economy; there are numerous intriguing secondary effects. One of the most intriguing is the influence interest rates have had on the political landscape. This is a relatively new phenomenon, but the evidence is compelling.

While there are many issues that can shape an election and thus the political landscape, I believe that the impact of interest rates is unmistakable. This is a relatively new phenomenon, dating back to the 1976 elections, when President Gerald Ford faced off against Governor Jimmy Carter. In every presidential administration since then there have been moments when interest rates played a major role in defining each President's place in history. While pundits have noticed that interest rates and politics cross paths now and then, few have noted the clear link that has undoubtedly existed over the last 25 years or so.

Judging the extent to which interest rates have affected politics is quite subjective, but few people argue against the notion that the health of the economy has played a substantial role in shaping the political landscape over the last 100 years. If the economy is known to influence politics, and interest rates are known to influence the economy, it stands to reason that interest rates must influence politics. In my view, the only debate should be about the degree of influence.

ECONOMIC ISSUES HAVE BEEN CORE POLITICAL ISSUES SINCE THE REVOLUTION

Throughout history economic factors have clearly been one of the most influential factors in U.S. politics. As far back as the Revolutionary War economic issues have been at the heart of the nation's political events. The Boston Tea Party in 1773, for instance, was a protest against taxes on tea imports, a tax the colonists felt was unfair. Interestingly, the tax was imposed by Britain to pay interest on its national debt. That debt had doubled during the Seven Years War between Britain and France, and interest payments were consuming more than half of Britain's annual budget. It was not the last time issues related to the economy and the national debt would affect America.

A clear example of the link between the economy and politics occurred during the presidency of Martin Van Buren. Within weeks of his inauguration the Panic of 1837 thrust Van Buren into a crisis from which he would never fully recover. Van Buren had the unfortunate luck of entering office when the U.S. economy was at the end of a boom period that had been fraught with excesses partly related to speculative demand for lands in the west. The banking system was soon in tatters, and hundreds of banks and businesses failed. The economy sunk into its first depression, and the economic weakness lasted about five years.

During those years the crisis might have been prevented and/or alleviated if the nation had had a means of smoothing the business cycle. Back then, the Federal Reserve did not exist and there was no real equivalent. There was, however, an equivalent in the private sector. Suffolk Bank of Boston served as a clearinghouse for virtually all the bank notes that circulated in New England, and it lent reserves to other banks and kept the payments system working. These functions are essential elements of the operations of today's Federal Reserve. Suffolk Bank's unique role as a "central bank" helps explain why New England and its banks were spared the economic distress that plagued the rest of the country. This episode is evidence of the importance of having a central bank such as the Federal Reserve to provide stability to the U.S. financial system. Interest rates, of course, are one of the Fed's most important tools, and there almost certainly would have been a role for the Fed in not only helping to prevent the speculative excesses that led to the Panic of 1837 but also helping the nation recover from them. The Fed could have raised interest rates to reduce the speculative fervor and then lowered them to bring stability to the financial system. The panic was a case where interest rates could have played an important role but did not because the mechanism for manipulating them did not exist.

As history has proved many times since the Panic of 1837, such a crisis can have major political repercussions. President Van Buren rolled from one crisis to the next and was alienated even in his own party. The economic distress fractured his party and hurt his popularity. In the election of 1840 Van Buren was defeated handily, losing in the Electoral College by a vote of 234 to 60.

THE GREAT DEPRESSION SPARKED A SEA CHANGE IN POLITICS

The panic of 1837 would be trumped almost 100 years later by an even worse set of economic circumstances during the Great Depression that began in 1929, and the political repercussions would again be dramatic.

On the heels of the booming economy of the 1920s, Herbert Hoover was swept into office as the 31st president of the United States, winning in the Electoral College by a vote of 444 to 87—the largest margin recorded up to that time. Hoover's Republican party was in complete control of the House, the Senate, and the executive branch of the government. That was a condition that would rarely be seen in the rest of the twentieth century, and it was the economy that was at the root of the power shift.

But on October 29, 1929, the stock market crashed, tumbling 11.7 percent and leading to the worst economic depression the country has ever seen. Unemployment skyrocketed to about 25 percent, putting nearly 14 million people out of work. The boom years of the Roaring Twenties were a distant memory. A lot of remedies were proposed at that time, many of which Hoover rejected. For the most part Hoover did not embrace the notion that the government could alleviate economic woes with new programs and fiscal initiatives. Most economists agreed with Hoover, as it was conventional wisdom at that time to expect the economy to right itself. Economists and the Treasury believed that new government spending ultimately would fail to revive the economy because the deficits created by the new spending would result in a decline in private investment. The notion that the economy would be better off if left alone, Hoover would learn, would become politically bankrupt. Laissez-faire was out.

As with the Panic of 1837, the Great Depression might have been less severe if the boom years that preceded it had been fraught with fewer excesses. The Federal Reserve, for instance, could have helped cool the speculative fervor that ran rampant in the 1920s, but the Fed did not fully grasp the powerful role interest rates could have played in cooling the excesses. If the Federal Reserve had raised interest rates during the 1920s, the excesses that built up almost certainly would have been reduced and the bubble would have burst more quietly. And once the bubble burst, the Fed could have used its interest rate tool again to soften the effects of the economic bust. But with the Federal Reserve having been established not too many years earlier in 1914, the Fed had little experience in handling the ups and downs of the business cycle. However, the Fed would be able to draw on its unfortunate experience for decades to come.

To Hoover, however, the invaluable lessons that the Fed learned from the Great Depression could not be redeemed for votes. In the 1930 election Hoover's Republican party lost the House to a previously weak Democratic party and won a plurality of just one vote in the Senate. In the 1932 election Hoover lost his bid for a second term in a landslide defeat to Franklin D. Roosevelt, losing in the Electoral College by 472 to 59. Roosevelt would go on to implement a series of government programs that ultimately would revive the economy. The failure of Hoover's laissez-faire approach and the success of Roosevelt's support for more proactive government helped define the two parties, particularly in the public's eye. Perceptions about the two major parties and their core beliefs about government involvement in the economy stand to this day. If the Federal Reserve had been more influential during that era and used its powerful interest rate tool, the political landscape might have evolved much differently over the subsequent years.

By the 1950s the Federal Reserve was playing a more active role in regulating the pace of the U.S. economy. Few people probably recognized it at the time, but the Fed's maturity probably had an influence on the stability the nation enjoyed in the 1950s. During that time interest rates were both low and stable. This probably encouraged investment, which helped raise productivity and thus the national standard of living.

As the 1960s unfolded, inflation and interest rates began to climb as the effects of the Vietnam War started to affect the economy. The Vietnam War affected the economy in two ways. First, the war was costly. The size of the public debt roughly doubled by the time the war ended, and interest rates rose in response to the increase in debt issuance. Second, the Federal Reserve allowed the money supply to expand through what in hindsight appears to have been an overly accommodating stance on monetary policy. The Fed was essentially monetizing the acceleration in inflation by providing the fuel needed to push up prices. The jumps in interest rates and inflation were arguably contributing factors in the 1969–1970 recession.

INTEREST RATES AND POLITICS IN THE MODERN ERA

Ford and Nixon

After the Vietnam War ended, the link between interest rates and politics grew stronger than ever, and for the first time interest rates became a campaign issue. During Ford's term as President the electorate began to view high interest rates not as a repercussion of the costly Vietnam War but as a symptom of bad economic policies and something it could control with its votes. The electorate came to see high interest rates as something that was detrimental to the national standard of living, as the recession of November 1974 to March 1975 would make clear. Of course, that recession was precipitated by the first of the two oil shocks in that decade, but the recession also can be attributed to excessive growth in credit and the money supply that was partly fueled by the Federal Reserve.

As it did in the late 1960s, the Fed monetized the acceleration in inflation of the mid-1970s by providing the fuel needed to push up prices. In turn, inflation drove interest rates higher and thus weakened demand for homes and other goods and services, resulting in rising unemployment and an economic recession.

Democrats, led by Governor Jimmy Carter of Georgia, pounced on Ford's economic record and made it one of their major campaign issues. Here's how Carter put it during one of the several presidential debates just weeks before the 1996 presidential election:

> Seven point nine percent unemployment is a terrible tragedy in this country. He [Ford] says he's learned how to match unemployment with inflation. That's right. We've got the highest inflation we've had in twenty-five years right now, except under this administration, and that was fifty years ago. And we've got the highest unemployment we've had, under Mr. Ford's administration, since the Great Depression.

Carter would repeat that theme many times during his campaign.

Ford clearly was on the defensive not only against Carter but also against a weary electorate. The mood of the electorate was captured in these pointed questions posed by the moderator of one of the debates:

> Mr. President, the country is now in something that your advisors call an economic pause. I think to most Americans that sounds like an antiseptic term for low growth; unemployment standstill at a high, high level; [for a] decline in take-home pay, lower factory earnings, more layoffs. Uh, isn't that a really rotten record and doesn't your administration bear most of the blame for it?

To which Ford responded, "Well, Mr. Kraft, uh—I violently disagree with your assessment. And I don't think the record justifies the conclusion that you come to."

Ford tried to explain how interest rate levels had not hurt the housing market and how inflation was trending lower. But Carter matched his explanation with a strong response. Here's the exchange:

> **Ford:** But now let's talk about the pluses that came out this week. We had an 18 percent increase in housing starts. We had a substantial increase in new permits for housing. As a matter of fact, based on the

announcement this week, there will be at an annual rate of a million, eight hundred and some thousand new houses built, which is a tremendous increase over last year and a substantial increase over the earlier part of this year. Now in addition, we had a very—some very good news in the reduction in the rate of inflation. And inflation hits everybody: those who are working and those who are on welfare. It means that the American buyer is getting a better bargain today because inflation is less.

Carter: With all due respect to President Ford, I think he ought to be ashamed of mentioning that statement, because we have the highest unemployment rate now than we had at any time between the Great Depression caused by Herbert Hoover and the time President Ford took office. Anybody who says that the inflation rate is in good shape now ought to talk to the housewives. One of the overwhelming results that I've seen in the polls is that people feel that you can't plan anymore. There's no way to make a prediction that my family might be able to own a home or to put my kid through college. Savings accounts are losing money instead of gaining money. Inflation is robbing us. And housing starts—he compares the housing starts with last year. I don't blame him, because in 1975 we had fewer housing starts in this country, fewer homes built, than any year since 1940.

At the root of Carter's assertions about the economy, particularly with regard to his statement on the housing sector—one of the most interest-rate-sensitive sectors of the economy—was his view that high interest rates were hurting the economy. Carter's message on the economy undoubtedly contributed to his victory over Ford in the 1976 election, given the narrowness of his victory. Indeed, Carter won by slim margins in many key northeastern states, no doubt helped by the weak economic conditions plaguing those states at that time. While this was not the first time the economy contributed to the outcome of an election, it was the most visible illustration up to that time of the power of interest rates and their subsequent impact on the economy and, hence, politics.

For Carter, High Interest Rates Became a Double-Edged Sword in the 1980 Campaign

While Carter clearly benefited from the high interest rates and weak economic conditions that prevailed in the years leading up to the 1976 election, those forces turned out to be a double-edged sword for him when he sought reelection in 1980. After over a decade of rising interest rates and accelerating inflation, the public was once again poised to show its discontent at the polls. The electorate merely needed a leader to champion its cause, and Ronald Reagan fit that mold.

To many people Reagan represented the best hope of restoring the American dream. The country had entered a slow but dangerous decline that was matched by similar conditions abroad. The economy was mired in an unusual slump consisting of high interest rates, high inflation, and high unemployment. The national standard of living was clearly in decline as a result of those major forces. High interest rates reduced housing affordability and hurt many other key interest-rate-sensitive sectors of the economy, such as business investment. The decline in business investment resulted in a decline in U.S. competitiveness, particularly in the automobile industry, where low-cost producers such as Japan began to make inroads on U.S. automakers, grabbing market share along the way. High inflation cut into wages and salaries, eroding the value of disposable income, while unemployment made those days even more difficult to bear.

There was a term used back then to define the unusual combination of high inflation and high unemployment that plagued the Carter years: *stagflation*. Stagflation became Carter's nemesis, and the nation looked to Reagan to lead it out of that dilemma.

Reagan saw to it that the public would recall Carter's criticisms of Ford's handling of the economy four years earlier. Carter was basically defenseless. Here's how Reagan, during one of the two presidential debates that took place in 1980, deftly turned an expression Carter had coined and benefited from in 1976 into an issue that he could use against Carter during the 1980 campaign:

> Now, as to why I should be [President] and he shouldn't be, when he was a candidate in 1976, President Carter invented a thing he called the misery index. He added the rate of unemployment and the rate of inflation, and it came, at that time, to 12.5% under President Ford. He said that no man with that size misery index has a right to seek reelection to the Presidency. Today, by his own decision, the misery index is in excess of 20%, and I think this must suggest something.

The misery index, which is the sum of inflation and unemployment, could easily be redesigned to include interest rates instead of inflation. Interest rates, after all, typically track inflation and therefore are a good proxy for inflation. Moreover, high interest rate levels relate to the miseries associated with the burdensome cost of borrowing. High mortgage rates, for example, can be disheartening to families hoping to realize the American dream of owning one's own home. Similarly, to individuals aspiring to own their own businesses, high interest rates can stymie their dreams. If the misery index were redefined to include interest rates, a more complete picture of the impact of a set of economic conditions would result.

Throughout the campaign Reagan offered a vision for better economic times. He repeatedly promised to adopt policies that ultimately would bring down both inflation and interest rates and thus restore economic prosperity to the nation. His economic plan would be dubbed "Reaganomics." Reaganomics consisted of four key elements. First, Reagan supported a restrictive monetary policy designed to purge inflation from the economy and ultimately result in lower interest rates. Lower interest rates, he argued, would spur investment and raise productivity levels, raising the nation's standard of living. Moreover, low interest rates would spur wider home ownership so that more families could realize the American dream. Initially, tight money policies also would help stabilize the value of the dollar and thus reduce the cost of imports and encourage foreign investment in U.S. assets. Second, Reagan proposed a 25 percent across-the-board tax cut to lift consumer buying power, increase savings and investment, and encourage work and worker productivity (this ultimately became the Economic Recovery Tax Act of 1981). Third, Reagan promised to reduce discretionary government spending. Fourth, he endeavored to reduce layers of government regulations that he felt were impeding productivity and, hence, economic growth.

With slow economic growth, high interest rates, inflation, and unemployment in mind, Reagan crystallized the 1980 election with these classic closing remarks at the debate on October 28:

> Next Tuesday is Election Day. Next Tuesday all of you will
> go to the polls, will stand there in the polling place and

make a decision. I think when you make that decision, it might be well if you would ask yourself, are you better off than you were four years ago? Is it easier for you to go and buy things in the stores than it was four years ago? Is there more or less unemployment in the country than there was four years ago?... And if you answer all of those questions yes, why then, I think your choice is very obvious as to whom you will vote for. If you don't agree, if you don't think that this course that we've been on for the last four years is what you would like to see us follow for the next four, then I could suggest another choice that you have. This country doesn't have to be in the shape that it is in. We do not have to go on sharing in scarcity with the country getting worse off, with unemployment growing... . All of this can be cured and all of it can be solved.

Reagan knew that when he asked people to ask themselves, "Are you better off than you were four years ago?" the public's discontent with high interest rates, inflation, and unemployment would be voiced at the polls. Reagan offered hope for a departure from the country's economic malaise and ultimately delivered on his promises.

Throughout Reagan's presidency, interest rates, inflation, and unemployment all fell. Reagan's prescriptions for those major ills proved to be the right remedies. During the 1984 election campaign Vice President George Bush summed up Reagan's accomplishments in regard to the economy, particularly with respect to interest rates, in his debates with vice-presidential candidate Geraldine Ferraro:

One of the reasons I think we're an effective team is that I believe firmly in his leadership. He's really turned this country around. We agree on the economic program. When we came into office, why, inflation was 21, 12 1/2 percent interest [rates] were wiping out every single American; [interest rates] were 21 1/2 percent if you can believe it. Productivity was down. Savings was down. There was despair... . The other day [Ferraro] was in a plant and she said to the workers, Why are you all voting for, why are so many of you voting for the Reagan-Bush ticket. And there was a long, deathly silence, and she said, Come on, we delivered. That's the problem. And I'm not blaming her except for the liberal voting record in the House. They delivered. They delivered 21 percent interest rates. They delivered what they called malaise. They delivered interest rates that were right off the charts. They delivered take-home pay, checks that were shrinking, and we've delivered optimism. People are going back to work: 6 million of them. And 300,000 jobs a month being created. That's why there was that deathly silence out there in that plant. They delivered the wrong thing. Ronald Reagan is delivering leadership.

Reagan's economic record would catapult him to a landslide victory in the 1984 presidential election.

As well as the economy performed during the Reagan years, the sharp rise in the government's budget deficit has been attributed to his policies. The large increase in defense spending that occurred during Reagan's tenure—the biggest peacetime defense buildup ever—often is cited as one of the main causes of the jump in the deficit. In addition, the massive tax cut implemented in 1981 often is cited as a cause. These assertions fall flat for a few reasons. First, the tax cuts did not result in a decrease in tax receipts; tax receipts actually increased in the 1980s. Indeed, tax revenue grew by a whopping 83 percent during his administration. Second, the defense buildup, which pushed defense spending up to 6.2 percent of the gross domestic product (GDP) during the 1980s, arguably helped win the Cold War. Once the cold war ended in the 1990s, the United States was able to reduce defense spending and enjoy a large peace dividend: Defense spending fell to just 2.9 percent of GDP by the year 2000. Thus, in the long run Reagan's defense buildup may have saved the nation hundreds of billions of dollars. Third, perhaps the biggest cause of the increase in the budget deficit was the sharp jump in entitlement spending. An increase in eligibility for entitlement programs and sharply increased costs for medical care contributed to the surge in entitlement spending. These were forces largely outside Reagan's control.

As large as the budget deficit was, it did not cost Reagan any votes, nor would it hurt the election chances of George Bush. One of the biggest reasons for this was that the surge in the deficit had little discernible effect on interest rate levels. In economic theory, budget deficits are supposed to result in an increase in interest rates because the government is competing with the private sector for capital. In a world with finite capital, investors would require higher interest rates to be enticed to invest in government bonds rather than in the private sector. In addition, simple economics suggests that if the supply of bonds increased as a result of a budget deficit, the price of those bonds would fall—and yields would rise.

Yet despite the increase in the U.S. budget deficit, interest rates began a long secular decline very early in Reagan's first term. This happened largely because inflation began a secular decline at that time. Moreover, Reagan's low-tax, low-regulation policies sowed the seeds for a sharp rise in business investment and innovation, resulting in a sharp rise in productivity. This is important because rising productivity levels tend to reduce the cost of labor and, hence, inflation and interest rates. These forces eventually would play a major role in laying the groundwork for the vigorous economic growth that occurred during the 1990s. Investors recognized this well in advance, and that helped to keep interest rates on a downward path during the 1980s. The growing budget deficits therefore had little impact on Reagan and Bush in the 1984 and 1988 elections. Falling interest rates had eased the public's concerns over the budget and therefore played a major role in the outcome of those elections. To most voters, as long as interest rates were falling, they could defer their concerns over the budget.

The Fed's Rate Increases: Slow Pace of Rate Cuts Hurt Bush

While declining interest rate levels undoubtedly played a role in helping George Bush become President in 1988, rising interest rate levels early in his term and their slow pace of decline late in his term probably hurt his reelection bid in 1992. As Bush entered office in 1989, interest rates began to climb. The Federal Reserve had embarked on a course of raising interest rates to combat a steady climb in inflation. Inflation had begun to occur as a result of economic forces that typically emerge when the duration of an economic expansion lengthens. The 1980s expansion, after all, was at the time the longest peacetime expansion since World War II. Nevertheless, Bush would have to contend with the political fallout higher interest rates would bring.

The Federal Reserve, led by its chair, Alan Greenspan, raised interest rates numerous times just before and soon after Bush took office in 1989. Indeed, the federal funds rate, the interest rate the

Fed controls, rose from about 6.5 percent in early 1988 to 9.75 percent in March 1989, the highest level since the early 1980s. The rate increases would seal Bush's political fate.

With the usual 12- to 18-month lag, the Fed's interest rate increases eventually slowed the economy. In July 1990 the economy entered into a recession, precipitated partly by Iraq's invasion of Kuwait and the sharp rise in oil prices that resulted from the increased tensions in the Middle East. The interest rate increases dealt a sharp blow to the housing market, where new housing starts fell to an annual level of about 800,000 (recent levels have been closer to 1.5 million). The reduced demand for new homes sparked a decline in home prices, and many individuals were saddled with mortgage debt that exceeded the values of their homes. This prompted a wave of foreclosures and bankruptcies, leading to the savings and loan crisis of the early 1990s. The bank failures were so extensive that the government established an institution, the Resolution Trust Company, to manage the orderly liquidation of failed banks.

The gloomy economy overshadowed Bush's many accomplishments in foreign policy, particularly his handling of the Gulf War and the important role he played in ending the Cold War. After the Gulf War ended, few people would have suspected that Bush might lose his reelection bid, especially in light of his 90 percent approval rating. But the ending of the war turned the public's attention back home, and the public did not like what it saw: The economy remained in recession, and unemployment was still rising.

There was very little Bush could do. The budget agreement he signed in 1990 gave him little leeway to stimulate the economy. Bush had agreed to a tax increase that broke his campaign pledge against new taxes (Bush famously said, "Read my lips: No new taxes"). Just as important was the framework of the budget agreement. It would permit new tax or spending initiatives only on a pay-as-you-go basis. In other words, if Bush wanted to cut taxes, he would have to cut spending to pay for the reduced revenue. The net benefit to the economy thus would be limited. Even without the budget agreement, it might have been political infeasible to try to stimulate the economy through fiscal initiatives. The budget deficit was already high—approaching $300 billion per year—and so there was basically no money in the till. There would be only one way to stimulate the economy: lower interest rates.

The Federal Reserve also recognized that lower interest rates were needed to stimulate the economy and cut interest rates many times during Bush's presidency. Yet Bush and members of his administration repeatedly voiced their discontent with the pace of the Fed's rate cuts. The administration recognized that owing to the long lag between interest rate cuts and their impact on the economy, the economy might not recover in time to help Bush in the 1992 election campaign. Bush wanted the Fed to move faster, as he stated during the 1992 presidential debates: "Alan Greenspan is respected. [But] I've had some arguments with him about the speed in which we have lowered interest rates."

Bush may have had a point. Despite the recession and the slow economic growth that followed, the Fed lowered rates in baby steps, mostly a quarter of a percentage point at a time. The slow pace of rate cuts was one of the reasons Greenspan became famous for his gradualist approach toward changing interest rates, at least until 2001. Indeed, Greenspan lowered interest rates 23 times during Bush's presidency, and 20 of those cuts were just a quarter of a percentage point. Baby steps, indeed. In fact, during the 1990–1991 recession Greenspan had lowered interest rates just seven times, a total of only 200 basis points, by the time the recession was over. More was clearly needed, but it would take time for the Fed to recognize that, and it would be too little, too late for Bush. The Fed probed for three and a half years before settling on an interest rate level it felt would help revive the ailing economy. The Fed eventually lowered the federal funds rate to 3 percent. Unfortunately for Bush, that equilibrium level would not be reached until he left office.

By taking so long to find the equilibrium interest rate level that would revive the economy, the Fed essentially validated the claim that it had moved too slowly. Greenspan must have learned from that experience, judging by the rapid pace of interest rate cuts that he and the Fed implemented in 2001, when the Fed lowered interest rates an unprecedented 11 times in a series of cuts, most of them a half percentage point.

If the Fed had responded as quickly and aggressively as it did in 2001 to the economic slowdown that began in 1990, there is a good chance that the economy might have recovered in time for Bush to be reelected in 1992, but the Fed did not lower interest rates fast enough to pull the economy out the recession that followed its interest rate increases years earlier. Interest rates clearly played a major role in Bush's political destiny.

Clinton Harnessed the Power of the Bond Market Like No President before Him

Bill Clinton masterfully used the powerful influence of interest rates as the centerpiece of his economic strategy. Clinton believed that if he adopted a fiscal strategy of reducing the budget deficit and encouraging investment, interest rates would fall and increase economic growth. Clinton's strategy, which was crafted with the help of Robert Rubin, who was Clinton's chair of the Council of Economic Advisors before becoming U.S. Treasury secretary, was a smashing success. Clinton turned deficits into surpluses, business investment soared, and interest rates fell in dramatic fashion. His policies helped create a virtuous cycle of economic growth, producing the longest peacetime expansion ever. It would be Clinton's crowning achievement. The remarkable set of economic conditions that prevailed during his presidency helped Clinton weather a number of personal and legal challenges. For Clinton, the dramatic role interest rates played in strengthening the economy helped save his presidency.

Before he entered office, Clinton once said that he would focus on the economy like a laser beam. He clearly had a strategy to help the economy early on. Hints of his strategy were revealed during the presidential debates with George Bush just weeks before the 1992 election. Note Clinton's apparent awareness of his central banklike ability to control long-term interest rates:

> We have low interest rates today. At least we have low interest rates that the Fed can control. Our long-term interest rates are still pretty high because of our deficit and because of our economic performance. And there was a terrible reaction internationally to Mr. Bush saying he was going to give us 4 more years of trickle-down economics—another across-the-board tax cut and most of it going to the wealthy, with no real guarantee of investment. But I think the important thing—the important thing—is to use the powers the president does have on the assumption that, given the condition of this economy, we're going to keep interest rates down if we have the discipline to increase investment and reduce the debt at the same time.

That is my commitment.... Give me a chance to do that. I don't have
to worry in the near term about the Federal Reserve. Their policies
so far, it seems to me, are pretty sound.

Clinton was a master of issues and seemed to know them
inside and out. His awareness of his ability to affect long-term
interest rates is evidence of this.

Clinton's fiscal plan eventually turned deficits into surpluses,
spurring a decline in long-term interest rates and freeing up money
for investment in the private sector. The result was a sharp increase
in capital spending—the so-called good growth that tends to foster
increases in productivity and, hence, cuts inflation and increases the
national standard of living. Of course, the low-tax, low-regulation
policies implemented during the Reagan-Bush years had helped
foster an environment conducive to achieving the solid economic
growth experienced in the 1990s, but Clinton advanced the cause
through his fiscal policies.

In Clinton's nomination speech at the 1996 Democratic con-
vention, he contrasted his record against Republican plans to cut
taxes by highlighting the impact interest rates were having on the
economy:

> This plan will explode the deficit, which will increase interest rates
> by 2 percent, according to their own estimates last year. It will
> require huge cuts in the very investments we need to grow, and to
> grow together, and at the same time slow down the economy. You
> know what higher interest rates mean. To you, it means a higher
> mortgage payment, a higher car payment, a higher credit card pay-
> ment. To our economy, it means business people will not borrow as
> much money, invest as much money, create as many jobs, create as
> much wealth, raise as many wages.

Time and time again Clinton reminded the American public
that his economic plan was working. Clinton illustrated his successes by highlighting the ways in which low interest rates were
helping the economy. Clinton often would note the sharp increase
in home ownership and business investment, for example.

It is notable that Clinton, a Democrat, achieved economic successes without having to resort to an increase in government spending. Clinton defied the traditional views of his party by adopting an
economic plan that depended more on the markets than on the gov-

ernment. Few people would have imagined this before he entered office, particularly people in the bond market. In fact, just before Clinton's election, when there was a sense that he would win, the bond market fell and interest rates jumped. George Bush made note of this: "There was a momentary fear that he might win and the markets went Phwee, down like that." However, despite its initial fears, the bond market eventually recognized that it was at the center of Clinton's strategy. For his plan to work, interest rates had to fall, and the best way for Clinton to accomplish this would be to reduce the budget deficit. As it became clear to bond investors that Clinton was more interested in reducing the deficit than in raising spending, interest rates fell and the economy soared.

The vibrant economy of the Clinton years benefited Clinton immensely, overshadowing some of his less dubious accomplishments, including his impeachment. In fact, if the economy had been weak at the time of his impeachment, it is conceivable that the political atmosphere might have been venomous enough to result in his removal from office. For Clinton, the economy played a crucial role in maintaining his popularity, which barely wavered through thick and thin. At the center of it all was the bond market. Like a chairman of the Federal Reserve, Clinton used his powers to control the interest rates that he could control in order to work wonders for the economy and for himself.

SUMMARY

Looking beyond the basics, in this chapter we discussed:

- Throughout history there have been many occasions when interest rates have played an unmistakable role in shaping the political landscape of this nation.
- In the more distant past, when interest rates were not yet ready for use as a policy tool or when their power was not yet fully understood, one can see how interest rates *might* have had a substantial influence on the economy and, hence, politics.
- In the more recent past interest rates have played an increasingly visible role in political campaigns and have become an issue in their own right.

- It is unconventional to think about the impact of interest rates on politics, but the evidence clearly suggests that the bond market has played a major role in shaping the political landscape and will continue to do so.
- As a practical matter, you should now be more cognizant of the ways in which interest rates can affect the political landscape and thus your personal life.
- In general, this chapter should remind you of the powerful role interest rates play in people's lives.

CHAPTER FIFTEEN

Utilizing Economic Data to Improve Your Investment Performance

In light of the important role economic data play in the behavior of the bond market, it is crucial for investors to understand the major economic reports that shape the bond market's daily movements. This chapter and the Appendix that follows will help give you that understanding. Gaining an understanding that is sufficient to be a material help to an investor is not all that difficult. In fact, you would be surprised at how little many Wall Street professionals know about the various economic reports. With a little work you can bring your knowledge level up to or above the standard that many on Wall Street have taken years to reach.

One of the things that make it easy to gain an understanding of the major economic reports is the frequency of their release; most of those reports are released monthly, and some are released quarterly. That frequency gives you an opportunity to learn more about them. Each month you can take a closer look at how a report is presented and observe its impact on the market. You also can begin to spot patterns in the way the data behave and learn to draw connections between one economic report and the next. Before you know it, it will all come together and you will see clearly how the reports are all intertwined. By simply paying close attention to the monthly economic reports, almost anyone can gain a high level of understanding of how the economy works. In many ways expert knowledge of economic reports is superior to the theoretical work done in college economics classes. In my eyes, there is no substitute for knowledge that can be applied to one's personal life. I strongly believe that knowledge about economic reports fits this mold.

The repetitive nature of economic reports is apparent from a quick glance at the monthly economic calendars. Figure 15-1 shows a typical economic calendar. In fact, if you looked closely at economic calendars from one month to the next, you would see that they look almost exactly alike, with most of the economic reports

F i g u r e   15–1

A typical economic calendar.

Monday	Tuesday	Wednesday	Thursday	Friday
		1 ISM Index Construction Spending Automobile Sales	2 Jobless Claims Factory Orders	3 Employment Situation ISM Non-Manufacturing Index
6	7 Consumer Credit	8	9 Jobless Claims	10
13	14 Producer Price Index Retail Sales	15 Business Inventories Industrial Production	16 Jobless Claims Consumer Price Index Housing Starts Philadelphia Survey	17 International Trade Consumer Sentiment
20 Leading Economic Indicators	21	22	23 Jobless Claims	24 Durable Goods New Home Sales
27 Existing Home Sales	28 Consumer Confidence	29	30 Jobless Claims Chicago Index Personal Income	

being released at about the same time each month. One of the more important things to note is the large role manufacturing-related data play in the makeup of the calendar. Manufacturing-related reports include durable goods orders, factory orders, the Chicago Purchasing Managers index, the Philadelphia Fed index, the Institute of Supply Management report (ISM) report, industrial production, and capacity utilization. The heavy concentration of manufacturing-related reports is unusual because the U.S. economy is largely a service-oriented economy. In fact, the manufacturing sector has been in a secular decline for over 20 years and now accounts for only 16 percent of the economy. In contrast, the service sector accounts for about 65 percent. The rest includes government (12.3%); construction (4.7 percent); mining (1.3 percent); and agriculture, forestry, and fishing (1.4 percent). The statistical discrepancy in this calculation is discussed in the section on the gross national product in the Appendix.

Despite the manufacturing sector's shrunken size and the service sector's rise, the economic calendar is almost completely devoid of economic reports that relate to the service sector. There are a couple of reasons for this. For one thing, the government agencies responsible for tracking the economy have been very slow to respond to the secular decline of the manufacturing sector. Indeed, the economic calendar has hardly changed despite the changed nature of the economy. In fact, the only relatively new service-related economic report is the nonmanufacturing report released monthly by the ISM, a private organization. A second reason is the fact that activity in the service sector is much more difficult to measure. It is easy to measure the monthly output of automobiles, but it is another matter to measure the plethora of services performed in the nation each day. It would be difficult, for example, to track the activity of landscapers, cleaning services, repairpersons, lawyers, hair salons, nail salons, and so on. As a result, the government focuses largely on tracking activity in the manufacturing sector. Most of the time this presents few problems for investors because the manufacturing data act as a microcosm of activity in the general economy. After all, if people are buying more cars, they probably are getting their hair and nails done more often too. However, there have been plenty of occasions in recent years when the manufacturing sector has sent misleading signals on the state of the overall economy. Thus, it would be a good idea for the government to put more focus on measuring activity in the service sector.

Although the manufacturing sector is a smaller part of the economy than the service sector is, the bond market tends to be swayed more by developments in the manufacturing sector. This is the case largely because of the unusually heavy presence of manufacturing-related reports in the monthly economic calendar. It is therefore important for bond investors to stay abreast of developments in the manufacturing sector most of all. A sustained jump in car sales, for example, tends to have a big impact on a wide variety of economic data. As developments in the automobile sector work their way into the monthly economic reports, the bond market will react accordingly. Therefore, it is important to think of the many ways in which developments in the economy may find their way into the monthly reports and spark movement in the bond market.

FORECASTING ECONOMIC DATA: NUMBERS DO NOT LIE

Forecasting trends in the economy is challenging, but the task is made easier when you let both your instincts and the facts guide your forecasts. I believe that many economic forecasters approach forecasting far too conservatively and rarely think outside the box. They tend to avoid making forecasts outside the cluster of forecasts around the mean, or consensus. As a result, they often miss the best calls and are more susceptible to being blindsided by surprises when the economic data are released. I suppose analysts feel more comfortable making conservative calls. After all, when their forecasts go awry, analysts are likely to be less open to criticism if their peers are also wrong. The investment strategies built around an analyst's forecasts are likely to be conservative, too, reducing volatility in investment portfolios. Analysts therefore are shielded against receiving partial blame for large trading losses related to the forecasts.

In some ways the conservatism of most economic forecasters is similar to the reticence shown by equity analysts before the financial bubble burst in 2000. Equity analysts stood by rosy forecasts on stocks that had few realistic growth prospects and were extremely reluctant to issue sell recommendations when the environment clearly called for it. In fact, fewer than 1 percent of analysts' stock recommendations are sells. While there is no doubt that analysts, like many others, were caught in a mania, there was little basis for clustering their forecasts together. Only a few broke away from the pack, delivering more honest and realistic forecasts about the future.

I have been known to be willing to make forecasts that are far removed from the consensus. I don't do this only for the sake of being contrary. I let my forecasts be dictated by numbers; numbers do not lie. In doing so, I have been able to deliver many accurate forecasts that few dared to make.

When making an economic forecast, try to think of yourself as a detective. You are on a mission to collect as many relevant facts as you can. I remember in my early working days taking drives to the local shopping mall just to look at the number of cars in the parking lot to get clues on the pace of consumer spending. Of course, it is best to get as much information on national trends as possible, but I want to underscore the point that you can never have too much information when you are putting a forecast together. The task has become simpler now that the information age has ushered in new means of obtaining various data. The Internet is particularly helpful, and I recommend utilizing Web sites created by trade associations to obtain information about the various sectors of the economy. Again, the key is to approach forecasting like a good detective and pull in as many facts as you can before drawing your conclusions.

Once you have the facts, it is very important to let them guide your forecasts and avoid being swayed by contradictory information. You must remain open-minded, of course, but there are many situations where your forecast may seem at odds with some of the more obvious facts that are guiding the decisions of other forecasters. I recall that in the middle of 2001, when most of the key indicators I use on the housing sector were pointing down, my forecast for imminent weakening was both counterintuitive and unproven. Mortgage rates had fallen sharply, leading many forecasters to say that the housing market, which had been strong despite the weakening in the economy, would remain strong. But the numbers simply did not point in that direction. Lumber prices were near a nine-year low, mortgage applications for home purchases were slipping, and home builders were saying that their business was softening, as evidenced by a sharp decline in the monthly housing market index released by the National Association of Home Builders. Those facts, along with a decline in consumer confidence and income growth—the two main pillars of the housing market—suggested that the housing market would slow. It did. There was simply no information to the contrary, and it was only a matter of time. (The housing market eventually rebounded very sharply when interest rates plunged after September 11th.) This is a good illustration of why it is important to stand by your numbers, especially if they make a compelling case.

BE FLEXIBLE: INVESTORS CHANGE THEIR FOCUS OFTEN

The bond market's focus on economic data is almost always intense, but the specific economic reports that get the most attention often vary with the shifts in the dominant influences on the economy. Occasionally, data that rarely are given more than a passing glance suddenly become a large force in shaping the bond market's direction. At other times big market movers such as the employment report carry little weight in shaping its direction. It is therefore important to be open-minded and flexible when weighing the potential impact of a set of economic reports.

Just before a recession, for example, bond investors tend to put a great deal of weight on the employment report because weakness in that report is a necessary prelude to a recession. In fact, it is a key criterion in the designation of the timing of the start of a recession. As a result, the market response to weak employment data released during the period leading up to a recession tends to be quite sharp. And since the market moves in advance of the release of the report as well as afterward, the cumulative response can be large. Importantly, however, there comes a point when bond investors start to look beyond the weakness and begin to anticipate an eventual recovery. Markets, after all, are known to anticipate and discount events before they occur. Investors therefore begin to look at the employment report as a lagging indicator. They recognize that if the underlying demand for goods and services begins to improve, employers will not quickly rehire workers until the pickup in demand is sustained. In this way, employment conditions can be a lagging indicator, or an indicator that lags actual turning points in the economy. Similarly, when the economy suddenly weakens after several years of expansion, employers generally do not let go of workers just because they had a bad month or two. They want to be sure that the trend will be sustained before they consider layoffs.

There are many different situations in which the market's focus will change, and the changes can occur frequently. It is therefore important to look several steps ahead at the chain of events that will affect the economy in future months. It is not enough to look at the economy's current problems. The way Wall Street works, that is like looking in the past. Instead, you must first identify the economy's key problems or key underpinnings and try to envision the chain of events that could alter its direction. The best way to accomplish this is to recognize that behind each economic event are a series of other events. Once you recognize the large degree of connectivity that exists in the economy, forecasting will be easier. Simply envision the series of events that you expect to occur and simultaneously envision the market response to both the individual events and the series of events. It is especially important to relate developments in the economy to the markets; *you cannot put being right in the bank.* You must apply your sense of the data to the markets in order to profit from accurate economic forecasts.

LEARN THE SURVEY METHODOLOGIES TO ENHANCE YOUR FORECASTING ABILITIES

Once you have a good sense of how the economy works and feel comfortable making economic forecasts, you can enhance your forecasting ability by having a better understanding of the methodology used by government agencies and private organizations to produce the major economic reports. By doing this, you will gain an edge on market participants who have scant knowledge about how the monthly reports are put together. The methodology used to produce the major economic reports is described in the Appendix.

A key point is that the actual economic data can differ greatly from the reported data. Statisticians see to it that the raw data that are captured in monthly surveys and the like are altered in a variety of ways to create consistencies in the data and smooth seasonal fluctuations. Consider the sale of Christmas trees. Sales increase substantially around the holiday season before nose-diving in January. The statisticians recognize this and therefore attempt to "smooth," or seasonally adjust, the fluctuations. They do this by adjusting the sales level for the holiday season downward by an amount close to the average percentage increase experienced in past years and by adjusting the sales level in January upward by an amount close to the average decrease seen in past years. Doing this removes the "noise," or volatility, from the data so that the data are easy to interpret. After all, if you heard that the sale of Christmas trees jumped 400 percent in December compared to November, you might get a tad confused. The point is that the reported data go through a series of changes before they are delivered in the economic reports. By recognizing the various ways in which the data are altered, you are more likely to spot situations where those adjustments may have a meaningful impact on the reported data and therefore affect the markets.

It also is important to learn how the data are collected. By doing this you are more likely to spot situations where the collection methodology could result in unexpected fluctuations in the reported data. Many economic reports, for example, are derived from samples and surveys with specific cutoff dates. This means that when a report is for, say, January, it is not necessarily for the full month of January but for some portion of January. Knowing the cutoff date therefore can help you know whether certain factors influenced the data. In January, for example, a snowstorm that occurs on the twenty-fifth of the month will have an effect on some economic reports for the month of January but not on others. In some cases the effects of the storm will not be captured until the February reports. If you are familiar with the survey methodology in advance, you are less likely to be fooled by the economic reports and can be opportunistic and use your extra insights to your advantage in trading and investing. We will look at the survey methodologies for each of the major economic reports throughout the Appendix.

SUMMARY

Looking beyond the basics, in this chapter we discussed:

- There is little doubt that the economic reports are at the root of most of the volatility in the bond market.

Recognition of this fact is the first step in using this simple notion to your advantage.

- The next step is to take advantage of the repetitiveness of the monthly releases to learn them inside and out. If you look closely at the reports month after month, your understanding of how the economy works will steadily increase, enabling you to forecast the future direction of the economy and the market more accurately.
- Utilize your understanding of the economy to envision the series of events that follows most economic events and weigh the potential market response to each individual event. Remember, however, that it is important to be open-minded. Investors change their focus frequently. What is important to investors today could mean much less to them tomorrow, and vice versa.
- When you have a good handle on how the economy works and feel comfortable making forecasts, enhance your abilities by learning more about how the monthly reports are put together. This will give a big edge over most market participants.
- Do all these things while remembering that in the economy everything is connected in one way or another. In the economy, for every action, there is a reaction. As an investor, your ability to anticipate these series of reactions will separate you from the pack.

Handbook of Economic Data: Power Tool for Investors

The following economic data is listed alphabetically.

BUSINESS INVENTORIES

Source: U.S. Census Bureau

Web address for report: *http://www.census.gov/mtis/ www/mtis.html*

Release date: Generally around the middle of every month

Time: 08:30 a.m. EST

Report covers: Inventory levels in retail trade, wholesale trade, and manufacturing as they stood in the calendar month two months before the report's release

Description of report: The business inventories report provides information about the extent to which businesses are accumulating or reducing their inventories. The data provide clues to whether inventory levels are too high or too low relative to demand. The more out-of-sync inventories are with demand, the more likely it is that manufacturers will alter their production schedules to fit demand, thereby influencing growth in personal income and spending. Imbalances in inventories have historically had a major influence on the business cycle. The markets use this report to forecast future activity in the manufacturing sector. Business inventories in the United States total approximately $1.2 trillion, and so even small percentage changes in the monthly data can have a large impact on the U.S. economy.

Survey methodology: The business inventories data are derived from three separate monthly surveys: retail trade, wholesale trade, and the survey of manufacturers' shipments, inventories, and orders. For the retail trade survey, which captures about a third of all business inventories, a mail-out/mail-back survey is sent to about 4000 retail businesses that meet minimum size requirements. Those businesses are asked to give information about their month-end inventory levels. The weighting of each response to the survey is dependent on the size of the companies that respond to the survey relative to the size of their respective industries. Inventories on wholesale trade, which account for about 25 percent of all business inventories, are calculated in a similar way, using a sample size of about 6500 wholesale businesses. Factory inventories, which account for about 40 percent of all business inventories, are calculated similarly, but there are some important differences; factory inventories are calculated by using data from three different stages of production: finished goods, work in process, and raw materials and supplies.

Key components of the report: As was mentioned above, total business inventories are derived from the data from three separate monthly surveys: *retail trade, wholesale trade*, and *manufacturers' shipments, inventories, and orders*. These are the most important components in the report on business inventories. Also important is the data on the *inventory-to-sales ratio*. This ratio provides a way to gauge the extent to which inventory levels may be too high or too low. A rise in the ratio indicates that inventories are rising relative to sales, while a drop indicates that inventories are falling relative to sales. There are inventory-to-sales ratios in each of the three main components, and they are useful for gauging possible inventory imbalances in those sectors of the economy.

How it affects the market: Reactions to the release of the business inventories report tend to be muted for a few reasons. First, the report is derived from three separate surveys, among which the market has some advance knowledge of when the business inventories data are released. Second, while there are important implications to changes in the level of business inventories, the market often anticipates those changes before they occur. Therefore, the data often merely confirm what the markets already expected. Third, inventory data are released well after the survey period. This makes the data less timely than the data in other economic reports. Nevertheless, inventory changes have been at the root of many economic cycles and are therefore critical to watch. Business inventory data tend to take on added importance in times when investors are formulating their views about upcoming data on the gross domestic product (GDP). This is the case because the report is often one of the last pieces of information forecasters need to finish their number crunching for their GDP forecasts.

What it means to you: From an investment standpoint, inventory data can help you recognize potential turning points in the economy, leaving you better able to shape your investment portfolio. From a consumption standpoint, the inventory data can help you be a smarter buyer. If, for example, retail inventories rise, you could take that as a signal that lower retail prices on everything from cars to clothes may be on the horizon. If, however, inventories fall, this could be taken as a signal that companies are in the driver's seat with respect to prices.

CHICAGO PURCHASING MANAGERS INDEX

Source: National Association of Purchasing Management–Chicago

Web address for report: *http://www.napm-chicago.org*

Release date: The last business day of every month

Time: 10 a.m. EST

Report covers: Manufacturing activity in the Chicago region in the month before the release of the survey results

Description of report: The Chicago Purchasing Managers index is a key gauge of the health of the nation's manufacturing sector. Its value is enhanced by the fact that the Chicago region has one of the heaviest concentrations of manufacturers in the country. In addition, because it is released just one business day before the national data on manufacturing conditions released by the Institute of Supply Management (ISM), the Chicago index provides a helpful advance lead on the ISM index. As with the ISM report, the Chicago Purchasing Managers report contains data that relate to important aspects of the manufacturing sector, including new orders, production, order backlogs, employment, delivery time, inventories, and prices.

Survey methodology: Each month the National Association of Purchasing Management–Chicago surveys more than 200 purchasing and supply executives in the Chicago region about their business conditions. The NAPM–Chicago uses the same methodology used to calculate the ISM index and asks the survey participants whether they experienced an increase or a decrease in important aspects of their business, including new orders, production, employment, delivery time, inventories, and order backlogs. The responses are compiled into a diffusion index, which is basically a number that reflects the percentage of firms that reported an increase in the respective components, minus those that saw a decrease. The diffusion indexes then are adjusted for seasonality and to equate a reading of zero to 50.

Key components of the report: As with the ISM index, the key component in the Chicago index is *new orders*. When new orders rise, for example, many forces are set in motion that lead to increases in the other key components of the survey, such as production and employment. Thus, as new orders go, so goes the Chicago index. Because of their ripple effects, new orders are a leading indicator for the economy.

How it affects the market: The timely release of the Chicago index provides an advance warning on the possible results of the ISM index. Although it is usually just one day, that is enough to enable investors to adjust their positions and boost the total return on their portfolios. As a result, market reaction to the Chicago index is often quite sharp. Moreover, although the Chicago index is a regional survey, because of the heavy concentration of manufacturing industries in the Chicago region, this index is a credible microcosm of national conditions. The Chicago index averaged a spread of about 3 points over the ISM index during the economic expansion of the 1990s and during that period the Chicago index was above the ISMM about 90 percent of the time. Thus, an investor can roughly estimate the ISM by taking the Chicago index and subtracting 3 points. When the economy is either very weak or in recession, one can expect the Chicago index to be below the ISM.

What it means to you: With the markets placing a high degree of emphasis on manufacturing statistics such as the Chicago index and the ISM report, the results of the Chicago index can directly affect your investment portfolio. You therefore should use the

Chicago index to get an advance lead on the ISM, especially when you are in the middle of making adjustments to your investment portfolio. In business, the report can help you navigate a variety of economic climates. However, while the Chicago index provides an advance lead on the ISM, it is important to wait for the ISM data to more accurately gauge national trends.

CONSTRUCTION SPENDING

Source: U. S. Census Bureau

Web address for report: http://www.census.gov/const/ c30_curr.html

Release date: Generally the first calendar day of every month

Time: 10 a.m. EST

Report covers: Construction activity in the calendar months two months before the report's release.

Description of report: The construction spending report details construction activity in both the public and private sectors. Construction spending, also known as construction put in place, represents approximately 8.5 percent of the U.S. economy. Construction spending is especially sensitive to interest rate levels because of the high cost of construction endeavors. The construction spending report tallies construction in a number of areas, including new buildings and structures; additions; renovations; alterations; mechanical and electrical installations; site preparation and outside construction of fixed structures or facilities such as sidewalks, highways, and streets; and parking lots. Excluded from the report are maintenance and repairs to existing structures or service facilities; the drilling of gas and oil wells, including the construction of offshore drilling platforms; and the cost and installation of some production machinery and equipment items. The report is quite volatile and is subject to large revisions.

Survey methodology: The construction data are calculated by combining data from several sources and surveys. The three most important sources of data are the Census Bureau's surveys on new private residential construction, private nonresidential construction, and construction by state and local governments. The data on residential construction are estimated by surveying approximately 900 permit-issuing places in the country. The Census Bureau contacts those places by using a mail-out/mail-back survey to obtain their monthly statistics. Where permits have been issued, the Census Bureau contacts the owners and builders to see if construction has been started. Once construction has begun, monthly construction progress reports are requested from the owner until a project is completed. The Census Bureau measures the "value of construction put in place," or the value of construction installed or erected at construction sites during a specific month. This can include the cost of materials, labor, and architectural or engineering work. Nonresidential data are collected in a similar manner. Some of the data are obtained from the F. W. Dodge Division of the McGraw-Hill Information Systems Company for projects valued at $75,000 or more in the United States except Hawaii, where data are obtained from permit-issuing places in that state. About 7000 projects are in the bureau's survey at any one time. The data on state and local governments are obtained largely from data produced by F. W. Dodge and are adjusted by benchmarking the tabulated estimates to annual construction expenditures data collected in the Census Bureau's Annual Survey of Government Finances. All the surveys are combined and adjusted for outliers and for construction projects not reported by F. W. Dodge as well as for seasonal fluctuations.

Key components of the report: There are two main components in the construction report: *private construction*, which accounts for about 75 percent of all construction activity, and *public construction*, which accounts for the remaining 25 percent. Residential construction activity represents about 45 percent of all private construction activity. The remaining portion consists of the construction of hotels, nonpublic schools, hospitals, office buildings, and religious buildings. Public construction activity consists largely of schools, highways and streets, and public buildings. These three areas represent about 80 percent of all public construction activity. Details such as the data on hotel and motel construction can shed light on trends in certain industries. The most important part of the construction report is the data on private construction not just because private construction accounts for such a large percentage of all construction activity but also because it is much more sensitive than public construction to the ups and downs of the business cycle.

How it affects the market: Although construction spending represents roughly 9 percent of the economy, there is generally little market response to the construction spending report for several reasons. First and foremost is the timing of its release. The report is almost always released on the same day and time as the ISM report, which is considered one of the most important economic indicators. As a result, the construction report essentially becomes an afterthought. Second, the report's sharp month-to-month volatility limits the significance of any single month's data. Investors tend to focus on the trends in this data series rather than on the monthly changes. Third, the report consists largely of information that the markets have discounted before it is released. The data on residential construction spending, for example, are largely captured in several high-profile housing-related reports released before the construction report.

What it means to you: The construction spending report should be used in tandem with other construction-related reports to help form your opinion about the economy. I suggest combining this report with the data on housing starts, new and existing home sales, and mortgage applications and the National Association of Home Builders' monthly housing market index to get the best picture of the construction industry. Also look at the monthly changes in construction jobs for additional clues. Once you have formed an opinion on the construction sector, you can incorporate it into your investment strategies. The construction sector tends to be quite interest-rate-sensitive, and so its strength or weakness can be used as a barometer of the impact of changing interest rates on the overall economy. However, construction activity can be a lagging indicator because some construction activity may have been planned and financed months in advance. The data on public construction can help you discern trends in public spending nationwide and compare them to trends in your local area.

CONSUMER CONFIDENCE INDEX

Source: The Conference Board
Web address for report: *http://www.conference-board.org/*
Release date: Usually the last Tuesday of every month
Time: 10 a.m. EST

Report covers: Generally reflect consumer sentiments in the first half of the month in which the report is released

Description of report: The Conference Board's consumer confidence survey attempts to measure overall consumer confidence as well as consumer sentiment about a variety of other issues. The index historically has been highly correlated with consumer spending patterns as well as developments in the labor market. In fact, this survey tends to be more closely correlated with labor market conditions than are most other consumer confidence surveys. Aside from consumer confidence levels, this survey captures consumer sentiment toward business conditions, the labor market, and buying plans. Investors and forecasters use the survey to anticipate changes in economic activity.

Survey methodology: At the end of every month the Conference Board mails out its survey to about 5000 households, of which about 3500 usually respond. The questionnaires are collected mostly during the first half of the month in which the final results are released. The Conference Board's consumer confidence index has two components: an index of consumers' assessment of the present situation, which is 60 percent of the overall confidence index, and an index of consumers' expectations, which is 40 percent of the overall index. Included in the questionnaire are five questions: two regarding current conditions and three regarding expectations. Consumers basically are asked how they currently feel about business conditions and the jobs market and where they see conditions six months in the future. They also are asked about their plans to buy a home, a new car, and major appliances. The data then are constructed into an index using a base year of 1985 (1985 = 100). A reading of 105 means that confidence is 105 percent of the level in 1985.

Key components of the report: There are a number of important components in the Conference Board's monthly survey, but their level of importance differs, depending on economic developments. My personal experience and various studies suggest that the most important component is the index of *the present situation*. This index tends to have the highest correlation with consumer spending patterns as well as the employment situation. This makes sense because the wherewithal to spend matters more than how consumers feel about the future. Confidence about the future, for example, can do little to spur spending by the unemployed. High expectations are clearly no substitute for a person's present state of finances. That is why it is important to beware of changes in consumer confidence that are rooted in changes in the expectations component rather than changes in consumers' assessment of the present. The expectations component often is affected by consumers' emotions rather than by economic realities. It is particularly important to look at whether consumers feel that jobs are "plentiful" or "hard to get." The responses to these questions tend to be highly correlated with the unemployment rate. The responses to questions about consumer buying plans tend to have loose but useful information about actual spending patterns.

How it affects the market: Investors are very interested in consumer confidence data because those data help them assess the likely direction of consumer spending. This is important to investors because they understand that consumer spending accounts for roughly two-thirds of the U.S. economy. The markets generally take the consumer confidence index at face value and react accordingly; the details of the report usually do not alter the initial reaction to the report. The bond market typically falls when consumer confidence rises on concerns that that rise could portend a strengthening of economic activity. Equity investors cheer strong consumer confidence data because the economic implications bode well for corporate profits. However, the markets are far more interested in how consumers behave than in how they feel. Therefore, it is important to look for data on consumer spending data to validate the conclusions an investor draws from the confidence data.

What it means to you: How you feel about the economy and your personal finances is extremely important, but it is also important to follow how others are feeling to assess the impact their assessments could have on you. As an investor, tracking the consumer, which, as was mentioned previously, accounts for roughly two-thirds of the economy, should be one of your top priorities. An accurate assessment of the consumer can go a long way toward helping you to formulate profitable investment decisions.

CONSUMER CREDIT

Source: Federal Reserve

Web address for report: *http://www.federalreserve.gov/releases/G19/*

Release date: Generally on or about the fifth business day of every month

Time: 3 p.m. EST

Report covers: The level of consumer credit in the calendar month two months before the release of the report

Description of report: The consumer credit report provides important information about trends in the level of consumer indebtedness. The report measures credit extended to consumers for the purchase of goods and services. Consumer credit consists of two main categories: revolving and nonrevolving credit. Revolving credit, which accounts for roughly 44 percent of all consumer credit, consists largely of credit cards, store charge accounts, and overdraft checking. Nonrevolving credit consists largely of automobile loans and other loans not included in revolving credit, such as loans for mobile homes, trailers, and vacations. Consumer credit does not include debts secured by real estate. Investors and forecasters use the consumer credit data as a gauge of both consumer confidence and potential excesses in consumer debt. Consumer credit stood at about $1.5 trillion at the end of 2001.

Survey methodology: Each month the Federal Reserve surveys commercial banks, consumer finance companies (including automobile finance companies), and credit unions to obtain the information it needs to produce the consumer credit report. The data are tabulated and then adjusted for seasonal variations. In December of each year, for example, consumers sharply increase their use of credit to make holiday purchases. In January, however, consumers sharply curtail their use of credit and begin paying down some of their debts. The Fed smoothes the reporting of these fluctuations by adjusting the December data downward and the January data upward. The Fed's adjustments are derived from patterns observed over prior years.

Key components of the report: The two main components of the consumer credit report are *revolving* and *nonrevolving debt*. The data on revolving credit can provide insight into the extent to which consumers are using their credit cards. This information can be used to assess consumer confidence and track potential excesses in consumer debt. The nonrevolving credit component can be used in the same way as well as to gauge the availability of credit, given the component's emphasis on consumer loans. The consumer credit report also contains interesting information on the *terms of credit* at commercial banks and finance companies. This includes the average interest rates charged on new car loans, personal loans, and credit card debt. The Fed also provides information on the average maturity and average dollar amounts financed at automobile finance companies.

How it affects the market: Market reaction to the consumer credit report tends to be muted. The report often is overlooked because investors are more concerned with how much consumers spent during a given month than with the means by which consumers paid for their purchases. When there is a reaction, it tends to vary with the market's focus primarily because the interpretation of the report is open to a great deal of subjective analysis. For example, a large increase in consumer credit can be looked at in two ways. On the one hand, it could be taken as a sign that consumers are confident about the economic outlook. On the other hand, it could be taken as a sign that consumers are building up excessive amounts of debt. Moreover, when the economy is weak, large increases in consumer credit can be taken as a sign that credit remains plentiful or that consumer finances are becoming so strained that consumers must resort to the use of debt to finance their expenditures. These varied interpretations reduce the market reactions to the report. Nevertheless, consumer credit is a hotly debated topic in the markets. I generally view growth in consumer credit positively as long as the economy is expanding. The increased use of credit cards for convenience purposes and to obtain frequent flier miles and the like probably is boosting consumer credit levels.

What it means to you: The consumer credit report can help you assess trends in consumer spending and help with your personal finances. In my experience steadily rising levels of consumer credit can be taken as a sign that consumers are confident and credit is plentiful. Both conditions are important for the economy to expand. You also can use the report to help with your personal finances. For example, you can utilize the information on the terms of credit at commercial banks and finance companies to assess whether the interest rate you pay on new car loans, personal loans, credit cards, and the like, is consistent with the national averages. This could help you comparison shop when obtaining credit.

CONSUMER PRICE INDEX

Source: Bureau of Labor Statistics

Web address for report: *http://www.bls.gov/news.release/cpi.toc.htm*

Release date: Generally around or slightly after the middle of every month, frequently on a Wednesday

Time: 8:30 a.m. EST

Report Covers: Consumer prices in the previous month; the survey period is the entire month

Description of report: The consumer price index (CPI) is a measure of changes in the prices of thousands of goods and services over time. These goods and services are grouped into more than 200 categories arranged in eight major groups: food and beverages, housing, apparel, transportation, medical care, recreation, education and communication, and other goods and services. Bond investors are particularly interested in inflation data because inflation erodes the value of money. Those investors constantly worry that their returns will be eroded by an acceleration of inflation. That is one of the main reasons why bond yields tend to be somewhat higher than the inflation rate. Investors often use the CPI as a reference point on inflation trends when they formulate their investment strategies. The CPI also is used by the U.S. government in its yearly adjustments of payments to the roughly 48 million Social Security benefits recipients, 4.1 million military and federal civil service retirees and survivors, and 22.4 million food stamp recipients. It is no wonder that the CPI is one of the most closely watched gauges of inflation.

Survey methodology: Starting in the first week of every month, the Bureau of Labor Statistics (BLS) visits or calls thousands of retail stores, service establishments, rental units, and doctors' offices to record prices on about 80,000 goods and services in 87 urban areas. Data on rents are collected from about 50,000 landlords or tenants. The BLS compares the prices recorded each month to the prices recorded in the previous month. In cases where the same item is no longer available, the BLS selects a new item. If the quality of an item changes (for example, if new features are added to an automobile), the BLS records the quality change to measure the effect of the change on the price of that item. Prices are recorded throughout each calendar month. The BLS then takes all the recorded prices and weights them by their importance; then it adjusts the data for fluctuations resulting from seasonality.

Key components of the report: The *housing* component is always important because it accounts for roughly 40 percent of the entire CPI and because everyone is affected by housing costs. It captures changes in the cost of shelter, rent, and fuel and utilities. This component often is unduly affected by sharp changes in energy prices and the health of the housing market. Another important component is the index on medical costs. *Medical costs* not only affect people personally but also affect employment costs, which account for about 70 percent of the cost of producing goods. The volatile *apparel* component often fluctuates because of the timing of new introductions of seasonal merchandise. An investor should keep an eye on the *other goods and services* component to gauge inflation in the service sector.

How it affects the market: Inflation is the bane of the bond market because it erodes the value of the interest payments bondholders receive. The inflation rate is therefore critically important to the bond market. To many people the CPI is their top inflation gauge, although others prefer to use the personal consumption deflator or the implicit deflator (both are released with the quarterly report on GDP). These other measures are very broad measures of inflation. Investors typically discount inflation trends before they occur, and so reactions to the monthly changes in the CPI are not always large. In fact, the bond market is generally more concerned with where inflation is headed than with where it is currently. Thus, inflation expectations are first and foremost in the bond investor's mind. Nevertheless, the CPI is one of the bigger market movers.

What it means to you: The inflation rate directly affects the purchasing power of your money. The more inflation there is, the less you can afford. Inflation in real estate prices, however, can be beneficial if you are a homeowner. In general, however, inflation is not a good thing for most people. The markets loathe high inflation rates, and investors typically root for low inflation. Investors worry that high rates of inflation not only will erode the value of their money but could prompt interest rate increases by the Federal

Reserve. Interest rate increases, of course, tend to weaken the economy, reducing job and income prospects. Low inflation, by contrast, tends to be good news for the economy, stock and bond prices, and job and income prospects. Inflation trends are therefore critical not only to the performance of your financial investments but also to your general economic well-being (Figure A-1).

UNIVERSITY OF MICHIGAN CONSUMER SENTIMENT INDEX

Source: University of Michigan

Web address for report: *http://www.umich.edu*

Release date: Preliminary results generally released to subscribers on or about the second Friday of every month; final results generally released on or about the last Friday of every month or the first Friday of the subsequent month

Time: 10 a.m. EST, but often leaked by subscribers 15 minutes earlier

Report covers: Reflects consumer sentiments throughout the month in which the report is released

F i g u r e   A—1

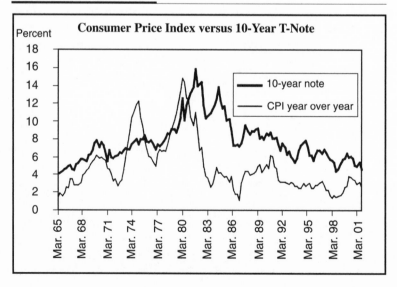

Description of report: The University of Michigan's (UOM) consumer sentiment survey attempts to measure overall consumer confidence as well as consumer sentiments about a variety of other issues. The index historically has been highly correlated with consumer spending patterns and developments in the labor market. However, the UOM's consumer sentiment survey is not as tightly correlated with labor market trends as the Conference Board's consumer confidence survey is. Aside from consumer confidence levels, the UOM's consumer sentiment survey captures consumers' sentiments about their personal finances, buying conditions, and inflation. Investors and forecasters use the survey to anticipate changes in economic activity.

Survey methodology: Each month the University of Michigan telephones 500 consumers to ask them about their sentiments toward their personal finances, business conditions, the buying climate, and the inflation outlook. The survey is conducted by using a rotating panel of participants; 60 percent of all participants are first-time participants, while the remaining 40 percent participated once before. The UOM telephones half the 500 consumers in the first half of each month and the remaining consumers in the second half of each month (about 125 persons per week). This index has two components: an index of consumers' assessment of the present situation, which is 60 percent of the overall confidence index, and an index of consumers' expectations, which is 40 percent of the overall index. Included in the questionnaire are five questions: two regarding consumers' assessment of current conditions and three regarding their expectations for future conditions. Regarding the present situation, the UOM asks consumers whether they feel it is a good time to buy a major household item and whether they are better or worse off financially than they were a year earlier. Regarding the future, consumers are asked about how they expect their financial condition to be in a year and how they see business conditions in the country as a whole. The data are constructed into an index using a base year of 1966 (1966 = 100). A reading of 105 means that confidence is 105 percent of the level in 1966. This survey is old, and it seems time for the UOM to update the base year.

Key components of the report: Not many details of the UOM survey are released to the public; the survey details are available only to subscribers, and the financial press rarely reveals all the survey results. Nevertheless, there are a few important components in the UOM survey. As with the Conference Board's consumer confidence survey, my experience and various studies suggest that the most important component is the index of *the assessment of current conditions*. This index tends to have the highest correlation with consumer spending patterns and the employment situation. This makes sense because the wherewithal to spend matters more than how consumers feel about the future. Confidence about the future, for example, can do little to spur spending by the unemployed. Moreover, the expectations component often is affected by consumer emotions rather than by economic realities. The UOM survey also includes a unique question about the consumers' inflation expectations.

How it affects the market: Investors are very interested in consumer confidence data because that information helps them assess the likely direction of consumer spending. This is important to investors because they understand that consumer spending accounts for roughly two-thirds of the U.S. economy. The bond market reacts to the preliminary results of the UOM survey as much as or more than it does to the final results, and reactions to the data are often sharp. Equity investors cheer strong consumer sentiment because the economic implications bode well for corporate profits. However, the markets are far more interested in how consumers behave than in how they feel. Therefore, it is important to let spending data be one's primary guide to consumer spending patterns.

What it means to you: How you feel about the economy and your personal finances is extremely important, but it is also important to follow how others are feeling to assess the impact their assessments could have on you. As an investor, tracking consumer spending, which accounts for roughly two-thirds of the economy, should be a top priority. An accurate assessment of the consumer can go a long way toward helping you formulate profitable investment decisions. The preliminary results of the survey can help give you an early lead on future spending trends.

DURABLE GOODS ORDERS

Source: U.S. Census Bureau

Web address for report: *http://www.census.gov/ftp/pub/ indicator/www/m3/index.htm*

Release date: Usually the last week of the month

Time: 8:30 a.m. EST

Report covers: Manufacturers' durable goods orders, shipments, and inventories in the previous month

Description of report: The durable goods report is considered an important leading economic indicator because it provides information about possible increases or decreases in industrial production; orders precede actual production and delivery. The relative strength or weakness of durable goods orders can provide important clues to consumers' degree of confidence in purchasing big-ticket items such as automobiles and appliances. The report also provides important clues to the pace of business spending. Durable goods orders account for a little more than half of all factory orders, and this report's release precedes the factory orders report, providing early clues to factory orders data. The durable goods data often fluctuate sharply from month to month.

Survey methodology: Each month the Census Bureau surveys manufacturing companies in approximately 473 manufacturing industries to obtain data on durable goods orders, shipments, and inventories. The companies surveyed have $500 million or more in annual shipments each. As with most government surveys, responses to the survey are voluntary. Because the companies that respond are generally large, diversified companies, many file separate reports for the different divisions within their companies. The Census Bureau derives its monthly data on durable goods orders not by tallying the respondents' orders data but by looking at the monthly change in shipments and unfilled orders and then estimating the level of new orders through the changes in shipments and unfilled orders. Consider, for example, a month in which shipments of a durable good were 100 units and unfilled orders were 90 units. If during the next month shipments increased to 110 units but unfilled orders remained at 90 units, this would imply an increase of 10 units in total durable goods orders (the increase in shipments should have reduced unfilled orders by 10 units; the fact that they held steady implies an increase in orders).

Key components of the report: The most important component in the durable goods report is the data on *nondefense capital goods orders*, a key gauge of capital spending (it is best to look at this component in isolation from the volatile aircraft component). Fluctuations in capital spending tend to coincide with changes in business confidence levels. The more confident businesses are about the economy, the more likely they are to engage in capital spending. Capital spending, which includes spending on plant and equipment, is critical to the nation's productivity. Another important component in the report is the data on *computers and electronics products*. This component yields important clues to the pace of economic activity in the technology sector. Also important are the data on *shipments*. This information is used in the computation of the quarterly data on GDP. *Unfilled orders* provide clues to the extent to which manufacturers may have to alter their production schedules to fit their order backlogs.

How it affects the market: Because of the sharp month-to-month volatility in the durable goods data, the bond market's reaction to this report varies but can be sharp. Sharp month-to-month changes that appear to be related to one-time factors often are quickly dismissed, especially if they are due to the report's two most volatile components: transportation (particularly aircraft orders) and defense. The bond market's reaction to the report is greatest when the data are well beyond expectations and lack these one-time influences. The reaction is even greater when the strength or weakness of the report is amplified by the data on nondefense capital goods orders. However, when the report's strength appears to be due largely to strength in capital spending, the bond market, which loathes strong economic activity, may not react as negatively as it would if the sources of strength were other sectors of the economy because capital spending is perceived to be conducive to productivity growth, which tends to dampen inflation.

What it means to you: The durable goods report can help you forecast future trends in the economy. Persistent strength in durable goods orders should be taken as a sign that both consumers and businesses are confident enough in the economy to engage in spending on big-ticket items. From this you can shape your investments in a way that reflects the likelihood of an economic expansion and increasing corporate profits. This means that you should consider the purchase of economically sensitive stocks and bonds in industries such as consumer cyclicals, basic materials, technology, and financials. By contrast, if durable goods orders are persistently weak, you might want to avoid these sectors in favor of defensive sectors such as utilities, health care, and consumer products. As a consumer, watch the durable goods data to weigh the climate for the purchasing of big-ticket items such as an automobile. The data will help you know how much bargaining power you may have when making such purchases.

EMPLOYMENT SITUATION

Source: Bureau of Labor Statistics

Web address for report: *http://www.bls.gov/news.release/empsit.toc.htm*

Release date: Generally the first Friday of every month

Time: 8:30 a.m. EST

Report covers: Employment conditions through the early part of the previous month

Description of report: The employment report provides one of the best summaries of current economic conditions and is one of the most closely followed economic reports. The employment situation is considered one of the most important determinants of the economy's performance. Employment growth provides the steady flow of fuel needed to keep the economy moving along a sustained growth path by supplying the income growth needed to sustain consumer spending, which accounts for two-thirds of U.S. economic activity. The monthly employment report provides important insights into both the health of the overall economy and key trends in the economy's major sectors. Trends in employment conditions historically have had a great impact on monetary policy and, hence, the bond market.

Survey methodology: The employment report is produced monthly by using two major surveys: the Current Population Survey and the Current Employment Statistics survey, popularly known as the household and establishment surveys, respectively. The household survey covers about 60,000 households and is used in the production of the monthly data on the unemployment rate, household employment, and the labor force. The establishment survey covers about 350,000 establishments and is used to produce the monthly data on payroll employment, hours worked, and workers' earnings. The reference period for the household survey is generally the calendar week that contains the twelfth day of the month, and the reference period for the establishment survey is the pay period that includes the twelfth, which may or may not correspond directly to the calendar week. The household survey is conducted by telephone or in person during the week after the reference period. Persons over age 16 are included in the survey and are selected in a way that the BLS considers representative of the entire population. Information on about 94k people is obtained each month. Households remain in the survey for four months, leave the survey for eight months, and return for four months before leaving it for good. People are considered employed if they did any work during the reference period. They are classified as unemployed if they had no employment during the reference period, were available to work, and made specific efforts to find employment during the four-week period ending with the reference week. The establishment survey includes entities that produce goods or services, and the data are collected by electronic means, mostly touch-tone phone, from about two-thirds of the survey participants. The submitted responses are returned to the respondents in mail form for use in the following month. This helps maintain consistency and increases the accuracy of the data. People are counted as employed if they received pay for any part of the reference week even if it was as little as one hour. People are counted in each job they hold. The data in both the household survey and the establishment survey are adjusted for seasonal fluctuations.

Key components of the report: There are many important components in the employment report, but the headline data grab most of the attention: the monthly change in *nonfarm payrolls* and the *unemployment rate*. Each of these components provides a quick snapshot of conditions in the labor market, and the jobless rate is perhaps the most frequently cited economic statistic. It is so widely understood that politicians frequently use it as a political tool; few economic statistics can match the political persuasiveness of the jobless rate. Another important area of the report is the breakdown of monthly payroll changes by industry. This information provides important insights into the levels of economic activity in the respective industries. The data on the manufacturing sector are watched particularly closely and are used as a gauge of industrial production. Another important component is the data on *average hourly earnings*. Expressed in terms of dollars earned per hour, the earnings data are used as a gauge of growth in personal income. The data also are used as an inflation gauge since labor costs account for roughly 70 percent of the cost of producing goods and services. Also important is the information on *hours worked*. The data on the average workweek and overtime hours, for instance, are good gauges of future changes in employment because businesses tend to increase or decrease the length of the workweek before they increase or decrease their payrolls. The data on *aggregate hours,* which basically sum up all the changes in employment plus hours worked, serves as a good proxy for GDP (crude formula: GDP = change in aggregate hours + productivity change). Other components that go in and out of vogue include the data on the pool of available workers (used when labor shortages develop) and the duration of unemployment (used when the labor market weakens).

How it affects the market: Few economic reports move the bond market more than the employment report does. Investors recognize that labor market trends are one of the most important determinants of the economy's performance and respond to jobs data accordingly. There are several reasons why the reaction to the report is often sharp. First, the employment report is one of the first major economic reports released at the start of each month (the widely followed ISM report almost always is released earlier but does not cast as wide a net on the broader economy). The data therefore often set the tone for expectations for the rest of the month. Second, analysts extrapolate data from the employment report to make forecasts on other data, and the data are used directly by several U.S. government agencies in their computations in many other economic reports. Third, investors recognize that the jobs data can influence the way both businesses and consumers perceive the economy. In a sense, the jobs data act as an advertisement for the health of the economy. Fourth, the forecasting record on the monthly jobs data is mediocre. A miss of only 0.1 percent on overall employment levels can translate into a miss of about 140,000 jobs in the headline data. The market response to the data often defies the headlines. The markets recognize that labor market trends sometimes lag other parts of the economy. If, for example, after a long period of economic strength a department store experienced weakness in sales, it would be unlikely to cut workers just because it had a bad month or two. The markets recognize that changes in demand are a better leading indicator of the economy, and that recognition sometimes results in a reduced response to the employment data. A large degree of the bond market's reaction to the jobs report is based on its potential impact on monetary policy. The bond market reacts negatively to strength in the labor market out of fear that the strength will lead to increased wage demands and, hence, inflation. Weakness in the labor market buoys bond prices because it suggests that there is excess capacity in the economy, a precursor to low inflation.

What it means to you: Obviously, employment trends are extremely important to almost everyone. We all need to be aware of conditions in the labor market to assure our own personal financial security as well as to assess our bargaining power when it is time to negotiate wages. It is essential for an investor to stay abreast of developments in the labor market because labor market trends are at the core of the health of the economy and therefore have an extremely large bearing on the performance of financial assets. Each month you should use the report to prepare yourself for upcoming economic reports and to help you formulate your investment strategies. Strong conditions in the labor market generally translate into strong growth in personal income, and this tends to be associated with strong economic growth, rising corporate profits, and rising bond yields. The opposite is true, of course, when the labor market is weak. In business, the employment data can help you navigate changes in the economic climate by keeping you aware of developments in the economy (Figure A-2).

EMPLOYMENT COST INDEX

Source: Bureau of Labor Statistics

Web address for report: *http://www.bls.gov/news.release/ eci.toc.htm*

Release date: Generally the final week of the month after the end of the previous calendar quarter

Time: 8:30 a.m. EST

Report covers: Employment costs in the previous calendar quarter

F i g u r e   A–2

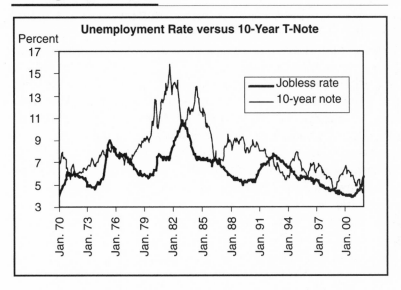

Description of report: The employment cost index (ECI) is perhaps the most comprehensive measure of changes in the cost of labor. The ECI measures most of the major labor costs incurred by employers, including wages and salaries and employee benefits. The report is a better gauge of employment costs than are the average hourly earning data included in the BLS's monthly employment statistics because it measures straight-time pay and therefore is not distorted by factors such as overtime pay and employment shifts among occupations and industries and because it contains data on benefit costs. The wages and salaries component accounts for roughly 70 percent of the overall ECI and includes production bonuses, commissions, tips, room and board, and cost-of-living allowances. Benefit costs covered by the ECI include paid leave such as vacations, holidays, and sick leave; overtime; nonproduction bonuses; insurance benefits, including life, health, and short- and long-term disability; retirement and savings benefits such as defined-benefit and defined-contribution plans; severance pay; and legally required benefits such as Social Security benefits. Employment costs account for roughly two-thirds of the cost of producing goods and services and therefore have a major influence on inflation and corporate profits. As a result, market participants and policymakers follow the ECI closely.

Survey methodology: During the last month of each calendar quarter data are collected during the pay period that includes the twelfth of the month from a probability sample of approximately 31,100 occupational observations within about 7400 establishments in private industry and approximately 3800 occupations within about 800 sample establishments in state and local governments. The occupational observations are placed into about 500 classifications according to the 1990 census of population. The individual classifications then are combined into broader occupational groups, including construction, manufacturing, transportation, executive, administrative, sales, and services. The occupational groups are more broadly defined as blue collar, white collar, and services. The ECI sample is rotated approximately every five years to make it more representative and assure the best response rate. The individual establishments included in the survey are selected in a way that assures that larger establishments are more likely to be part of the survey than smaller establishments are. Occupations within the establishments are selected by using a process that gives occupations with higher employment a greater chance of being selected. In the near future occupations will be classified even more narrowly by using a points system based on ten factors that determine the work level of the occupation, including the complexity, physical demands, and personal contacts needed for the occupation. The data collected for the ECI are seasonally adjusted, and the reported data are subject to revision.

Key components of the report: There are two main components in the ECI: *wages and salaries* and *benefits*. The more important of the two, of course, is the wages and salaries component. Wages and salaries are the biggest expense for most businesses and are therefore critical to monitor for clues on inflation pressures and the potential impact on profit margins. The benefits component is unique among economic indicators because it captures trends that are not captured elsewhere. For example, scant data are available on trends in the costs of providing health insurance. The benefits component can be skewed at the start of each year because a large percentage of insurance companies set their rates at the start of the year. Rate changes that are above or below trend can therefore skew the benefit component. In the early 1990s, for example, as companies migrated to managed-care insurance plans, they experienced a one-time reduction in their benefit costs. This skewed the ECI sharply lower for several years in the first quarter of those years. Large fluctuations in stock prices also can skew the benefit component because they affect the amount of money large corporations must pay into their pension plans. Occasionally, large quarterly changes in commissions in various occupations can skew the wages and salaries component of the ECI.

How it affects the market: The market reaction to the ECI report is often quite sharp for a few reasons. First, since the ECI is a quarterly report, the markets get relatively few chances to react to it and this sharpens the reaction to its release. Second, the data contained in the report are not readily available elsewhere because much of it is unique to the ECI report. Thus, in a sense, the ECI report provides a first look at previously unknown data. This is unusual for the markets, which generally have a good bead on many other economic reports before they are released. Third, the ECI is used as a key barometer of inflation, the bond market's nemesis. The bond market's reaction to the report is generally consistent with the notion that employment costs are the single biggest determinant of inflation. Fourth, investors recognize that the Federal Reserve closely follows the ECI to gauge inflation pressures. The market reaction to the ECI report therefore reflects sentiments about the future direction of Fed policy.

What it means to you: The ECI report should be one of your top economic indicators. Its correlation to inflation is strong enough that you can use it as a key gauge of inflation risks and draw conclusions about the outlook on both interest rates and the economy. There are other ways to utilize the ECI report. For one thing, you can use it to get a better sense of prevailing wage rates, putting yourself in a better position to negotiate your wages. You also can use the benefits data to compare the benefits you receive with the nationwide average. Businesses can use the ECI data to determine compensation rates for pay ranges or annual pay increases. They also can use the data to evaluate and improve their benefits packages to remain competitive in the labor market. Labor organizations can use the report's data on mean and median wages as a reference point for wage negotiations.

EXISTING HOME SALES

Source: National Association of Realtors

Web address for report: *http://www.nar.realtor.com/research*

Release date: Generally the last week of every month, often on the twenty-sixth or twenty-seventh day

Time: 10 a.m. EST

Report covers: Existing homes sold in the previous calendar month

Description of report: The existing home sales report provides information on the number of existing homes sold and their median and average sales prices. This report is considered very important because of the enormous contribution the housing sector makes to the overall economy. Existing home sales, however, have a smaller economic impact than do new home sales for obvious reasons. New homes must be built, whereas existing homes already exist. Therefore, the economic activity that results from the sale of an existing home is far less than that from the sale of a new home. Nevertheless, the sale of an existing home provides meaningful benefits to the economy through brokers' sales commissions, for example. In addition, individuals who move into an existing home tend to purchase new carpeting, appliances, paint, and other home products. The existing home sales data provide important clues to the level of both consumer confidence and income growth, the two main pillars of a strong housing sector. The data also can be used to gauge the impact of changes in interest rates.

Survey methodology: Each month the Research Division of the National Association of Realtors (NAR) collects data on existing home sales and prices from a representative sample of approximately 160 of the 700 boards, or multiple listing services (MLSs), that regularly participate in its monthly surveys. The 700 board/MLSs represent approximately 25 percent of all existing home sales that occur in the United States during a given month and are situated in every region of the country. The survey participants reflect the regional breakdown of sales reported by the Census Bureau in its American Housing Survey and are therefore a microcosm of the existing home sales market. The NAR's monthly data are based on its representative sample of 160 boards/MLSs. The NAR tallies the data it receives from the 160 boards/MLSs and adjusts the data for various outliers and "problematic data" such as erroneous data and missing responses. The NAR divides the home sales data into four census regions: Northeast, South, Midwest, and West. It then weights the aggregated raw volume figures to accurately represent sales activity in each region of the country. The data is then adjusted for seasonality. The data on the median and mean sales prices are not adjusted, however, because their seasonality is difficult to gauge. Existing home sales are reported when a home sale closes. This contrasts with new home sales, which are reported when the sales contract is signed. This means that the existing home sales data tend to lag trends in home sales captured in the new home sales report by approximately one or two months.

Key components of the report: The existing home sales report is a relatively simple report containing few key details. Existing home sales are reported at a seasonally adjusted annual rate. Because of this, a slight variation in the actual sales level can have a big impact on the annualized number reported each month. Thus, it is important to consider all of the possible ways in which the headline data may have been affected by unusual factors such as extreme weather and sharp fluctuations in interest rates. An important detail that can expose potential flaws in the reported data is the regional data. If one looks at each region, inconsistencies between the regions can be captured. Another important detail is the data on the *median sales price*. This component is important because for most people, the bulk of their net worth consists of the equity in their homes. Home prices therefore can have an impact on consumer spending because the wealthier a homeowner feels, the more likely it is the homeowner will be confident about spending. Also important are the data on the *supply of homes* available for sale. Measured in total months of supply remaining on the market, this information provides insight into whether there is either an excess or a shortage of homes on the market.

How it affects the market: Investors are keenly aware of the importance of the housing sector to the U.S. economy. They recognize that the effects from the housing sector can ripple throughout the economy. They also recognize that the condition of the housing sector speaks volumes about consumer confidence and income growth. It is no wonder that data on the housing sector often spark fairly large reactions in the bond market. The existing home sales report, however, does not always provoke a large response in the markets. One of the biggest reasons for this is the somewhat lagging nature of the report. As was mentioned above, unlike new home sales, existing home sales are reported at closing instead of at contract signing. Obviously, since the contract signing precedes the closing of the sale, the contract signing gives an earlier indication than does the closing, making the new home sales report a better leading indicator of housing activity. In addition, the data in the report tend to be volatile and sometimes are distorted by the regional data. The home sales data also are often foreshadowed by the data on mortgage applications released weekly by the Mortgage Bankers Association as well as by the monthly survey of home builders conducted by the National Association of Home Builders.

What it means to you: Although it is not the best leading economic indicator, the existing home sales report provides important clues to the economic outlook. You therefore should utilize the report when formulating your investment strategies, particularly with respect to economically sensitive sectors of the economy. Beyond your investments, you can use the existing home sales report to get a general idea about the behavior of home prices. This information could be useful in assessing the value of your home and, hence, your net worth. Moreover, by tracking the pace of existing home sales, you can improve your sense of the pricing power that exists in areas such as general contracting, appliances, and building materials. In addition, if you are in the market to buy a new home, you can improve your bargaining abilities by tracking the level of unsold homes.

FACTORY ORDERS

Source: U.S. Census Bureau

Web address for report: *http://www.census.gov/indicator/www/ m3/index.htm*

Release date: Usually the last few days of the month or the very beginning of the subsequent month

Time: 10 a.m. EST

Report covers: Manufacturers' durable and nondurable goods orders, shipments, and inventories for the previous month

Description of report: Factory orders data are considered an important leading economic indicator because they provide advance indications of possible increases and decreases in industrial production. Factory orders are a leading indicator because orders for manufactured products generally precede their actual production and delivery. Factory orders data include data on both durable and nondurable goods. These data tend to mirror the trends in the manufacturing sector. Although the factory orders report provides clues to the direction of the manufacturing sector, the report's late release puts it on a lower scale than other manufacturing reports.

Survey methodology: Each month the Census Bureau surveys manufacturing companies in approximately 473 manufacturing industries to obtain data on durable and nondurable goods orders, shipments, and inventories. The companies surveyed have $500 million or more in annual shipments each. As with the data on durable goods orders, the Census Bureau generates its monthly data on factory orders not by tallying the respondents' orders data but by looking at the monthly changes in shipments and unfilled orders and then estimating the level of new orders through the changes in shipments and unfilled orders. Consider, for example, a month in which shipments of factory goods were 100 units and unfilled orders were 90 units. If during the next month shipments increased to 110 units but unfilled orders remained at 90 units, this would imply an increase of 10 units in total factory orders (the increase in shipments should have reduced unfilled orders by 10 units; the fact that they held steady implies an increase in orders).

Key components of the report: Factory orders consist of both *durable* and *nondurable goods*. The more important of the two is the durable goods component, which accounts for about 55 percent of all factory orders. Durable goods orders provide clues to the willingness of consumers and businesses to spend on big-ticket items such as automobiles, appliances, and new equipment and structures. The data on business spending can be found in the component called *nondefense capital goods orders*. Also important are the data on *shipments*. This information is used in the computation of the quarterly data on the GDP. The report includes data on *factory inventories*, which account for about 40 percent of all business inventories. Unwanted inventory buildups often foreshadow slowing industrial production, while inventory shortfalls foreshadow increases in production.

How it affects the market: Data on factory orders are very important to the market and are considered a leading indicator for the economy. Despite the importance the market places on factory orders, the report does not always provoke much of a market response for a couple of reasons. First, durable goods orders, which account for more than half of factory orders, are known days in advance of the release of the factory orders report. Second, factory orders data often are foreshadowed by trends in the regional and national purchasing managers surveys that are released weeks earlier. Nevertheless, the data on nondurable goods orders are never truly completely known until the data on factory orders are released, and so the report always has the potential to move the markets. Moreover, as with the data on durable goods, the market reaction to strong data can vary with the composition of the strength. The bond market, which tends to loathe strong economic activity, may not react as negatively to strong data if the source of the strength is capital spending because capital spending is perceived to be conducive to productivity growth, which tends to dampen inflation.

What it means to you: Because trends in factory orders tend to precede trends in production and, hence, the economy, the factory orders report therefore can help you forecast economic trends. Moreover, because factory orders are driven by demand, the report can reinforce your sense of the underlying strength in the economy. Data on factory orders are best used in concert with other key manufacturing-related economic reports. A broad analysis of the manufacturing sector can be very helpful in assessing where the economy is with respect to the business cycle. That analysis can help you formulate investment strategies that will benefit from fluctuations in the economy. Be watchful of trends in the manufacturing sector and the signals the sector sends about the future pace of job and income growth.

GROSS DOMESTIC PRODUCT

Source: Bureau of Economic Analysis
Web address for report: *http://www.bea.doc.gov/ bea/dn1.htm*

Release date: Generally during the final week of the month after the end of the previous calendar quarter

Time: 8:30 a.m. EST

Report covers: The gross domestic product for the previous calendar quarter

Description of report: The gross domestic product report is the most comprehensive measure of economic activity available. Comprehensive data on inflation also are included in the report. GDP measures the total value of the output of goods and services produced by labor and property in the United States. The textbook formula for GDP is: GDP = C + I + G + (X − M), or GDP = consumption + investment + government + (exports − imports). Personal consumption expenditures (PCE) account for roughly two-thirds of GDP, and this explains why there is such a sharp focus on consumer spending. About 60 percent of all consumer spending is on services. Nonresidential fixed investment accounts for about 13 percent of GDP, but in recent years it has made a disproportionate contribution to overall economic growth. Nonresidential fixed investment, also known as capital spending, includes investments in structures (3 percent of GDP) and equipment and software (10 percent of GDP). Over the last 20 years GDP has expanded at an annual rate of about 3.1 percent. Monetary policy often is shaped by the extent to which economic growth exceeds or falls short of the economy's long-term growth rate. This elevates the importance of the GDP report.

Survey methodology: As one might expect, tabulating the methodology used to compute the GDP statistics is complex and requires the use of a wide variety of sources and methods. The Bureau of Economic Analysis (BEA) assembles the GDP data by measuring GDP on both ends of the transaction spectrum. Specifically, GDP is measured by using estimates of both income and spending. Consider the sale of apples at a grocery store. On the income side the BEA would measure the labor, capital, and other costs involved in the sale. On the spending side the BEA would measure the value of the apples sold. Theoretically, the dollar value of the income received and that of the expenditures should be equal, but this is not usually the case. In 2000, for example, the income side exceeded the spending side by about $110 billion. The data sources are independent and are merely estimates; the BEA

does not count every apple sold in the country. A fairly large proportion of the PCE data is obtained from the monthly survey of
retail trade conducted by the Census Bureau. Many other sources
are utilized to obtain data on gasoline sales, home sales, medical
spending, and the like. Most of the data are obtained from U.S.
government agencies. The inflation data in the GDP report are calculated basically by comparing current prices and quantities with
those in a base year (currently 1996). Current prices are "deflated"
to equate the current value of the output of goods and services to
the past value. The extent to which the price of a good must be
deflated is the inflation rate. In calculating quantities and prices of
goods and services, the BEA uses a system that incorporates
weights used in two adjacent quarters. This helps assure that the
quarterly changes are not affected by the choice of the base year.

Key components of the report: There are a number of important components in the GDP report. First, the PCE component is
important because it is the biggest component of the economy,
accounting for about two-thirds of economic activity. Second, *nonresidential fixed investment* is a key gauge of overall business spending and of technology spending in particular. Strength in business
spending often is called "good growth" by bond investors because
it helps lift productivity and thus contain inflation. Third, the *final
sales* component, which is *GDP minus the change in inventories*, gives
a clean read on the underlying strength in demand. Inventory
changes can distort the GDP data because the fluctuations sometimes result from changes in demand. In fact, unwanted inventory
buildups, while a net plus for GDP in the quarter in which they
occur, can be looked at as a negative sign on the economy because
a buildup can draw from future production. The *net exports* component is used as an important gauge of the impact of trade on the
economy, and that impact can vary widely from quarter to quarter.
The data on the *government sector* are also important and should be
watched to gauge the true underlying condition of the private sector. The *price index* in the GDP report is considered one of the
broadest measures of inflation available. The *PCE deflator* is
watched particularly closely and is the preferred consumer inflation
gauge among many analysts as well as Federal Reserve Chairman
Alan Greenspan.

How it affects the market: As a quarterly report, the GDP report contains a blend of familiar and unfamiliar news. The familiar news comes from digesting three months of data related to the GDP report during the months covered by the report. In essence the report can be looked at as a summation of previously released data. This lessens the reaction to the report to some extent. However, investors recognize that the GDP report is more comprehensive than the summation of the monthly economic reports and therefore justifies changes in their portfolio positions. In general, the reaction to the report is often quite sharp. The bond market generally trades lower on strong GDP data, but the magnitude of the reaction depends on the composition of the report. If, for example, GDP is strong but final sales are weak, the bond market often views the data as weak and trades higher. In addition, if GDP is strong but appears to have been boosted by capital spending, or so-called good growth, the bond market generally will be quite forgiving, recognizing that capital spending helps boost productivity and cut inflation.

What it means to you: For those who would rather steer clear of daily ruminations on the constant flow of economic news, the GDP report is the perfect choice because it provides a broad summary of the main macroeconomic themes affecting the economy. However, the monthly data can give you an earlier lead on developments in the economy than the GDP report will, and so it is probably not a good idea to focus mostly on the GDP data. Moreover, the monthly data contain useful details that are not in the GDP report. Nevertheless, the GDP report is a good foundation for formulating your investment plan. The biggest thing to keep in mind while analyzing the GDP data is the potential impact on the Federal Reserve. The Fed bases its policies largely on the extent to which GDP is above or below the economy's so-called speed limit, or growth potential. The economy's growth potential is computed basically by adding growth in the labor force (about 1 percent per year) to productivity growth (about 1.7 percent over the long term but much stronger than that in recent years). Thus, as a rough guide, you can shape many of your financial decisions by comparing the economy's growth rate to its growth potential.

HOUSING STARTS

Source: U.S. Census Bureau

Web address for report: *http://www.census.gov/indicator/ www/newresconst.pdf*

Release date: Generally the last calendar week of every month

Time: 10 a.m. EST

Report covers: New residential housing construction begun in the previous calendar month

Description of report: The housing starts report provides statistics on the construction of new privately owned residential structures in the United States. The data included in the press release are (1) the number of new housing units authorized by building permits, (2) the number of housing units authorized to be built but not yet started, (3) the number of housing units started, and (4) the number of housing units under construction. The data exclude hotels, motels, and group residential structures such as nursing homes and college dormitories. The housing starts report basically mirrors trends in new and existing home sales, especially in recent years, when home builders have attempted to reduce their levels of "speculative building," or unsold homes. The housing starts report nonetheless can provide indications on whether home construction is running above or below the underlying level of demand and in forecasting GDP.

Survey methodology: Each month the Census Bureau attempts to estimate the number of housing starts by surveying approximately 900 of the approximately 19,000 permit-issuing places in the country. The Census Bureau utilizes a mail-out/mail-back survey to obtain these monthly statistics. The 900 permit-issuing places are selected from a sample of 8500 permit-issuing places that are deemed to be representative of all 19,000 of those places. The Census Bureau first estimates the number of housing units for which building permits have been issued in all 19,000 permit-issuing places. It then queries the owners and builders to determine whether construction on the units covered by the permits has started. In places where permits are not required, the Census Bureau visits nonpermit land areas at least every three months to see if there has been any new construction. Units authorized by permits but not yet started in the survey month are reviewed again in successive months to determine if they have actually started. Estimates are made for units started before permit authorization and for late reports. The data collected are used to make an estimate of the total number of housing starts in both permit-issuing and non-permit-issuing areas. All the data are adjusted for seasonal fluctuations.

Key components of the report: The housing starts report is constructed in a manner similar to that of both the new and existing home sale reports. In particular, the details of the report are broken down into four regions: the Northeast, Midwest, South, and West. The *regional breakdown* provides clues than can expose potential flaws in the headline data caused by inconsistencies between the regions. Sharp fluctuations in the regional data can distort the overall figures, and so it is important to keep tabs on the reasons behind the fluctuations. This is especially true of construction activity, which can be affected by regional weather events since it is an outdoor activity. Another important detail in the report is the breakdown of starts by *type of structure*. Specifically, the report details the number of starts in single-family structures with two to four units and five units or more. Single-family units represent about 80 percent of all starts, and so it is important to focus there. The data on multifamily units tend to be volatile and therefore can distort the overall data. Also important in the report are the data on *building permits*, a leading economic indicator. Permits are a leading indicator of housing conditions because most state and local governments require that a permit be filed before a new home is built. The permits data are relatively immune to the many factors that can cause starts to fluctuate (the weather, for example). This makes the permits data helpful in weeding out distortions of the true underlying trend. Because some states do not require a permit, starts typically exceed permits by about 30,000 to 50,000 units. When the gap is wider, it portends weakness in starts in the months ahead. When the gap narrows, it portends strength.

How it affects the market: Although the housing sector is considered important to the economy, the housing starts report does not always provoke a large market response for a couple of reasons. First, housing starts are largely an offshoot of new home sales activity. This makes the housing starts data of secondary importance compared to the new home sales data. After all, a home will not be built unless there is or is expected to be a buyer for it. Second, distortions in the data often result from volatility in the multifamily data, regional data, and weather-related factors. Third, the housing starts data often are foreshadowed by data on mortgage applications released weekly by the Mortgage Bankers Association as well as by the monthly survey of home builders conducted by the National Association of Home Builders. In fact, each month the home builders' survey is released the day before the release of the housing starts report.

What it means to you: On its own the housing starts report provides useful information about current levels of residential construction activity and therefore can be used to form an opinion about the economy. When combined with other housing data, housing starts can provide important clues about the economic outlook. You therefore should utilize the report in formulating your investment strategies. Beyond your investments, you can use this report to get a general idea about the behavior of home prices and in assessing the value of your home and, hence, your net worth. Moreover, by tracking the pace of existing home sales, you can improve your sense of the pricing power that exists in areas such as general contracting, appliances, and building materials.

INDUSTRIAL PRODUCTION AND CAPACITY UTILIZATION

Source: The Federal Reserve

Web address for report: *http://www.federalreserve.gov/releases/ G17/Current/*

Release date: Around the fifteenth calendar day of every month

Time: 9:15 a.m. EST

Report covers: Manufacturing output and utilization rates for the previous month

Description of report: The industrial production and capacity utilization report measures the monthly change in output in U.S. manufacturing, mining, and electricity, gas, and utilities. The changes in output are measured in physical terms rather than by multiplying the output by prices. This makes the data reliable in terms of reflecting actual changes in physical output. The industrial production report does not include production in a variety of industries, including agriculture, construction, trade, finance, and the service industries. The industrial production report is used as a key gauge of the health of the economy; increases and decreases in production tend to reflect changes in the underlying demand for goods and services. The capacity utilization data measure the extent to which available capacity is being utilized.

Survey methodology: Each month the Federal Reserve constructs indexes on industrial production by using two main sources: (1) output measured in physical units and (2) output inferred from data on inputs to the production process. The Fed attempts to obtain as much of the data as possible from output measured in physical units by obtaining data from private trade associations and government agencies. In cases where obtaining data on physical output is not possible, the Fed estimates the physical output by using data on hours worked by production workers. This information is collected monthly by the Bureau of Labor Statistics when it conducts its monthly payroll survey. The Fed weights the components in the industrial production index by their relative importance and then adjusts the data for seasonality. The weights are updated monthly to eliminate distortions in the contributions of several high-technology industries, where weights shift a great deal. Capacity utilization rates are designed to be consistent with the production data, and the Fed utilizes its own estimates on productive capacity in its calculations.

Key components of the report: Two components in the industrial production report often have a large impact on the report and should be watched closely for unusual effects on the data: the indexes on *utilities* and *automobiles*. The utilities component can be volatile because of weather conditions. Unseasonably cold weather in the winter months, for example, can push utilities' output up sharply and distort the true underlying levels of industrial production. The automobile component also can be quite volatile. Automobile manufacturers change their production schedules often in response to changes in demand for automobiles, and this often distorts the monthly data. However, the automobile sector is one of the most important sectors of the economy, and developments in that sector should not be dismissed. A component that has received an increased focus in recent years is the index for *business equipment*. This component contains important information about the technology sector. Particularly close attention is paid to production in selected high-tech industries.

How it affects the market: The industrial production report provides important information about the level of national output and therefore is an important gauge of the state of the economy. Investors thus put a great deal of weight on these data. The market reaction, however, sometimes is muted by a few factors. First, as was mentioned above, some of the industrial production data are assembled using data from the monthly jobs report, which is released about a week or so before the industrial production report. This gives the markets advance warning of the potential results of the report. Second, while the industrial production report indicates plenty about current production levels, it does not provide much guidance on future trends. The market prefers to get that guidance from data on manufacturing orders, a key leading economic indicator.

What it means to you: Changes in the level of industrial production can directly affect both your income and your investments. For example, if you work in the production sector of the economy, your workweek and overtime hours could fluctuate with production levels. Others could be affected secondarily when their customers who work in the production sector of the economy alter their spending in response to their fluctuating income. You also should watch the capacity utilization rate, which has averaged about 81 percent over the last 20 years, with levels below 80 percent indicating excess capacity in the economy. In such cases a decreased rate of job creation or an increase in unemployment becomes a risk as companies look to reduce their excess capacity.

INITIAL JOBLESS CLAIMS

Source: U.S. Department of Labor
Web address for report: *http://www.dol.gov/dol/media/main.htm*
Release date: Every Thursday

Time: 8:30 a.m. EST

Report covers: Initial filings for state unemployment insurance filed in the week ended five days before the release of the report

Description of report: The weekly jobless claims report is an important gauge of employment trends. It measures the number of new persons who file for state unemployment benefits and provides an early lead on the closely watched monthly employment statistics. Indeed, the correlation between the jobless claims data and the monthly employment is very strong. Included in the report are a four-week moving average, a state-by-state breakdown of the claims filed along with comments by states where new claims increased or decreased by more than 1000 persons, the cumulative total of persons continuing to receive unemployment benefits, and the unemployment rate for insured workers. Jobless claims of about 380,000 per week or lower are consistent with increases in the monthly payroll statistics. Jobless claims averaged about 450,000 per week during the 1990–1991 recession and moved into that territory in late 2001.

Survey methodology: Unlike most economic data, the data on jobless claims are derived using very little estimation and therefore accurately reflect actual conditions in the labor market. To obtain the weekly data, the Department of Labor (DOL) essentially tallies all the data provided to it by the nation's state unemployment offices. The data provided to the DOL are based on actual filings, and the states do not seasonally adjust the data they submit to the DOL. The seasonal adjustments are made by the DOL before the data are released to the public. An unemployment rate for insured workers is calculated by dividing the number of persons receiving jobless benefits by the number of persons eligible to receive them. The unemployment rate for insured workers tends to be lower than the national unemployment rate because not all workers are eligible to receive unemployment benefits. Self-employed persons, for example, are ineligible. The rate has been declining over the years as a result of an increase in the number of ineligible workers. This has been caused by a decline in unionization, tighter eligibility requirements, and other factors.

Key components of the report: Most of the components of the initial claims report contain useful information. The data on *continuing claims*, for example, track the cumulative number of people receiving unemployment benefits rather than only new recipients. This component can help an investor assess the extent to which people who filed for unemployment benefits in the last few weeks are having difficulty finding a new job. I like to use the continuing claims data to predict changes in the monthly employment data. Another important component is the *state-by-state* breakdown. States with weekly changes of more than 1000 persons provide details about the industries most responsible for those changes. This detail provides important clues to the health of the various industries and the economy in general. The *four-week average* is also important since it weeds out the weekly variability and provides greater clarity on developments in the labor market. However, the weekly data provide the best insight into emerging developments in this important data series. The *unemployment rate for insured workers* serves as a good proxy for trends in the national unemployment rate.

How it affects the market: Market participants keenly watch the jobless claims statistics. They recognize that trends in the labor market have a substantial bearing on the economy. Data that reflect the labor market are therefore among their most important economic indicators. The jobless claims report is considered particularly important because its timely release helps investors formulate their views on the monthly employment data. The market response to the claims data is therefore often quite palpable. The reaction can be especially sharp if the weekly data that immediately precede the monthly employment report are compelling enough to alter or reinforce views about it. The market reaction to weekly data that have been affected by unusual factors suggests that market participants are generally quite aware of the many special factors that cause the data to fluctuate.

What it means to you: Obviously, employment trends are extremely important to almost everyone. We all need to be aware of conditions in the labor market to assure our personal security and assess our bargaining power when it is time to negotiate our wages. For an investor it is essential to stay abreast of developments in the labor market because those trends are at the core of the health of the economy and therefore have an extremely large bearing on the performance of financial assets. Strong conditions in the labor market generally translate into strong growth in personal income. This tends to be associated with strong economic growth, rising corporate profits, and rising bond yields. In business, the jobless claims data can help in navigating changes in the economic climate.

INDEX OF LEADING ECONOMIC INDICATORS

Source: The Conference Board

Web address for report: *http://www.conference-board.org/ economics/index.cfm*

Release date: Generally between the seventeenth and twenty-second calendar days of every month

Time: 10 a.m. EST

Report covers: Economic indicators from the previous calendar month

Description of report: As its name suggests, the index of leading economic indicators (LEI) is meant to act as a barometer of economic activity three to six months in the future. The index is designed to signal peaks and troughs in the business cycle. An increase or decrease in the index over a period of three or more months generally signals growth or contraction, respectively, in economic activity. The index consists of ten indicators that are considered top leading economic indicators. Because the index is composed of indicators that are widely followed, the LEI index is largely a summation index and therefore provides minimal value to the markets. Nevertheless, the LEI index provides confirmation of the economic trends discerned from its components.

Survey methodology: The LEI index is constructed by combining a weighted average of ten well-regarded economic indicators: the average workweek of production workers in the manufacturing sector, average initial weekly claims for state unemployment benefits, new orders for consumer goods and materials, vendor performance (the speed at which companies make deliveries of goods), new orders for nonmilitary capital goods, new building permits issued, an index of stock prices, money supply data (M2 index), an index of consumer expectations, and the spread between rates on 10-year Treasury bonds and federal funds (the Fed's target rate). The month-to-month change in each of these components is multiplied by the assigned weighting. This produces the monthly changes in the index, which are expressed in percentage terms and generally average about 0.1 to 0.2 percent per month.

Key components of the report: The key components of the LEI report are its ten indicators. The relative importance of each indicator is largely a subjective matter; the indicators provide few clues to the future direction of the overall index. Predicting the future direction of the index requires close scrutiny of the trends in the individual components. It is important, however, to scan the components to determine if they may be exerting an unusual impact on the overall index. While the details of the LEI report say little about the index itself, the Conference Board releases two additional indexes along with the LEI: the indexes of lagging and coincident indicators. These indexes are meant to give indications of the economy in the past and the present, respectively. The coincident index measures various aspects of production that reflect the current pace of economic activity. The lagging index reflects the cost side of the equation, including production costs, inventories, and debt costs. Many analysts like to look at the ratio of the coincident to the lagging indicators to gauge future economic activity. A rising ratio is considered a positive signal for the economy because it indicates that business costs are falling at the same time that revenues are rising, indicating the likelihood of increases in corporate profits.

How it affects the market: The LEI report rarely has much of an impact on the markets but often reinforces sentiments about the economy. Investors often yawn at the report because it largely summarizes information with which the markets are largely familiar. Unlike most economic reports, the LEI index contains no fresh information on the economy. Nevertheless, to the extent that the LEI report reinforces convictions about the future direction of the economy, its value is greater than might be surmised from the market reaction that follows the report's release. Moreover, media coverage of the report puts the LEI report in the public's eye, thus affecting consumer confidence.

What it means to you: The LEI index is best used as a barometer of the future direction of the economy. You can use it as the equivalent of an executive briefing on some of the best time-tested indicators for the economy. The index can be especially helpful if you find it difficult to put much time into following the economy or would rather steer clear of the daily ruminations on economic data. However, it is best to use as many indicators as possible when formulating a view on the economic outlook. Although the LEI report consists of ten indicators, there are many more factors that need to be weighed, including factors that go beyond the traditional scope of economic analysis. Psychological factors, for instance, are not easy to gauge by looking at market indicators alone.

INSTITUTE FOR SUPPLY MANAGEMENT REPORT ON BUSINESS

Source: Institute for Supply Management

Web address for report: http://www.ism.ws

Release date: First business day of every month

Time: 10 a.m. EST

Report covers: Manufacturing activity for the month before the release of the survey results

Description of report: The ISM report, formerly known as the NAPM report, is one of the most closely followed economic reports and a top leading economic indicator. Federal Reserve Chairman Alan Greenspan, for example, is known to look at the report very closely. The report contains meaningful indications of the pace of economic activity in the manufacturing sector and therefore provides extremely valuable information on the health of the overall economy. The ISM releases an index on the findings of its survey that consists of five components that carry varying weights: new orders (30 percent of the overall index), production (25 percent), employment (20 percent), delivery time (15 percent), and inventories (10 percent). An index above 50 is consistent with expansion in the manufacturing sector; one below 50 is consistent with contraction. Over time, a reading above 42.6 has indicated expansion in the overall economy.

Survey methodology: Each month the ISM surveys purchasing and supply executives in approximately 400 industrial companies. Twenty diverse industries from various geographic areas of the nation are represented in the survey, including primary metals, transportation equipment, rubber and plastics, food and kindred products, and printing and publishing. The 20 industries are weighted according to their contributions to the economy. The ISM asks the purchasing and supply executives whether they experienced an increase, a decrease, or no change in nine important aspects of their businesses, including the five listed above. Separate questions are posed on prices paid, order backlogs, export orders, and import orders. The responses are compiled into a diffusion index, which is basically a number that reflects the percentage of firms that reported an increase in the respective components plus half the firms that reported no change. The diffusion indexes are adjusted for seasonality.

Key components of the report: The most important component in the ISM report is *new orders*. New orders are the lifeline of the manufacturing sector. When new orders rise, many forces are set in motion that lead to increases in the other key components of the survey, such as production and employment. Thus, as new orders go, so goes the ISM index. The *inventory* component is also very important because it indicates whether inventory levels are becoming too high or too low. Inventory levels can indicate whether an increase or a decrease in manufacturing output may be in the offing. To gauge export activity, an investor should watch the *export orders* component closely. The *price index* is a helpful guide to the producer price index.

How it affects the market: As a leading indicator for the economy, the ISM report is one of the most respected economic reports, and its release often sparks very large market moves. The bond market generally receives a strong report poorly because it fears that strong economic growth will stoke inflation and perhaps cause the Federal Reserve to raise interest rates. A weak report, in contrast, usually receives a positive response in the bond market, as it could indicate economic weakness and, hence, low inflation and perhaps interest rate cuts by the Federal Reserve. The market tends to shift its focus on the details of the report but basically stays focused on the new orders component. Nevertheless, mood shifts in the market can shift the market's attention from month to month. When this happens, it is usually the employment component or the price index that grabs attention, especially since the national employment report usually follows the ISM release by a matter of days.

What it means to you: With the markets placing a lot of emphasis on the ISM report, its impact on the markets can directly affect your investments. Investors recognize that the ISM is a top leading indicator for the economy and therefore respond accordingly. You should pay close attention to trends in this important indicator because of its substantial influence on the behavior of both bond and stock prices. Moreover, you should follow the report closely to make assessments about the economy. A strong series of reports generally indicates economic prosperity for months to come, while a weak series of reports points to economic weakness and possibly job layoffs. In business, the report can help you navigate a variety of economic climates.

INSTITUTE FOR SUPPLY MANAGEMENT NONMANUFACTURING INDEX

Source: Institute for Supply Management

Web address for report: *http://www.ism.ws*

Release date: The third business day of every month

Time: 10 a.m. EST

Report covers: Nonmanufacturing activity in the month before the release of the survey results

Description of report: The ISM's nonmanufacturing report is a relatively new indicator that is meant to mirror the construct of the ISM's widely followed manufacturing index, a top leading economic indicator. Over the years the manufacturing sector's share of the U.S. economy has been declining steadily. In recognition of this in 1997 the ISM created a nonmanufacturing index. The index captures trends in key service industries such as entertainment, communication, insurance, finance and banking, health services, retail trade, and real estate. The index has been gaining recognition as a key gauge of economic activity in the service serctor, where economic data are not readily available. The ISM's nonmanufacturing report contains indexes for new orders, production, employment, delivery time, inventories, and order backlogs. A reading above 50 is consistent with expansion; a reading below 50 is consistent with contraction.

Survey methodology: Each month the ISM surveys purchasing and supply executives in approximately 370 nonmanufacturing companies. Over 62 diverse industries from various geographic areas of the nation are represented in the survey. The 62 industries are weighted according to their contribution to the economy. The ISM asks the purchasing and supply executives whether they experienced an increase or a decrease in nine important aspects of their businesses, including the six mentioned above. The responses are compiled into separate diffusion indexes, which are basically numbers that reflect the percentage of firms that reported an increase in the respective components minus those which saw a decrease. The diffusion indexes are adjusted for seasonality and to equate a reading of zero to 50. Unlike the ISM's manufacturing index, the headline number on the nonmanufacturing index is not composed of subcomponents; it is currently a stand-alone number. The ISM expects eventually to compute its overall nonmanufacturing data by assigning weights to the various subcomponents after several years of observing the behavior of the data.

Key components of the report: The most important component in the ISM's nonmanufacturing report is the *new orders* component because new orders precede actual output as well as employment. The *inventory* component is also very important because it indicates whether inventory levels are becoming too high or too low. Inventory levels can indicate whether an increase or a decrease in output may be in the offing. It is unclear, however, how useful the inventory component is in the ISM's nonmanufacturing survey. When inventories increase in the legal sector, for example, the economic implications are not nearly as important as they are when inventories increase in the manufacturing sector. To gauge export activity, an investor should watch the *export orders* component closely. The *price index* is a helpful guide to inflation pressures in the service sector.

How it affects the market: As a leading indicator on the economy, the ISM's manufacturing report is one of the most respected economic reports, and its release often sparks very large market moves. Its nonmanufacturing index, however, does not yet command the same respect, largely because the report is relatively new. Over time, however, the index is expected to become an increasingly prominent gauge of economic activity in the service sector. Recent market reactions to the ISM's nonmanufacturing report appear to indicate that investors are beginning to recognize the value of the report. The market tends to shift its focus on the details of the report but basically stays focused on the new orders component. Nevertheless, as with the ISM's manufacturing report, mood shifts in the market can shift the market's attention from month to month. When this happens, it is usually the employment component or the price index that grabs attention.

What it means to you: In light of the intense interest that the markets have in the ISM's manufacturing index, it would be prudent to keep an eye on the ISM's nonmanufacturing index as it becomes more widely recognized. The more the markets respond to the index, the more that will affect your investments. Moreover, you should follow the report closely to make assessments of the service sector of the economy. This is especially important in light of the fact that the economic calendar is laden with manufacturing statistics and relatively devoid of statistics that reflect the service sector. Because the U.S. economy is largely service-oriented, keeping tabs on the health of the service sector is an important endeavor for both your investments and your personal finances. Strength in the ISM's nonmanufacturing report should be taken as a positive sign for the broader economy, while weakness will point to economic weakness and possibly job layoffs. Business managers can use the report to monitor economic trends.

NEW HOME SALES

Source: U.S. Census Bureau

Web address for report: *http://www.census.gov/const/ newresales.pdf*

Release date: Generally the last calendar week of every month

Time: 10 a.m. EST

Report covers: New homes sold in the previous calendar month

Description of report: The new home sales report provides information on both the number of new homes sold and their median and average sales prices. This report is considered very important because of the enormous contribution the housing sector makes to the overall economy. The multiplier effects of the housing sector are arguably bigger than those of any other sector in the economy. In other words, when the housing sector strengthens or weakens, it can have a profound effect on the overall economy. A new home sale affects the economy in many ways. First, the building of new homes creates jobs; the construction of 1000 single-family homes generates an estimated 2448 full-time jobs in construction and construction-related industries. Another boost to the economy comes when home buyers furnish their homes with new appliances, tools, carpeting, outdoor equipment, and the like. The new home sales data provide important clues to the level of consumer confidence and income growth, the two main pillars of a strong housing market. The data also can be used to gauge the impact of changes in interest rates. The data on new home sales often are subject to large monthly revisions.

Survey methodology: Each month the Census Bureau attempts to estimate the number of building permits issued by the approximately 19,000 permit-issuing places in the country by sampling about 900 permit-issuing places that are considered representative of all permit-issuing places. The Census Bureau's field representatives obtain the data they need for their estimates by visiting the 900 permit-issuing places. In places where permits are not required, the Census Bureau visits nonpermit land areas at least once every three months to see if there is any new construction. For each permit issued in the 900 permit-issuing places, the Census Bureau asks the owner or the builder whether the house has been sold or is for sale. If it has been sold, the date of sale is recorded. Unsold homes are reviewed again in successive months to determine if they have been sold. The data collected are used to make an estimate of the total number of home sales in both permit-issuing and non-permit-issuing areas. The data are adjusted upward by 3.3 percent to account for homes that may have been built in permit-issuing areas but without permit authorization. The data then are adjusted for seasonal fluctuations.

Key components of the report: The new home sales report contains just a few details. Nevertheless, a few details in the report shed light on the condition of the housing market. An important detail that can expose potential flaws in the headline data is the *regional data*. Sharp fluctuations in the regional data can be misleading, depending on the possible causes of the sales drop in that region, which can sometimes experience sharp fluctuations due to the weather and other factors. Another important detail is the information on the *median sales price*. This component is important because for most people, the bulk of their net worth consists of the equity in their homes. Fluctuations in home prices impact a homeowner's net worth and this affects consumer confidence and spending; the wealthier a homeowner feels, the more likely it is the homeowner will be confident about spending. Also important are the data on the *supply of homes* available for sale. Measured in total months of supply remaining on the market, this information provides insight into whether there is an excess or a shortage of homes on the market.

How it affects the market: Investors are keenly aware of the importance of the housing sector to the U.S. economy. They recognize that the effects of the housing sector can ripple throughout the economy. They also recognize that the condition of the housing sector speaks volumes about consumer confidence and income growth. It is no wonder that the new home sales report often sparks fairly large reactions in the bond market. Large revisions to the report often magnify the market impact. However, reactions to the new home sales report sometimes are muted by its volatile nature and by occasional distortions related to the regional data. Moreover, the new home sales report often is foreshadowed by the weekly data on mortgage applications released by the Mortgage Bankers Association and the monthly survey of home builders conducted by the National Association of Home Builders, thereby limiting the market's reaction at times.

What it means to you: As a leading economic indicator, the new home sales report provides important clues about the economic outlook. You therefore should use the new home sales report when formulating your investment strategies, particularly with respect to forming opinions about the economically sensitive sectors of the economy. Beyond your investments, you can use the new home sales report to get a general idea about the behavior of home prices. This information could be useful in assessing the value of your home and, hence, your net worth. By assessing the pace of new home sales, you can assess the widespread implications that the housing sector might have for the pricing power in areas such as general contracting, appliances, and building materials. Moreover, if you are in the market to buy a new home, you can improve your bargaining abilities by tracking the level of unsold homes.

PERSONAL INCOME AND CONSUMPTION

Source: U.S. Census Bureau

Web address for report: *http://www.bea.doc.gov/bea/rels.htm*

Release date: Generally the last week of each month or the very first days of the subsequent month

Time: 8:30 a.m. EST

Report covers: Personal income and consumption in the previous calendar month, except when the release is delayed until early in a subsequent month (see above)

Description of report: The report on personal income (PI) and personal consumption expenditures (PCE) provides important information about the household sector, which accounts for about two-thirds of the U.S. economy. Trends in personal income growth are particularly important since income is at the root of all spending. Personal income consists of more than wages and salaries. In fact, about one-third of all personal income comes from sources other than wages, salaries, and other personal income, including rental income, dividend income, interest income, disability and health insurance benefits, and Social Security payments. The data on personal consumption are quite comprehensive, but the monthly report provides few details. It merely breaks the consumption data into three parts: durable goods, nondurable goods, and services. The data on both PI and PCE are used in the quarterly computations of GDP.

Survey methodology: Obtaining the data necessary to produce the report on personal income and consumption is a comprehensive task. Data must be collected from numerous sources, including the housing stock, insurance premiums, mortgage debt, interest rates, unit sales, receipts, and tax collections. The data on personal consumption are generated by using what the BEA calls the retail-control method. This method is used to estimate over one-third of PCE and basically captures spending on a wide variety of goods. Consumption data in many areas are estimated by using data obtained from the Bureau of Labor Statistics. Spending on dental and other medical services, for example, is estimated by using data on wages and salaries derived from the monthly employment data collected by the BLS. The data on personal income are estimated by using many of the sources described above.

Key components of the report: The details of the personal income and consumption report provide insight into whether the trends in each of these two key areas are as strong or weak as the headlines suggest. The data on personal income, for example, occasionally are skewed by *transfer payments*, which include Social Security payments. A delay of just a few days can push these payments out of one month and into the next, distorting the data on personal income. Similarly, the timing of payments of *farm subsidies* often skews the data. During expansions growth in PI tends to be strong. PI grew at an annual rate of about 5.5 percent during the expansion of the 1990s, fluctuating in a range of about 4 to 8 percent. It rarely slips much below 4 percent except during recessions. The details of the data on personal consumption help in assessing trends in spending on *durable* and *nondurable goods*, and this can shed light on consumer confidence levels. Strong growth in spending on durable goods, for example, suggests that consumers are confident about their personal finances. Another key detail of interest is the information on the savings rate. The savings rate has been in a secular decline for many years and was essentially zero in the late 1990s. Rising stock prices emboldened consumers to consume more than they earned, but when stocks faltered, the savings rate began to rise again as consumers tried to steady their finances. The savings rate is likely understated by the absence of capital gains in the equation.

How it affects the market: Market reaction to the release of the report on personal income and consumption tends to be relatively muted, but there are times when that response is quite palpable. The reaction tends to be muted because it is derived from data to which the markets have already reacted. Personal income data, for example, often are foreshadowed by the monthly data on average hourly earnings reported each month in the employment report. Similarly, the data on personal consumption are foreshadowed by the monthly retail sales report. The reaction to the report on personal income and consumption tends to be greatest when the release occurs just before the release of the quarterly GDP statistics. Market participants recognize that the PCE data are directly plugged into the GDP statistics, and this increases the market's focus on the PCE data when the GDP release is around the corner.

What it means to you: Obviously, personal income growth is important to almost everyone, and so it is important to keep tabs on the data that reflect it. This can help you determine whether you believe you are leading or lagging the pack. It can help you plan your career as well as your personal finances. Moreover, in business, a good sense of trends in personal income growth can help you anticipate consumption patterns. You should consider using the data on the personal savings rate as a key indicator. A sharp decline in the savings rate, characterized by a break from the secular trend, indicates that consumption is exceeding income; this is generally an unsustainable trend. If the savings rate increases, it suggests that consumers have the wherewithal to spend, boding well for the long-run health of the economy.

PHILADELPHIA FED'S BUSINESS OUTLOOK SURVEY

Source: Federal Reserve Bank of Philadelphia

Web address for report: *http://www.phil.frb.org/econ/ bos/index.html*

Release date: The third Thursday of every month

Time: 12 p.m. EST

Report covers: Manufacturing conditions through the first week of the month in which the report is released

Description of report: The Philadelphia Survey provides an early glimpse of manufacturing conditions every month. Included in the survey are manufacturers in the Fed's Third District: eastern Pennsylvania, southern New Jersey, and the entire state of Delaware. The survey contains important information about business conditions in the manufacturing sector. In a questionnaire, the Philadelphia Fed asks manufacturers about their overall business conditions, new orders, shipments, backlogs, the average length of their employees' workweek, employment conditions, inventories, the prices they pay and receive for goods and services, and delivery time. Market participants use the report to assess economic conditions in the manufacturing sector and to predict the monthly ISM index.

Survey methodology: Near the end of every month the Philadelphia Fed mails its survey questionnaire to about 250 large manufacturing firms (firms with 100 or more employees) in the Fed's Third District, and about 100 firms respond to each survey. Although the responses are due back to the Fed by about the fifth day of the following month, the Fed normally accepts responses received after the due date. The survey asks the manufacturers whether they experienced an increase or a decrease in the important aspects of their businesses (mentioned above). The responses are compiled into a diffusion index, which is basically a number that reflects the percentage of firms that reported an increase in the respective components minus those which saw a decrease. Thus, a reading of over zero in the survey and its components indicates expansion, while a reading below zero indicates contraction.

Key components of the report: The Philadelphia Survey consists of the various indicators mentioned above, the most important of which is *new orders*. When new orders rise, many forces are set in motion that lead to increases in the other key aspects of a manufacturer's business, resulting in a rise in many of the other components of the Philadelphia Survey. The new orders component is so important that it has the largest weighting (30 percent) of any component in the national survey on manufacturers' conditions conducted each month by the Institute for Supply Management, which is considered one of the most important economic indicators. Market participants therefore watch the details of the Philadelphia Survey closely for hints to the possible outcome of the ISM survey.

How it affects the market: The timely release of the Philadelphia Survey gives it added importance to the financial markets. The report generally is released fully two weeks before the release of the ISM data as well as other regional manufacturing surveys and therefore can provide an early indication of national conditions in the manufacturing sector. Thus, at times market reaction to the Philadelphia Survey is often sharp. However, because the survey is merely a regional survey and since the results of the survey often fluctuate sharply from month to month, the market often reacts skeptically to the report, producing a muted response.

What it means to you: The markets pay close attention to data on the manufacturing sector. Investors recognize that the manufacturing sector is highly sensitive to fluctuations in the business cycle and is often a microcosm of activity in the broader economy. Manufacturing data such as the Philadelphia Survey therefore can have a great effect on your investments. Generally, the stronger the manufacturing sector is, the more likely it is that stock market will be rising and the bond market will be falling (with the yield curve flattening). Businesses can use the data to gauge the health of the economy.

PRODUCER PRICE INDEX

Source: Bureau of Labor Statistics

Web address for report: *http://www.bls.gov/news.release/ ppi.toc.htm*

Release date: Generally slightly before the middle of every month

Time: 8:30 a.m. EST

Report covers: The previous month's data, mostly for prices on the Tuesday of the week containing the thirteenth of the month.

Description of report: The producer price index (PPI) measures price changes in the prices received by domestic producers on the goods they produce. It basically tracks the prices manufacturers pay on the commodities, parts, and raw materials they use to manufacture their products. The PPI therefore tends to be a good gauge of the manufacturing sector and fluctuations in commodities prices. PPIs are available for products of virtually every industry in the mining and manufacturing sectors of the economy. New PPIs are gradually being introduced for the products of industries in the transportation, utilities, trade, finance, and service sectors of the economy.

Survey methodology: Each month the BLS collects data from approximately 500 manufacturing and mining industries on over 10,000 specific products and product categories at three stages of the production process: crude, intermediate, and finished. To grasp what happens at these three stages, one can think about the production of a shirt. In this example the crude good would be cotton from the field, the intermediate good would be cotton yarn, and the finished good would be the shirt. The prices on goods at the crude and intermediate stages of production are called *pipeline* numbers since they hint at price changes in finished goods in future months. For most items in the PPI, establishments report their selling prices for the Tuesday of the week containing the thirteenth of the month. This means that the PPI report can be slow to capture the most current developments. That is why it is important for market observers to follow commodities futures prices closely to stay abreast of the most recent developments. As with the CPI, the BLS assigns weights to the surveyed products and adjusts its findings for quality changes and seasonality.

Key components of the report: Because of their predictive value, the indexes for *crude* and *intermediate goods* are important to watch. *Core intermediate prices*, which are intermediate prices excluding food and energy, have a very good correlation to the data on finished goods, the headline number that is so widely followed. An investor should look at the details of the report for indications on how various sectors of the economy are performing. For example, sharp declines in the price of copper, a metal widely used for industrial purposes, indicate that the manufacturing sector is weak. It is also important to track *prescription drug* costs. This component has a high correlation with trends in overall health care costs, which are a key factor in the cost of labor and, hence, economywide inflation pressures. One also should keep an eye on the *automobile* component. This component tends to fluctuate a great deal, particularly during the fall and winter months, when the introduction of new models can cause volatility in automobile prices.

How it affects the market: The PPI report is important, but it does not always grab the market's attention for two main reasons. First, since producer prices tend to reflect the behavior of commodities prices and commodities prices generally are easy to track on a day-to-day basis, the markets are generally well prepared for the PPI report. Second, the PPI is a less valuable inflation indicator than the consumer price index because the CPI captures service inflation far better. The PPI largely captures trends in commodity prices, which account for only 10 percent of the cost of producing goods and services (wages are the biggest cost at about 70 percent). As a result of these two factors, the PPI does not have a large impact on the market, but the report is important nonetheless, particularly in light of the bond market's sensitivity to inflation trends.

What it means to you: As with the CPI, it is important to keep tabs on key inflation gauges such as the PPI for many reasons, particularly because of the way it can affect your purchasing power as well as your investments. Keeping in mind that inflation trends tend to lag fluctuations in the economy, the PPI should be used in tandem with other inflation indicators to assess the likely direction of interest rates. You can use the PPI as a gauge of manufacturing activity, a sector that is very sensitive to fluctuations in the business cycle. The more you know about where the economy stands in relation to the business cycle, the better you will be at formulating investment strategies. In addition, tracking the PPI can help you know the trends in the prices of many of the goods you buy, making you a smarter shopper.

PRODUCTIVITY AND COSTS

Source: Bureau of Labor Statistics

Web address for report: *http://www.bls.gov/news.release/prod2. toc.htm*

Release date: Usually within 40 days of the close of the reference period

Time: 8:30 a.m. EST

Report covers: Labor productivity and costs in the calendar quarter before the report's release

Description of report: The productivity report measures the productivity of the American workforce. In technical terms, labor productivity is the ratio of the output of goods and services to the labor hours devoted to the production of that output. The BLS has been studying output per hour in individual industries since the 1800s; 1898 a study titled "Hand and Machine Labor" provided compelling evidence of the savings in labor resulting from mechanization in the latter part of the nineteenth century. Advances in productivity are extremely important to the economy. The more productive workers are, the more their earnings are likely to increase. Advances in productivity increase the national standard of living because they enable workers to produce more goods and services without having to increase labor time. Advances in productivity keep inflation low by keeping a lid on the labor costs required to produce goods and services. The productivity report provides data on the productivity of workers in the major sectors of business, nonfarm business, and nonfinancial corporations, along with the subsectors of durable and nondurable goods manufacturing. Investors and policymakers closely follow productivity trends to gauge the long-term health of the economy. Annual growth in productivity has averaged roughly 1.7 percent over the last 20 years but has grown more rapidly in recent years.

Survey methodology: The quarterly data on productivity and costs are estimated by using data on output, hours worked, and compensation costs compiled by a variety of sources. Output data are provided by the Bureau of Economic Analysis and the Census Bureau of the Department of Commerce, the Bureau of Labor Statistics, and the Federal Reserve Board. Data on compensation and hours are provided by the Bureau of Labor Statistics and the Bureau of Economic Analysis. Productivity is calculated by comparing labor output to labor input, measured as hours at work. The primary source for data on output is the data on the real gross domestic product prepared by the BEA. The primary source for the data on labor input is the BLS Current Employment Statistics program. Unit labor costs are calculated by relating hourly compensation to output per hour. To assure reliability, the BLS revises the data as more complete information becomes available. Revisions appear 30 days after the initial release, and second revisions appear after 60 days.

Key components of the report: The details of the productivity report take a backseat to the headlines. The headline data, which include the quarterly change in *nonfarm business productivity* and *unit labor costs*, are essentially the crux of the report. This is a bit different from most other economic reports, where the headlines often are distorted by the details. One key detail is the breakdown by industry of quarterly changes in productivity and costs. It is helpful, for instance, to observe the data on the *manufacturing sector,* where details on the *durable* and *nondurable goods sectors* are included. Also included in the report are details for each of the covered industries on: quarterly changes in productivity, output, hours, hourly compensation, real hourly compensation, and unit labor costs. All quarterly changes are expressed as percentage changes at a seasonally adjusted annual rate.

How it affects the market: Since this is a quarterly release, the markets get only four chances a year to react to the productivity data. One might think this would sharpen the reaction to its release. But unlike other quarterly economic releases, the reaction to the productivity data is often difficult to measure for a few reasons. First, the markets are interested mostly in long-term trends in productivity. Investors do not react much to the quarterly changes unless they feel there has been a change in the trend. Second, productivity trends tend to last many years, rendering short-term trends less meaningful to investors. In fact, some studies suggest that over the last 100 years productivity cycles have averaged about 20 years in duration. These long productivity cycles have been sparked by innovations such as the automobile, air travel, and the computer. The most recent productivity cycle is believed to have started in 1995, when more widespread use of technology began to significantly lift productivity. It is easy to understand how innovations can raise productivity levels for many years, especially since it usually takes years for enhanced applications of these innovations to begin to appear. It stands to reason, then, that investors generally take the long view when quarterly data are released. The bond market benefits when productivity advances because such advances help keep unit labor costs in check, reducing pressures on businesses to raise prices.

What it means to you: Most people endeavor to be more productive in everything they do and therefore can relate to the concept of productivity as it pertains to the business world. Like individuals, businesses want to produce more in the same or a shorter amount of time. Personal familiarity with the concept of productivity can help people recognize the importance of changes in national productivity trends. By doing so, people can more readily spot opportunities to invest in companies and industries that are the most productive. In addition, a good sense of productivity trends is an essential element in the formulation of long-term investment strategies. An accelerating productivity trend normally is associated with sustained economic growth, rising corporate profits, low inflation, and low bond yields.

RETAIL SALES

Source: Census Bureau of the Department of Commerce

Web address for report: *http://www.census.gov/svsd/ www/retail.html*

Release date: Usually nine working days after the end of the previous month

Time: 8:30 a.m. EST

Report covers: Sales through the end of the previous month

Description of report: The retail sales report provides an indication of sales by retail companies such as department stores, automobile dealers, clothing stores, and drugstores. Retail sales data contain important information about the pace of consumer spending, which accounts for about two-thirds of the U.S. economy. Data from the retail sales report are used in the computation of quarterly data on GDP. Retail sales are considered a leading indicator for the economy because sales tend to lead production. Retail sales recently have averaged about $297 billion per month. The markets use the report as a key gauge of consumer spending, one of the most important elements of the economy.

Survey methodology: Five working days before the end of every month the Commerce Department collects its data by mailing a survey to about 4100 firms, 900 of which are surveyed regularly because of their relatively large size. Sales of all merchandise at the surveyed firms are included except for sales taxes. The Commerce Department utilizes the data it collects from the surveyed companies to derive estimates of sales in various retail industries. The data then are adjusted to account for seasonal fluctuations. The short time between the survey mailing and the data release often results in large revisions since only about one-fourth of all responses to the survey are received by the time the report is released. The revisions appear in the report released in the subsequent month.

Key components of the report: The *automobile* component is important but also is volatile; that is why the Commerce

Department also releases data on retail sales excluding automobiles. Nevertheless, one should not overlook this key component, which accounts for almost 25 percent of all retail sales. Strength or weakness in automobile sales can provide evidence of consumers' willingness to spend on big-ticket items and therefore hints at consumer confidence levels. Also important is the *general merchandise* component, which accounts for about 12 percent of all retail sales. This component is a gauge of consumer spending at department stores. One should look closely at the *gasoline* component because fluctuations in gasoline prices can distort the overall data. Investors also should watch the *apparel* component for fluctuations related to unusual weather.

How it affects the market: The retail sales report can have a large impact on both the stock and bond markets depending on their sensitivity to the pace of consumer spending at the time the report is released. If, for example, the bond market was worried about an acceleration of consumer spending (which could ultimately cause inflation to accelerate), the retail sales report would be watched closely and could produce a relatively large reaction in the markets. The market's response often is dictated by the large revisions to the last two months of data that accompany each monthly release. An investor therefore should look closely at the revisions to the report before drawing conclusions based solely on the headline data. The markets react least to the retail sales reports that cover the two clearance months of January and July.

What it means to you: The pace of consumer spending is one of the most important determinants of the health of the economy. Since everyone is affected in one way or another by the health of the economy, it is critical to track consumer spending activity. You should use the retail sales report as a leading indicator of the economy. A strong pace of retail sales, for instance, should indicate to you that the economy is likely to grow strongly, causing stock prices and bond yields to rise. It is especially important to watch the pace of retail sales during the holiday season. The pace of sales often sets the tone for the economy at the start of the new year. Moreover, if sales exceed or fall short of expectations, this tends to affect the manufacturing sector because of the impact of the sales pace on retail inventories. Watching retail sales also can make you a better shopper since strength or weakness in retail sales can affect your ability to obtain goods and services as well as the prices you pay for them. For example, if by watching retail sales closely you learn that automobile sales are weak, you could use that knowledge to your advantage when bargaining for a new automobile.

U.S. TRADE BALANCE

Source: U.S. Census Bureau and Bureau of Economic Analysis

Web address for report: *http://www.bea.doc.gov/ bea/rels.htm*

Release date: Generally around the third week of every month

Time: 8:30 a.m. EST

Report covers: U.S. trade in goods and services two calendar months before the release of the report

Description of report: The trade report provides information on U.S. international trade in goods and services. The report contains details on the dollar value of the goods and services exchanged between the United States and its trading partners and a breakdown of that trade by expenditure category. The report is a useful barometer of the health of the global economy and its impact on the U.S. economy and potential impact on foreign exchange rates. The report is also a useful gauge of the impact of changes in U.S. trade policy and therefore can be used in the political arena to galvanize opinion for or against various trade policies. The details of the trade data can be used to assess the outlook for various sectors of the economy, particularly the manufacturing sector. U.S. exports represent about 9 percent of GDP, while imports total around 13 percent.

Survey methodology: The trade report requires data from many sources. This partly explains why the Bureau of Economic Analysis and the U.S. Census Bureau jointly produce the report. The BEA estimates the merchandise trade balance by using data compiled by the Census Bureau and the Department of Commerce. The data recorded include the movement of goods across U.S. customs boundaries but not always the change in ownership; the BEA assumes that goods moving across boundaries change ownership;

in other words, it assumes that physical possession indicates actual ownership. This applies even if goods are shipped between U.S. firms and their affiliates abroad. Examples of sources of data are the Commerce Department's shipper's declaration forms filed at the point of export, surveys conducted by the U.S. Travel and Tourism Administration, and the Treasury Department's International Capital Reporting system. Services are recorded when performed. Investment income is recorded on an accrual basis regardless of when the income is paid or received. Transactions denominated in foreign currencies are reported in their dollar equivalents, generally converted at the exchange rates prevailing at the time of the transaction.

Key components of the report: The details on the monthly percentage changes in *exports and imports* are followed closely. U.S. exports are particularly important to the manufacturing sector, which does the bulk of exporting in the United States. Export activity augments the manufacturing sector's domestic activity. The data on U.S. imports of foreign goods and services are watched for signals on the condition of the U.S. economy. A strong pace of imports, for example, generally indicates that the U.S. economy is strong as it suggests that U.S. businesses and consumers are prospering and therefore buying foreign products. However, the data on imports can be used as a gauge of potential overstocking of goods. Other important details include the *country-by-country breakdown* of activity. There tends to be a great deal of focus on trading activity with Japan, China, and Mexico. Politicians often seize upon the chronic trade deficits that the United States has had with those countries to tout their views on trade policy. Also important is the breakdown of trade by category. Roughly 45 percent of all U.S. exports are *capital goods*. Capital goods include many of the goods in which the United States is highly competitive, including semiconductors, computer accessories, medicinal equipment, and industrial engines. The fact that so many U.S. goods are capital goods is good news for the U.S. economy since those goods are likely to remain in demand even when the global economy slows.

How it affects the market: As with the report on business inventories, the trade report has the greatest impact when investors are formulating their views about upcoming data on GDP because the trade data are often one of the last pieces of information forecasters need to finish their number crunching on the GDP report.

In fact, because the trade data are released well after the calendar month that they cover, the trade data are unavailable when the advance estimate on GDP is released, and so an estimate is used instead. This puts added focus on the trade data just ahead of the revision to GDP, which incorporates the actual trade data for that final month in the revision. The market reaction to the trade report often is muted by the market's informed sense of the many messages contained in the report. For example, the export data are known to have implications for the manufacturing sector. Data for this sector can be readily observed through many other, more timely economic reports. Occasionally, the trade report serves as a catalyst for volatility in the foreign exchange market. In recent years, however, investors have recognized that currency values are dictated by many other factors, including capital flows, fiscal policy, and foreign direct investment.

What it means to you: The trade report is important to you for a number of reasons. As an investor, you can use the trade report to gauge the competitiveness of U.S. businesses. An accurate assessment of where U.S. companies stand in the global economy will help you make more informed investment decisions. The report also can help you gauge any risks to the U.S. dollar from chronic trade deficits. By definition, the trade deficit means that the United States is buying more goods from its trading partners than they are buying from the United States. Ordinarily, this should put downward pressure on the U.S. dollar, since dollars are sold to buy the currencies needed to purchase the foreign goods. Luckily, however, the U.S. trade deficit, which recently approached $400 billion annually, has been offset by huge net purchases by foreigners of U.S. stocks, bonds, and companies. This has resulted in net inflows of money into the United States and a strengthening of the U.S. dollar. The trade report can help you assess U.S. trade policies. In business, the report can also help you to assess trends in the global economy.

INDEX

Note: Boldface numbers indicate illustrations.

Anthony Crescenzi is chief bond market strategist at Miller Tabak & Co. and founder and daily market analyst of Bondtalk.com. Widely respected by the nation's top institutional investors, Crescenzi is one of today's most visible and influential bond market commentators. He makes frequent appearances on CNBC, CNN*fn*, and Bloomberg Television and is regularly quoted in *The Wall Street Journal, Barron's, The New York Times,* and other national periodicals.